Lectures on the History
of Political Philosophy

JOHN RAWLS

Lectures on the History of Political Philosophy

Edited by

Samuel Freeman

THE BELKNAP PRESS OF
HARVARD UNIVERSITY PRESS

Cambridge, Massachusetts, and London, England
2007

ISBN-13: 978-0-674-02492-2
ISBN-10: 0-674-02492-3

The Cataloging-in-Publication data is available from
the Library of Congress.

To my students

—John Rawls

Contents

Contents

Editor's Foreword

THESE LECTURES derive from John Rawls's written lectures and notes for a course in Modern Political Philosophy (Philosophy 171) that he taught at Harvard University from the mid-1960s until his retirement in 1995. In the late 1960s and 1970s Rawls would teach his own theory of justice, justice as fairness, in conjunction with other contemporary and historical works. For example, in 1971 he taught, in addition to *A Theory of Justice*, works by Locke, Rousseau, Hume, Berlin, and Hart. Later in the 1970s and early 1980s this course consisted entirely of lectures on most of the major historical political philosophers in this volume. In 1983, the last year he taught historical figures alone without *A Theory of Justice*, Rawls lectured on Hobbes, Locke, Hume, Mill, and Marx. In earlier years Sidgwick would often be discussed (1976, 1979, 1981), as would Rousseau, but in that case Hobbes and/or Marx would not be discussed. In 1984 Rawls again taught parts of *A Theory of Justice* in conjunction with Locke, Hume, Mill, Kant, and Marx. Soon thereafter he dropped Kant and Hume from his political philosophy course, and added the lectures on Rousseau. During this period he wrote final versions of the lectures presented here on Locke, Rousseau, Mill, and Marx, along with the lectures that were published in 2000 as *Justice as Fairness: A Restatement*. (This explains the occasional comparisons with justice as fairness found in the present lectures.) Since they were regularly taught during the last ten to twelve years of Rawls's teaching career, the lectures in this volume on Locke, Rousseau, Mill, and Marx are the most finished and complete. Rawls typed them into computer files and adjusted and refined them over the years, until 1994. As a result, they required very little editing.

Somewhat less finished are the earlier lectures on Hobbes and Hume from 1983. They do not appear to have been written out as a continuous and complete set of lectures (with the exception of most of the first Hume

lecture). The Hobbes and Hume lectures presented here were mainly derived from transcriptions of recording tapes of Rawls's lectures for that
term, which have been supplemented by Rawls's handwritten lecture notes
and class handouts.[1] Rawls typically provided students with summaries that
outlined the main points in his lectures. Prior to the early 1980s (when he
started typing his lectures on a word processor), these handouts were handwritten in a very fine script which, when typed out, filled more than two
single-spaced pages. These handouts have been used to supplement the lectures on Hobbes and Hume, and they also provide most of the content of
the first two Sidgwick lectures in the Appendix.

One great benefit of these lectures is that they reveal how Rawls conceived of the history of the social contract tradition, and suggest how he
saw his own work in relation to that of Locke, Rousseau, and Kant, and to
some degree Hobbes as well. Rawls also discusses and responds to Hume's
utilitarian reaction to Locke's social contract doctrine, including Hume's argument that the social contract is superficial and an "unnecessary shuffle"
(Rawls), an argument that established a pattern of criticism that continues
down to the present day. Another substantial benefit of this volume is
Rawls's discussion of J. S. Mill's liberalism. It suggests many parallels between his own and Mill's views, including not just the palpable similarities
between Mill's principle of liberty and Rawls's first principle of justice, but
also the less tangible parallels between Mill's political economy and Rawls's
account of distributive justice and property-owning democracy.

The Marx lectures evolved perhaps more than others over the years. In
the early 1980s Rawls endorsed the position (held by Allen Wood, among
others) that Marx did not have a conception of justice but rather regarded
justice as an ideological concept necessary to sustain the exploitation of the
working class. He revises that position in the lectures included here, under
the influence of G. A. Cohen and others. Rawls's interpretation of Marx's
Labor Theory of Value seeks to separate its outmoded economics from
what he regards as its main aim. He construes it as a powerful response to
the Marginal Productivity Theory of Just Distribution and other classical

1. The editor served as one of Rawls's graduate teaching assistants (along with An-
drews Reath) in the spring term of 1983, and recorded the Hobbes and Hume lectures
transcribed here. The lectures on Locke, Mill, and Marx were also recorded in 1983. These
tapes, as well as tapes of Rawls's 1984 lectures, have been preserved in digital format and
deposited in the Rawls Archives at Widener Library, Harvard University.

liberal and right-wing libertarian conceptions which regard pure ownership as making a tangible contribution to production. (See Marx, Lecture II.)

Rawls's lectures on Bishop Joseph Butler and Henry Sidgwick were not left as finished as the other lectures in this volume. Nonetheless, he agreed to their publication shortly before he died in November 2002, and they have been included in the Appendix to this volume. Rawls taught Sidgwick for a number of years (including 1976, 1979, and 1981) in his political philosophy course, along with Hume and J. S. Mill, to give students an idea of the works of (what he regarded as) the three major utilitarian philosophers. He saw Sidgwick as the culmination of the classical utilitarian tradition that began with Bentham. He also regarded Sidgwick's comparative method in *The Methods of Ethics* as providing a pattern for moral philosophy to emulate. The first two Sidgwick lectures included here were for the most part taken from the handwritten notes that Rawls duplicated and handed out to students. He used these handouts as his lecture notes, and then elaborated upon them orally when delivering the lectures. For this reason, the first two Sidgwick lectures cannot be considered by any means complete lectures. The third lecture on Sidgwick (1975) goes over some of the same material as in the brief discussion of utilitarianism in Sidgwick, Lecture II, but discusses in much more detail the assumptions and implications of the classical utilitarian position. There is a good deal of material on utilitarianism in this lecture and in the brief fourth lecture (1976) that is not available in any of Rawls's other published discussions of utilitarianism in *A Theory of Justice,* "Social Unity and Primary Goods,"[2] or elsewhere.

The five lectures on Butler were among Rawls's handwritten papers. These lectures were used in Rawls's course on the history of moral philosophy in the spring of 1982, when he also taught Kant and Hume. Rawls thought that Butler provided the major non-utilitarian response to Hobbes by an English philosopher. He also regarded Butler as among the major figures in modern moral philosophy. Among Rawls's handwritten notes to himself (not incorporated into the lectures themselves) is the following: "Important Points in Butler: (Hobbes and Butler, the two great sources of modern moral philosophy: Hobbes as posing the problem—the writer to refute. Butler supplied a deep answer to Hobbes)." In addition, Rawls found

2. See John Rawls, *Collected Papers,* ed. Samuel Freeman (Cambridge, Mass.: Harvard University Press, 1999), chap. 17.

some connection between Kant's and Butler's doctrine of conscience, and this perhaps provided Rawls with grounds for believing that Kant's non-naturalistic, non-intuitionistic account of morality was not peculiar to German Idealist philosophy.[3] Finally, the Butler lectures are suggestive of the central role that the idea of a "reasonable moral psychology" had in Rawls's conception of moral and political philosophy. (There are parallels in the lectures on Mill and Rousseau too.) One of the main ideas behind Rawls's work is that justice and morality are not contrary to human nature, but rather are part of our nature and indeed are, or at least can be, essential to the human good. (See *A Theory of Justice,* chapter 8, "The Sense of Justice," and chapter 9, "The Good of Justice.") It is noteworthy that Rawls's discussion of Butler's reconciliation of moral virtue and "self-love" parallels Rawls's own argument for the congruence of the Right and the Good.

Rawls left among his papers a short piece called "Some Remarks About My Teaching" (1993), which discusses his lectures on political philosophy. Relevant portions of it are as follows:[4]

> For the most part I taught moral and political philosophy, doing a course in each one every year over the years. . . . I came gradually to focus more and more on political and social philosophy, and I came to talk about parts of justice as fairness, so-called, in tandem with earlier people who had written on the subject, beginning with Hobbes, Locke and Rousseau, and occasionally Kant, although Kant was very difficult to work into that course. I included at times Hume and Bentham, J. S. Mill and Sidgwick. However, usually Kant's moral philosophy was

3. Thanks to Joshua Cohen for this suggestion. It is confirmed by notes that Rawls made to himself. Among the references to Kant in Rawls's notes on Butler are the following two entries:

> (4) Egoism contra Hobbes: Butler holds moral projects as much a part of the self as other parts of the self: our natural desires, etc. Kant deepens this by connecting ML [Moral Law] with the self as R+R [Rational and Reasonable]. . . .
> (9) Connect this up with Kant; including his notion of reasonable faith.

4. A somewhat similar version of Rawls's account of his teaching is excerpted in the Editor's Foreword to the companion volume, *Lectures on the History of Moral Philosophy,* ed. Barbara Herman (Cambridge, Mass.: Harvard University Press, 2000), pp. xvi–xviii. That account derives from Rawls's published remarks on his teaching as found in John Rawls, "Burton Dreben: A Reminiscence," in *Future Pasts: Perspectives on the Place of the Analytic Tradition in Twentieth-Century Philosophy,* ed. Juliet Floyd and Sanford Shieh (New York: Oxford University Press, 2000).

taken up in a separate course along with other writers, who changed from time to time, but often it covered Hume and Leibniz as examples of strikingly different doctrines which Kant certainly knew something about. Other writers occasionally considered were Clarke and Bishop Butler and other British 18th century people, such as Shaftesbury and Hutcheson. Sometimes I used Moore and Ross, Broad and Stevenson, as modern examples.

In talking about these people I always tried to do two things especially. One thing was to pose their philosophical problems as they saw them, given what their understanding of the state of moral and political philosophy then was. So I tried to discern what they thought their main problems were. I often cited the remark of Collingwood in his *An Autobiography,* to the effect that the history of political philosophy is not that of a series of answers to the same question but of a series of answers to different questions, or, as he actually put it, it is "the history of a problem more or less constantly changing, whose solution was changing with it."[5] This remark is not quite right, but it tells us to look for a writer's point of view on the political world at that time in order to see how political philosophy develops over time and why. I saw each writer contributing to the development of doctrines supporting democratic thought, and this included Marx, whom I always discussed in the political philosophy course.

Another thing I tried to do was to present each writer's thought in what I took to be its strongest form. I took to heart Mill's remark in his review of [Alfred] Sedgwick: "A doctrine is not judged at all until it is judged in its best form" (CW: X, p. 52). So I tried to do just that. Yet I didn't say, not intentionally anyway, what to my mind they should have said, but what they did say, supported by what I viewed as the most reasonable interpretation of their text. The text had to be known and respected, and the doctrine presented in its best form. Leaving aside the text seemed offensive, a kind of pretending. If I departed from it—no harm in that—I had to say so. Lecturing that way, I believed that a writer's views became stronger and more convincing, and would be for students a more worthy object of study.

Several maxims guided me in doing this. I always assumed, for ex-

5. R. G. Collingwood, *An Autobiography* (Oxford: Clarendon Press, 1939), p. 62.

ample, that the writers we were studying were always much smarter than I was. If they were not, why was I wasting my time and the student's time by studying them? If I saw a mistake in their arguments, I supposed they [the philosophers] saw it too and must have dealt with it, but where? So I looked for their way out, not mine. Sometimes their way out was historical: in their day the question need not be raised; or wouldn't arise or be fruitfully discussed. Or there was a part of the text I had overlooked, or hadn't read.

In doing this I followed what Kant says in the *First Critique* at B866. He says that Philosophy is a mere idea of a possible science and nowhere exists *in concreto*. So how can we recognize and learn it? ". . . we cannot learn philosophy, for where is it, who is in possession of it, and how shall we recognize it? We can only learn to philosophize, that is, to exercise the talent of reason, in accordance with universal principles, on certain actually existing attempts at philosophy, always, however, reserving the right of reason to investigate, to confirm, or to reject these principles at their very sources." So we learn moral and political philosophy, and indeed any other part of philosophy by studying the exemplars—those noted figures who have made cherished attempts—and we try to learn from them, and if we are lucky to find a way to go beyond them. My task was to explain Hobbes, Locke, and Rousseau, or Hume, Leibniz, and Kant as clearly and forcefully as I could, always attending carefully to what they actually said.

The result was that I was loath to raise objections to the exemplars—that's too easy and misses what is essential—though it was important to point out objections that those coming later in the same tradition sought to correct, or to point to views those in another tradition thought were mistaken. (I think here of the social contract view and utilitarianism as two traditions.) Otherwise philosophical thought can't progress and it would be mysterious why later writers made the criticisms they did.

In the case of Locke, for example, I remarked on the fact that his view allowed for a kind of political inequality we would not accept—inequality in basic rights of voting—and that Rousseau had tried to overcome this, and I discussed how he had done so. Yet I would emphasize that Locke in his liberalism was ahead of his time and opposed royal absolutism. He didn't flinch from danger and was loyal to his friend Lord Shaftesbury, following him even in taking part, it seems, in the Rye House plot to assassinate Charles II in the summer of 1683. He fled for his life to Holland and barely escaped execution. Locke had the courage to put his head where his mouth was, perhaps the only one of the great figures to take such enormous risks.

None of these lectures were written with the intention that they would be published. Indeed Rawls said, in discussing Kant in the paragraph that immediately follows his remarks about Locke quoted above: "The last version of the [Kant] lectures (1991) is no doubt better than earlier ones but I couldn't bear to have it published as it stands (as some have urged). It doesn't begin to do Kant justice on those questions, or to measure up to what others can now do." As this sentence indicates, Rawls resisted the publication of his lectures for years. It was only after he was prevailed upon to publish his *Lectures on the History of Moral Philosophy* (edited by Barbara Herman and published by Harvard University Press in 2000), and that volume was substantially complete, that he agreed to allow his lectures on the history of political philosophy to be published as well.

Finally, in the conclusion to Rawls's "Some Remarks About My Teaching," he said (and what he says of Kant here, he, in all his modesty, also would have said of the philosophers in this volume):

Yet, as I have said, I have never felt satisfied with the understanding I could gain of Kant's overall conception. This leaves a certain unhappiness and I am reminded of a story about John Marin, a great American watercolorist along with Homer and Sargent. Marin's paintings, which most of you must have seen, are a kind of figurative expressionism. In the late forties he was highly regarded as perhaps our leading artist, or among the few. Looking at his watercolors one can tell what they are of: say, a skyscraper in New York City, the Taos mountains of New Mexico, or the schooners and harbors of Maine. For eight years in the 1920s Marin went to Stonington, Maine, to paint; and Ruth Fine, who wrote a splendid book on Marin, tells of going there to see if she could find anyone who had known him then. She finally found a lobsterman who said, "Eeah, eeah, we all knew him. He went out painting in his little boat day after day, week after week, summer after summer. And you know, poor fellah, he tried so hard, but he never did get it right."

That always said it exactly for me, after all this time: "Never did get it right."[6]

Mardy Rawls did much of the work in editing these lectures, and without her help and advice I could not have completed them. Particularly from 1995 (after Jack's first stroke), Mardy assumed an invaluable role in bringing to fruition many projects. She read each of these lectures carefully and worked arduously to clarify and point out sentences that could be misconstrued. Before Jack asked me in 2000 to undertake the editing of this volume, Mardy had already more or less completed the editing of the lectures on Locke, Rousseau, Mill, and Marx. Jack went over these lectures carefully and gave his approval. Anne Rawls transcribed (in 2001) from the recording tapes the 1983 lectures on Hobbes and Hume. Mardy then put them into readable form, whereupon I made further revisions and additions taken from Rawls's typed and handwritten notes and handouts. The lectures on Sidgwick and Butler were typed up from Rawls's handwritten lecture notes. I made additions to the first Sidgwick lecture, relying upon other notes on Sidgwick in Rawls's lecture files. In general, any editorial emendations in these lectures involve the repositioning of paragraphs and sentences written by Rawls himself.

I am grateful to Mark Navin for deciphering and typing the handwritten lecture notes on Sidgwick and Butler, and also for entering the editing corrections made to the Locke, Rousseau, Mill, and Marx lectures. I am also especially grateful to Kate Moran, who typed up handwritten lecture notes on Hobbes and Hume, checked carefully the quotations by all philosophers, and prepared the manuscript for final submission. Matt Lister, Thomas Ricketts, and Kok Chor Tan helped in a number of ways as well. Thanks to Warren Goldfarb and Andy Reath for helpful advice regarding Rawls's syllabi. T. M. Scanlon and especially Joshua Cohen gave me much helpful advice on editing the lectures, regarding what to include and what to leave unpublished, and I am most grateful to them both.

Finally, I am, once again, grateful to my wife, Annette Lareau-Freeman, for her sage counsel and constant support in helping me bring the publication of these important documents to fruition.

Samuel Freeman

6. [Note by Mardy Rawls: Thinking of the many times Jack told that story to his classes, we chose Marin's painting, "Deer Isle, Islets," for the cover of *Justice as Fairness: A Restatement.*]

Introductory Remarks

In preparing these lectures, developed over a number of years of teaching Political and Social Philosophy, I have considered how six writers, Hobbes, Locke, Rousseau, Hume, Mill, and Marx, treat certain topics discussed in my own writings on political philosophy. Originally, I devoted about half of the course's lectures to relevant topics from *A Theory of Justice*.[7] Later, as I was developing the text of *Justice as Fairness: A Restatement*,[8] those lectures concerned the more recent work instead, and I made available to the class Xerox copies of the manuscript.

Because the *Restatement* has now been published, I am not including those lectures in this book. There are only a few places where I have pointed out in any explicit way the connection between the works and ideas discussed and my own work; but where justice as fairness is mentioned, references to sections of the book are in footnotes, and where it seems useful, important ideas or concepts are defined or explained in those footnotes. An introductory lecture including some general remarks on political philosophy, and some thoughts on the main ideas of liberalism, may help lay the groundwork for a discussion of the six writers.

I shall try to identify the more central features of liberalism as expressing a political conception of justice when liberalism is viewed from within the tradition of democratic constitutionalism. One strand in this tradition, the doctrine of the social contract, is represented by Hobbes, Locke, and Rousseau; another strand, that of utilitarianism, is represented by Hume and J. S. Mill; whereas the socialist, or social democratic strand, is represented by Marx, whom I will consider largely as a critic of liberalism.

7. John Rawls, *A Theory of Justice* (Cambridge, Mass.: Harvard University Press, 1971; revised edition, 1999).

8. John Rawls, *Justice as Fairness: A Restatement* (Cambridge, Mass.: Harvard University Press, 2001).

The lectures are narrow in focus, both from a historical and from a systematic point of view. They do not present a balanced introduction to the questions of political and social philosophy. There is no attempt to assess different interpretations of the philosophers discussed; interpretations are proposed that seem reasonably accurate to the texts we study and fruitful for my limited purposes in presenting them. Moreover, many important questions of political and social philosophy are not discussed at all. It is my hope that this narrow focus is excusable if it encourages an instructive way of approaching the questions we do consider and allows us to gain a greater depth of understanding than would otherwise be possible.

JOHN RAWLS

Texts Cited

Joseph Butler, *The Works of Joseph Butler*, ed. W. E. Gladstone (Bristol, England: Thoemmes Press, 1995).

Thomas Hobbes, *De Cive*, ed. Sterling P. Lamprecht (New York: Appleton-Century-Crofts, 1949).

Thomas Hobbes, *Leviathan*, ed. C. B. MacPherson (Baltimore: Penguin Books, 1968).

David Hume, *Enquiries Concerning the Human Understanding and Concerning the Principles of Morals*, 2nd ed., ed. L. A. Selby-Bigge (Oxford: Oxford University Press, 1902).

David Hume, *Treatise of Human Nature*, 2nd ed., ed. L. A. Selby-Bigge (Oxford: Oxford University Press, 1978).

Immanuel Kant, *Groundwork of the Metaphysics of Morals*, trans. and ed. H. J. Paton (London: Hutchinson, 1948).

John Locke, *A Letter Concerning Toleration*, ed. James H. Tully (Indianapolis: Hackett, 1983).

John Locke, *Two Treatises of Government*, ed. Peter Laslett (Cambridge: Cambridge University Press, 1960).

Karl Marx, *Capital: A Critique of Political Economy* (New York: International Publishers, 1967).

John Stuart Mill, *Collected Works* (cited as *CW*) (Toronto: University of Toronto Press, 1963–1991).

Jean-Jacques Rousseau, *The First and Second Discourses*, ed. Roger D. Masters, trans. Roger D. and Judith R. Masters (New York: St. Martin's Press, 1964).

Jean-Jacques Rousseau, *On the Social Contract, with Geneva Manuscript and Political Economy*, ed. Roger D. Masters, trans. Judith R. Masters (New York: St. Martin's Press, 1978).

Henry Sidgwick, *The Methods of Ethics* (London: Macmillan, 1907).

Robert C. Tucker, ed., *The Marx-Engels Reader*, 2nd ed. (New York: W. W. Norton, 1978).

INTRODUCTION

Remarks on Political Philosophy

§1. Four Questions about Political Philosophy

1. We begin by asking several general questions about political philosophy. Why might we be interested in it? What are our reasons for thinking about it? What, if anything, do we expect to gain by doing so? In this spirit I review some more definite questions that might prove helpful.

Let's ask first: What is the audience of political philosophy? To whom is it addressed? Since the audience will vary from one society to another depending on its social structure and its pressing problems, what is the audience in a constitutional democracy? Thus, we begin by looking at our own case.

Surely, in a democracy the answer to this question is: all citizens generally, or citizens as the corporate body of all those who by their votes exercise the final institutional authority on all political questions, by constitutional amendment, if necessary. That the audience of political philosophy in a democratic society is the body of citizens has important consequences.

It means, for one thing, that a liberal political philosophy which, of course, accepts and defends the idea of constitutional democracy, is not to be seen as a theory, so to speak. Those who write about such a doctrine are not to be viewed as experts on a special subject, as may be the case with the sciences. Political philosophy has no special access to fundamental truths, or reasonable ideas, about justice and the common good, or to other basic notions. Its merit, to the extent it has any, is that by study and reflection it may elaborate deeper and more instructive conceptions of basic political ideas that help us to clarify our judgments about the institutions and policies of a democratic regime.

2. A second question is this: In addressing this audience, what are the credentials of political philosophy? What are its claims to authority? I use

the term "authority" here because some have said that writers in moral and political philosophy claim a certain authority, at least implicitly. It has been said that political philosophy conveys a claim to know, and that the claim to know is a claim to rule.[1] This assertion is, I believe, completely mistaken. In a democratic society at least, political philosophy has no authority at all, if by authority is meant a certain legal standing and possession of an authoritative weight on certain political matters; or if, alternatively, it means an authority sanctioned by long-standing custom and practice, and treated as having evidential force.

Political philosophy can only mean the tradition of political philosophy; and in a democracy this tradition is always the joint work of writers and of their readers. This work is joint, since it is writers and readers together who produce and cherish works of political philosophy over time and it is always up to voters to decide whether to embody their ideas in basic institutions.

Thus, in a democracy, writers in political philosophy have no more authority than any other citizen, and should claim no more. I take this to be perfectly obvious and as not needing any comment, were it not that the contrary is occasionally asserted. I mention the matter only to put aside misgivings about this.

Of course, one might say: political philosophy hopes for the credentials of, and implicitly invokes the authority of, human reason. This reason is simply the shared powers of reasoned thought, judgment, and inference as these are exercised by any fully normal persons beyond the age of reason, that is, by all normal adult citizens. Suppose we agree with this and say political philosophy does invoke this authority. But so likewise do all citizens who speak reasonably and conscientiously in addressing others about political questions, or indeed any other question. Seeking what we have called the authority of human reason means trying to present our views with their supporting grounds in a reasonable and sound manner so that others may judge them intelligently. Striving for the credentials of human reason does not distinguish political philosophy from any kind of reasoned discussion on any topic. All reasoned and conscientious thought seeks the authority of human reason.

Political philosophy, as it is found in a democratic society in texts that

1. See the interesting review by Michael Walzer of Benjamin Barber's *The Conquest of Politics: Liberal Philosophy in Democratic Times* (Princeton, N.J.: Princeton University Press, 1988), in the *New York Review of Books*, February 2, 1989, p. 42.

endure and continue to be studied, may indeed be expressed in unusually systematic and complete statements of fundamental democratic doctrines and ideas. These texts may be better argued and more perspicuously presented than those that do not endure. In this sense they may more successfully invoke the authority of human reason. Yet the authority of human reason is a very special kind of authority. For whether a text in political philosophy makes this appeal successfully is a collective judgment, made over time, in a society's general culture, as citizens individually, one by one, judge these texts worthy of study and reflection. In this case there is no authority in the sense of an office or court or legislative body authorized to have the final say, or even a probative say. It is not for official bodies, or bodies sanctioned by custom and long-standing practice, to assess the work of reason.

This situation is not peculiar. The same is true in the community of all scientists, or to be more specific, of all physicists. There is no institutional body among them with the authority to declare, say, that the theory of general relativity is correct or incorrect. In matters of political justice in a democracy, the body of citizens is similar to the body of all physicists in this matter. This fact is characteristic of the modern democratic world and rooted in its ideas of political liberty and equality.

3. A third question is: At what point and in what way does political philosophy enter into and affect the outcome of democratic politics? How should political philosophy view itself in this respect?

Here there are at least two views: the Platonic view, for instance, is the view that political philosophy ascertains the truth about justice and the common good. It then seeks a political agent to realize that truth in institutions, irrespective of whether that truth is freely accepted, or even understood. On this view, political philosophy's knowledge of the truth authorizes it to shape, even to control, the outcome of politics, by persuasion and force if necessary. Witness Plato's philosopher king, or Lenin's revolutionary vanguard. Here the claim to truth is understood as carrying with it not only the claim to know, but also the claim to control and to act politically.

Another view, the democratic view, let's say, sees political philosophy as part of the general background culture of a democratic society, although in a few cases certain classic texts become part of the public political culture. Often cited and referred to, they are part of public lore and a fund of society's basic political ideas. As such, political philosophy may contribute to the culture of civic society in which its basic ideas and their history are discussed and studied, and in certain cases may enter into the public political discussion as well.

Some writers[2] who dislike the form and style of much current academic political philosophy see it as trying to avoid and to render unnecessary the everyday politics of democracy—the great game of politics.[3] Academic political philosophy is said by these writers to be, in effect, Platonic: it tries to provide basic truths and principles to answer or to resolve at least the main political questions, thus making ordinary politics unnecessary. These writers, critical of philosophy, also think that ordinary politics best proceeds by itself, without the benefit of philosophy, or without worrying about its controversies. They think that proceeding in that way would lead to a more vibrant and lively public life and a more committed citizen body.

Now, to say that a liberal political philosophy is Platonic (as defined above) is surely incorrect. Since liberalism endorses the idea of democratic government, it would not try to overrule the outcome of everyday democratic politics. So long as democracy exists, the only way that liberal philosophy could properly do that would be for it to influence some legitimate constitutionally established political agent, and then persuade this agent to override the will of democratic majorities. One way this can happen is for liberal writers in philosophy to influence the judges on a Supreme Court in a constitutional regime like ours. Liberal, academic writers, such as Bruce Ackerman, Ronald Dworkin, and Frank Michelman, may address the Supreme Court, but so do many conservatives and other non-liberal writers. They are engaged in constitutional politics, we might say. Given the role of the Court in our constitutional system, what may look like an attempt to override democratic politics may actually be the acceptance of judicial review, and of the idea that the Constitution puts certain fundamental rights and liberties beyond the reach of ordinary legislative majorities. Thus, the discussion of academic writers is often about the scope and limits of majority rule and the proper role of the Court in specifying and protecting basic constitutional freedoms.

Much depends, then, on whether we accept judicial review and the idea that a democratic constitution should put certain fundamental rights and

2. For example, Benjamin Barber as mentioned above.

3. "The Great Game of Politics" was the name of a column in the *Baltimore Sun* by Frank R. Kent in the 1920s and 30s.

liberties beyond the reach of the legislative majorities of ordinary, as opposed to constitutional, politics. I incline to accept judicial review in our case, but there are good arguments on both sides and it is a question that democratic citizens must themselves consider. What is at stake is a decision between two conceptions of democracy, constitutional democracy and majoritarian democracy. In any case, even those who support judicial review take for granted that, in ordinary politics, legislative majorities are normally governing.

Our third question was: At what point and in what way does political philosophy enter into and affect the outcome of democratic politics? To this let's say: in a regime with judicial review, political philosophy tends to have a larger public role, at least in constitutional cases; and political issues that are often discussed are constitutional issues concerning basic rights and liberties of democratic citizenship. Beyond this, political philosophy has an educational role as part of the background culture. This role is the subject of our fourth question.

4. A political view is a view about political justice and the common good, and about what institutions and policies best promote them. Citizens must somehow acquire and understand these ideas if they are to be capable of making judgments about basic rights and liberties. So let's now ask: What basic conceptions of person and political society, and what ideals of liberty and equality, of justice and citizenship, do citizens initially bring to democratic politics? How do they become attached to those conceptions and ideals, and what ways of thought sustain these attachments? In what way do they learn about government and what view of it do they acquire?

Do they come to politics with a conception of citizens as free and equal, and capable of engaging in public reason and of expressing through their votes their considered opinion of what is required by political justice and the common good? Or does their view of politics go no further than thinking that people simply vote their own economic and class interests and their religious or ethnic antagonisms, supported by ideals of social hierarchy, with some persons viewed as by nature inferior to others?

It would seem that a constitutional regime may not long endure unless its citizens first enter democratic politics with fundamental conceptions and ideals that endorse and strengthen its basic political institutions. Moreover, these institutions are most secure when they in their turn sustain these conceptions and ideals. Yet surely citizens acquire those conceptions and ideals in part, although only in part, from writings in political philosophy, which themselves belong to the general background culture of civic society. They come across them in their conversation and reading, in schools and universities and in professional schools. They see editorials and discussions debating these ideas in newspapers and in journals of opinion.

Some texts achieve a rank that puts them in the public political culture, as opposed to the general culture of civic society. How many of us had to memorize parts of the Declaration of Independence, the Preamble to the Constitution, and Lincoln's Gettysburg Address? While these texts are not authoritative—the Preamble is not part of the Constitution as law—they may influence our understanding and interpretation of the Constitution in certain ways.

Moreover, in these texts, and others of this status (if there are any), the values expressed are, let's say, political values. This is not a definition, just an indication. For example the Preamble to the Constitution mentions: a more perfect union, justice, domestic tranquility, common defense, the general welfare, and the blessings of liberty. The Declaration of Independence adds the value of equality and connects it with equal natural rights.

It is safe to call these political values. I shall think of a political conception of justice as trying to give a reasonably systematic and coherent account of these values, and to set out how they are to be ordered in applying them to basic political and social institutions. The vast majority of works in political philosophy, even if they endure a while, belong to general background culture. However, works regularly cited in Supreme Court cases and in public discussions of fundamental questions may be viewed as belonging to the public political culture, or bordering on it. Indeed a few—such as Locke's *Second Treatise* and Mill's *On Liberty*—do seem part of the political culture, at least in the United States.

I have suggested that citizens had best learn from civic society its fundamental conceptions and ideals before they come to democratic politics. Otherwise a democratic regime, should one somehow come about, may not long endure. One of the many reasons why the Weimar constitution failed was that none of the main intellectual currents in Germany was prepared to defend it, including the leading philosophers and writers, such as Heidegger and Thomas Mann.

To conclude: Political philosophy has a not insignificant role as part of general background culture in providing a source of essential political principles and ideals. It plays a role in strengthening the roots of democratic thought and attitudes. This role it performs not so much in day-to-day politics as in educating citizens to certain ideal conceptions of person and political society before they come to politics, and in their reflective moments throughout life.[4]

5. Is there anything about the politics of a society that encourages the sincere appeal to principles of justice and the common good? Why isn't politics simply the struggle for power and influence—everyone trying to get their own way? Harold Lasswell said: "Politics is the study of who gets what and how."[5] Why isn't that all there is to it? Are we naive, as the cynic says, to think that it could be anything else? If so, then why isn't all talk of justice and the common good simply the manipulation of symbols that have the psychological effect of getting people to go along with our view, not for good reasons, plainly, but somehow mesmerized by what we say?

What the cynic says about moral and political principles and ideals cannot be correct.[6] For if it were, the language and vocabulary of morals and politics referring to and appealing to those principles and ideals would long since have ceased to be invoked. People are not so stupid as not to discern when those norms are being appealed to by certain groups and their leaders in a purely manipulative and group-interested fashion. This is not to deny, of course, that principles of justice and fairness and the common good are often appealed to in a manipulative way. Such an appeal often enough rides piggy-back, so to speak, on those same principles' being invoked sincerely by those who mean them and can be trusted.

Two things, it seems, make an important difference in what ideas citizens have when they first come to politics: one is the nature of the political system in which they grow up; the other is the content of the background culture, how far it acquaints them with democratic political ideas and leads them to reflect on their meaning.

The nature of the political system teaches forms of political conduct and political principles. In a democratic system, say, citizens note that party

---

4. My answer to this question has followed that of Michael Walzer, referred to in note 1 above.

5. Harold Lasswell, *Politics: Who Gets What, When, and How* (New York: McGraw-Hill, 1936).

6. See Jon Elster, *The Cement of Society* (Cambridge: Cambridge University Press, 1989), pp. 128ff.

leaders, in forming working majorities, are constrained by certain principles of justice and the common good, at least as regards their explicit public
political program. Here again the cynic may say that these appeals to public
principles of justice and the common good are self-interested, because to
remain relevant, a group must be recognized as "inside the system," and
that means that its conduct must respect various social norms consistent
with those principles. This is true, but it overlooks something: that in a reasonably successful political system, citizens in due course become attached
to these principles of justice and the common good, and as with the principle of religious toleration, their allegiance to them is not purely, even if it is
in part, self-interested.

6. An important question, then, is: what features, if any, of political and
social institutions tend to prevent the sincere appeal to justice and the common good, or to fair principles of political cooperation? Here I conjecture
that we can learn something from the failure of Germany to achieve a constitutional democratic regime.

Consider the situation of German political parties in Wilhelmine Germany of Bismarck's time. There were six noteworthy features of the political system:

(1) It was a hereditary monarchy with very great though not absolute
powers.
(2) The monarchy was military in character as the army (officered by
the Prussian nobility) guaranteed it against an adverse popular will.
(3) The chancellor and the cabinet were servants of the crown and not
of the Reichstag, as would be the case in a constitutional regime.
(4) Political parties were fragmented by Bismarck, who appealed to
their economic interests in return for their support, turning them
into pressure groups.
(5) Since they were no more than pressure groups, political parties
never aspired to govern, and they held exclusive ideologies which
made compromise with other groups difficult.
(6) It was not considered improper for officials, not even the chancellor,
to attack certain groups as enemies of the empire: Catholics, Social
Democrats, national minorities: French (Alsace-Lorraine), Danes,
Poles, and Jews.

Consider the fourth and fifth features, that political parties were nothing more than pressure groups, and because they never aspired to rule—to

form a government—they were unwilling to compromise or to bargain with other social groups. The liberals were never ready to support programs wanted by the working classes, while the social democrats always insisted on the nationalization of industry and dismantling of the capitalist system, which frightened off the liberals. This inability of the liberals and the social democrats to work together to form a government was fatal in the end to German democracy, because it persisted into the Weimar regime with its disastrous outcome.

A political society with a structure of this kind will develop enormous internal hostility between social classes and economic groups. They never learn to cooperate in forming a government under a properly democratic regime. They always act as outsiders petitioning the chancellor to meet their interests in return for their support of the government. Some groups, like the social democrats, were never thought of as possible supporters of the government at all; they were simply outside the system, even when they came to have the greatest number of votes, as they did before the First World War. Since there were no genuine political parties, there were no politicians: people whose role is not to please a particular group but to put together a working majority behind a political and social democratic program.

Beyond these features of the political system, the background culture and the general tenor of political thought (as well as the social structure) meant that no major group was willing to wage a political effort to achieve a constitutional regime; or if it did support one, like many of the liberals, its political will was weak and it could be bought off by the chancellor by the granting of economic favors.[7]

---

7. As texts on (1)–(5) above, see the following: Hajo Holborn, *History of Modern Germany: 1840–1945* (New York: Knopf, 1969), e.g. pp. 141f, 268–275, 296f, 711f, 811f; Gordon Craig, *Germany: 1866–1945* (Oxford: Oxford University Press, 1978), Chs. 2–5, and see his comments on Bismarck, pp. 140–144; Hans-Ulrich Wehler, *The German Empire: 1871–1918* (New York: Berg, 1985), pp. 52–137, 155–170, 232–246; A. J. P. Taylor, *The Course of German History*, 1st ed. 1946 (New York: Capricorn, 1962), pp. 115–159; and his *Bismarck: The Man and the Statesman*, 1st ed. 1955 (New York: Vintage Books, 1967), Chs. 6–9; D. G. Williamson: *Bismarck and Germany: 1862–1890* (London: Longman, 1986). On (6), regarding Jews: Peter Pulzer, *Rise of Political Anti-Semitism in Germany and Austria before WW I*, 2nd ed. (Cambridge, Mass.: Harvard University Press, 1988); Werner Angress, "Prussia's Army and Jewish Reserve Officer's Controversy before WW I," essay in *Imperial Germany*, ed. J. T. Sheehan (New York: Watts, 1976).

§2. Four Roles of Political Philosophy

1. I see four roles that political philosophy may play as part of a society's public political culture. These are discussed at length in §1 of the *Restatement*. So I will only briefly recount them here.

(a) The first is its *practical role* arising from divisive political conflict when its task is to focus on deeply disputed questions and to see whether, despite appearances, some underlying basis of philosophical and moral agreement can be uncovered, or differences can at least be narrowed so that social cooperation on a footing of mutual respect among citizens can still be maintained.

(b) The second role, which I call *orientation*, is one of reason and reflection. Political philosophy may contribute to how a people think of their political and social institutions as a whole, of themselves as citizens, and of their basic aims and purposes as a society with a history—a nation—as opposed to their aims and purposes as individuals, or as members of families and associations.

(c) A third role, stressed by Hegel in his *Philosophy of Right* (1821), is that of *reconciliation:* political philosophy may try to calm our frustration and rage against our society and its history by showing us the way in which its institutions, when properly understood, from a philosophical point of view, are rational, and developed over time as they did to attain their present, rational form. When political philosophy acts in this role, it must guard against the danger of being simply a defense of an unjust and unworthy status quo. This would make it an ideology (a false scheme of thought), in Marx's sense.[8]

(d) The fourth role is that of *probing the limits of practicable political possi-*

---

8. For Marx an ideology is a false scheme of thought that sometimes helps to obscure from those within the social system how it works, making them unable to penetrate beneath the surface appearance of its institutions. In this case it buttresses an illusion, as classical political economy helped, in Marx's view, to obscure the fact that a capitalist system is a system of exploitation. Or an ideology serves to firm up a necessary delusion: decent capitalists do not want to believe that the system is exploitative; so they believe the classical doctrine of political economy, which assures them it is a scheme of free exchanges in which all factors of production—land, capital, and labor—appropriately receive what they contribute to social output. In this case ideology buttresses a delusion. [See Marx, Lecture III in this volume, for a discussion of ideological consciousness. —Ed.]

bility. In this role, we view political philosophy as realistically utopian. Our hope for the future of our society rests on the belief that the social world allows at least a decent political order, so that a reasonably just, though not perfect, democratic regime is possible. So we ask: What would a just democratic society be like under reasonably favorable but still possible historical conditions, conditions allowed by the laws and tendencies of the social world? What ideals and principles would such a society try to realize given the circumstances of justice in a democratic culture as we know them?

§3. Main Ideas of Liberalism: Its Origins and Content

1. Since a good part of these lectures will be concerned with conceptions of liberalism and four of its main historical figures and one of its greatest critics, I should say something about how I understand it. There is no settled meaning of liberalism; it has many forms and many features, and writers characterize it in different ways.

Liberalism's three main historical origins are the following: the Reformation and the religious wars of the sixteenth and seventeenth centuries ending with the, at first, reluctant acceptance of the principle of toleration and liberty of conscience; the gradual taming of royal power by the rising middle classes and the establishment of constitutional regimes of limited monarchy; and the winning of the working classes to democracy and majority rule.[9] These developments occurred in different countries in Europe and North America at different times; yet thinking of England, it is roughly true that liberty of conscience was well on its way to being won at the end of the 17th century, constitutional government during the 18th, and democracy and majority rule with universal suffrage during the 19th. This movement is not, of course, complete. Important aspects of it have not yet been won even today, and some still seem a long way off. All existing allegedly liberal democracies are highly imperfect and fall far short of what democratic justice would seem to require.

For example, five reforms needed in the United States are indicated here: campaign finance reform to overcome the present system of money

---

9. This is a philosopher's schematic version of speculative history, and to be recognized as such.

buying access to power; fair equality of educational opportunity; some form of assured health care for all; some form of guaranteed and socially useful work; and equal justice for and equality of women. These reforms would greatly mitigate if not remove the worst aspects of discrimination and racism. Others will have their list of essential reforms whose importance is also undeniable.

2. Expressed in broad terms, the content of a liberal political conception of justice has three main elements: a list of equal basic rights and liberties, a priority for these freedoms, and an assurance that all members of society have adequate all-purpose means to make use of these rights and liberties. Note that the liberties are given by a list. Later we try to make these elements more definite.

To give the general idea: the equal basic liberties include the equal political liberties—the right to vote and to run for public office, and the right of free political speech of all kinds. They include also the civic liberties—the right of free non-political speech, the right of free association and, of course, liberty of conscience. Add to these freedoms equality of opportunity, freedom of movement, the right to one's own mind and body (integrity of the person), the right of personal property, and finally, the liberties covered by the rule of law and a right to a fair trial.

This list of the basic liberties is, of course, familiar. The difficult part lies in specifying them more exactly and in ordering them in relation to one another when they conflict. At the moment the essential thing is to stress the great significance that liberalism attaches to a certain list of liberties, rather than to liberty as such. With this in mind, the second element of the content of liberalism is that the liberties are assigned a certain priority, that is, a certain force and weight. This means, in effect, that they cannot normally be sacrificed in order to gain greater social welfare, or for the sake of perfectionist values; and this restriction is, practically speaking, absolute.

The third element of liberalism's content is that, as indicated above, its principles assign to all members of society claims to adequate all-purpose material means to make use of their freedoms, as detailed and given priority by the preceding elements. These all-purpose means fall under what I shall call primary goods. They include, in addition to the basic liberties and equal opportunities: income and wealth, and as appropriate, claims to goods in kind, for example, to education and health care.

By saying that the content of liberal views has these three elements I mean that the content of any familiar liberal view would more or less fit this broad description. What distinguishes different liberalisms is how they specify these elements and the general arguments used to do this. There are views, often described as liberal, for example, libertarian views, that don't exemplify the third element of assuring to citizens adequate all-purpose means to make use of their freedoms. But the fact that it does not is, among other things, what makes a view libertarian and not liberal. Libertarianism doesn't fit the third element. Of course, this is not an argument against it, but simply a comment about its content.

§4. A Central Thesis of Liberalism

1. There are, no doubt, several candidates for the central thesis of liberalism—the securing of the basic liberties is certainly one of them—and writers will differ on this. One central element is certainly the following:

A legitimate regime is such that its political and social institutions are justifiable to all citizens—to each and every one—by addressing their reason, theoretical and practical. Again: a justification of the institutions of the social world must be, in principle, available to everyone, and so justifiable to all who live under them. The legitimacy of a liberal regime depends on such a justification.[10]

While political liberalism (of which justice as fairness[11] is an example) does not reject or question the importance of religion and tradition, it insists that political requirements and obligations imposed by law must answer to citizens' reason and judgment.

This requirement of a justification to each citizen's reason connects with the tradition of the social contract and the idea that a legitimate political order rests on unanimous consent. The aim of a contractual justification is to show that each member of society has a sufficient reason to agree to that order, to acknowledge it, on the condition that other citizens acknowl-

10. For a discussion of this matter, see Jeremy Waldron's instructive essay, "The Theoretical Foundations of Liberalism," *Philosophical Quarterly,* April 1987, pp. 128, 135, 146, 149.

11. Justice as fairness is the name I have given to the political conception of justice developed in *A Theory of Justice* and in *Justice as Fairness: A Restatement.*

edge it as well. This yields unanimous consent. The reasons invoked must be reasons from the point of view of each reasonable and rational person.

"Men being, as has been said, by Nature, all free, equal and independent, no one can be put out of this Estate, and subjected to the Political Power of another, without his own *Consent*. The only way whereby any one divests himself of his Natural Liberty and *puts on the bonds of Civil Society* is by agreeing with other men to join and unite into a Community, for their comfortable, safe, and peaceable living one amongst another, in a secure Enjoyment of their Properties, and a greater Security against any that are not of it." Locke: *Second Treatise on Government*, ¶95.

In this passage from Locke it seems that consent is something citizens actually do at some point; or at any rate this interpretation is not excluded. In Kant we get a different idea. He says that we cannot assume the original contract arises from an actual coalition of all private individuals existing, for this cannot possibly be so.

> [The original contract] is in fact merely an *idea* of reason, which none the less has undoubted practical reality; for it can oblige the legislator to frame his laws in such a way that they could have been produced by the united will of the whole nation. . . . This is the test of rightfulness of every public law. For if the law is such that a whole people could not *possibly* agree to it (for example, if it stated that a certain class of *subjects* must be the privileged *ruling* class), it is unjust; but if it is at least *possible* that a people could agree to it, it is our duty to consider the law as just, even if the people is at present in such a position or attitude of mind that it would probably refuse to consent to it were it consulted. Kant, *Theory and Practice* (1793): Ak:VIII:297 (Reiss, 79).[12]

2. Now I note some distinctions that enable us to understand the meaning of different social contract views and to separate them from one another.

First, the distinction between *actual and non-historical agreements:* The former is found, it seems, in Locke (we shall discuss whether this is so when we come to Locke). The latter is found in Kant, who has in mind an agree-

---

12. Immanuel Kant, *Political Writings*, ed. H. S. Reiss and H. B. Nesbit (Cambridge: Cambridge University Press), p. 79.

ment that could arise only from a coalition of all wills; but since historical conditions never allow for this, the original contract is non-historical.

Second, the distinction as to how the content is determined: whether by the terms of *an actual contract, or by analysis* (that is, by figuring out from the situation of those making the contract what they could, or would agree to), or by some combination of the two ways. In part, Kant calls the original contract an idea of reason because it is only by reason—both theoretical and practical—that we can figure out what it is possible for people to agree to. In this case the contract is *hypothetical.*

A third distinction is whether the content of the social contract concerns what people *could do*—or could not possibly do—or what they *would do.* These are very different: often it is much harder to work out the content of a hypothetical contract saying what people would do rather than what they could do, or could not possibly do. Thus, when Locke is attacking Charles II, he is mainly interested in showing that in setting up a form of government, the people could not possibly have agreed to royal absolutism. So the King's behaving as a sovereign with such powers makes his conduct illegitimate. Locke need not show what the people would have agreed to, other than inferring what they would not do from what they could not possibly do. (Here he relies on: if we could not possibly do X, we would not do X.)[13]

A fourth distinction is whether the content of the social contract is seen as specifying when a form of government is *legitimate,* or whether that content is seen as determining the *(political) obligations* that citizens have to their government. The idea of the social contract can serve two distinct purposes: either as yielding a conception of *political legitimacy,* or as giving an account of *citizens' political obligations.* Of course, a social contract doctrine may do both; but the distinction between the two is significant: for one thing, the idea of the social contract works differently in the two cases, and can be quite satisfactory in one case but not the other.[14] I think Hume's critique of the social contract view is effective for Locke's account of political obligation,[15] but it doesn't touch Locke's account of legitimacy, or so I believe.

13. Thus: could not do X implies would not do X; but, could do X does not imply would do X.

14. On this point, see Waldron, "Theoretical Foundations of Liberalism," pp. 136–140.

15. See Hume's *Of the Original Contract* (1752).

There are other distinctions and aspects of a social contract. For example, who are the parties to the contract? Is it all citizens with each other, or is it all citizens with the sovereign? Or are there two or more contracts: first citizens with each other and then citizens with the sovereign? In Hobbes and Locke, the parties are all citizens contracting with each other; the sovereign is not a party at all. There is no second contract. But this and further distinctions can be considered as we proceed.

§5. Initial Situations

1. Every social contract doctrine needs an account of the situation in which the social contract, whether historical or non-historical, is to be made. Let's refer to this situation as the initial situation. To develop a contract doctrine at all clearly, numerous aspects of this situation have to be expressly filled in. Otherwise, they are left to be inferred from the nature of what is agreed to, or from what must be presupposed if the reasoning is to be sound, and this risks misunderstanding.

We have many items to specify: for example, What is the nature of the parties involved in the initial situation, and what are their intellectual and moral powers? What are the parties' aims and wants? What are their general beliefs, and how much do they know about their particular circumstances? What alternatives do they face; or what are the several contracts they may enter into? Answers to these questions and to many others must in some way be provided. And in each case there are various possibilities.

2. Consider first the nature of the parties. Are they persons in a state of nature, as with Locke? Are they all the members of society, as with Kant? Are they neither of these but the representatives of the individual citizens of society, as supposed in justice as fairness?

What is the original contract an agreement about? Is it agreement as to what is a legitimate form of government, as with Locke? Or is it, as with Kant, an understanding as to what all members of society collectively could possibly will, with this understanding to be used by the legislator as a test of just law? (In Kant this test is to be followed by the sovereign in enacting laws.) Or is it perhaps, as with Rousseau, an agreement about the content of what he calls the general will, that is, what it is that the general will wills?

Or is it, as justice as fairness says, an agreement about the content of a political conception of justice—the principles and ideals of justice and the common good—to be applied to the basic structure of society as one unified system of social cooperation? And beyond this, as justice as fairness also says, an understanding about the restrictions of public reasoning concerning fundamental political questions and the duty of civility? Any social contract doctrine has to decide on these questions and adopt an approach to them that ties them into a consistent unity.

3. Next consider the question of how much the parties know. One might think that the most reasonable answer is to suppose the parties know all that is known to them in ordinary life. We may think: surely it leads to a worse agreement for everyone when people are deprived of information! How can a lack of knowledge lead to an agreement that is more reasonable and better for all?

Now, it is usually correct that in applying a conception of justice already accepted and on hand, we normally want all the information available. Otherwise we cannot apply its principles and standards properly.[16] But agreeing to, or adopting a conception of justice in the first place is another matter. Here we want to achieve consensus, and full knowledge often stands in the way of doing this. The explanation is that the kind of knowledge that people often have may lead to endless wrangling and enable some to drive hard bargains, setting the stage for the nastiest individuals getting more than their share.

It is easy to see how this happens by looking at cases where people have too much information. In Elster's example of the tennis game, rain intervenes after the third set with the first player ahead 2 sets to 1. How are they to divide the prize, as the match must now end? The first player claims the whole prize; the second player says it should be divided equally, claiming to be in excellent shape and always reserving energy and coming on strong in the fourth and fifth sets; the spectators say it should be divided in thirds with the first player getting 2/3 and the second 1/3. Plainly the matter should have been settled before the game started, when no one knew the particulars of current circumstances.[17]

---

16. An exception is in a criminal trial where rules of evidence may exclude some kinds of available information, as when spouses may not testify against each other. This is to help ensure a fair trial.

17. See Jon Elster, *Local Justice* (New York: Russell Sage Foundation, 1992), pp. 205f.

Even then, though, it might not have been easy, since the second player will strongly prefer dividing the prize equally, given the facts above mentioned, and especially should the first player be older and tend to tire more quickly, and both know this. Also, if the prize is very large, and one player is wealthy and the other poor, knowledge of this will make for additional difficulties. Thus, the players need to imagine a situation in which no one knows their capacities, their physical condition, or their wealth, and many other things, and settle the rules apart from the particular circumstances, and for players generally. In this way they are led to something approaching the veil of ignorance of justice as fairness.

4. I shall note two cases of genuine political importance to illustrate the same points. Consider the case of gerrymandering election districts. Gerrymandering means the drawing up of state, county, or local voting districts in such a way as to gain partisan advantage. The term originated in 1812 when the Jeffersonian followers of Governor Elbridge Gerry of Massachusetts (an Anti-federalist) sought to keep their political control of the state. To do this they redrew election districts to include Anti-federalist enclaves. This resulted in a grotesque shape, suggesting a salamander to one cartoonist of the day—hence, "Gerrymander."

Here is a clear case where strict rules about electoral districts are best adopted in advance. It also illustrates the crucial distinction between what knowledge is appropriate in adopting rules and what knowledge is appropriate in applying them. Different and less information is needed in one case than the other.

The same point explains why it is so difficult to pass laws reforming elections and establishing public financing. In this instance it is obvious that the party that can raise the most money will have less desire for reforms of this kind, and if it is in power, can block reform efforts. If both parties in a two-party system are corrupt and can raise large funds, such efforts at reform may be practically impossible without a major political change via, say, a third party.

I note also Daniels's treatment of medical care and Dworkin's insurance scheme.[18] Here the general idea is that people should decide how

---

18. See Norman Daniels, *Am I My Parent's Keeper?* (New York: Oxford University Press, 1988), with summaries on pp. 63–67 and 81f; and Ronald Dworkin, "Will Clinton's Plan Be Fair?" *New York Review of Books,* January 13, 1994 [republished as "Justice and the High Cost of Health Care," Ch. 8 in Ronald Dworkin, *Sovereign Virtue* (Cambridge, Mass.: Harvard University Press, 2000)].

much health care society should provide in a situation in which no one knows their age, but only that they will live through different phases of life—from youth to old age—during which their need for health care will vary. They must balance their needs at one time against their needs at another, as well as society's needs for other things. I follow a similar approach in discussing the flexibility of primary goods.[19]

5. All these examples suggest the need for something like the so-called veil of ignorance. Yet there are many veils of ignorance, some thicker than others (excluding more information) and some excluding different kinds of information. Note Elster's meritocratic veil of ignorance, which allows information about citizens' natural abilities and skills, and Dworkin's restrictions, which still allow citizens to know their ambitions and aspirations. I only mention these views, but they may be expected to lead to different conclusions.[20]

I should mention also that much the same effect as that of a veil of ignorance may result from a combination of other elements. Thus, rather than exclude information, we can allow people to know whatever they now know and yet make the contract binding in perpetuity and suppose the parties to care about their descendants, indefinitely into the distant future.[21] In protecting their descendants as well as themselves, they face a situation of great uncertainty. Thus, roughly the same arguments, somewhat modified, pertain as with a thick veil of ignorance.

Finally, I call attention to the idea of discourse ethics of Jürgen Habermas and a related idea of Bruce Ackerman.[22] The thought here is that with certain rules of discourse restricting the participants in an ideal speech situation, only norms with a suitable moral content can be generally endorsed by everyone. A valid norm is one that can be established, or redeemed, as

---

19. See Rawls, *Justice as Fairness: A Restatement* (Cambridge, Mass.: Harvard University Press, 2001), pp. 168–176.

20. See Elster, *Local Justice*, pp. 206f.

21. This was actually the form the limits on information took in my first articles stating justice as fairness. See "Justice as Fairness" in Rawls, *Collected Papers*, ed. Samuel Freeman (Cambridge, Mass.: Harvard University Press, 1999), pp. 47–72.

22. See Jürgen Habermas, *Moralbewusstsein und kommunikatives Handeln* (Frankfurt am Main: Suhrkampf, 1983), esp. 3, entitled "Diskursethik—Notizen zu einem Begründungsprogramm. Erläuterungen zur Diskursethik" (Suhrkamp, 1991), and esp. 6: 119–222. See also Bruce Ackerman, *Social Justice and the Liberal State* (New Haven: Yale University Press, 1980); "What Is Neutral about Neutrality?" *Ethics*, January 1983; "Why Dialogue?" *Journal of Philosophy*, January 1989.

Habermas says, in such an ideal discourse situation. There is no veil of ignorance, or other restrictions beyond the rules of ideal discourse. It is these rules that serve to filter out all norms that cannot be generally accepted and, in this sense, do not further generalizable interests.

The reason for mentioning these various views is to indicate how widespread is the idea of an initial situation. Indeed, it is not a strange idea, a philosopher's fancy, but a rather common and I think highly intuitive idea. It is clearly foreshadowed, I believe, in Rousseau and Kant, and no doubt in other classical writers as well.

The initial situation of justice as fairness I refer to as "the original position." It is characterized so that the agreement reached there by the parties, who are viewed as representatives of citizens, expresses the content—the principles and ideals—of the political conception of justice that specifies the fair terms of social cooperation.

As a concluding remark, I stress that the original position, as I have often said, is a device of representation. Were we to look through the history of the tradition of the social contract we would find many different things the initial situation has been used to represent, even if the idea of a device of representation is not made clear, or possibly even understood by the author. It has been so used whether so understood or not.

HOBBES

HOBBES I

Hobbes's Secular Moralism and the
Role of His Social Contract

§1. Introduction

Why do I begin a course in political philosophy with Hobbes?[1] It isn't that Hobbes began the social contract doctrine, of course. That goes back to the classical Greeks, and then in the sixteenth century there was a marvelous development of it by the later Scholastics, by Suarez, de Vittoria, Molina, and others. By Hobbes's time it is a quite highly developed doctrine. My reason is that in my own view and that of many others, Hobbes's *Leviathan* is the greatest single work of political thought in the English language. By saying that, I don't mean that it comes the closest to being true, or that it is the most reasonable. Rather, I mean that taking everything together—including its style and its language, its scope and its acuteness and interesting vividness of observation, its intricate structure of analysis and principles, and its presentation of what I think is a dreaded way of thinking about society which almost might be true and which is quite a frightening possibility—adding all those together, the *Leviathan* makes, to me, a very overwhelming impression. Taken as a whole, it can have a very overwhelming and dramatic effect on our thought and feeling. There are other writers one might prize more. In a way, I tend to value J. S. Mill's work more highly than Hobbes's, but then there is no single work of Mill's that can be compared to the *Leviathan*. There isn't anything he did that begins to have this overall effect. Locke's *Second Treatise* may be more reasonable, more sensible, in some ways, and one might think closer to being accurate, or true. But again, it lacks the scope and power of presentation of a political conception on the order of Hobbes. And while there are other impressive writ-

---

1. [Transcription of February 11, 1983 lecture, with additions from John Rawls's handwritten lecture notes of 1979 and 1983. —Ed.]

ers, like Kant and Marx, they did not write in English. In the English language this is, I think, the most impressive single work. Therefore it would be a shame to have a class on political philosophy and not try to read it.

A second reason for opening with a study of Hobbes's work is that it is useful to think of modern moral and political philosophy as beginning with Hobbes, and with the reaction to Hobbes. Hobbes wrote the *Leviathan* during a period of great political upheaval. He published it in 1651, during the period of transition between the English Civil War (1642–48), which defeated Charles I, and the restoration of the monarchy with the crowning of Charles II in 1660. Hobbes's work called forth a strong intellectual reaction. Hobbes was regarded by his critics to be the chief representative of modern infidelity to Christian beliefs. That was a Christian age, and Christian orthodoxy saw their opposition to Hobbes along a number of very important and sharp lines (see Figure 1).

For example, orthodoxy would, of course, hold a theistic view, while they regarded Hobbes as atheistic. Orthodoxy holds a dualist view, making a distinction between soul and body, whereas they regarded Hobbes as a materialist. Orthodoxy also believed in freedom of the will, freedom of the soul and mind, but they regarded Hobbes as a determinist who would reduce the will to a sequence of appetites or some sort of cultural change. Orthodoxy also held a corporative conception of human society (it would not be correct to call it "organic"). They regarded society as intrinsically an aspect of human nature, whereas they regarded Hobbes as having an individualist conception of society. He is still regarded as having a rather radically individualistic view. Orthodoxy also held to a view of eternal and

Cudworth and Orthodoxy	Hobbes
Theism	Atheism
Dualism (mind and body)	Materialism
Free will	Determinism
Corporate conception of the state and society	Individualist conception of the state and society
Eternal and immutable morality	Relativism and subjectivism
Persons as capable of moral sensibility and benevolence	Persons as rational egoists and incapable of benevolence

Figure 1.

immutable morality. That is to say there were certain moral principles based on God's reason that were possible for us, in virtue of our reason, to grasp and to understand, and there was but one interpretation of these principles. Moral principles were like the axioms of geometry in that they could be grasped by reason alone. Hobbes, on the other hand, was seen as relativistic and subjectivistic, totally the opposite view. To make a final point, orthodoxy regarded persons as capable of benevolence and being concerned with others' good, and also as capable of acting from moral principles of eternal and immutable morality for their own sake; whereas Hobbes, as they thought, presumed persons to be psychological egoists and concerned only with their own interests.

I don't think that this picture of Hobbes, this interpretation of his view, is particularly accurate, but I mention it because it was what people in Hobbes's time, even a number of sophisticated people, took Hobbes to be saying. It explains why he was so severely attacked and even dreaded. It was a matter of personal affront in some circles if someone took you to be a Hobbist. That was an accusation against which many felt they had to defend themselves, much as people felt around 1950 in this country that they had to defend themselves from being thought to be a communist. Locke thought that Newton took him for a Hobbist, and this was something that they had to straighten out before they could be friends. It was a very serious matter to have others regard you in this light.

What one will find is that immediately after Hobbes there are two lines of reaction against him. One is the orthodox reaction by Christian moral philosophers, those who belonged or were sympathetic to the church. Perhaps the most important among them were Cudworth, Clarke, and Butler. They attacked what they took to be Hobbes's leading views, e.g.:

1. his presumed psychological and ethical egoism;
2. his relativism and subjectivism and denial of free will;
3. and what they took to be the *result* of his doctrine: the idea that *political authority* is made legitimate by *superior power* or else by *agreements* made when *confronted* by such power.

They also rejected the idea that political authority *could* rest on anything like a social *contract* at all.

The other line of reaction was the utilitarian line: Hume, Bentham, Hutcheson, Adam Smith, and on down. They did not disagree with

Hobbes for orthodox reasons, and they on the whole, with the exception of Hutcheson, took a secular standpoint. The utilitarians wanted to attack Hobbes's egoism. They wanted to argue that the principle of utility is an objective moral principle, and in that way attack Hobbes's presumed subjectivism or relativism. And they also argued for the principle of utility as a principle that could decide between and justify and explain the grounds of political authority. One of the ways in which Hobbes was interpreted was that he based political obligation and political authority on superior power. Again, I am not saying that any of these things are what Hobbes actually said, but that they are what he was widely regarded as saying.

So Hobbes was attacked then from all sides—by the orthodox and the non-orthodox—and because the *Leviathan* is such a tremendous work, it initiated a kind of reaction: his system of thought was something in regard to which one *had* to decide where one stood. Given these circumstances, it is useful to think of Hobbes and the reaction to Hobbes as the beginning of modern British political and moral philosophy.

§2. Hobbes's Secular Moralism

In order to have time to discuss some of the essential points in this work, I shall focus on what I shall call "Hobbes's Secular Moral System." I am going to omit certain things, and I will explain why I am going to do so. The first thing I am going to ignore are Hobbes's theological assumptions. Hobbes often talks as though he were a Christian believer, and I don't question or deny that in some sense he was, although as you read the work you will understand why there are some who did deny that. At any rate they wondered how he could say the things he did and yet believe, in any orthodox sense. So I am going to leave these orthodox theological assumptions aside and assume that there is within the book a secular political and moral system. This secular political and moral system is fully intelligible as regards its structure of ideas and the content of its principles when these theological assumptions are left aside. In other words, we do not need to take these assumptions into account in order to understand what the secular system is. Indeed, it is precisely because, or in part because, we can leave these assumptions aside that his doctrine was an offense to orthodoxy of his time. In orthodox thought, religion ought to play some essential part in understanding the political and moral system of ideas. If it does not, then that it-self is a troublesome matter.

Religion, the orthodox thought, played no *essential* role in Hobbes's view. I believe, then, that all the notions that Hobbes uses, for example the notion of natural right, of natural law, the state of nature, and so forth, can all be defined and explicated apart from any theological background. And the same is also the case in regard to the content of the moral system, where by the content I mean what its principles actually say. This means that the content of the laws of nature, which right reason bids us to follow, and also the content of the moral virtues, such as the virtues of justice, honor, and the like, can all be explained without resorting to theological as-sumptions and can all be understood within the secular system.

Hobbes thinks of a law of nature as "a Precept, or general Rule, found out by Reason, by which a man is forbidden to do, that, which is destructive of his life, or taketh away the means of preserving the same" (*Leviathan*, p. 64 in the original 1651 edition).[2] These precepts, when generally fol-lowed, are the means of achieving peace and concord, and are necessary for the "conservation" and defense of "men in multitudes" (*Leviathan*, Ch. 15, p. 78). The laws of nature can all be understood without mentioning theo-logical assumptions. This does not mean, however, that we cannot add cer-tain theological assumptions to Hobbes's secular scheme; and when such assumptions are added they may lead us to describe parts of this secular system in a different way. For example, Hobbes says that *in the secular system* (my term) the laws of nature are properly speaking "dictates of reason," conclusions or "theorems" concerning what is necessary for our conserva-tion and for the peace of society. They are properly called "laws" *only* when we think of them as the *commands* of God who has by right legitimate au-thority over us (*Leviathan*, Ch. 15, p. 80). But the crucial point is this: think-ing of these dictates of reason as the Laws of God in no way changes their *content*—what they *direct* us to do; they still say exactly the same thing to us

2. Page references are to the first edition of Hobbes's *Leviathan*, the Lionshead (or "Head") edition of 1651 [these are included within the text of the Penguin edition edited by C. B. MacPherson, which was used by Rawls in his course]. Pagination from the Head edition is included in the margins of all principal modern editions of *Leviathan*. "The prin-cipal modern editions (those of A. R. Waller in 1904, the Oxford University Press in 1909, Michael Oakeshott in 1946, and C. B. MacPherson in 1968) all based themselves, correctly, on the Head edition," as did Molesworth in his 1839 edition. Richard Tuck, p. xviii from his edition of *Leviathan* (Cambridge: Cambridge University Press, 1991).

about what we ought to do as they said before. Nor does it change the content of the virtues. Nor does thinking of them as God's laws change the *way* in which we are *bound* to follow them. We are already bound by right reason to follow them (at least *in foro interno*) and justice and covenanting is a *natural* virtue.[3] As God's laws, the dictates of reason simply acquire a peculiarly forceful *sanction* (cf. *Leviathan*, Ch. 31, pp. 187f). In other words there is another forceful and compelling reason, the threat of God's punishment, for why they ought to be followed. But the sanction does not affect the content and the notions involved.

The background theological system *would* change the content and formal structure of Hobbes's secular scheme only if what is *necessary* for our salvation from a religious standpoint is different from and would conflict in some way with the dictates of reason about what is necessary for the peace and concord of society. If the theological view were that you had to do certain things that would conflict with the precepts of the laws of nature, or the dictates of reason, in order to be saved, then you would have a conflict. But Hobbes does not I think believe this. He would say that any religious view that is incompatible with the dictates of reason, regarded as theorems for what is necessary for the conservation of men in groups, is a superstition and irrational. In Chapter 12 (pp. 54–57) he discusses religion, and here he notes how the first founders and legislators of the commonwealth among the ancients took pains to make it publicly believed that what is necessary for the peace and unity of society is also pleasing to the gods, and that the *same* things were displeasing to the gods that were forbidden by the laws. It is clear that Hobbes approves of this policy and thinks that this is what they ought to have done.

Later in Chapter 15 Hobbes gives an answer to the so-called fool who believes that there is no justice (*Leviathan*, pp. 72f). He has the fool say, among a number of other things, that the secure and perpetual felicity of heaven may be gained by not keeping covenants (for instance, with heretics). (It was a common practice at the time to say that we are not obligated to keep our covenants with heretics, that they are an exception.) Hobbes replies that this idea is frivolous. He says that there is no imaginable way to attain salvation except by honoring our covenants (*Leviathan*, p. 73). Then he goes on to reject the views of those who think that covenants with here-

3. "The Laws of Nature oblige *in foro interno;* that is to say, they bind to a desire they should take place: but *in foro externo;* that is, to the putting them in act, not always." *Leviathan*, p. 79.

tics and others are not binding, and who think that the dictates of reason, that is the laws of nature, may be overridden for religious ends (*Leviathan*, pp. 73–74). For Hobbes, then, such a breach of covenant would not be justified. Thus the quest for our salvation does not in any way, in his view, change the content of the Laws of Nature regarded as the dictates of reason. Theological assumptions may *enforce* this secular system by adding God's sanctions to the dictates of reason, and they may enable us to describe it in a somewhat different fashion so that the dictates of reason are called "laws," but they do not alter the fundamental structure of concepts and the content of its principles, or what they require of us. In sum, it is on those grounds that I propose that we can put aside the theological assumptions.

Another aspect of Hobbes's view that I am going to put aside is his so-called materialism. I don't believe that this had any significant influence on the content of what I am calling his secular system. Hobbes's psychology derived mainly from common sense observation, and from his reading of the classics, Thucydides, Aristotle, and Plato. His political thought, that is, his conception of human nature, was probably formed there. It doesn't show any signs of actually having been thought out and derived on the basis of mechanical principles of materialism, the so-called method of science. Although occasionally it is mentioned, it did not actually affect his account of human nature and the passions, and the like, that motivate it.[4]

We may allow that Hobbes's materialism, and the idea of there being a mechanical principle that explains causation, gave him greater confidence in the social contract idea as an analytic method. He may have felt that the two went together. For example: in the *De Cive*, which is an earlier, less full, less elaborate work than the *Leviathan*, presenting much the same view, he starts with a discussion of "the very matter of civil government," and then proceeds to discuss its generation and form and the first beginnings of justice, and then he adds the phrase that "everything is best understood from its constitutive causes."[5] In order then to understand civil society, that is, the

---

4. Thus, what Robertson said long ago seems largely right: "The whole of his political doctrine . . . has little appearance of having been thought out from the fundamental principles of his philosophy . . . it doubtless had its main lines fixed when he was still a mere observer of men and manners, and not yet a mechanical philosopher." George Croom Robertson, *Hobbes* (Philadelphia: J. B. Lippincott, 1886), p. 57.

5. Thomas Hobbes, *De Cive*, ed. Sterling P. Lamprecht (New York: Appleton-Century-Crofts, 1949), pp. 10–11. Hobbes says that he starts from the "very matter of civil government" and proceeds to "its generation and form, and the first beginning of justice; for everything is best understood by its *constitutive causes*."

great Leviathan, we must take it apart, break it down into its separate elements, or its matter—that is human beings—and view these elements as if dissolved. Doing this enables us to understand what the qualities of human nature are, and in what way they make us fit or unfit to live in civil society, and to see how men must be agreed among themselves if they are to form a well grounded state (id.). His idea is that viewing civil society as if dissolved, or broken into its elements, leads to the idea of the State of Nature. Then having the notion of a State of Nature, he then suggests the social contract as a way of conceiving of the unity of a well-grounded state. Mechanical notions and principles of causal materialism may have reinforced this train of thought in Hobbes, and it may even in some sense have prompted him to have these thoughts. But clearly such a mechanical basis is not essential, and they do not affect the content of these ideas. The ideas of the State of Nature and of the Social Contract can stand on their own feet. And numerous writers have espoused these notions who have rejected mechanism and materialism.

In conclusion, I am going to discuss Hobbes's secular moral system as essentially self-contained, and independent of theological assumptions and principles of mechanics (materialism).

§3. Interpretations of the State of Nature and the Social Contract

Before taking up the problem of how one might interpret the social contract, let me begin first with Hobbes's account of the State of Nature. We should not interpret the state of nature as an actual state, nor should we interpret the social contract as an agreement that actually took place. No doubt Hobbes supposes that something like the state of nature did obtain at one point, and he says that it now exists in some parts of the world, and it also exists between nation-states, princes, and kings at the present time (*Leviathan*, p. 63). So in that sense the State of Nature exists. But I do not think Hobbes is concerned with giving an historical account or explanation of how civil society and its government came about. His social contract doctrine is best viewed, not as explaining the origin of the Leviathan and how it came to be, but rather as an attempt to give *"philosophical knowledge"* of the Leviathan so that we can better understand our political obligations and the reasons for supporting an effective Sovereign when such a Sovereign exists.

Near the end of the *Leviathan,* Hobbes says, "Philosophy is . . . the Knowledge acquired by Reasoning, from the Manner of the Generation of any thing to the Properties; or from the Properties, to some possible Way of Generation of the same; to the end to be able to produce, as far as matter, and human force permit, such Effects, as human life requireth" (*Leviathan,* p. 367). The idea is that we would have philosophical knowledge of something when we understand how we could generate from its parts the properties of that thing as we now know it. Hobbes's aim in the *Leviathan* would be to give us philosophical knowledge of civil society, in that sense.

To accomplish this Hobbes considers society as if broken apart, dissolved into its elements, that is, human beings in a state of nature. Then he examines in detail what that state of nature would be like, given the propensity and features of these human beings, the innate drives or passions that motivate their actions, and how they would behave when they are in that state. The aim is then to see how civil society with its government *could be* generated and come about, given the State of Nature as he has described it. If we can explain how civil society and the Sovereign could come about from a state of nature, this then gives us philosophical knowledge of civil society, in Hobbes's sense. That is, we understand civil society when we understand a possible mode of its generation that accounts for its recognized and observable properties. On this interpretation, the idea of a Social Contract presents a way in which civil society *could* have been generated— not how it was actually generated, but how it could have been. There are recognized properties of society and requirements of society—for example, the necessary powers of the Sovereign, the fact that the Sovereign must have certain powers if society is to cohere; that is a property of the great Leviathan. We recognize these properties and account for them as things that rational persons in a state of nature would regard as essential if the Social Contract is to achieve its intended aim of establishing peace and concord. Thus, the Social Contract grants these necessary powers to the Sovereign. He thinks that spelled out in full, all of this provides *philosophical knowledge* of civil society.

So the idea again is that we should view the Social Contract as a way of thinking about how the state of nature could be transformed into civil society. We explain the present properties of the state, or the great Leviathan, and understand why the Sovereign has to have the powers that he does by seeing why rational persons in a state of nature would agree to the Sovereign's having those powers. This is how we are to understand the properties of the state, from the process of its generation, and also understand why its powers are as they are. On Hobbes's definition of philosophical knowledge that then provides philosophical knowledge of the nature of the state, or of the great Leviathan. This is a much broader definition of philosophy or of philosophical knowledge than now exists. Then it covered science, or "natural philosophy" as it was then called.

Now consider a second way to think of Hobbes's social contract. In Chapter 13 of *Leviathan* (p. 63), Hobbes recognizes the possible objection, that there never was a state of nature. ("There never was such a time, nor condition of war as this.") To this he replies that at least Kings and Sovereigns are in a State of Nature with respect to one another: the State of Nature obtains between nation-states. Moreover, he indicates that it is sufficient for his argument that the State of Nature be a state that *would* come about *now* if there were no sovereign authority to keep people in awe.[6] In this way, the state of nature is a condition that always *would* exist if effective exercise of sovereignty were to break down. So conceived, the State of Nature is an *ever present possibility* of degeneration into discord and civil war, although in a "well-grounded" society it is very unlikely (improbable). Now because the State of Nature is in effect a state of war, the constant possibility of a State of Nature provides for all *sufficient reason* for wanting an effective Sovereign to continue to exist. We all have strong grounds for fearing the collapse of our current arrangements, Hobbes thinks, and this yields a sufficient reason for everyone to support them. Thus, on this interpretation, the State of Nature is not some *past* state of affairs, or indeed any actual condition, but an *ever present possibility* to be *avoided*.

The second interpretation of the social contract is this: Suppose all are fully rational and understand the human condition as Hobbes describes it. Let's suppose also that an effective Sovereign now exists with the requisite powers to maintain current arrangements. Then Hobbes thinks that all have a sufficient reason based on their own self-preservation and fundamental interests to enter into a covenant with all to *authorize* the Sovereign to continue to exercise his powers in perpetuity. Entering into such a covenant

6. "It may peradventure be thought, there was never such a time, nor condition of war as this; and I believe it was never generally so, over all the world: but there are many places, where they live so now. . . . Howsoever, it may be perceived what manner of life there would be, where there were no common Power to fear; by the manner of life, which men that have formerly lived under a peaceful government, use to degenerate into, in a civil War." *Leviathan*, p. 63.

is rational for all to do; it is (let's say) *collectively* rational since rational for each and all.

Looked at in this way, we don't need to see the social contract as made *in* the State of Nature. So we don't need to consider whether a social contract is *enough* to transform the state of nature into civil society. (For example, how can we be sure that people's promises will be honored?) Rather, we can think of the social contract as a covenant that serves to secure and renders secure an already existing stable government. Hobbes's point is that given the *normal* conditions of human life, and given the ever present danger of civil conflict and collapse into the State of Nature, every rational person has a sufficient and fundamental interest in supporting an *effective Sovereign*. And given this interest, every rational person *would* enter into the Social Contract, should the occasion arise.

Here we should ask, must there be an actual social contract on Hobbes's view? Isn't it enough to think of the social contract in this hypothetical way, that all members of an existing society with an effective Sovereign *would* have sufficient reason for entering into a covenant to authorize this Sovereign, etc.? This suggestion regards the *Social Contract* itself, as well as the State of Nature, as purely hypothetical: that is, as a covenant we *would* have sufficient reason to enter into if this were possible, etc. Now certainly Hobbes doesn't explicitly express his Social Contract doctrine in this way. And we should be cautious in putting words into his mouth. Nevertheless, you might consider the question whether this hypothetical interpretation of the Social Contract suffices to express what is essential to Hobbes's view. After all, the Social Contract, when understood in this way, does give a conception of social unity and explains how civil society could hang together and why once an effective Sovereign exists, citizens might support current arrangements etc. While it may not explain how civil society could be *generated* from its parts, it might explain why it doesn't *degenerate* back into its parts. The Social Contract provides a point of view for showing why everyone has an *overriding* and *fundamental* interest in supporting an effective Sovereign. Why isn't this enough for Hobbes's aims, seeing the social contract in this way?

This depends, of course, on what Hobbes's aims were. I think he meant to present a convincing philosophical argument to the conclusion that a *strong and effective Sovereign*—with *all* the powers Hobbes thinks a Sovereign should have—is the *only remedy* for the great evil of civil war which all persons must want to avoid as contrary to their fundamental interests. Hobbes wants to convince us that the existence of such a Sovereign provides the only way to civil peace and concord. And given this conclusion, and given that the Fundamental Law of Nature is "to seek Peace, and follow it" (*Leviathan*, p. 64) and that the second Law of Nature is to "be contented with so much liberty against other men, as [we] would allow other men against [us]" we all have an *obligation* (not based on the Social Contract) to comply with the Sovereign's laws. The focus of Hobbes's thought is the turmoil and civil strife of his day; this is what immediately concerns him. He thinks an understanding of the Sovereign's necessary powers and a clear view of the Laws of Nature as based on our fundamental interests can help to address this situation. The Social Contract, interpreted purely hypothetically, enables Hobbes to make his argument. For this purpose, the hypothetical interpretation does *seem* to suffice.

To sum up, there are three possible interpretations of the social contract. First, it is an account of what actually happened and of how the state actually was formed. This is not Hobbes's intention as I interpret him. A second, more plausible interpretation, for which there is a good deal of evidence in the text, is that he was attempting to give a philosophical account of how the state could arise. I say "could arise," or how it might have come about, and not how it actually did. He wanted to give us philosophical knowledge of the state, by dissolving it into its parts and depicting human beings as they are psychologically constituted, and then showing how the state of nature could be transformed into the great Leviathan, or into a society of people under a state. Finally, a third possible interpretation I suggested is the following: Suppose that the great Leviathan actually exists already. Then we should think of the state of nature as an ever-present possibility that might come about if the effective Sovereign should cease to be effective. Given that possibility, and in view of what he takes to be everyone's fundamental interests in self-preservation, their "conjugal affections," and their desire for the means of a commodious life, Hobbes is explaining why everyone has a sufficient and overriding reason to want the great Leviathan to continue to exist and to be effective. On this interpretation, Hobbes is trying to urge us into accepting an existing effective Sovereign. We can understand this intention in light of the climate of the times and the English Civil War.

These two interpretations are suggestions as to how to understand the social contract. I suggest these interpretations somewhat hesitantly. I am never altogether satisfied that what I say about these books is correct. This is a very large and complicated view, and there are various ways it can be read. We ought to be suspicious of any pat account of how it is supposed to be taken.

Hobbes Lecture I: Appendix A

HANDOUT: FEATURES OF HUMAN NATURE WHICH
MAKE THE STATE OF NATURE UNSTABLE

A. Two Introductory Remarks:

1. I shall discuss only *The Leviathan* and no other works of Hobbes; and I assume that Hobbes's Social Contract doctrine as presented in this work can be fully understood apart from any theological or religious view. Neither the formal structure nor the material content of Hobbes's doctrine is affected by these background notions. This is, of course, debatable; and I don't argue the point. You should consider carefully Chapters 12, 31.

2. I shall also leave aside Hobbes's materialism and his other metaphysical theses except insofar as occasional remarks may help to clarify his Social Contract and how it is put together.

B. Two Ways of Regarding the State of Nature in Hobbes:

1. First, as the *state of affairs* that *would* come about if there were no effective political authority, or Sovereign, with *all* the powers which on Hobbes's view, it is necessary for an effective Sovereign to have.

2. As a *point of view* which persons in society may assume and from which each can understand why it would be rational to covenant with every other person to set up an effective Sovereign (as Hobbes describes this Sovereign). In this sense the Social Contract is collectively rational; from the point of view of the State of Nature, the conditions which reflect permanent (and so present) features of human nature, each member of society *now* has a sufficient reason to want the effective Sovereign to continue to exist, and thereby to ensure the stability and viability of existing institutions.

C. Destabilizing Features of Human Nature (when taken together in a State of Nature):

1. Human beings are sufficiently equal in natural endowments and mental powers (including prudence), and also sufficiently vulnerable to one another's hostility, to give rise to fear and insecurity. 13: 60–62.

2. Human desires and needs are such that together with the scarcity of

the means of satisfying them, people must find themselves in competition with one another. 13: 60–62.

3. Human psychology is in various ways self-centered and self-focused, and when people take careful thought all tend to give priority to their own *preservation* and security, and to gaining the means to a commodious life.

4. Human beings are in several ways unfit for peaceable association in society:

i. They have a liability to pride and vainglory which association with others arouses and which is irrational. That is, this liability often prompts them to act contrary to the principles of right reason (the Laws of Nature), and these passions tempt them to actions highly dangerous both to themselves and to others.

ii. They have, it seems, no original or natural desires for association, or natural forms of fellow-feeling. What appears to be such feelings derive from our self-concern. On the other hand, Hobbes does not think we're malicious, that is, enjoy the suffering of others for its own sake.

5. Defects and Liabilities of human reasoning:

i. Those arising from lack of a proper philosophical (scientific) method: 5: 20–21. Note here Hobbes's attack on the Schools (Aristotle via scholasticism).

ii. Liability of human reasoning, presumably even when a proper philosophy is known, to be distorted and undermined by our proneness to pride and vainglory: 17: 86–87.

iii. Fragile nature of practical reason when it concerns the conduct of human beings in groups and the appropriate social institutions. This form of practical reason is fragile because Hobbes thinks it must be given a *conventionalist* basis. That is, everyone must agree *who* is to decide what is for the common good and everyone must abide by this person's judgments. There is no possibility of all freely recognizing by the exercise of reason what is right and wrong, or for the common good, and abiding by this knowledge. Social cooperation for the common good requires an effective Sovereign.

Hobbes Lecture I: Appendix B

[Rawls's 1978 version of this lecture contained the following discussion, which supplements section 2, "Hobbes's Secular Moralism," above from the 1983 lecture. —Ed.]

Simplifications: I propose to make *two* simplifications in my discussion of Hobbes:

1. *First,* I shall assume that the *essential formal* structure and *content* of Hobbes's political philosophy (as a Social Contract conception) can be understood as addressed to *rational* human beings who can grasp its sense and interpretation by the correct use of their *natural reason.* Thus, I suppose that Hobbes's view is *fully intelligible,* as regards its structure and content within a *secular* as opposed to a *theological* or religious view.

Thus for the most part I shall leave aside the disputed question of the interpretation of Hobbes which is raised by the Taylor-Warrender thesis that Hobbes's account of political authority and obligation is tied at bottom to natural laws as the laws of God, who has *rightful* authority over us.[7]

Now by the *secular character* of Hobbes's political philosophy I mean roughly the following.

(a) The *formal structure of concepts* and definitions of Hobbes's account of the Sovereign, etc., of right and liberty, etc., is independent from *theological presuppositions.* This structure can stand on its own. For example, as a definition of natural right, we can say:

α has a *natural right* to do x = df α's doing x is in accordance (initially, i.e. prior to events or actions that limit the right) with *right reason.*[8]

(b) The *material* content of Hobbes's political conception and of his supporting moral philosophy is likewise independent from theological presuppositions. This content can also stand on its own and be understood by natural reason given Hobbes's psychological account of human nature. For example, consider the *material* definition of natural right:

α has a natural right to do x = (material df) α's doing x is (conscientiously *believed* by α to be) advantageous or necessary for α's preservation.

There is no reason offhand, however, why Hobbes's view cannot be *supplemented* by theological doctrines. But if such assumptions are introduced, there are two possibilities:

---

7. A. E. Taylor, "The Ethical Doctrine of Hobbes," *Philosophy* 53 (1938); reprinted in *Hobbes Studies,* ed. Keith Brown (Cambridge, Mass.: Harvard University Press, 1965); and Howard Warrender, *The Political Philosophy of Hobbes* (Oxford: Clarendon Press, 1957). The point of view I follow is roughly that of David Gauthier, *The Logic of Leviathan* (Oxford: Clarendon Press, 1969).

8. ["= df" is standardly used to introduce definitional equivalences; it should be understood as "is defined to mean." Rawls's sentence above should thus be read as: "'α has a natural right to do x' is defined to mean: 'α's doing x is in accordance . . . with right reason.'" —Ed.]

(i) The first case is this: the conclusions drawn when these doctrines are *adjoined* to the system of formal structure and material content are *not* fully *compatible* with the conclusions drawn from the *secular system* alone. (Should this happen, the material conditions of the system would not be independent (in a suitably strong sense) from theological doctrine. Thesis (b) above although not (a) would need revision.)

(ii) The second case is this: the conclusions drawn when theological doctrines are adjoined are the *same* as those of the purely secular system (without theological presuppositions). Should this happen, both (a) and (b) hold. (cf. what Hobbes says: *Leviathan*, Book I: Ch. 12, 96–97; I: 15, last paragraph, pp. 57, 80.)

Now the important point is that Hobbes accepts case (ii). In the *secular system* the conclusions drawn depend upon what institutions, etc., are required for the *peace* and *concord* of people living in society. In the *theological system* the conclusions depend upon not only what is required for peace and concord but *also* upon what is necessary for human *salvation*. The first case (i) would hold, then, *only if* what is necessary for peace and concord in society is *different from* what is *necessary* for *salvation*.

I believe that Hobbes would deny the truth of *any* theological doctrine that made the prerequisites of salvation *incompatible* with conditions of the preservation of people in groups. A religious view that declares them incompatible is (on Hobbes's view) a *superstition* and as such *irrational*. It is based on an unreasoning fear springing from a lack of true knowledge of the natural causes of things. (See his whole discussion of the natural seeds of religion in I: 12—"Of Religion.")

In Chapter 12 of Book I Hobbes discusses how "the first Founders, and Legislators of Commonwealths amongst the Gentiles, whose ends were only to keep the people in obedience, and peace" took care "to make it believed, that the same things were displeasing to the Gods, which were forbidden by the Laws" (*Leviathan*, p. 57). There is every reason to suppose that Hobbes approves of this policy of the ancient world (Greeks and Romans) of using religion to strengthen the conditions necessary to preserve social peace and concord. In this sense, Hobbes's doctrine is secular. (See also II: 31, 528f re obedience to Laws of Nature as worship) [1st edition, 192f].

One must be careful, however, not to question that Hobbes is (so far as one can tell) a sincere and believing Christian. We must interpret his Christianity so that it is not incompatible with the *secular structure* and content of his moral and political conception. In conclusion, the whole order of Hobbes's exposition seems to imply that the *secular structure and content* of his doctrine is regarded by him as basic. If theological presuppositions were *fundamental*, he would, it seems, have started with them.

So much then, for why it seems correct to focus on Hobbes's view as addressed to *rational* human beings, etc.

2. The second simplification (about which I shall be brief) is that one can (perhaps) interpret Hobbes's method in the *Leviathan* (and in his other political works) as the application to a moral and political conception of a *general mechanistic* doctrine of the workings of *nature*. Hobbes is often seen as trying to work out a *unified science* (unified not only in *general methodology* but also in its *first principles*).

Thus we might interpret him as beginning with the study of bodies and their motions in general (explained in some mechanistic fashion) and then taking up the study of that particular kind of body—that of individual human beings—and finally coming to the study of artificial bodies, namely civil governments which are human-made. They are the result of *human artifice*. The *Leviathan* is the commonwealth, a human artifice.

In studying artificial bodies—commonwealths and civic governments, etc.—Hobbes's method is to look at the <u>parts</u> of these bodies which he takes to be human beings (individuals with their faculties and desires, etc.). He says in *De Cive* that everything is best understood by its constitutive causes, and he illustrates this remark by noting that we understand a watch by grasping how its various parts are put together and work mechanically. Similarly, to understand a commonwealth, it is not necessary *actually* to take it apart (for that is hardly possible, or can be done at too great a cost), but we are to consider it *as if it were dissolved*: State of Nature.

That is, we want to understand what the features of human beings are and in what ways these features (qualities, etc.) render people either *fit* or *unfit* for civil government. We want to understand also how people must be *agreed* among themselves if their intention and aim to become a well-grounded state is to be realized (EW, p. xiv; ed. Lamprecht, pp. 10f).

I shall more or less leave aside the rest of Hobbes's philosophy and how far his moral and political philosophy fits into his overall metaphysics.

Hobbes Lecture I: Appendix C

PASSAGES RELEVANT TO THE IDEAL OF GENEROUS NATURES
[References to Head ed.]

A. *Possibility of Affections:*

Hobbes asserts the possibility of *benevolence* and it seems to man generally; when to men generally, it is "good nature" (26).

Recognizes various passions of love, including love for particular persons (26).

Recognizes conjugal affections, as of second in order of importance after self-preservation and *before* riches and means of living: 179.

B. *Related to above:* it is not to take pleasure in the misfortunes of others: (said re cruelty): 28.

Curiosity as a delight in the continual generation of knowledge; distinguishes man from animals: 26, cf. 51, 52.

C. *Generous Attitude Expressed in the Virtues:*

1. On the *"relish"* of justice: when a man *scorns* to be beholden for the contentment of his life to fraud and breach of promise: 74.

2. For great minds one of the proper works is to help people, and free them from the scorn of others; such minds compare themselves only with the most able: 27.

3. Two ways to secure that men honor their covenant: fear of consequences of breaking them; or: "a glory or pride in appearing not to need to break it." But "this latter is a *Generosity too rarely found to be presumed on* . . ." (70).

4. Honor of great persons is to be valued for their beneficence, and the aids they give to persons of inferior ranks; or not at all. Greatness makes our violences, oppressions worse, as we have *less need* to commit them: Ch. 30 (180).

HOBBES II

Human Nature and the State of Nature

§1. Preliminary Remarks

Hobbes had the general thesis, very important to his view, that a state of nature tends to pass over very readily into a state of war. He often talks about a state of nature (which is a state in which there is no effective Sovereign to keep men in awe and keep their passions in check) as being essentially a state of war. It is important to note here that for Hobbes, a state of war consists "not in battle only, or the act of fighting . . . but in the known disposition thereto, during all the time there is no assurance to the contrary" (*Leviathan*, p. 62). What I will call "Hobbes's Thesis" is the thesis that a state of nature is, essentially and for all practical purposes, a state of war. Why does Hobbes think this is so?

Hobbes remarks that it may seem strange to us "that Nature should thus dissociate, and render men apt to invade, and destroy one another" (that is, it may seem strange to us that the State of Nature *so readily* becomes a State of War). But, he says that we can understand why this is so by what he calls an "Inference, made from the Passions" (*Leviathan*, p. 62). We can confirm that we make this inference from the passions by looking at actual experience in everyday life, by noting how we conduct ourselves as we do now, in civil society, when the Sovereign actually exists and there are laws and armed public officers. He says that when we travel we arm ourselves, when we go to sleep we lock the door, even in our house we lock up our chest, and so on (*Leviathan*, p. 62). By these actions we accuse one another and show that we accept, as it were, this inference from the passions, which says: *If a state of nature obtains, then a state of war also obtains*, for all practical purposes.

Thus what Hobbes says, I think, is that if we take human nature as it is, we can infer that the State of Nature becomes a State of War. What human nature is Hobbes takes to be demonstrated by the essential features and abilities and desires and other passions of people as we observe them *now* in civil society; and so he supposes, for the purposes of his political doctrine, that these essential features of human nature are more or less given or fixed. Hobbes is not denying that social institutions and education and culture can importantly change our passions and alter our aims, at least in some very important sorts of cases. But he supposes that, for the purposes of his political doctrine, that is, of what I call his secular moral system, that the main outlines and essential features of human nature are more or less fixed or given. The existence of social institutions and, in particular, of an effective Sovereign, changes our objective circumstances and hence changes what it is prudent and rational for us to do. For example, given the Sovereign we are now protected and have no reason not to honor our covenants. That is to say, supposing the Sovereign actually exists, we have reasons we did not have before to honor our covenants, to keep our promises, and so on. However, social institutions are not thought of as though they change the more essential aspects of our nature. They don't change our most fundamental interests in self-preservation, in conjugal affections, and in the means for commodious living. So, taking those elements as more or less fixed, for the purpose of his political doctrine, what Hobbes then does is to infer what a state of nature would be like, taking people as they are, or as he thinks they are; and he describes a state of nature as a state of "continual fear, and danger of violent death; And the life of man, solitary, poor, nasty, brutish, and short" (*Leviathan*, p. 62), but still probably all too long under those conditions. From what *features* of (actual) human beings is this *inference from the passions made?*

§2. Main Features of Human Nature

I am going to mention and comment on four features of human nature as he characterizes them and then will go over fairly quickly the basic argument of what I earlier called "Hobbes's Thesis."

The first feature is the fact of human equality in natural endowments, strength of body and quickness of mind. Of course, Hobbes has not regarded these natural endowments as literally, or strictly equal; but, his point is that they are equal enough. Thus, even the weakest in bodily strength is still strong enough to kill the strongest, either by secret means or by plotting along with others who are similarly threatened by the strongest. Note here now that "equal enough" means, not strict equality, but sufficiently equal to support this inference from the passions, where people feel themselves threatened, and are led to attack one another. This is sufficient to give rise to the fears and the dangers of the state of nature. Note also that Hobbes thinks that in quickness of mind people are even more equally endowed, in many regards, than they are in strength of body. Here the attributes in question are wit and prudence, which Hobbes thinks to be derived from experience; and here all individuals have, he thinks, equal opportunity to acquire experience and to learn.

Again, Hobbes doesn't think that all people have equal quickness of mind. But the differences arise, on Hobbes's view, from differences in custom and education and in bodily constitution, which in turn cause differences in the passions, that is, in the desire for riches, glory, honor, knowledge, and so on. Hobbes has a tendency in the political doctrine to reduce all these desires that cause difference of wit to one: namely, the desire for "power after power," where power in this case stands for the means for attaining our good or the object of our desires (*Leviathan*, pp. 35, 41). Many different kinds of things, the things that we think will make us happy, are forms of power for Hobbes, in the sense that they enable us to attain our good. It is the different strengths of people's desires for power that determine, Hobbes thinks, their quickness of mind. Since these differences are equal enough, so is their quickness of mind. Here again, equal enough means equal enough to make the state of nature into a state of war.

A final observation concerning equality of endowments is that Hobbes assumes that if there were, in fact, substantial natural inequality, so that one person or a few persons could dominate the rest, then that person would simply rule. He says that they would rule by natural right. Or, if this seems unrealistic, then a dominant group of persons, provided they could stay united and be of one mind, could also rule. Hobbes says as much in discussing the rights whereby God reigns over us. God does not have this right by virtue of the Right of Creation, which Locke, whom we will be discussing later, assumes is a moral principle. That is, if God created us, as Locke believes, then, being created by God, we have a moral obligation to obey, which obligation depends on the principle that if A creates B then B has an obligation to A. In Hobbes we don't find such a Right of Creation.

We don't find an obligation to God based on either God's creation or our gratitude, but simply on God's irresistible power. Hobbes says, "Whereas if there had been any man of Power Irresistible; there had been no reason, why he should not by that Power have ruled . . . according to his own discretion. To those therefore whose Power is irresistible, the dominion of all men adhereth naturally by their excellence of Power; and consequently it is from that Power, that the Kingdom over men . . . belongeth Naturally to God Almighty; not as Creator, and Gracious; but as Omnipotent" (*Leviathan*, p. 187).

Now what Hobbes has to show, then, is that given the state of equality, among other things, in the state of nature, the tendency is to lead to a state of war; and to avoid that happening, the great Leviathan with its effective common power or sovereign is necessary.

The second feature or element of human nature has to do with the fact that the scarcity of resources and the nature of our needs introduces competition. We could put it this way: Given the nature of people's needs and desires, and given the tendency of needs and desires to change and to expand (although not necessarily to expand without limit), there is a permanent tendency for these needs and desires to require more for their fulfillment than is available in nature. This makes for a scarcity of natural resources, which is, of course, a relation wherein the amount, or total aggregate of needs and desires is larger than the amount of resources available. This scarcity, Hobbes believes, leads to competition between people. If we wait until others have taken all they want, there will be nothing left for us. So, in a state of nature we must be ready to stake out and to defend our claims.

Civil society, on Hobbes's view, does not eliminate this relation of scarcity. He believes, or at least assumes, that scarcity is a permanent feature of human life. Scarcity is relative and it may be more or less urgent, so that the wants and needs that remain unsatisfied in civil society are less pressing, less urgent than those that remain unsatisfied in a state of nature. Thus, the civil state wherein an effective Sovereign exists is more agreeable.

Hobbes says at the end of Chapter XIII that "The Passions that incline men to Peace, are Fear of Death; Desire of such things as are necessary to commodious living; and a Hope by their Industry to obtain them" (*Leviathan*, p. 63). The existence of an effective Sovereign removes the fear of violent death; and through the establishment of the conditions wherein industry is rewarded and is secure, the Sovereign's existence encourages the means for a commodious life. On this Hobbes says at the beginning of Chapter XXX that the end, or purpose, for which the office of the Sovereign is entrusted with sovereign power, is the "procuration of the *safety of the people;* to which he [the Sovereign] is obliged by the Law of Nature, and to render an account thereof to God, the Author of that Law, and to none but him. But by Safety here, is not meant a bare Preservation, but also all other Contentments of life, which every man by lawful Industry, without danger, or hurt to the Commonwealth, shall acquire to himself" (*Leviathan*, p. 175).

Therefore, one thing that civil society does, and one thing that makes it collectively rational, is that it introduces conditions that make it much easier to produce the fruits of labor, or the means of a commodious living. This does alter, or render less urgent, the scarcity of natural resources. Scarcity does still exist. The Sovereign does not eliminate scarcity, but does produce the objective conditions, on Hobbes's view, for lawful industry and for the holding of property and making it secure, and so forth.

The third feature of human nature supporting the inference from the passions, in Hobbes's view, is that the psychological makeup of human beings is largely, or predominantly, self-centered. In particular, when people deliberate about basic political and social matters, they tend to give priority in their thought and action to their own preservation and security, to that of their families, and, to use his phrase again, to "the means of a commodious life." It can be hard to get this point straight in Hobbes, and it's worth spending some time on. Hobbes does not say in the *Leviathan* that people are psychological egoists, or that they pursue or care only about their own good. He does say in Chapter VI that we are capable of benevolence; of desire of good to another, or goodwill; and of charity (*Leviathan*, p. 26). He says that we are capable of loving people, and in Chapter XXX, he ranks conjugal affections as second in importance after our own self-preservation and before the means of a commodious life (*Leviathan*, p. 179). He therefore does think that people are capable of benevolence and of genuine affection for other people, or concern for their good. He also says that some persons are virtuous, or that we are capable of virtue—that people do what is just or noble or honorable because they want to be, and to be recognized as, someone who acts in that way. An important example of this is in Chapter XV, where Hobbes writes about the virtue of justice and of acting in accordance with it. He equates justice with keeping our promises, honoring our covenants, and he says, "That which gives to human Actions the relish of Justice, is a certain Nobleness or Gallantness of courage, (rarely found,) by which a man scorns to be beholding for the contentment of his life, to fraud, or breach of promise" (*Leviathan*, p. 74).

That is an important statement. There are several others in the *Leviathan*, where Hobbes clearly asserts that we have the capacity to act justly for its own sake. He does not, then, deny that capacity, nor does he deny that we have capacities of benevolence or affection. Often, however, he appears to do so. One might say, perhaps, that his views are inconsistent when strictly read. But, I think that it is better to say that he is emphasizing certain aspects of human nature in ways that are suitable for his purposes, that is, for his political doctrine. He wants to give an account of what holds civil society together and to explain why an effective Sovereign is necessary for peace and concord. He is concerned, that is, primarily with politics, with political questions, and with basic sorts of institutional structures of government.

Politics is, of course, only part of human conduct; and Hobbes need not deny that we can be, and often are, benevolent, and that we are capable of the virtues of justice and fidelity, and so forth. His point is that one should not rely on these human capacities in an account of civil society and in the basis of social unity. That is, there are other fundamental interests upon which one ought, if one can, to base the unity of civil society. His view would then be that political institutions must be rooted in, and congenial to certain fundamental interests: our interest first in preserving our life, then our interest in securing the good of those who are close to us (what Hobbes calls "conjugal affection"), and finally, our interest in acquiring the means of a commodious life (*Leviathan*, p. 179). He lists these three things I am calling "fundamental interests" in that order of importance. It is those three fundamental interests to which he appeals. To say that we give great weight to these interests in political matters, and that the account of civil society should focus on these interests, is not to deny that we are capable of other desires and often act on them in other circumstances. Perhaps, in those other circumstances they may be extremely strong.

Thus, I am assuming that Hobbes's largely self-centered, or self-focused, account of human nature serves, in effect, as an emphasis for the purposes of a political conception. It is an emphasis that goes with his stress on the desire for power, where a person's power is defined as a person's present means to obtain some future apparent good (*Leviathan*, p. 41). These means include all sorts of things. They include natural faculties of body or mind, or things that are acquired by those faculties. The latter include riches, reputations; they even include "Friends, and the secret working of God, which men call Good Luck" (*Leviathan*, p. 41). It is small wonder then, with this broad definition of "power," that we should desire to have it.

The weight that Hobbes assigns to our self-preservation in his political theory is used by him to explain why certain rights, in his sense, are inalienable. He says that no one can be understood deliberately and intentionally to do anything contrary to their self-preservation. Contracts (the transferring or renouncing of rights in consideration of some other right or good) are deliberate, voluntary acts, and as such, Hobbes says, they must have as their object, some good to the agent. He then continues, "Therefore there be some Rights, which no man can be understood by any words, or other signs, to have abandoned, or transferred." He gives as an example, the right of resisting those who actually assault us. And he says, "And lastly the motive, and end for which this renouncing, and transferring of Right is introduced, is nothing else but the security of a man's person, in his life, and in the means of so preserving life, as not to be weary of it. And therefore if a man by words, or other signs, seem(s) to despoil himself of the End, for which those signs were intended; he is not to be understood as if he meant it, or that it was his will; but that he was ignorant of how such words and actions were to be interpreted" (*Leviathan*, p. 66).

Here, Hobbes is more or less regarding it as a principle of legal interpretation within his political doctrine that persons must be presumed to intend their own good and so to preserve their own lives. However, at least from things he says elsewhere, he knows perfectly well that people sometimes do irrational things; and he believes that some persons, with full knowledge, prefer death rather than disgrace or dishonor. He says that most men would rather lose their lives than suffer slander; and that a son would rather die than obey an order to kill his father, on the grounds that if he were to do obey such an order, he would look infamous and would be hated by all the world; and that, from shame or dishonor, he cannot bear (this is in the earlier work, *De Cive*).

Perhaps what Hobbes is saying is that the desire for self-preservation is the strongest of all natural desires, but that while this will explain the primacy that he gives to it in his political theory, this doesn't imply that it is always the strongest of all desires, when everything is taken into account. In other words, I am making a contrast between saying something is the strongest of natural desires and saying something is the strongest of all of our desires; everything considered. Thus, he says in *De Cive,* an earlier work, that we seek to avoid death by a certain impulsion of nature, no less than whereby a stone moves downwards. But, as we all know, stones sometimes move sideways, or they get thrown upward. Social institutions and social customs and education and culture can, as it were, work on us in a certain way, so that as civilized persons we act non-naturally or contrary to nature, if you like, affected by institutions and culture as much as by the word of reason.

Hobbes seems to allow this, and he says as much in various places. However, in his political conception he wants to emphasize very basic things. He is aware that he lives in an age in which people appeal to many different kinds of interests—to religious interests, to political interests, to interests that he thinks are based in the end on pride and vainglory and love of dominion—and he is trying to introduce a class of interests common to everyone. That is, although we may differ from the standpoint of our religious and political views, and may have other various interests that are very important to us, we nevertheless share certain fundamental interests in self-preservation, conjugal affection, and the means of a commodious life. Hobbes wants to put all other interests aside and see the kind of argument that we would get for an effective Sovereign based only on these interests. The point is that Hobbes is not saying that other important interests, religious interests for example, don't exist or are not important to people. He knows perfectly well that they exist and are important. He sees them all around him. But he is trying to give a basis upon which people might agree that an effective Sovereign is over all, over everything else, a desirable thing to have—thinking of the social contract in the third sense I discussed earlier (as an argument why people should accept an existing Sovereign to avoid degeneration back into the state of nature were the Sovereign to lose his power).

§3. The Argument for Hobbes's Thesis

I shall now pull all this together and give, in a more concise form, Hobbes's argument for his thesis that the state of nature leads to, and in fact is, a state of war. First, however, remember that in the state of nature there is no effective Sovereign to keep men in awe and discipline their passions, and that a state of war is a condition in which the will to contend by battle is publicly recognized. Furthermore, as I quoted Hobbes earlier, a state of war consists "not in battle only or the act of fighting . . . but in a known disposition thereto, during all the time there is no assurance to the contrary. All other time is Peace" (*Leviathan,* p. 62). I take "publicly recognized" to mean that everybody knows, and everybody knows everybody else knows, that this is a state of war; it is common knowledge.

The argument for Hobbes's Thesis can be summarized as follows:

(a) Equality of natural endowments and mental powers leads to equality of hope in attaining our ends, given the central place in Hobbes's political doctrine of the desire for self-preservation and for the means of a commodious life. Equality of hope, given the scarcity of natural and produced means of sustaining life, puts people in competition with one another, and makes them potential enemies.

(b) Competition, given the great uncertainty concerning the aims of others and the possibility of their forming alliances and coalitions against us, gives rise to "diffidence," which in modern usage means a general state of mutual distrust.

(c) Diffidence, made greater by the possibility that some may be moved by pride and vainglory to gain dominion over others, together with the fact that no covenants or contracts can provide security in the absence of a Sovereign to enforce them, makes productive industry seem less worthwhile and predation seem more productive, and this leads people to believe that their security is best secured by anticipatory attack.

(d) Anticipation—as the state of affairs in which the disposition to strike first when the circumstances seem propitious—is generally and publicly known, and is, by definition, a state of war.

Now I'll comment on this outline of Hobbes's argument:

(i) Note the meaning of *diffidence.* Nowadays it means shyness, timidity, or lack of self-confidence. But the derivation from the Latin is: *diffidere,* which means to mistrust. This is what it means in Hobbes. (Compare Hobbes's use of "mediocrity of the passions" (*Leviathan,* p. 80) in the next to last paragraph of Chapter 15, meaning *moderation* of the passions.)

(ii) Note carefully that as I have stated the argument for Hobbes's thesis, it assumes that everyone in the State of Nature *conducts* themselves in a perfectly *rational manner.* (I shall discuss this in more detail in a moment.) No one is assumed actually *to be* moved by the love of dominion, or to have their deliberations actually *distorted* by *pride and vainglory.* No one is assumed to act irrationally in this argument. Indeed, given the opportunity, anticipatory attack is one's most rational response to the circumstances. Nor does the argument assume that people have boundless desires for ever greater means to a commodious life. All that is assumed is that they desire to have enough to secure their present and future needs and wants.

At step (d) it is assumed that it is possible that some people are moved by pride and vainglory to seek dominion over others, and that this possibility must be taken into account in one's deliberations. It may be that no one is actually so moved; what is important is that many believe that some are. If we cannot exclude the possibility, we have to take it into account and guard against it. The possibility is a basis for mutual suspicion. For example, in the case of two national powers in competition, they naturally tend to distrust each other. It may be that neither power is motivated to dominion or has any of these sorts of passions influencing those who govern it. But still the other side thinks so, and that is enough to exacerbate the state of nature and transform it into a state of war. That is the way I would interpret Hobbes's emphasis on pride and vainglory. He does not for his purposes need to base his political theory on it, as some interpreters might think. We can say that if pride and vainglory, and the will to dominion is a possibility, then that is enough for his purposes. Thus, the difficulty in the State of Nature is the great *uncertainty* about the aims and intentions of others. As long, then, as love of dominion and vainglory are *psychologically possible,* these passions are a complicating factor in the State of Nature. A *general state of uncertainty* about others' aims and intentions characterizes the State of Nature, so that a concern for our self-preservation forces us to consider the *worst* possibilities.

(iii) Hobbes also does not need to assume that people generally desire more "power" (as means for their good = means to fulfill their desires) without *bound.* Most people may be content with moderate means (for a commodious life). So long as *some* do strive for dominion, all must strive for dominion as means to their *own* security. Gibbon said: "Rome conquered the ancient world in self-defense." (*He* meant this in sarcasm.)

(iv) The significance of Hobbes's argument lies in part in the fact that it rests on quite plausible assumptions about the normal conditions of human life. For example, again it does not assume that everyone is actually moved by pride and vainglory to seek dominion over others. That would be a questionable assumption. It would give his conclusion, but much too easily. What makes his argument frightening and gives it significance and dramatic power is that he thinks that normal, even quite nice, people can be put in this sort of situation, and it will degenerate into a state of war. You lose the significance of the view if you overemphasize the desire for power and domination. The *force* of Hobbes's thesis, and why it is so *significant* an achievement (even though Hobbes does not frame it in such a careful and rigorous fashion), is that the premises rest solely on *normal* and more or less permanent circumstances of human life as they *quite plausibly* might be in a State of Nature. The point is: we don't have to be *monsters* to be in deep trouble.

(v) Remember that Hobbes's psychological and other assumptions need not be strictly true of all human conduct. He is not a thoroughgoing psychological egoist, as we have seen. His assumptions about basic human interests need only be accurate enough to represent the major influences on human conduct in the kinds of social and political situations he is concerned with. On the interpretation proposed, Hobbes's secular moral system is meant as a political doctrine; and as such, it is appropriate that it stress certain aspects of human life. The relevant question is, are his assumptions true enough to model some of the major psychological and institutional forces that influence human behavior in political situations?

(vi) Hobbes is trying to convey to us that, even if *all* were moved by *normally* moderate wants and we were perfectly rational people, we are still in danger of a State of War in the absence of an effective Sovereign with *all* the powers Hobbes says the Sovereign *must* have to be effective. However *bad* some Sovereigns may be, the State of War is *still* worse. Greed, love of dominion, pride, and vainglory can be serious complicating elements; but they are not actually necessary to bring it about that the State of Nature will become a State of War. At best, the *possibility* that *some* are so moved is enough.

(vii) A *useful exercise* is to see how far the assumption of Hobbes's thesis can be weakened still further in the sense that people in a State of Nature are in a State of War even though their psychology is *less* self-centered and they are more virtuous, or moved by wider attachments and affection. For example, suppose all are motivated according to Hume's account of limited *altruism*. Consider here the case of *religious wars,* for example in the 16th and 17th centuries. We can suppose that all are devout and faithful to their conception of religious obligation and still they can be thrown into a State of War. Remember that Hobbes is writing against the background of this history and the English Civil War.

Finally, as an aside, let me say that in looking at a text of this sort, which is so large, and with so many elements in it, if you are to get as much out of it as you can, you must try to interpret it in the best and most interesting way. There is no point in trying to defeat it, or to show the author was wrong in some way, or that his argument doesn't follow. The thing is to make as much out of it as you can and to try to get a sense of how the overall view might go, if you put it in the best way. Otherwise, I think it is a waste of time to read it, or to read any of the important philosophers.

Hobbes Lecture II: Appendix A

HANDOUT: OUTLINE OF HOBBES'S CLAIM THAT THE STATE OF NATURE → A STATE OF WAR

1. State of Nature = df. state of affairs in which there is no Sovereign power to keep everyone in awe. State of War = df. state of affairs in which the will to contend by battle is publicly recognized. A State of War consists not in actual fighting but in a known disposition thereto during a stretch of time in which there is no assurance to the contrary. All other time is peace.

2. Argument for the Claim that the State of Nature → State of War:

(a) Equality (of natural endowments and mental powers)—given the central place in Hobbes's political doctrine of the desire for self-preservation and the desire for the means of a commodious life—leads to equality of hope in attaining our ends.

(b) Equality of hope—given the scarcity of natural and produced means of life—puts people in competition with one another and makes them potential enemies.

(c) Competition—given the great uncertainty concerning the aims of others and the possibility of their forming alliances and coalition against us—gives rise to diffidence, that is, to a general state of distrust.

(d) Diffidence—made greater by the possibility that others may be moved to gain dominion by pride and vainglory, together with the fact that no covenants can provide security—makes productive industry seem less worthwhile (predation may be more productive) and leads people to find their security by anticipatory attack.

(e) Anticipation, as the state of affairs in which the disposition to strike first when the circumstances seem propitious is generally and publicly known, is by definition a State of War.

3. Observe these points:

(i) In this argument no one is assumed to act irrationally. Nor does the argument assume that people have boundless desires for ever greater means of a commodious life.

(ii) At step (d) it is assumed that it is possible that other people are moved by pride and vainglory to seek dominion, and that this possibility must be taken into account; but no one may actually be so moved. (One should also consider the question whether the assumption of this possibility is necessary for Hobbes's argument.)

(iii) The significance of Hobbes's claim lies in part in the fact that it rests in quite plausible assumptions about the normal conditions of human life. For example, it does not assume that everyone actually is swayed by pride and vainglory to seek dominion over others. This questionable assumption would give the conclusion but make it much less interesting.

(iv) We should recall that Hobbes's psychological and other assumptions need not be strictly true of all human conduct. We have seen that he is not, for example, a psychological egoist. His assumptions need only be accurate enough to model the major influences on human conduct in the kinds of political and social situations that Hobbes is concerned with. Don't forget that, on the interpretation proposed, Hobbes's secular moral system is meant as a political doctrine; and as such, it is appropriate that it stress certain aspects of human life.

HOBBES III

Hobbes's Account of Practical Reasoning

§1. The Reasonable and the Rational

Today I will discuss Hobbes's account of practical reasoning as it arises within what I call his secular moral system, or within his political doctrine. He views practical reason as a kind of rationality and has a view, which I will attribute to Locke, of practical reason as involving a kind of reasonableness. That is, it is my view that we can distinguish between two forms of practical reasoning. We can think of practical reason as rational, or as reasonable. For the moment "rational" and "reasonable" are simply words, labels, and we do not know what the difference between them might be. In ordinary English both mean being consistent with or based on reason, in some way. But, in everyday speech we do seem to have a sense of the difference between them. We don't usually use these terms synonymously. One might say of somebody, "He was driving a very hard bargain and being extremely unreasonable, but I had to concede that from his point of view he was being perfectly rational." In that, we recognize the distinction, to some extent. We tend to use "reasonable" to mean being fair-minded, judicious, and able to see other points of view, and so forth; while "rational" has more the sense of being logical, or acting for one's own good, or one's interests. In my own work, and in this discussion, the reasonable involves fair terms of cooperation; while the rational involves furthering the good or advantage of oneself, or of each person cooperating.

Hobbes illustrates the view that *practical reasoning* is *deliberating* concerning what is the *rational* thing to do (where rational ≠ reasonable). Many of the Laws of Nature Hobbes lists fall under what intuitively we consider the *Reasonable*. The Laws of Nature formulate precepts of fair cooperation, or dispose us to virtues and habits of mind and character favorable to such cooperation. For example, the first law is to seek peace and follow it and to defend ourselves as necessary; the second says that a man should be willing, when others are too, to lay down his right to all things, and be contented with as much liberty against other men as he would allow other men against himself; the third concerns honoring our covenants. The fourth through the tenth all have to do with one virtue or another involving cooperation: gratitude, accommodation to others, forgiveness and pardon; not showing contempt for other people, acknowledging others as equals, and the like. The 10th Law of Nature says *not* to reserve to ourselves a right we are not content that others should have as well, and so on. All have to do with the precepts of cooperation necessary for social life and a peaceful society (*Leviathan*, Chapters 14 and 15). But these *reasonable* principles, Hobbes urges, are *rational* for us to follow, on the condition that others follow them likewise. The role of the Sovereign is in part to guarantee that (enough) others follow them, so that it *is rational* for each to follow them. Thus Hobbes justifies *Reasonable* principles (with reasonable *content*) in terms of the *Rational*.

Hobbes, however, urges that it is rational for us to follow these reasonable principles, only on the condition that others also follow them. They will help us to achieve our own good. In other words, he is making an argument to the effect that this group of principles that we could accept as reasonable, in my sense of that term, are rational principles for us to follow, based on our fundamental interests, provided others follow them also. The appeal is to what is conducive to our self-preservation, conjugal affections, and means for commodious living, or in other words, to our own essential good. The role of the Sovereign is then, in part, to guarantee that enough others follow the laws of nature so that it is rational for us to follow them also, thus ensuring peace.

Later we will take up the social contract and what that actually does, which is to set up the Sovereign with sufficient powers to effectively achieve the conditions necessary to such a guarantee. The existence of the Sovereign changes the circumstances in such a way that there are no longer reasonable grounds, or rational grounds, for not complying with the laws of nature. But, the difficulty, which Hobbes, I believe, was one of the first to see, is that within the state of nature itself, it is hard to see how such agency could exist that would make it rational to make or to follow through on our covenants. Therefore, one of the basic arguments of the book is that we take these reasonable principles of social cooperation and justify them in terms of the rational.

Let me try to explain in a bit more detail the contrast between rational principles and reasonable principles. There are two ways to do this:

(a) By their distinctive *role* in practical reasoning and in human life; and

(b) By their *content,* or what they actually say and direct us to do, which content we can usually intuitively recognize as belonging to the Rational or the Reasonable.

The distinction of (a) the role these principles play is this: I think of conceptions of social cooperation as being quite different from another notion, which would be merely *efficient and productive coordination of social activity,* for example, bees in a hive, or workers on an assembly line in a factory. They are engaged in coordinated activity, it's productive, and certainly we'd say it's social. But, it's not necessarily cooperation. It is *socially coordinated,* and perhaps there are public rules of some kind which people know they're supposed to follow, but they're not cooperating in the normal sense. What, then, is the notion of cooperation that distinguishes it from socially coordinated and even productive activity?

Every conception of *social cooperation* (as opposed to the merely *efficient* and *productive and coordinated* social activity) has *two* parts:

(a) One part defines a notion of *rational advantage* for those engaged in cooperation, some idea of each *individual's* or *each association's,* good or well-being etc. An enumeration of *principles of rational choice* enters here as an *essential,* but not the *sole,* element in defining rational advantage. Rational advantage involves some idea of what each individual, or each association engaged in cooperation is going to gain from taking part in this activity. We suppose that they are rational and have reflected on this. It is an idea of their own good that hasn't been imposed on them by other people, but that they hold on their own part, after reflection; and it leads them to be willing to accept the second aspect of the notion of cooperation;

(b) This second part defines *fair* terms of *social cooperation,* or *just* terms of cooperation, as may be appropriate. These terms involve some notion of *mutuality* or *reciprocity,* and how specifically this notion is to be interpreted *in practice.* This does not mean that there is a single interpretation of reciprocity, or of mutuality. There might be a number of them appropriate to different situations. These will be expressed in terms of the *constraints* that fair terms impose on efficient and productive and coordinated social activity so that this activity is *also* fair social cooperation. The *principles* defining these terms of *fair social cooperation* we define as the *reasonable*. This is their *role:* to interpret such a notion of reasonableness.

Note too that a conception of social cooperation also supposes that people are *capable* of *engaging* it and honoring its terms, and has some view of what makes their cooperation possible. Later we will discuss the role of a sense of right and wrong, a sense of justice, in enabling people to engage in social cooperation.

Now, the precepts or principles that specify the fair terms of cooperation in any particular case will be reasonable. So, when we describe someone as being unreasonable when he is bargaining with someone else, although perfectly rational from his own point of view, what we are saying is that somehow he took advantage of some, perhaps accidental, fortunate position on his part to impose unreasonable (unfair or unjust) terms on the bargain. Although, we have to grant that given the situation and looking at things from his point of view, perhaps it was rational (furthering his own good) for him to do that.

I have already touched on some of the features of Hobbes's account of practical reasoning as *rational,* in the sense that we discussed the self-related nature of the ends of human beings that Hobbes focuses on. Recall that those ends were those of our own self-preservation, conjugal affections, and the means of a commodious life. I will now go over these in somewhat more detail.

In Hobbes's secular moral system, or in his political conception, people's final ends are the states of affairs and activities which they strive for and enjoy for their own sake. These ends are focused on the self, being concerned with our desires for our own health, strength, and well-being; with the well-being of our family; or with obtaining the means to live a comfortable life. It is a relatively narrow concern, and it is in that sense that Hobbes gives a self-interested account of human nature for the purpose of his political view. Two points about these final ends or desires:

First, (a) these final ends or desires are all self-related, and *object-dependent,* as I define them. To say they are object-dependent means they can all be described without referring to or mentioning any reasonable or rational principle, or any moral notions generally. For example, take the desire for food and drink; or for friendship and company. I can describe a state of affairs that I care about in terms of these and other "objects" in a broad sense; as one in which I have all I want to eat, or all I want to drink, in which I am secure, or my family is secure, and the like. There is no reference to notions like being treated justly, or to rights or other notions that have a moral character. (b) In Hobbes's view, the most important final ends or desires that people have are non-social; that is, they are desires they are presumed to have in a state of nature, and not as members of civic society. They would remain as characteristics of human beings even if we were to think of society as if dissolved or degenerated back into its elements. What that means is that Hobbes's social theory, or his account of the political doctrine, is not, on the whole, going to rely on ends and desires that have been created by social institutions. He thinks of these desires as more basic, as parts of the elements, the human beings, that go to make up society. These ends are features of the parts—the individuals—out of which the *commonwealth* is, as it were, *mechanically assembled* as an *artificial* body (cf. passage in *De Cive EW* ii, p. xiv). (Recall here the *three* parts of Hobbes's scheme: *body, man, citizen*—each built up from the preceding.)

Second, on Hobbes's view, people also have, in addition to these object-dependent desires, certain *principle-dependent desires*. These are higher-order desires and presuppose lower-order desires such as the object-dependent desires discussed above. In Hobbes, the only principle-dependent desires are those defined by the principles of rational choice as opposed to the principles of reasonable conduct. I call them principle-dependent because in order to describe them, we must cite some principle or other. They are rational as opposed to reasonable because they are desires to act in accordance with, or to deliberate in accordance with, a principle of rationality that we can describe and state. For example, a rational principle might be that we should take the most effective means to achieve our ends. The desire to deliberate and to act in accordance with that principle would be a rational desire. I think of these also as final desires or ends in the sense that we desire to act from such a principle and to deliberate in accordance with it for its own sake.

Now, let's recall what Hobbes says at Ch. 11, p. 47 (1st paragraph): ". . . the object of man's desire, is not to enjoy once only, and for one instant of time; but to assure forever, the way of his future desire. And therefore the voluntary actions, and inclinations of all men, tend, not only to the procuring, but also to the assuring of a contented life." Thus we have, each of us, a *general inclination* which Hobbes describes as: ". . . a perpetual and restless desire of Power after power that ceaseth only in Death." There is no utmost aim which, once achieved, we can *rest* in the repose of a mind satisfied.

There are several points to be noted here:

(1) First, I understand Hobbes to be saying also that because of our capacity for reason, we have a conception of ourselves as an individual living a life over time and see ourselves as having a future and perhaps a far distant future. Not only do certain final desires move us now, but we foresee and we understand the possibility of a whole unending series of desires moving us in the future. These future desires are not desires that we actually have now. They are not now psychologically active, but we do foresee *now* that we shall have, or most likely shall have, such desires at certain times in the future. For example, I may know that in the future I am going to want food to eat, and I may want to assure that I can make provision for making sure the larder is filled; but that desire is not based on a present state of hunger. There is a *higher-order* desire which we do now have and always will have, to the extent that we are rational, and that is our desire to assure ourselves now, by some appropriate conduct in the present, based on some rational principle as earlier described, to make provision for these future desires. It is not the future desires, but rather, the higher-order desires that move us now; and in order to describe its object, that is, what it tries to do, it is necessary to refer to certain principles of rational deliberation. Higher-order desires move us and express themselves in actions just as other desires do.

Hobbes describes men as having "a perpetual and restless desire of Power after power, that ceaseth only in Death. And the cause of this, is not always that a man hopes for a more intensive delight, than he has already attained to; or that he cannot be content with a moderate power: but because he cannot assure the power and means to live well, which he hath present, without the acquisition of more" (*Leviathan*, p. 47). Remember here that "*the Power of a Man* . . . is his present means, to obtain some future apparent Good" (*Leviathan*, p. 41). The desire for "power after power" suggests that there is no utmost aim that, once achieved, we can rest and suppose ourselves to be completely satisfied with.

(2) The second point is: the general inclination that expresses itself as a desire for power after power (given the circumstances of human life) is a

principle-dependent desire in the sense that in order to *describe* the *object* of this desire, what it strives to achieve, it is necessary to refer to certain *principles of rational deliberation* (or rational choice) in the forming of our plans and intentions. The higher-order desires are desires to form and to pursue a scheme of conduct that is *rational* as defined by certain *principles*. Basic, self-centered (lower or 1st order) desires *cannot* account for these higher-order desires, or *explain* the conduct in which they are expressed.

Some examples here will help: consider these *principles* of *rational choice:* Perhaps we can only define these by a *list*.

(i) Principle of Transitivity etc: (Complete Ordering) applied to Preferences (or over alternatives)
(ii) Principle of effective means
(iii) Principle of Preferring the Greater Probability for the more preferred outcome
(iv) Principle of the Dominant alternative

A *rational* being understands and applies these and other *rational* principles; and their higher-order desires as defined by these principles can be viewed as the desire to *regulate* their pursuit of the totality of their object-dependent (and natural) desires by these principles.

Thus it seems appropriate to call these desires *rational* desires. I shall not try to *define* "rational" or "rationality." Instead, we proceed via *examples* and *lists*. For such a list consider the principles just enumerated. Contrast *rational* principles with other kinds of principles, for example, *reasonable* principles. Consider the principle that Hobbes uses to state a kind of *directive* for discerning the *force* of the laws of nature:

"Do not that to another, which thou wouldest not have done to thy self." I: 15: p. 79 (This comes after 19th Law of Nature and last Law of Nature L: 79).

This can be given as an example of a *reasonable* principle: someone who does not take effective means to advance their ends is being (let's say) *irrational* (other things equal); whereas those who do to others what they would not have done to themselves (perhaps because they think they can get away with it) are being *unreasonable*. This does not imply that they are being *irrational*, given the aims of theirs they are seeking to further. But in violating this principle they are being *unreasonable*.

All of the principles Hobbes calls "the Laws of Nature" could plausibly be called *reasonable* principles. See especially the following:

(i) *Leviathan*, p. 64, The first part of the first Law of Nature: everyone ought to endeavor peace, as far as they have hope of obtaining it.

(ii) *Leviathan*, pp. 64–65, the second Law of Nature: that we be willing, when others are so too, to lay down our right to all things and be content with so much liberty against others as we would allow others against ourselves. This is a principle of *reciprocity*.

And so on: Note numbers 10 through 19 of the Laws of Nature.

We may not accept these principles quite as Hobbes states them; but still, as stated, or as modified above, it seems fitting to call them *reasonable* principles and the desire to act from these principles for their own sake *reasonable* desires. Reasonable desires also are *principle-dependent* desires in the same sense that *rational* desires are. Desires of both kinds are specified by reference to rational or reasonable *principles*.

Now, let's turn to what Hobbes says about *voluntary actions:*

(a) He states that the object of voluntary actions of human beings, when they are fully rational and have time to deliberate, is always some apparent good to themselves. Hobbes says: ". . . and of the voluntary acts of every man, the object is some *Good to himself*" (*Leviathan*, p. 66). In other words, we do not act *voluntarily* contrary to our own good. When the apparent good turns out not to be an actual good, then, leaving aside the cases where people are motivated by pride and vainglory, he supposes that there is some error or misfortune in the situation, which although the action turned out badly is not to be attributed to the agents themselves (*Leviathan*, p. 66). Hobbes grants that *some* voluntary acts are *against reason*. Our deliberations at some point come to an end and the last (effective) desire at that point Hobbes defines as the *will;* and our deliberations and hence our will may be distorted by pride and vainglory, for example. But Hobbes thinks, I believe, that in *any case,* voluntary acts have as their tacit object some *apparent* good of ourselves. Even someone moved by pride and vainglory still strives for something they *think* is for their own good, although their reasoning is incorrect.

Hobbes makes this claim about voluntary actions in the context of explaining how some rights can never be abandoned or transferred. For example, we always have the right to resist the Sovereign in self-defense and to do what we think necessary to preserve our own life. Hobbes says that "The mutual transferring of Right is that which men call Contract" (*Leviathan*, p. 66), and in contracts, some basic rights are always reserved for ourselves.

(b) How, then, can we define a *rational* human being, for someone's reasoning *may also* be incorrect, i.e. we have a false conclusion. The difference lies in the *explanation* for the incorrectness of their reasoning, of *why* the apparent good is not the true good for them. If the explanation is their failure to discipline and to allow for their tendencies to vainglory etc., then they are not (fully) rational. If however the explanation lies (for example) in *lack of information* that *cannot be avoided* and is *no fault* of the agent, the person is still acting *perfectly rationally,* even though the conclusion they arrive at is incorrect.

To summarize, in Hobbes's *Political Conception:*

(i) The *object* of the voluntary actions of perfectly rational persons is *always* viewed by these persons as some *apparent good to themselves* (as individuals). This good is identified by the principles of rational deliberation in conjunction with the array of our *object*-dependent self-related desires (which belong to us as individuals), taking into account both present and foreseeable future desires. (Recall here our fundamental interests, in order of priority: self-preservation, conjugal affections, riches, and means of life.)

(ii) When the *apparent good* turns out not to be the *real* good, the explanation, in the case of *rational* individuals, does not lie in some *fault* or *failure* of reasoning that is *properly* attributable to them (e.g. not the result of pride and vainglory). But it lies in unavoidable lack of information or some other unavoidable circumstance.

(iii) The voluntary acts of rational persons are moved in part by highest-order, principle-dependent desires and not solely by object-dependent desires. In a perfectly *rational* person these higher-order desires are *fully regulative—fully effective and in control.*

Thus *rational deliberation* may reach a *false* conclusion and when acted upon may lead to *disaster.* But that the conclusion is false and leads to disaster is the result of *misfortune* and not the person's fault: there were no *errors* in reasoning or *distortions* via the passions, etc.

§2. The *Rational* Basis of the *Reasonable* Articles of Civic Concord

A conception of social cooperation is a conception of how coordinated social activity may be arranged to further everyone's (rational) good in ways that are fair (reasonable) to each. It involves a notion of fair terms of cooperation (the reasonable), and a notion of the good or advantage of each person cooperating (the rational). In the political conception, the way in which Hobbes thinks of human beings determines in more detail how the notion of social cooperation is to be understood and how the notions of rationality and reasonableness are to be understood. Our problem is to discover how Hobbes understands the relation between the rational deliberation of individuals on the one hand, and on the other the laws of nature whose contents are intuitively reasonable since they formulate precepts of fair cooperation or dispose us to habits of mind favorable to such cooperation. Traditionally, the Laws of Nature are thought of as follows:

(a) The *Laws of Nature* are the (*legislative*) enactments (norms) of that person, namely God, who has *rightful authority* over the world and all its creatures, including human beings.

(b) As enactments of this rightful authority, these enactments are *commands,* and are therefore *laws* in the strict sense (vs. principles), since by definition "law" is understood as the command of someone with rightful authority.

(c) These laws are *natural* laws (vs. *revealed*) because *what* they command and *that* they *are* commands, can be ascertained by the correct use of the *natural* powers of reason, which are possessed by human beings as *rational* beings when we use our powers to reflect upon the facts of *nature* which are *open* to our view, and draw suitable inferences. That is, it is possible by natural reason to work out that God exists, and that God must have intended people to be happy, and to live in society, and so forth. Therefore, if certain precepts are necessary for that fundamental purpose, then they would be laws of nature, natural laws, and they would have the force of law.

Understood this way: Hobbes says: The commands of God, who has rightful authority over us, are the *Laws of Nature* when these commands are proclaimed to us, as it were, by and through our natural reason in view of the fact of nature, e.g. the facts of our human nature, etc.

Hobbes has this interpretation of the Laws of Nature in mind (or a similar interpretation) when he says at the end of Chapter 15, p. 80: "These dictates of Reason, men use to call by the name of Laws, but improperly; for they are but Conclusions, or Theorems concerning what conduceth to the conservation and defense of themselves; whereas Law, properly is the word of him, that by right hath command over others. But yet if we consider the same Theorems, as delivered in the word of God, that by right commandeth all things; then are they properly called Laws."

At the beginning of the last lecture I explained why I believe the *secular* interpretation of Hobbes's system is the *primary* one. The supplementary theological interpretation affects *neither* the *formal* structure of Hobbes's account of political institutions *nor* its *substantive content:* what is required for the *self-preservation of each* in the world does *not* conflict with what is *necessary* for *salvation.* So understood, Hobbes's argument is addressed to *rational* people who are to use their *natural* reason. Hobbes's reference to the Laws of Nature as *also,* from another point of view, laws of God may be taken to mean: the introduction of theological concerns will not affect or change these laws, nor will it affect the generation of the commonwealth.

Thus I suggest that we regard the Laws of Nature as *primarily* conclusions about what principles and standards of social cooperation it would be *rational* for *everyone* to comply with in order to *preserve* themselves and to attain the means for a contended life. This compliance is rational for *each* person provided that *other persons likewise comply.* Thus the Laws of Nature, when *generally* complied with by everyone and when this general compliance is publicly *known* to each, are *collectively rational.* Or referring back to the discussion of practical reasoning we can say: the Laws of Nature define a family of *reasonable* principles, so far as their content and role discern, the *general* compliance with which is *rational* for each and every person.

Another way of describing the Laws of Nature is the following:[1] The Laws of Nature are *much like* what Kant calls *assertoric* hypothetical imperatives. These are Hypothetical Imperatives that are *valid* for all in virtue of the fact that we all have, as rational beings, a certain end, namely, our own *happiness* (which for Kant is the orderly fulfillment of our many and various ends).[2] For Kant the end of our own happiness is one that, as a *rational* being, we have by *natural necessity.* I am not sure what Kant means by this. The idea of happiness involves for him some conception of how to order and to plan for the satisfaction of our various desires over time. So in this respect, Kant's account of practical reason is similar to that of Hobbes's as earlier described. That our own happiness is an end for us may just mean

1. This reading of Kant is proposed by J. W. N. Watkins, *Hobbes's System of Ideas* (New York: Barnes and Noble, 1968), pp. 55–61.

2. Immanuel Kant, *Groundwork of the Metaphysics of Morals,* trans. and ed. H. J. Paton (London: Hutchinson, 1948), II: 21, Ak. 4: 15f.

that as natural beings we cannot *help but care* whether or not our desires are satisfied. To make this account fit Hobbes, we replace the end of happiness with that of our felicity now understood as our *own self-preservation and the means of a contented life.*

The distinction between a Hypothetical Imperative and a Categorical Imperative lies in how the corresponding principle or directive is *justified* and not in its form or mode of expression. Thus suppose we always write a principle or directive as: *To do so and so.* Whether the directives: "To honor one's covenants" or "To keep oneself in a state of good health" are Hypothetical Imperatives or Categorical Imperatives for a person is decided by the *grounds* upon which they are affirmed. One person may hold either as a Hypothetical Imperative, another as a Categorical Imperative. Some one who *honors their covenants* on the grounds that it is *necessary* to *preserve* one's *good reputation,* etc., holds this directive as a Hypothetical Imperative, since reputation is a kind of power. Whereas to keep *oneself healthy* because this it *necessary* if one is to discharge one's moral duties is to hold that injunction as a Categorical Imperative.

Thus in *Kant's* ethics there are *two* procedures of practical reasoning: *One* is defined by the way in which *particular* Hypothetical Imperatives are justified, which involves the general *principle of rational choice* and the *idea of our own happiness;* and the *other* is defined by the way in which *particular* Categorical Imperatives are justified, which invokes the *CI-procedure.*[3] This procedure expresses the requirements of *reasonableness:* that is, restrictions for the specification of principles with which *everyone* is to comply insofar as their conduct is social. Hypothetical Imperatives are justified to each in view of their *own* particular ends, which are diverse between individuals. Categorical Imperatives are justified as requirements that *all* are to follow, *whatever* their more particular ends.

Thus the interpretation of the Laws of Nature as Hypothetical Imperatives (on Hobbes's view) comes to this: the Laws of Nature have the kind of *content* that we intuitively associate with *reasonable* principles, that is, principles with which we think everyone is to comply (whatever their more particular ends). Thus the Laws of Nature are reasonable principles. Yet for Hobbes these principles are *justified* to *each* individual in view of their hav-

---

3. For a detailed account of Kant and his Categorical Imperative Procedure, see John Rawls, *Lectures on the History of Moral Philosophy,* ed. Barbara Herman (Cambridge, Mass.: Harvard University Press, 2000), pp. 162–181.

ing the end of self-preservation. And so they are justified as Hypothetical Imperatives and indeed assertoric Hypothetical Imperatives. In sum: reasonable principles are collectively rational.

So, summing up Hobbes's view in contrast with e.g. Kant, we get something like this:

(a) What traditionally were considered Laws of Nature (as defined at the beginning of this section) have the *content and role* we associate with the *Reasonable*. Let's call them the *Articles of Civic Concord (or peace)*. These articles can be understood as articles for the *conservation of human beings* as they live in society. These articles are the *subject of moral science* for Hobbes—the science of what is *good and evil*. The goodness of these principles consists in their being means to *peaceful, sociable*, and *comfortable living*, which peace *all* human beings (when rational) agree is good.

(b) But although the *content* and role of articles of civic concord are standard enough, the grounds upon which Hobbes justifies them *fall solely* under the *Rational:* these articles are justified to *each* person by appealing to their *rational deliberation* as described above. This is what I take Hobbes to mean by calling them "but Conclusions, or Theorems concerning what conduceth to the conservation and defense of themselves" (*Leviathan*, p. 80). They become *laws* when viewed under the aspect of the commands of God. Thus for Hobbes: the *grounds* of the Reasonable is the Rational.

(c) For this reason I don't believe (one can question this certainly) that there is any room in Hobbes for a notion of *moral* right and obligation, as this notion is normally understood. The *formal* structure of rights and obligations and so on is there; but if moral right and obligation involves grounds different from the Rational, as I believe it does, Hobbes has no place for it in his *official* view. This explains in part his offense to traditional doctrine. (See Appendix A to this chapter.)

As to our obligation to obey the laws of nature, Hobbes says that the laws of nature bind to a desire they should take place *(in foro interno)*, but not always to putting them into action *(in foro externo)*, because if a man performs all he promises and no one else does, he is "mak(ing) himself a prey to others, and procur(ing) his own certain ruin, contrary to the ground of all Laws of Nature" (*Leviathan*, p. 80).

Finally, Hobbes gives a definition of moral philosophy when he says,

"Peace is Good, and therefore also the way, or means of Peace, which . . . are *Justice, Gratitude, Modesty, Equity, Mercy* . . . that is to say, *Moral Virtues;* and their contrary *Vices,* Evil. Now the science of Virtue and Vice, is Moral Philosophy; and therefore the true Doctrine of the Laws of Nature, is the true Moral Philosophy" (*Leviathan,* p. 79). So, he is defining moral philosophy as the science of these dictates of reason, the Laws of Nature, which it is necessary for everyone to follow if peace is to be achieved. Or, to put it in another way, he thinks of moral philosophy as the science of what is necessary to preserve the good of men in groups. He is claiming that the object of moral philosophy is to work out and explain the content of these precepts, the Laws of Nature—to explain why they are based on rationality. The account we could then give for why they are reasonable principles is that they turn out to be the kinds of precepts that are required to make social life possible.

Hobbes sees himself as explaining the basis of these principles, not as the schools do via Aristotle (mediocrity, passions), nor by an appeal to religion or to revelation etc; nor by an appeal to *history,* e.g. Thucydides. The Laws of Nature as dictates of reason are not arrived at by *induction,* by a survey of the history of nations, etc. They are arrived at by deductive *science:* by going back to first principles of *body and of human nature,* and seeing how *political society must* (the citizen or the Leviathan) work, looking at its parts viewed when society is, so to speak, *dissolved.* He analyzes the basic elements of society, human beings, attempting to identify fundamental interests by which everyone is moved. Then, basing everything on that analysis, he concludes that in order to realize these fundamental interests, it is necessary that these dictates of reason, or laws of nature, should be followed by everyone. In order to achieve that, of course, there must be a Sovereign. The Sovereign, or the Leviathan, is an artificial person who must fulfill a certain *end.* As we'll see next time, the task of the Sovereign is to make it reasonable for all of us to honor these dictates because we know that the existence of an effective Sovereign is going to guarantee that others are going to honor them also. In the absence of that guarantee it would not be reasonable or rational for anyone to honor them. The Sovereign is the necessary condition of its being rational for any of us to act on and to follow these reasonable principles. If this artificial person is to serve this end or role effectively, political society must be *constructed, as it were,* in a certain way. And what this way is, Reason as Science (moral philosophy) must discern.

Hobbes Lecture III: Appendix A (1979)

WHETHER THERE IS MORAL OBLIGATION IN HOBBES

I shall begin the discussion of this question by looking at Hobbes's reply to the fool who says there is no justice: S: 120–130 in I: Ch. 15 [1st ed., 72f].

1. Hobbes's thesis is this: that in the case of covenants where the other party has performed *already,* or where there is a *power* to compel the other party to perform (or to render compensation), then it is *always* in accordance with *right reason* for us to honor our covenant. (Let's assume the making of the covenant was rational for both parties.) As we expressed it earlier: in these conditions, it is (always) *rational* to be *reasonable*. Keeping (valid) covenants is always a dictate of *right reason*.

2. Hobbes makes three points in support of this thesis:

(a) He does not deny that one might violate one's covenant and, as things turn out, *profit* thereby enormously; but Hobbes thinks that we can never *reasonably expect* to profit. Given the way the social life *is*, the *only reasonable expectation* is that of loss to ourselves. The fact that infidelity *sometimes* succeeds does not show otherwise. And those who gain from infidelity still act contrary to right reason, since they *could not reasonably* have expected to gain.

This holds, Hobbes remarks, in the case of successful rebellion that deposes the Sovereign and sets up working government eventually. Events of this sort are not unknown but those who engage in rebellion nevertheless act contrary to reason: they had no *reason to expect* that they would be successful, or that having been successful, their example won't encourage others to overthrow them to their *ruin in the end*.

(b) Hobbes's other argument is that we depend *utterly* on the help of confederates to defend us against others; and anyone who violates their covenant either *declares* in effect their readiness to infidelity (makes their duplicity public, so to speak), in which case they cannot expect the help and aid of others; or else if they break their covenant in silence (and others do not learn of it), they are accepted by their confederates by *mistake,* or by *error,* which error or mistake cannot be *reasonably* relied upon not to be found out, with the consequent loss in one's security. Thus the violation of valid covenants, whether openly or in secret must reasonably be supposed to be to our loss eventually: fidelity we should *assume* is *always* a necessary means to our self-preservation.

(c) Hobbes argues further that theological considerations (re our salvation and eternal felicity) cannot be invoked to give a different conclusion. There is no *natural* knowledge of our life after death and so breach of covenants on the basis of such considerations (e.g. infidelity to those of another belief regarded as heretics) is contrary to reason.

3. I have summarized Hobbes's argument contra the fool who says there is no justice simply to emphasize that in this very crucial passage the appeal is solely to our primary interest in our security and self-preservation (including here the desire for a commodious life). Hobbes is maintaining that:

It is never *reasonable to expect* to gain (as judged by our self-preservation) from the breach of *valid* covenants, even though it *sometimes* happens that infidelity is, in fact, profitable.

Hobbes makes the argument turn on a question of fact and upon what it is reasonable to expect given the *standing* conditions of human life and the propensities of human psychology.

Hobbes's argument can be strengthened by emphasizing two matters he himself stresses elsewhere:

(a) *First,* the very great *uncertainty* of human life whenever the conditions of peace and security are threatened or undermined. Given this uncertainty and the severe losses that are possible *without* peace, a rational person will appropriately *discount* the prospects of present and immediate gains from breaches of trust, *given conditions of peace.*

(b) *Second,* a rational person will also recognize that *pride and vainglory* is most likely what is *prompting* us to infidelity (when peace obtains and valid covenants hold). Pride and vainglory distorts our perception and skews our deliberations, which when corrected we can see to be erroneous and destructive of our self-preservation.

4. Many of us may, no doubt, still find Hobbes's argument unpersuasive on the *facts* of the matter. Prisoner's Dilemma examples in political affairs may appear to rebut his claims. But we should resist the idea, I think,

that Hobbes is unaware of these kinds of cases, that he is less shrewd than us and hasn't seen the darker possibilities.

My guess is that Hobbes's basic idea of trying to show that it is *rational*, as defined by his account of practical reason, to be *reasonable* either led him to overlook these cases or to pass over them as unimportant, really. His error in this regard, if it is error, is not surely *stupidity;* but springs from his underlying idea. Hobbes wants to appeal solely to our interest in self-preservation because he wants to appeal only to the most fundamental interests which he thinks *none* will question are fundamental. Thus, Hobbes drastically simplifies, but intentionally.

5. The argument against the fool shows, I think, that Hobbes does not in fact appeal to a notion of moral obligation (as normally understood) *in this argument.* But have we yet shown that his conception of practical reason would not *permit* him to do so? What is it that his conception of rationality seems to exclude? Let's say that it is the notion of the *reasonable* in the following sense:

(a) *First,* there are different *kinds* of reasons that we can have for violating covenants. Hobbes does not argue contra the fool that the fool appeals to the *wrong kind* of reasons; he disputes the fool's suppositions of *fact.* By contrast, a *reasonable* person does not think it is a *sufficient* [reason] for violating their promise that they thereby gain *some* permanent, long-run advantage. Perhaps the situation has so changed that had they foreseen the change they would not have promised; a different undertaking would have been more to their advantage. Nevertheless, this is *not enough* to go back on the undertaking. Thus, one feature of a *reasonable* person's thought is this: promises are to be [kept] even at some *loss,* as things turn out, to one's advantage, even when this is a *certain overall* loss.

(b) *Second,* a reasonable person has some concern for what, vaguely speaking, are considerations of *fairness* and the distributions of gains and losses among, e.g., the parties to an agreement. Important here is the balance of advantages at the time the agreement was made, what we might call people's *bargaining power.* A reasonable bargain is one which satisfies certain conditions of background fairness. Later on we shall try to discuss what these conditions might be on certain views. But it is notable that in his reply to the fool Hobbes does not mention this element; and indeed the tenor of his political conception is against it. Hobbes says that a promise is binding even when one is *coerced* into making it (I: Ch.14, p. 69], or has no other genuine alternative; for it is still a *voluntary* act, and like all such acts, done with a prospect to our *own* advantage.

Thus, I conclude that Hobbes's view, as expressed in his reply to the fool, does not *permit* room for the *ordinary* notion of moral obligation (re promises, e.g.) because this notion involves some concern for fairness (e.g. re the circumstances under which promises are given) and for honoring promises even when *we* might do better. And if we take Hobbes's account of practical reason strictly, it seems that both of these are *ruled* out.

Hobbes Lecture III: Appendix B

HOBBES'S LAWS OF NATURE: *LEVIATHAN*, CHAPTERS 14–15

Law of Nature = defined as a Precept found out by Reason that forbids us to do what is destructive of our life, etc. (*Leviathan*, p. 64).

1st Law of Nature: 1st branch: to seek peace; 2nd branch: to defend ourselves (64)

2nd Law of Nature: that we be willing, when others are also, to lay down right to all things, for the sake of peace (64f)

3rd Law of Nature: to perform covenants made (71)

4th Law of Nature: Gratitude: cause no one to reject their good will (75–76)

5th Law of Nature: Mutual accommodation (76)

6th Law of Nature: Pardon offenses, when repented (76)

7th Law of Nature: To punish only for future good, not revenge (76)

8th Law of Nature: Not to show contempt and hatred of others (76)

9th Law of Nature: To acknowledge others as equals by nature, contra pride (76–77)

10th Law of Nature: At time of the Social Contract, no one to reserve any right that he is not willing others to reserve as well, contra arrogance (77)

11th Law of Nature: That judges are to judge equally between men (77)

12th Law of Nature: Use of Commons (77)

13th Law of Nature: Use of Lot (78)

14th Law of Nature: Use of lot natural: primogeniture (78) (11–14 re dist. justice)

15th Law of Nature: Mediators to be allowed safe conduct (78)

16th Law of Nature: To submit controversies to mediation (78)

17th Law of Nature: No man judge in his own case (78)

18th Law of Nature: No man to be judge who is partial by natural causes (78)

19th Law of Nature: Judge in controversies of fact, to credit no one witness than another, etc. (78) (15–19 re Natural Justice)

Summary of Laws of Nature: Do not do that to another which we would not have done to us. (79)

Laws of Nature bind *in foro interno* (79)

Def. Moral Philosophy: Science of what is good and evil in society of mankind (79f)

Argument for Laws of Nature from Necessary Conditions of Peace (80)

Laws of Nature improperly called Laws: they are dictates of Reason, theorems regarding our conservation (80)

[1983] As to our obligation to obey the laws of nature, Hobbes says that the laws of nature bind to a desire they should take place *(in foro interno),* but not always to putting them into action *(in foro externo),* because if a man performs all he promises and no one else does, he is "mak(ing) himself a prey to others, and procur(ing) his own certain ruin, contrary to the ground of all Laws of Nature" *(Leviathan,* p. 79).

He thinks that each of the natural laws is to each individual's rational good. So you have an argument, in effect, that the reasonable features of the social life are justified by each person's rational advantage. Hobbes is making an argument in which he wants to justify all of the precepts that come under the laws of nature as imperatives of this kind, but only if everyone else can also be assumed to follow them.

HOBBES IV

The Role and Powers of the Sovereign

I have examined the grounds that led Hobbes to think that a state of nature must in due course become a state of war so that, effectively, they are the same thing. The state of war is a state that is mutually destructive, and let's assume that it is on the whole destructive for everyone. So far as people are rational, then, they will want to avoid having things collapse back into a state of nature. What I have tried to do was to give a more instructive interpretation of Hobbes's argument by stressing those aspects of it that only appeal to the normal and permanent features of human life, and by avoiding drawing on some of the more dramatic elements which put emphasis on pride and vainglory and other elements of that sort. Although, of course, we have to allow that those are possibilities that have to be guarded against; even if we don't know that they are actually the case we still have to take them into account.

Plainly then, it seems that in Hobbes's view the *role of the Sovereign* is to *stabilize*, and thereby to maintain, that social state in which everyone, normally and regularly, adheres to the Laws of Nature, which state Hobbes calls the "State of Peace." The Sovereign stabilizes society by effectively imposing sanctions that keep everyone "in awe." It is the *public knowledge* that the Sovereign is effective that makes it rational for each person then to obey the laws of nature. He provides all with the *assurance* that the Laws of Nature will be enforced. Most people then comply, *knowing* that the others are also going to comply with them.

Now I should like to say some things about the formal structure of the situation in the state of nature, and to do so by comparing it to the Prisoner's Dilemma game, an idea that seems to have been invented in 1950 by a Princeton mathematician, A. W. Tucker. The Prisoner's Dilemma is a case of a two-person, non-cooperative, non-zero-sum game. It is non-cooperative because agreements are not binding (or enforceable), and non-zero-sum because it is not the case that what one person gains the other loses. It is often discussed in the context of political institutions, and also in the case of moral notions. Many of you have perhaps heard of it.

A standard example of the Prisoner's Dilemma is the following payoff matrix (see Figure 2). Imagine that two prisoners have been apprehended for a crime, held for interrogation, and brought in separately to the District Attorney whose aim is to get them both to confess. To achieve this end, the DA makes each one aware, separately, of the following options and consequences: if neither of them confesses, they are each going to be charged with some lesser offense and be in jail for two years. If they both confess, they are each going to be in jail for five years. If one of them confesses and the other does not, the one who confesses is to be released, and the other one will go to jail for ten years. All of this is indicated in Figure 2. In each square there are two numbers: the first number is the number of years in jail for the first prisoner; the second number is the number of years in jail for the second prisoner.

The prisoners' dilemma is how to weigh and balance the unhappy outcomes for each of them in this situation. The action 'to confess' is said to "dominate" the action 'not to confess' for both prisoners. What this means is that the most rational thing for each to do is to confess, no matter what the other does. So, it pays the first prisoner in each case to play the second row; that is, to confess. For if the second prisoner does not confess, then the first prisoner gets off entirely, as indicated by the '0, 10' pair in the second row. Whereas, if he does not confess and the second prisoner also does not confess, then the first prisoner would get two years (as indicated by the '2, 2' pair in the first row). Moreover, confessing and getting five years is better than having the other one squeal and have you get ten years. And it is symmetrical for each one. So, they each have then an incentive to confess on

	Prisoner 2: Not Confess	Prisoner 2: Confess
Prisoner 1: Not Confess	2, 2	10, 0
Prisoner 1: Confess	0, 10	5, 5

Figure 2. Prisoner's Dilemma 1.

the grounds that the second row dominates the first row, and the second column also dominates the first column. The most reasonable course of action for them jointly—that neither should confess—is unstable, as neither of them can trust the other to do the same; and the consequence of pleading innocent while the other confesses is ten years in jail. By confessing, one guarantees either release or at most a five-year jail term, as is indicated by the '5, 5' in the southeast pair. By not confessing, one chances a ten-year sentence in the hopes of getting only two years. So the action to confess is said to *dominate* the action not to confess, for both of them equally.

The outcome that results for both prisoners, if they choose the dominant alternative, is a *stable equilibrium*. That is to say, either prisoner stands to lose if he does not confess and the other does. So the southeast pair is a stable point in the sense that it does not pay either of them to deviate from that. On the other hand, if they both thus act rationally and confess it will nevertheless turn out that they are *both worse off* than if somehow they could stabilize the most reasonable course of action—if they could make and then enforce a prior agreement not to confess. The two prisoners are isolated, but, even if they could get together before they go in and say, "I promise not to confess," still neither of them can trust the other to keep the promise. So, it doesn't help to promise unless there are some prior ties of friendship or affection or bonds of trust that have been established between them. Or if they belonged to a group or a gang, whose leader will make sure that whoever squeals will be "fed to the fishes." Otherwise, they are going to be tempted to confess, and that's the point.

The relevance of this to Hobbes is that people who contemplate making promises in the State of Nature are looking at somewhat the same situation (although it's not exactly the same by any means). One difference is that the state of nature is going to be a recurrent game. In other words, one is going to be involved in this situation with confederates normally not only once, but time and time again, and that kind of case is going to be different than where there is just one encounter. Still, I take it to be Hobbes's view that the general condition of mankind is that there are only two stable states, one of them being the state of nature, which is a state of war. The other one we might call a "state of the Leviathan," in which there is, as Hobbes sometimes says, an absolute Sovereign who enforces the laws of nature, and makes sure that everyone acts on them.

The reason why the state of nature becomes a state of war, and the reason that is a stable state, meaning that it is hard to get out of it, is that there is no effective Sovereign. Covenants do not do any good, for, as Hobbes said, words of that sort are of no effect because no one can trust anyone else to keep them. The reason is that the person who performs first has no way to ensure that the other party will perform in the absence of a Sovereign. In a covenant, the performance required is ordinarily divided in time. One person performs earlier, and then some weeks or months afterwards someone else performs. In between the time the first person performs and the time that the other person is to do their part, the situation may alter, and that person will then have some reason for not honoring the covenant. The first person, knowing that, doesn't have grounds for keeping their part of the covenant in the first place. So, normally there would then be no point to making covenants in that state. The way Hobbes puts it is "Therefore he which performeth first, does but betray himself to his enemy; contrary to the Right (he can never abandon) of defending his life, and means of living" (*Leviathan*, p. 68).

Now, to understand why Hobbes makes performing first in a covenant a case of betraying oneself, just consider again the Prisoner's Dilemma. Hobbes's thesis is that the state of nature, which is a state of war, is a stable state, much in the same way that the lower right-hand corner of the Prisoner's Dilemma is also stable. It doesn't pay anyone to depart from that choice. Therefore, in the absence of some change in the background conditions, it will be a stable state. That is, if there isn't some external sanction like those discussed that is outside of the whole situation that the prisoners are in, then they're both going to confess, even though both would be better off if both did not confess.

As an example of an actual situation where the state of nature still exists, Hobbes mentions the relationship between nation-states (*Leviathan*, p. 63). Consider this matrix (Figure 3) to represent that state. In the upper left-hand corner put in a P for peace, put in the lower left 'E, S' where 'E' is

	Nation 2: Comply	Nation 2: Not Comply
Nation 1: Comply	P, P	S, E
Nation 1: Not Comply	E, S	W, W [D, D]

Figure 3. Prisoner's Dilemma 2.

empire and 'S' is submission. And put in the upper right 'S, E', which is submission and empire; one reverses it. Then in the bottom right, put 'W, W' which should be 'war-war', or if it's bad enough you could put 'D, D', which would be 'destruction-destruction'.

Now if 'D, D' were bad enough that might be the case of [nuclear] deterrence. One might never then want to violate the agreement. But otherwise in the case of an armament agreement, one would have the same situation as the Prisoner's Dilemma; that is, the agreement to disarm, or to reduce arms, is very unstable. If both parties can honor it then you are in the upper left and everyone would be better off. But there is always the danger that you cannot trust the other party to do their part. So, it is a case of where the violator picks up all the marbles and in that situation you are going to end up, or tend to end up, on the bottom right, with war or even worse, mutual destruction.

The problem then, as Hobbes sees it, is *how to lift ourselves out of the state of nature* and into a state of the Leviathan-society. How are we going to do that, given the fact that in the state of nature agreements between individuals are subject to the kind of instability that we have just discussed? Hobbes views this problem as one of defining what is needed to lift us out of the state of nature.

What we have to do first would be to define a mutually beneficial social state, which includes a stable and secure civil peace and concord. What is that state and what are the precepts that characterize it? On Hobbes's view, it would be characterized, first, by the precepts of the dictates of reason, which are the Laws of Nature (*Leviathan*, p. 63), and second, by the idea that those laws are effectively enforced by a Sovereign or common power who has all the necessary powers to do so. So, the laws of nature would give the background precepts, and then would come the Sovereign with these necessary and effective powers, and then of course, on top of all that there would be the Sovereign's particular enactments, that is, civil law.

Then the third thing that one would have to do would be to move to set up this mutually beneficial state. This Hobbes thinks of as being done by the Social Contract, by which is meant the establishment of the Sovereign by "institution," or by authorization. Notice that he thinks that a Sovereign can come about also by conquest, or by "acquisition" as he puts it. This is a very important point to mention, namely the Sovereign has the same powers in either case, whether brought about by conquest, or by authorization or institution via the social contract. Hobbes mentions that if we have two countries ruled by the same Sovereign, but in one of them the Sovereign's rule is by acquisition or by conquest, and in the other by a social contract brought about by authorization or institution, the Sovereign has precisely the same powers in both countries (*Leviathan*, p. 102). There is no difference. It will be effectively the same constitutional regime. (I am using the term "constitutional" here rather broadly, not as implying any bill of rights or anything of that sort.)

What happens next then, is that this mutually beneficial state must be stabilized by instituting an agency which then would ensure that every person normally has a *sufficient motive* to comply with the rules and that these rules are ordinarily complied with. The Sovereign does not do this by changing anyone's character, as it were, or by changing human nature. What it does rather is to *alter the background conditions* against which people reason and against which they are going to make contracts and decide to honor them and to adhere to the other precepts of reason or laws of nature. In effect, given the Sovereign's existence, it now becomes rational to do what, in the state of nature, it is not rational to do, namely to adhere to the laws of nature. So, to repeat, what the Sovereign does is not to reform human beings, or alter their character, but to change the background conditions against which they reason.

Perhaps a good example might be a familiar one. Take the case of voluntary payment of one's income tax. I am now making some assumptions that we think our taxes are spent wisely for things that we all need, also that the income tax is drawn up fairly, so that people do not have various sorts of reasons that people might have for not wanting to pay them. Make those assumptions that the income tax that is being collected is being spent on things that people need, for the common benefit, and make the assumption that the schedule of taxation is fair. If you had a voluntary income tax scheme, it might be that everyone would be happy to pay their tax if they thought that everyone else was doing the same. But, in the large society one might reason, "I don't know that everyone else is paying their taxes and I don't want to be taken advantage of by others. I don't want my honesty taken advantage of by those who might be going to renege and not pay." It is a case where even though everyone is honest, and even though everyone is prepared to pay their tax if other people do, it still would be a reasonable thing for everyone to agree to set up a Sovereign with the necessary powers to make sure that everyone pays their tax. It is perfectly rational for us all to agree to do that, agree to a Sovereign, because otherwise none of us has a way of being sure that everyone else is going to pay the tax.

In this example I have not assumed that there are actually any cheaters. I have assumed that everyone is happy to pay their taxes, but only if they know that everyone else is going to. What the Sovereign does, then, is to *stabilize* this scheme so that everyone does what is actually to their mutual advantage. One often finds in ordinary life many examples of this sort. The idea is that it becomes *rational* for each of us to *want* some kind of *coercive sanction* to be imposed, even though there is not anyone who is actually unwilling to do what they are supposed to be doing. I think that Hobbes is one of the first to have a clear understanding of these situations.

Now let's look at the notion of *authorization* and then go on to say something about just and good laws. The notion of authorization is discussed in Chapter 16 at the end of Book One of the *Leviathan*. Here Hobbes is writing about the generation of the commonwealth as a way of overcoming the state of nature in which everyone's behavior is, as we have just described, self-defeating. Hobbes begins Chapter 16 with a definition of "person": A person, is he *whose words or actions are considered, either as his own, or as representing the words or actions of another man, or of any other thing to whom they are attributed, whether Truly or by Fiction.* When they are considered his own, then he is called a *Natural Person:* And when they are considered as representing the words and actions of another, then he is a *Feigned* or *Artificial Person.*

The Sovereign, or the assembly, Hobbes thinks of as an artificial person, because the Sovereign is someone whom members of society have *authorized* to act on their behalf. Having authorized them, we *own* the actions of the Sovereign and recognize them as our own. Representatives and agents are said to be actors in those words and actions of theirs which are owned by those they represent. The Sovereign, then, is a kind of actor, and the Sovereign's actions are *owned by us,* as the Sovereign represents us.

The notion of *authority* has been introduced in the following way. An action of the Sovereign is done by authority when it is performed by a licensed public person whose right it is. In other words, a certain person, A, does action x by the authority of B if B has the right to do x and B has *authorized* or granted the right to do x to A. So to *authorize* someone as your representative or your agent is to give that person the use of your rights. It means that you have given them *the authority* to act in some capacity on your behalf. Now, the Sovereign is going to be the person whom *everyone* has authorized to act on his or her behalf in certain ways; in that sense, the Sovereign is *our agent*, and acts *with authority*.

Now I'll make some points about authorization. First, authorization is not simply the renunciation of a right on my part. Rather, authorization enables someone else to use my right to act in a certain way. Thus we do not renounce or abandon our rights in authorizing the Sovereign; rather we authorize the Sovereign to use our rights in certain ways.

Second, the person who has the use of my right and who is my agent now has a right which that person did not have before. That is, if we authorize the Sovereign to use our rights, then the Sovereign has rights that the Sovereign did not have before.

Third, authorization can be for a longer or shorter period of time and that, of course, depends on the grant of authority and its purpose and the like. In the case of the Sovereign it will, of course, be a long period of time. As Hobbes says, the life of the authorization will be in perpetuity.

This then brings us to the *authorization of the Sovereign*. Hobbes says, "The Essence of the Commonwealth . . . is *One Person, of whose Acts a great Multitude, by mutual Covenants one with another, have made themselves every one the Author, to the end he may use the strength and means of them all, as he shall think expedient, for their Peace and Common Defense*" (*Leviathan*, p. 88). He makes certain further points about this, one being that the Sovereign must be the only actor upon whom these rights are conferred. That is, there cannot be two or more sovereigns. All parties in the original covenant have authorized identically the same person, or the same assembly of persons, as the actor who has the authority to use their rights. And this sovereign person or assembly has the use of rights that he or they did not have before the covenant was made.

A second point is the use of rights of many persons the Sovereign enjoys has been conferred on the Sovereign by a *covenant among themselves*. That is, in Hobbes, this original covenant, or sovereignty by institution, is a covenant between everyone in the society, but not with the Sovereign. Everyone covenants with everyone else, except the Sovereign, to authorize the Sovereign as their agent and to confer on the Sovereign the use of their rights. The relation that holds between the Sovereign and members of society is that of *authorization*, not covenant. The Sovereign is the actor and each citizen is the author of the Sovereign's act, or is the owner of the Sovereign's actions. The Sovereign is their agent, and there is not, Hobbes contends, a contract between members of society and the Sovereign. I do not believe that this in itself is a very important point, because in the case of the act of submission, where sovereignty is by acquisition or conquest, there *is* a pact between those who submit and the Sovereign. There is not the same kind of agreement that occurs in the case of authorization, but there is some agreement. Still, for Hobbes, in the case of institution of the Sovereign by authorization, the covenant is not with the Sovereign but between everyone in the society with each other.

So far this account is rather informal and concerns only what the notion of authorization is. It is a different account than Hobbes gives in his earlier *De Cive* (1647), where the Sovereign becomes the Sovereign by everyone's renouncing their right to resist the Sovereign. So, it is not that the Sovereign isn't authorized in *De Cive;* it's just that everyone renounces certain rights that would enable them in some conditions to resist the Sovereign. In the *Leviathan* everyone confers the use of their right on the Sovereign by means of a contract with each other, so the Sovereign becomes their agent; and Hobbes believes that in this case one has a different and stronger sense of social community than one has in *De Cive*.

Now, next, it is a useful exercise to try to work out what the social contract is supposed to say. If we think of A and B as being any two members of society, and if try to write out a hypothetical contract, it might be something like the following:

The first clause would be: "I, A, do hereby covenant with you, B, to authorize F (who is the Sovereign, or some sovereign body) as my sole political representative, and therefore I covenant to own henceforth all the Sovereign's actions so far as this is compatible with my inalienable right of self-preservation and my natural and true liberties" (see *Leviathan*, pp. 111–112; see also p. 66). In Chapter 21 Hobbes mentions certain liberties that we cannot alienate; so, what I have done here is to say that I covenant to own and support all the actions of the Sovereign except in these special cases.

The second clause would be: "I covenant to maintain this authorization of the Sovereign as my sole political representative continually and in perpetuity and to do nothing incompatible with this authorization."

The third: "I covenant to recognize all the necessary powers of the Sovereign enumerated below, and therefore that the powers listed are justifiable and recognized as such." And here we can go through the *Leviathan* and make a list of all the powers that Hobbes says the Sovereign must have. As you can see, the list is quite extensive.

The fourth clause would be: "I covenant not to release you, B, from your similar authorization of F made in your covenant to me, nor shall I ask you, B, to release me." In other words, we are tying ourselves into this. We are not going to ask the other to release us and we are also undertaking not to release them. There may be some logical puzzles about this, but I'll skip over those at the moment.

As the next to last clause: "I covenant to forgo my right of exercising my discretion in matters of the common good of the commonwealth and to forgo the right to private judgment as to whether the enactments of the Sovereign are good or bad, and to recognize that all these enactments are just and good so far as this is compatible with my inalienable right of self-preservation and the like."

And then to end it: "All this I do for the final end of setting up the Sovereign, for the preserving of my life, the objects of my affections, and the means of commodious living." The introduction of these constraints on myself is required, in Hobbes's view, for the existence of an *effective* Sovereign, and so one regards all of these conditions as necessary.

Note that the next to last clause, about forgoing the exercise of my discretion in deciding whether the laws of the Sovereign are good, is a very strong clause. That is, normally, what one would do would be to agree to comply with the Sovereign's laws. One would say that would be a reasonably normal thing to do in this sort of covenant. But, to add to that that I will not *judge,* nor even think about, whether or not the Sovereign's laws are good—that is a much stronger condition. Let's say we can presume that I have an obligation to obey the law even though I do not necessarily think it is a very good law, or perhaps I do not think it is even a just law; we can recognize that bad consequences might result if we each regard ourselves as justified to disobey laws that we do not think would be just or good. However, to covenant that I will not even consider *judging* a law *at all* unless it is incompatible with my retaining certain inalienable rights such as the right of self-preservation, is a very strong condition. There are, however, statements in Chapters 29 and 30 where Hobbes implies just this.

What Hobbes requires then is quite a lot, and while it would be wrong to characterize Hobbes's view as totalitarian (because that is a term that can only make sense in a nineteenth-century or twentieth-century government), it is, nevertheless, an absolute regime, in the sense that he is requiring very strong conditions and is saying that the Sovereign must have very strong powers if it is to be effective. What one wants to do in examining Hobbes is to try to work out how plausible his argument is for including under the Sovereign all these powers, and think what assumptions he is making that make the requirement of all these powers plausible to him.

Now, I want to say a few things about the relation between the Sovereign and the notions of *just* and *good* laws. Often, Hobbes says that the Sovereign's laws are *necessarily* just. But, it is possible for the Sovereign to enact laws that are *not good*—laws that are bad. So the problem arises as to how we are to understand the notion of justice so it that can happen that the Sovereign's laws are necessarily just, but may not be good. And how are we to understand the notion of good which also allows for that? Some people have thought that Hobbes is saying that the Sovereign has all this power and in effect that power makes right—that the reason the Sovereign's laws are always just is that the Sovereign has all the power. I believe that is a rather bad distortion of what Hobbes is saying. His thinking is that, if you take his idea of how the state is put together, then everyone has, by *covenant,* agreed with each other to authorize the Sovereign; and by Hobbes's third law of nature we know that covenant is the foundation of justice. Anything characterized in Hobbes to be just is normally related somehow to the notion of covenant (*Leviathan,* pp. 71–75).

I think then, that it is Hobbes's view that the Sovereign's laws are just because the Sovereign is the person upon whom everyone has granted the use of their rights for certain purposes, and among those purposes are those of making laws. He says that the law is made by the sovereign power, and that all that is done by such power is warranted and owned by every one of the people; and that that which every man will have so, no man can say is unjust. Therefore, the Sovereign being the person whom everyone has covenanted as that person who is to make laws, it follows that the Sovereign's laws are just. He also comments: "In the Laws of a Commonwealth, as in the Laws of Gaming: whatsoever the Gamesters all agree on, is Injustice to none of them" (*Leviathan,* p. 182). So, if we have all agreed to make the Sovereign the one who has the use of our rights, then it follows that the Sovereign's laws are just.

Of course Hobbes has another idea about the notion of good altogether. He says that in a state of nature each of us calls those things good that favor our interests. One might say roughly that in a state of nature, when I say that something is good, I mean that it is favorable to my rational concerns as I now see them. Hobbes believes that people don't have any agreed notion about what is good. The same person at different times will say that different things are good. Different people at the same time also say that different things are good. It is not the case that men are like beasts, say, where all in pursuing their private interests also realize the common good (*Leviathan,* pp. 86–87). We are not that fortunate, and there is no common good that we recognize by reason. We have no common insight into a notion of that sort. What we require is some agency, some impartial arbitrator or impartial judge, to decide what is in the common good. When Hobbes says that some laws are bad and not good, I think he has a very simple notion of good that one might characterize in the following way: What is to the common good are those enactments and those laws that will secure the background conditions that enable everyone to find it reasonable or rational to adhere to the laws of nature. Good laws would then be specific enactments that on the whole further the interests of the vast majority of the members of society, on the presumption that a civil state exists.

If that is right, if we give a characterization of the notions of justice and goodness in this way, then it is easy, I think, to see how Hobbes could say that the laws that the Sovereign enacts are always just even though the Sovereign may enact bad laws, and sovereigns have often done so. The Sovereign is the rightful arbitrator or judge of what is just and unjust since subjects have agreed to authorize him to exercise those powers, and subjects have also given up their right to question the Sovereign's discretion; but still the Sovereign *may in fact* do injury and enact *bad and not good* laws, as decided by the subjects' *rational* interests.

Finally, Hobbes contends bad laws are never as bad as a State of War.

Closing Remarks on Hobbes and Constitutional Democracy (1978)

Hobbes's political conception is likely to strike us as extremely unsatisfactory: we are compelled to choose between *absolutism* and *anarchy:* an unlimited Sovereign or the state of nature. For Hobbes insists:

(a) The *only* way to escape the State of Nature is to set up a Sovereign that is as absolute as *can* be (consistent with our inalienable rights to self-preservation, etc.); and,

(b) The State of Nature is the *worst* of all calamities that can befall us.

It is essential to see that these two theses are *not* required by Hobbes's *formal* theory but from his *substantive* views about *human* psychology and how he thinks political institutions will *actually* work. And, of course, he may be wrong in thinking that his own theory hangs together: it may be internally inconsistent.

After all, we *know,* I think, that Hobbes's substantive theory can't be, *in general,* correct; since *constitutional democratic* institutions that violate his conditions for the Sovereign *have actually* existed and have not been noticeably less stable and orderly regimes than the kind of absolutism that Hobbes favored. I shall conclude with some observations on this theme by way of making the transition to Locke and his form of Social Contract theory.

1. *First,* let's note some of the distinctive features of a constitutional democratic regime (with or without private property in the means of production) illustrated so far as possible by reference to our own regime.

(a) The constitution is understood as *written and supreme law* that regulates the scheme of government as a whole and defines the *powers* of its various agencies: executive, legislative, etc. This is a different notion than that of the constitution as simply the scheme of laws and institutions which form the system of government. Perhaps any regime has a constitution in the latter sense; but the idea of fundamental written law is distinctive, at least when combined with other features: e.g. with judicial review (a constitutional agency with certain powers to *interpret* the constitution).[1]

(b) One purpose of a written constitution (*interpreted* say by judicial review) is to *secure* certain *basic rights* from being overridden by the *highest legislative* agency. Enactments of the legislature that violate certain rights and liberties can be held void or unconstitutional, etc., e.g. by a supreme court, or other agency.

(c) So let's assume (for our purposes here) some form of *judicial review* (as we find it in our constitutional system). And finally

(d) The idea of a *constitutional convention* and of various constitutional *procedures* for *amending* the constitution. A constitutional convention is regarded as having regulative power to *adopt* or to put to adoption by the people (by *ratification,* etc.), or to amend etc., the constitution; and it is superior

---

1. Cf. Gordon Wood, *The Creation of the American Republic* (Chapel Hill: University of North Carolina Press, 1969), pp. 260f.

to the *normal* process of legislation by the highest legislature. The constitutional convention and the amending powers express in working institutions the so-called *sovereignty of the people*. This sovereignty need not be expressed by resistance and revolution but has an available *institutional* expression.

2. Now in a constitutional regime with these *four features* there is *no* absolute Sovereign in Hobbes's sense. Presumably Hobbes would not deny this, since he regards the idea of *mixed* government with a *balance of powers* as violating his principle of good government (cf. *Leviathan* II:29:S:259 [1st ed., 170]; and II:18:S:150 [1st ed., 92]): the rights and powers of the Sovereign should lie in the *same* hands and be inseparable.

(a) Sometimes, however, Hobbes uses a familiar *regress argument* for the Sovereign: such an unlimited power must exist, for if the supposed Sovereign is limited, it must be limited by some superior agency and then *that* agency is unlimited. This argument is suggested at two places: first (p. 107) where Hobbes says, "And whosoever thinking Sovereign Power too great, will seek to make it less; must subject himself, to the Power, that can limit it; that is to say, to a greater." And second, in arguing that the Sovereign is not subject to laws, Hobbes says that it is an error to think the Sovereign is subject to law (p. 169). "Which error, because it setteth the Laws above the Sovereign, setteth also a Judge above him, and a Power to punish him; which is to make a new Sovereign."

It is not *clear* that Hobbes intends a regress argument here, but he apparently fails to make two distinctions that are crucial:

(i) Between a *supreme* (or final) e.g. legislative power and an *unlimited* one. Thus Congress may be the *supreme* legislative authority for *normal* law making, but it is *not unlimited:* it is subject to veto, to judicial review, to constitutional limitations, etc.

(ii) Between the idea of a *personal* Sovereign or agency whom *all* obey and who in turn obeys *no one* (Bentham's definition of the Sovereign) and the idea of a *legal system* defined by a scheme of *rules* that specify a constitutional regime. This scheme of rules will contain certain *basic* or *fundamental* rules which serve to define which rules are *valid* rules; and these basic rules are accepted and followed, deliberately and publicly, by the various constitutional bodies. Thus we have to distinguish between the idea of a *personal* Sovereign (or sovereign body) identified by habits of obedience and who in turn obeys no one, and the idea of a *constitutional system* revealed by certain *basic rules* which everyone (or enough people) accept and use to direct their conduct.[2]

(b) Now the point of making these distinctions is that we can see (by applying these distinctions) that in a constitutional democratic regime (of the U.S. type) there *is* no personal Sovereign (in Hobbes's or Bentham's sense); nor is there one constitutional body or agency that is supreme *and* unlimited in all matters. There are different powers and agencies which are assigned different tasks and authorities, and are put in a position where they can check each other in certain ways (via balance of powers, etc.).

3. Now a constitutional system of this kind, if it is to work, requires a kind of institutional *cooperation*, and the conception of this cooperation must be understood and accepted by those who take part in these institutions and work them. This ties in with what we said earlier (in Lecture III) about Hobbes's political conception having no room for the notion of moral obligation; this we interpret to mean that:

(i) Hobbes has no room for a notion of *reasonable self-restraint* in the sense of a willingness to forgo permanent and long-term benefits as judged by one's own rational self-interest (in Hobbes's sense); and that

(ii) Hobbes has no place for a *sense of fairness*, as illustrated by his having no account of fair background conditions of binding covenants. Hobbes comes close to saying: To each according to their (rational) threat advantage.

These two notions—that of reasonable self-restraint and that of fairness—are essential to the notion of *social cooperation*, where cooperation is understood as distinct from mere social coordination and organized social activity. The idea of cooperation involves an idea of *mutuality* and *reciprocity* (another way to refer to fairness), and a willingness to do one's part, *provided* others (or enough others) do theirs (another way to refer to reasonable self-restraint).

4. In view of these remarks, we can interpret Hobbes's doctrine that people are not *fit* for society this way: it means that people are not *capable* of social *cooperation* in the sense defined above. While Hobbes argues that it is *rational* for each to be reasonable, that is, to comply with the Laws of Nature (as articles of peace) when others do likewise, Hobbes supposes that

2. For these distinctions, see H. L. A. Hart, *The Concept of Law* (Oxford: Clarendon Press, 1965), pp. 64–76, 97–114.

people have no attachment, no desire etc., to act from principles of reasonable self-restraint or mutuality (fairness) for their own sake. These *reasonable desires* (as you might call them) have no part in his account of human psychology, at least insofar as political questions are concerned. Hobbes need not, perhaps, deny that these desires exist; he may say that they are too *weak* and *unreliable* to matter. In any case, Hobbes's account of practical reason as rationality has no place for them.

If we reject Hobbes's doctrine, one thing we can do is to see how the Social Contract view might be recast so as to provide not merely a perspective from which political institutions can be seen to be collectively rational, but a framework within which the content of the notions essential to social cooperation—reasonable self-restraint and fairness—can be defined or outlined. And this brings us to Locke.

Hobbes Lecture IV: Appendix A

HANDOUT: THE ROLE AND POWERS OF THE SOVEREIGN

A. The Role of the Sovereign

1. The Role of the Sovereign is to stabilize civic life as a state of peace and concord; and while the Sovereign's laws may not be always good, and may often be bad, the state of civic peace is always better than the State of Nature, which readily falls into a mutually destructive State of War.

2. There are some analogies between Hobbes's account of why the making of covenants cannot remove the destructive instability of the State of Nature and the now well-known problem of the Prisoner's Dilemma. This is an example to illustrate the problems that can arise in a two-person, non-cooperative, non-zero-sum, perfect-information, non-recurrent game (see Figure 4).

	2nd prisoner not confess	2nd prisoner confess
1st prisoner not confess	2, 2	10, 0
1st prisoner confess	0, 10	5, 5

Figure 4. Prisoner's Dilemma 3.

(a) Note that the action: to confess dominates the action: not to confess. This means that the first prisoner does better by confessing, whatever the second prisoner does. And similarly, the second prisoner does better by confessing, whatever the first prisoner does.

(b) The pair of actions of both prisoners confessing is a stable pair in the sense that when either knows the action (to confess), that prisoner does better to confess. Thus the SE cell is the only stable cell.

(c) Yet the result of both prisoners' following their rational strategies and therefore confessing leads to a situation in which they are both worse off. They would both do better if they could agree not to confess and somehow have that agreement enforced.

(d) That such an agreement needs to be enforced is shown by the fact that both prisoners are at least tempted to break it; and the temptation is greater or less depending, of course, on the stakes involved.

3. Hobbes's account of why covenants in the State of Nature are in general invalid (14:68) resembles a Prisoner's Dilemma situation. For if the party to perform first honors the agreement, the other party, knowing this, has an incentive not to honor the agreement. The temptation not to honor it may be very great; as shown by the problem of arms-limitation agreements. The country that succeeds in cheating may gain empire; and the other knowing this is afraid, on rational grounds, to limit its armaments.

4. Thus Hobbes's view is that the general condition of humankind is such that there are but two stable states: the State of Nature (which is a State of War) and the State of the Leviathan: a state of civic peace maintained by an effective Sovereign equipped with all the powers which Hobbes says the Sovereign must have. The reasons why the State of Nature (which is a State of War) and the State of the Leviathan are the only two stable states are explained by Hobbes in ways analogous to the features of Prisoner's Dilemma situations. Be careful, however, to recognize that the State of Nature is far more complicated as a fuller discussion would show. For example, Hobbes thinks of the State of Nature as like a recurrent (repeated) Prisoner's Dilemma game, which introduces other considerations. On this, see his reply to the fool, 15:72f.

B. *The Problem to be Solved:*

1. On Hobbes's view what we must do, if a State of Nature exists, is to lift ourselves out of this State of Nature and into a State of the Leviathan. And we must do this despite the fact that in the State of Nature covenants

between individuals puts parties in a dilemma analogous to the Prisoner's Dilemma situation.

2. This lifting process, if it is to succeed, must solve three problems:

(a) It must define a mutually beneficial and peaceful social state which is recognizably better for each than the State of Nature. This is done by the Laws of Nature and the idea of an effective Sovereign; if this Sovereign is at all rational, and recognizes its own good, it will enact good, or sufficiently good laws.

(b) As already indicated, once an effective Sovereign exists, it stabilizes the state of civic peace, the State of the Leviathan. This it does by being an effective Sovereign: for when such a Sovereign exists, citizens have a sufficient reason for relying on others to comply with the Laws of Nature and the Sovereign's enactments. The general nature of human motives is not changed; rather, given these motives, citizens now have good reasons for adhering to their covenants. The public knowledge that an effective Sovereign exists solves the problem of instability. The Sovereign makes it possible for us to stay in the Northwest box and not to be trapped in the Southeast box.

(c) The lifting process must move us to a State of the Leviathan. Hobbes envisages this happening in two ways. One is that an effective Sovereign may come to exist by conquest, or by acquisition; or by some similar process. The other is that an effective Sovereign may be set up by the Social Contract, or by institution.

3. But how is it possible for the lifting process of Sovereign by institution, by Social Contract, to succeed? Or is it purely notional in Hobbes's view, and therefore intended only as a point of view from which citizens can understand why they each have a sufficient reason for wanting an effective Sovereign to continue to exist, and therefore to comply with the laws of such a Sovereign when one does exist?

4. Possibly Hobbes thinks the lifting process via Social Contract might work as follows:

(a) Given that everyone in a State of Nature recognizes that general compliance with the Laws of Nature is collectively rational, and hence rational for each, and that an effective Sovereign is necessary for a (stable) State of the Leviathan, each person covenants with everyone else (except the Sovereign) to authorize the Sovereign (as designated) and to own all the Sovereign's actions, on the condition that others also do this.

(b) Given that the Social Contract is entered into and publicly recognized on some occasion, any one person who contemplates not adhering cannot presume that, from that moment on, sufficiently severe sanctions to ensure general compliance will not follow. Reputation of power is power: that is, the general and public recognition that the Social Contract has been made may, in Hobbes's view, give everyone sufficient reason for believing that, from now on, the designated Sovereign will be effective, or will probably be effective. When the probability is great enough, general compliance results; and with the passage of time, as the effectiveness of the Sovereign is demonstrated, this probability increases. Eventually everyone has strong inductive grounds for believing the Sovereign is and will be effective. (Is this line of reasoning plausible?)

5. Note that the Sovereign is not a party to the Social Contract as Hobbes describes it. But this actually is not the crucial point because when the Sovereign is established by acquisition, the Sovereign is a party to the pact of acquisition: 20:103f. What is crucial is that both in authorization by the Social Contract and in pact by submission before a victor, those who become subjects accept the Sovereign's discretion and give up to the Sovereign the right to govern themselves, that is, to exercise their judgment, for example, to judge whether the Sovereign's laws and policies are good, and to voice their opinions accordingly.

6. Thus, it is perhaps best to say (or is it?) that in Hobbes the Social Contract is purely notional: the end result of both ways of setting up the Sovereign are the same, practically speaking. However historically the Sovereign may have been established, citizens are equally subject to the Sovereign's discretion, and have now and henceforth, the same reasons for compliance with the Sovereign's authority, namely, the assured prospects of a stable State of the Leviathan and the avoidance of the evils of the State of Nature.

C. *The Relation between Justice and the Public Good:*

1. How are we to understand Hobbes's repeated assertions that although the Sovereign's enactments are necessarily just and the Sovereign cannot injure its subjects, the Sovereign may enact laws that are bad and not good, and the Sovereign may do iniquity? Plainly we must distinguish between the justice and the goodness of the Sovereign's laws so that the statements referred to above are not incompatible.

2. When Hobbes says that the Sovereign's laws are necessarily just, he

is not saying, I think, that the fact that the Sovereign has effective power is what makes the Sovereign's laws just. The existence of an effective Sovereign does not alter the content of the Laws of Nature. These are unchanging and rooted in the deep and general facts of human nature and the normal circumstances of human life. The role of the Sovereign (see above in *A*) is to stabilize civic life and to make it safe for us to honor our covenants; and this renders them valid. The third Law of Nature, the foundation of justice, which is to honor covenants, is not itself the creation of the Sovereign.

3. The Sovereign's laws are just, and the Sovereign cannot injure its subject, because the Sovereign arises either by authorization or by pact of submission, which authorization or pact gives the Sovereign all necessary powers to make the Sovereign effective. Thus, in either case, the Sovereign's powers are authorized by a valid covenant which is such as to authorize all that the Sovereign does. Hence, by the third Law of Nature, the Sovereign's enactments and deeds are just. See 30:181f.

4. Yet the Sovereign may enact laws that are not good and do things that hurt the commonwealth, or the public good. For the public good is, roughly speaking, the furtherance of those institutions and social conditions under which rational citizens may act to secure their self-preservation and the means of a commodious life. And of course about these institutions and social conditions the Sovereign, being human, may make mistakes or grievous errors either from ignorance, or, of course, from pride and vainglory, and so on.

Hobbes Lecture IV: Appendix B

Regarding Contrast Between *De Cive* and *Leviathan* re institution of the Sovereign

1. As noted above, Hobbes does describe the Social Contract that institutes the Sovereign differently in the two works. In the first he says we *surrender* our rights; in the other we authorize the Sovereign as our agent. Thus the formal system of notions is different.

2. At first the change seems to affect Hobbes's conception of the unity of society; it appears to provide more unity since the same public person is *our* authorized *agent*.

3. But while the formal notions used to describe the covenant are different, and do yield greater unity formally speaking; Hobbes so *stretches* the usual notion of authorization—or deputizing someone as our agent—that there is no *material* or *substantive* difference between the two accounts.

4. This is so because:

(a) The authorization is so comprehensive: we *give up* the right of *governing ourselves* to the Sovereign, which goes well beyond deputizing another.

(b) Because it is *permanent* and *irrevocable,* which no authorization is (normally understood).

(c) Because we even give up our *right of judging* whether the Sovereign is doing properly (rationally) those things the Sovereign was authorized to do; which again no authorization does.

(d) Because in effect as Hobbes describes it authorization of the Sovereign is *submission* (and?) a mutual pact thereto; we submit our wills every one to the Sovereign's will, our judgments to the Sovereign's judgments.

(Citation for a–d: Ch. 17, p. 142)

(e) Because authorization has all the same formal consequences and yields the Sovereign the same Powers, as pact of submission to a victorious conqueror.

(f) In both Sovereign by Authorization and by acquisition, the motive is *fear,* in the former fear of one another, in the other fear of the conqueror who is victorious. Thus in practical effect, the Social Contract, however described, is a *Pact of Submission.*

(Citation for d–e: Ch. 20:2, p. 163)

Appendix: Hobbes Index

[Page references are to Schneider edition][1]

LIBERTY

1. *Liberty*—Physical concept of absence of *external* impediments to motion, called by Hobbes *natural* liberty: 170ff, cf. 212
> and deliberation: 59
> and free will: 171f
> free man df: 171
> relation to *power,* absence of internal impediments: 171
> liberty is true only of the *person,* the man: not to will or anything not a
> > person, man: 171
2. *Liberty and Right:* contrasted with Law and Obligation: 228f
3. *Liberty of Subjects:* 170–180, 212f
> (i) Liberty of Silence, liberty of exemption from laws: 172f, 228f, cf.
> > 211f, 228, some enumerated 173
> (ii) *True* Liberties of Subject df: 175; see 117f
> —may resist Sovereign's punishment: 176 (cf. 117 on contracts to con-
> > trary *void*)
> —may resist demand to confess: 176 (cf. 117 on contracts to contrary
> > *void*)
> —may refuse dangerous mission when commonwealth not at stake:
> > 177, 289f
> —rebels in self-defense singly and together do no further unjust act:
> > 177f
> —includes right to be honored by one's children, for such right not
> > nec sov: 267

---

1. Hobbes, *Leviathan,* Parts I and II, ed. Herbert W. Schneider (New York: Library of Liberal Arts, 1958).

Liberty of the Commonwealth ≠ liberty of subjects: 174f

Liberties incompatible with Sovereign power cannot be granted (are void): 179

Liberty of Nature returns after Sovereign relinquishes Sovereignty: 180

Obligation of Subjects lasts so long as Sovereign can protect them: 179f

Aim of Law is to limit the natural liberties so they assist one another: 212f

Liberty and Equity: it is equity that in whatsoever not regulated, each equal enjoys natural liberty: 228

Liberty of conscience: 17–20 (re inquisition, etc.)

    Right of Sovereign to limit: 18ff

Right to Educate one's children: 267

    Does it limit the Sovereign? Or does Hobbes mean a Sovereign who makes *good* laws allows it: 267

4. Liberties that cannot be relinquished by covenant:

    (i) right to be honored by one's children: 267

    (ii) right men have by nature to protect themselves: 179

        (hence obligation to Sovereign ceases when Sovereign power breaks down [or is relinquished] 180)

5. Liberty and fear consistent: 171

JUSTICE

Justice, natural science of, only science needed by Sovereigns to govern: 287

Justice, foundation and original of: that men perform their covenants made: 3rd law of nature: violation of laying down right by covenant injustice and absurdity: 111; 119f; 122; 212; Reply to Fool 120–123

Why Injustice presupposes the erection of Sovereign power: otherwise mutual trust and covenants are not valid: 120, cf. 115, where no common power, no law, no justice 108

That which all will have so is not unjust; justice compared to laws of gaming: 272; cf. 146, 212

Justice as keeping of covenants a Law of Nature: 122; 139; Unjust to vow contrary to Laws of Nature: 116; he that fulfills the Laws of Nature is just: 131

Justice applied to persons and their character: 123f; 215

Justice applied to actions: 123ff

    commutative justice: 124f

    natural justice: 129f, 216, 190, 194f

    distributive justice: 124f, 225

    just price (value): 125

Justice as right reason relies on conventional standard: 46 (cf re good: 53, 54)

    Justice in arbitration: 125

Justice as defined by (existing) law:

    Just = he that in his actions observes the laws of his country: 39

    Laws are rules of just and unjust: 211; 7; 15

    Obedience to the civil law is just since required by covenant: 212

    Justice and Propriety: both presuppose Sovereign power: 198, 120 as giving each their due: 198, 120

    Just law ≠ good law 271f

    Law requires interpretation and this is Sovereign's reason and *just* judgments look to this: 214

Justice as an inconstant name: and signifies disposition and interest of speaker: 45

Natural Punishment of Injustice as violation of Laws of Nature: the violence of enemies: 287

Justice and Injustice are not faculties of body or mind; they are qualities that relate men in society: 108

    No justice in a State of Nature: 108; no injustice in a State of Nature: 120

    In State of Nature men are judges of justness of their own fears: 115

    In State of Nature people fought and plundered one another *justly:* 140

Subject cannot accuse Sovereign of Injustice since subject is *author* of all the Sovereigns and it is impossible to do injury to oneself: 146, cf. 173, 178, (cf. 212); 144; 149; 184

Sovereign may commit injury but not injustice: 146; 173f

In a commonwealth justice and force must lie in *one* hand: 214

Sovereign's reason decides the law and judges must look to that, else their judgments unjust: 214

Justice as an end of the Social Contract: 150

Reply to the Fool: justice (as keeping covenants) not contrary to reason: 120–123

Rebels in resisting Sovereign commit no further unjust acts: 177f

Unjust to have private forces: 191

Cowards act dishonorably, not unjustly: 177

Association and leagues of private men for evil intent is unjust: 191

SOVEREIGN AND SOVEREIGN'S POWERS

1. *Aim of the Social Contract* in setting up Sovereign: 139, 143, 147, 150, 159, 176, 262

    State of Nature as determining Prerequisites of Sovereign: 139–142

    Social Contract: Formal and material def: 142, 143f

2. *Rights and Powers of Sovereign:* 144–150

    (General)

    As great as possibly can be imagined 169, as unlimited is given authority without stint: 135, 142, 181, 252, 151f

    Powers of same wherever placed: 151, 152

    Powers and Establishment of not revocable: 144f

    Regress argument for absolute Sovereign: 170, 225

    Contra Balance of Powers (in const): 259

    Rights of succession: 159–162; 180

    Sovereign grants of right must be interpreted consistent with Sovereign Power: 179

3. *Rights and Powers of Sovereign*

    (*Particular* Powers)

    Sovereign cannot be punished: 147; is not subject to civil law: 211f, 254f

    Sovereign has right to *judge means* of peace and war: 147f

    Sovereign has power to regulate *speech* and *books:* 147f

    Sovereign determines rules and definition of propriety (property): 148; 198f; and of trade and contracts: 200f

    Sovereign has judicial authority: 148

    Sovereign has rights of appointment, rewards and honor: 149

    Sovereign is legislator of the laws: 211f

    Sovereign judges what is reasonable customs: 212

Sovereign determines liberties of silence: 173, 228

Sovereign determines what is to be obeyed as divine law: 226ff (when not contrary to moral law 226)

4. *Office and Duties of Sovereign*

Sovereign bound by Laws of Nature: 158, 173, 182, 244, 262, 270, 199

Sovereign cannot treat subjects unjustly nor do them injury: 144, 146, 173, 178

... but can do them iniquity: 146, 199

... and may err in equity: 219

Duty of Sovereign to make good laws: 262, 271ff, 275f

Good laws what: 271ff, cf. Def good and evil: 15, 53f, 131f, 253f; and 46

Making law rational faculty of commonwealth: 259, 23, 214

Sovereign via civil law is judge of good and evil: 253, 259

End of Sovereign's laws safety of the people: 262, and by general providence: 267

Good of Sovereign and People cannot be separated: 272

Sovereign fit arbitrator: as agreed upon in Social Contract: 194; cf. 129, 46, 274

LAWS OF NATURE

0. Def. Law of Nature = precept or rule, found out by reason by which forbidden to do that destructive of our life etc: 14:3

1. Laws of Nature dictate peace for the means of the conservation of men in multitudes. I:15:25 (S. 130)

2. These laws summed up: Do not do to another etc. I:15:26

3. Laws of Nature bind *in foro interno* to a desire they should be followed: I:15:27–28

4. Science of Laws of Nature is the true and only moral phil: I:15:30

5. Laws of Nature are improperly so-called, being but conclusions concerning what conduces to our conservation: 15:30

CONTENT OF LAWS OF NATURE

1. 1st and 2nd Laws: (i) to seek peace and follow it, (ii) to lay down one's right subject to rule reciprocity. These branches of general rule to endeavor peace: 14:6–7

2. 3rd Law: to perform covenants made: 15:1–3
    Def. covenant and their validity: 14:12–29; 15:3
    Justice: 15:1–9
    Reply to Fool: 15:4
3. 4th–10th Law: injunction to virtues and dispositions of sociable reasonable association: 15:10–18
4. 11th–19th Laws: Precepts of Equity and Natural Justice: 15:17–25

LOCKE

LOCKE I

His Doctrine of Natural Law

§1. Introductory Remarks

1. The early 20th-century philosopher R. G. Collingwood said: "The history of political theory is not the history of different answers to one and the same question, but the history of a problem more or less constantly changing, whose solution was changing with it."[1] This interesting remark seems to exaggerate a bit, since there are certain basic questions that we keep asking, such as:

What is the nature of a legitimate political regime?
What are the grounds and limits of political obligation?
What is the basis of rights, if any? and the like.

But these questions, when they come up in different historical contexts, can be taken in different ways and have been seen by different writers from different points of view, given their political and social worlds and their circumstances and problems as they saw them. To understand their works, then, we must identify those points of view and how they shape the way the writer's questions are interpreted and discussed.

Construed this way, Collingwood's remark helps us to look for the answers different writers give to their (not our) questions. To this end we must try to think ourselves into each writer's scheme of thought, so far as we can, and try to understand their problem and their solution from their point of view and not from ours. When we do this, it often happens that their answers to their questions strike us as much better than we might otherwise have supposed. Indeed, I think that, given their way of thought and the problems of their day, the writers we discuss—Hobbes, Locke, Rous-

---

1. R. G. Collingwood, *An Autobiography* (Oxford: Clarendon Press, 1939), p. 62.

seau, Hume, Mill, and Marx—give very good, though not perhaps perfect, answers to the questions that concern them. This is why we still read their texts and find what they say instructive.

2. The criticisms I shall make do not consist in pointing out fallacies and inconsistencies in, say, Locke's or Mill's thought, but rather in examining a few basic respects in which we, from our own point of view and concerned with our own questions or problems, do not find their answers or solutions altogether acceptable, as instructive as they are. Therefore, when we discuss these writers our first effort is to understand what they say, and to interpret them in the best way their point of view seems to allow. Only then shall we regard ourselves as ready to judge their solution from our point of view. I believe that unless we follow these guidelines in reading the works of these six philosophers, we fail to treat them as conscientious and intelligent writers who are in all essential respects at least our equals.

In taking up Locke[2] I shall consider but one main difficulty which arises from the fact that, as described in the Second Treatise, Locke's social contract doctrine may justify or allow for inequalities in basic political rights and liberties. For example, the right to vote is restricted by a property qualification. The constitution he envisages is that of a class state: that is, politi-

2. Useful secondary sources on Locke are: Richard Ashcraft, *Revolutionary Politics and Locke's "Two Treatises of Government"* (Princeton: Princeton University Press, 1986), and *Locke's Two Treatises of Government* (London: Unwin, 1987); Michael Ayres, *Locke: Epistemology-Ontology*, 2 vols. (London: Routledge, 1991); Joshua Cohen, "Structure, Choice and Legitimacy: Locke's Theory of the State," *PAPA*, Fall 1986; John Dunn, *The Political Thought of John Locke* (Cambridge: Cambridge University Press, 1969); Julian Franklin, *John Locke and the Theory of Sovereignty* (Cambridge: Cambridge University Press, 1978); Ruth Grant, *John Locke's Liberalism* (Chicago: University of Chicago Press, 1987); Peter Laslett, Introduction to *Two Treatises of Government* (Cambridge: Cambridge University Press, Student Edition, 1988); Wolfgang von Leyden, *John Locke, Essays on the Law of Nature* (Oxford: Oxford University Press, 1954); C. B. MacPherson, *Political Theory of Possessive Individualism* (Oxford: Oxford University Press, 1962); J. B. Schneewind, *Moral Philosophy from Montaigne to Kant* (Cambridge: Cambridge University Press, 1990), 2 vols., in Vol. 1, pp. 183–198; Peter Schouls, *The Imposition of Method: A Study of Descartes and Locke* (New York: Oxford University Press, 1980); John Simmons, *The Lockean Theory of Rights* (Princeton: Princeton University Press, 1992), and *On the Edge of Anarchy* (Princeton: Princeton University Press, 1993); Richard Tuck, *Natural Rights Theories: Their Origin and Development* (Cambridge: Cambridge University Press, 1979); James Tully, *A Discourse on Property: John Locke and His Adversaries* (Cambridge: Cambridge University Press, 1980); Jeremy Waldron, *The Right to Private Property* (Oxford: Clarendon Press, 1988), esp. Ch. 8, and "Locke, Toleration, and the Rationality of Persecution," in *Liberal Rights: Collected Papers* (Cambridge: Cambridge University Press, 1993).

cal rule is exercised only by those who own a certain amount of property (the equivalent of a 40s. freehold, which in Locke's day was roughly 4.5 acres of farmable land). How a class state is permissible in his doctrine we shall examine in the third lecture on Locke.

But before we can raise this question we must understand his doctrine in its best light. Remember here J. S. Mill's aphorism: "A doctrine is not judged at all until it is judged in its best light."[3]

3. To this end, we must ask what problem Locke, and each of the other writers, is especially concerned with and why. Hobbes, for example, is concerned with the problem of civil war between contentious religious sects, made worse by conflict between political and class interests. In his contract doctrine Hobbes argues that everyone has sufficient rational grounds, rooted in their most basic interests, for creating, by agreement among themselves, a state, or Leviathan, with an effective sovereign with absolute powers, and for supporting such a sovereign whenever one exists. These basic interests include not only our interest in preserving ourselves and obtaining the means of a commodious life, as Hobbes says, but also, and this is important for Hobbes, who was writing in a religious age, our transcendent religious interest in our salvation. (A transcendent religious interest is one that may override all secular interests.) Taking these interests as basic, Hobbes thinks it rational for everyone to accept the authority of an existing and effective absolute sovereign. He views such a sovereign as the only sure protection against destructive civil strife and the collapse into the state of nature, the worst condition of all.

Locke's problem is altogether different, and so, as we might expect, are his assumptions: Locke's aim is to provide a justification for resistance to the Crown within the context of a mixed constitution. This is a constitution in which the Crown has a share in legislative authority, and therefore, the legislature (that is, Parliament) cannot alone exercise full sovereignty. Locke is preoccupied with this problem because he is involved in the Exclusion Crisis of 1679–81, so named because the first Whigs, led by the Earl of Shaftesbury, tried to exclude Charles II's younger brother James, then Duke of York, from succeeding to the throne.

James was a Catholic, and the Whigs feared that he was bent on establishing in England a royal absolutism and restoring the Catholic faith, using

3. See Review of Sedgwick's *Discourse*, in Mill's *Collected Works*, Vol. X, p. 52.

force, and with French help. The Whigs were defeated in this crisis in part because they were divided as to whom to name King in James's place (the Duke of Monmouth, Charles's illegitimate son, or William of Orange), and in part because Charles was able to rule without Parliament with the aid of large secret subsidies paid him by Louis XIV of France.

4. Locke, who was trained as a physician, first met the Earl of Shaftesbury when he was called to the Earl's bedside in that capacity. They became very close, and for a number of years beginning in 1666, Locke was a member of his household. He had an apartment in Exeter House (Shaftesbury's London residence) on the Strand in London, and there he wrote in 1671 the first draft of the *Essay on Human Understanding*. The *Two Treatises* were written during the Exclusion Crisis of 1679–81 (and not later in 1689 as was once believed) as a political tract defending the Whig cause against Charles II. This date explains their tone and preoccupations.[4]

Sir Robert Filmer,[5] a committed royal absolutist with personal connections to the church and the court, who had died in 1653, had written in defense of the absolute monarchy at the time of the English Civil War. Most of his works were published between 1647 and 1653, but they were republished in 1679–1680, at which time his most important manuscript, *Patriarcha*, was published for the first time. His writings were very influential between 1679 and 1681, when Locke was writing his *Two Treatises of Government*. Locke's avowed philosophical aim (see the title page of the *First Treatise*) is to attack Robert Filmer's defense of the royalist position and his argument that the King has absolute power that comes from God alone, and to establish that royal absolutism is incompatible with legitimate

4. Laslett thinks that most of the *Second Treatise* was written during the winter of 1679–1680, including Chapters 2–7, 10–14, and 19. Early in 1680, after Sir Robert Filmer's *Patriarcha* appeared (see note 5 below), the *First Treatise* was written, as a response to that book. In the summer of 1681 Locke added to the *Second Treatise* a part of Chapter 8 and Chapters 16, 17, and 18. Finally, in 1689, before publication, he added Chapters 1, 9, and 15 to the *Second Treatise*. See Laslett's Introduction to *Locke's Two Treatises*, p. 65.

5. For Robert Filmer see the following: *Patriarcha and Other Writings*, ed. Johann Somerville (Cambridge: Cambridge University Press, 1991), which now replaces the earlier edition of *Patriarcha* by Peter Laslett (Oxford: Blackwell, 1949); besides the many references in Laslett's Introduction to the *Two Treatises*, see Gordon Schochet, *Patriarchalism and Political Thought* (Oxford: Oxford University Press, 1975); John Dunn in his *Political Thought of John Locke*, Ch. 6, considers the place of Filmer in Locke's thought; see also Nathan Tarcov, *Locke's Education for Liberty* (Chicago: University of Chicago Press, 1984), Ch. 1, which has much to say about Filmer and his relation to Hobbes and Locke.

government. Very briefly, on Locke's view, legitimate government can arise only from the consent of the persons subject to it. He views these persons as by nature free and equal, as well as reasonable and rational. Hence they cannot agree to any change unless it improves their condition. Locke believes that absolute government can never be legitimate because he, as opposed to Hobbes, believes that (royal) absolutism is even worse than the state of nature. See ¶¶90–94, esp. ¶91, where Locke distinguishes between the ordinary state of nature, and the unrestrained state of nature to which absolutism leads.[6]

5. To sum up: in Hobbes, the idea of the social contract is used as a point of view from which rational persons, looking to their most basic interests (including here their transcendent religious interest in salvation) can see that they have sufficient reason for supporting an effective sovereign (and for Hobbes this means an absolute sovereign, because only such can be effective) whenever such a sovereign exists.

In Locke the idea of the social contract is used to maintain that legitimate government can be founded only on the consent of free and equal, and reasonable and rational persons, starting from the state of nature regarded as a state of equal political jurisdiction, all being, as it were, equally sovereign over themselves. In this way Locke seeks to limit the form of a legitimate regime to exclude royal absolutism and so to justify resistance to the Crown under a mixed constitution.

This contrast between Hobbes and Locke illustrates an important point: that what may seem the same idea (the idea of the social contract) can have a very different meaning and use, given its role within a political conception as a whole.

---

6. All references within the text, unless otherwise stated, are to numbered paragraphs of the *Second Treatise*. While for the most part I shall refer only to the *Second Treatise*, the *First* is not without its interest and contains a number of passages very important for Locke's view. To wit: property does not imply authority, I: ¶¶41–43; property related to liberty of use, ¶¶39, 92, 97; on fatherhood and authority, with the mother having an equal share, ¶¶52–55; Locke says that for Filmer, men are not born naturally free, ¶6; and cites him as saying that men are born subjects, ¶50; Locke argues against primogeniture, ¶¶90–97; he gives a summary of Filmer's system, ¶5, and says that if this system fails, government must be left again to the old way of being made by contrivance and the consent of men making use of their reason to unite into society, ¶6; and finally, that public good is the good of every particular member of society, as far as by common rules it can be provided for, ¶92.

6. In reading Locke we should be aware that he was engaged in what increasingly became politically dangerous business. As Laslett tells us, principally on pages 31 and 32 of his Introduction to the *Two Treatises,* when the third Exclusion Parliament met at Oxford in March of 1681, armed resistance to the Crown seems to have been decided on if the Exclusion Bill failed again (as it did). Locke took an active part; he even went from house to house seeking accommodations for Shaftesbury's entourage, including a man named Rumsey, chief of Shaftesbury's desperadoes.

Subsequently, when Shaftesbury, after a period of imprisonment, engaged in what bordered on treasonous consultations, Locke went along with him. He was with Shaftesbury the whole summer of 1682, and he traveled with him to Cassiobury (the seat of the Earl of Essex) where they met with Whig leaders at the height of the so-called Insurrection Plot. And he went there again in April of 1683, after Shaftesbury had died in exile in Holland, when preparations for the Assassination, or Rye House Plot, are alleged to have been under way. After the Rye House Plot was discovered Locke became a fugitive, and lived in exile until 1689. The *Two Treatises,* a work against the government, had been written earlier, probably while he was still with Shaftesbury, well before the Glorious Whig Revolution of 1688.[7] I recount this by now well-known story to give you a sense of the man whose work we are about to discuss. It is quite remarkable that anyone could write such a reasonable work, one of such imperturbable good sense, while actively engaged, at great personal risk, in what may have been treason.

7. I call your attention to what Locke says in the first sentence of the Preface to the *Two Treatises:* namely, that there had been a middle part of the work, longer than what he publishes here as the *Two Treatises.* He says that it is not worthwhile to tell us what happened to that middle part; but Locke was a cautious man and perhaps had reason to destroy it. Perhaps it contained constitutional doctrines that might have cost him his head. A list of books in Locke's library suggests that to mislead the King's agents he may have called the whole work *De Morbo Gallico* (the French disease), in those days a name for syphilis. Locke and Shaftesbury did think of royal ab-

---

7. See note 4 above. For an interesting discussion concerning when and why Locke wrote the *Two Treatises,* see Laslett's Introduction, pp. 45–66.

solutism as a French disease, and certainly the French had a bad case of it under Louis XIV.[8]

§2. The Meaning of Natural Law

1. As background to what Locke calls "The Fundamental Law of Nature" (FLN) I should first make some remarks about the meaning of natural law. In the natural law tradition, natural law is that part of the law of God which can be known by us by the use of our natural powers of reason. These powers discern both the order of nature open to our view and the intentions of God which are disclosed through that order. And on this ground, it is said that natural law is promulgated, or made known to us, by God through our natural reason (¶57).[9] The following points explain why the terms "natural" and "law" in the term "natural law" are appropriate.

(a) First as to "law": a law is a rule addressed to rational beings by someone with legitimate authority to regulate their conduct. (Here one might add to the definition of law the phrase: "for their common good," as this would fit Locke's view, given his definition of political power in ¶3 as the right to make and enforce laws—"all this only for the public good.") Natural law is literally law, that is, it is promulgated to us by God who has legitimate and supreme legislative authority over all mankind. God is, as it were, the sovereign of the world with supreme authority over all its creatures; thus natural law is universal and associates mankind into one community with a law to govern it.[10] To speak of natural law as promulgated is, of course, metaphorical, since natural law is not literally promulgated like the

8. See Laslett's Introduction, pp. 62–65, 76f.

9. See also ¶124 where Locke says that the law of nature is plain and intelligible to all rational creatures; and ¶136 where he says that the law of nature is unwritten and found only in the minds of men.

10. Locke says: "What duty is, cannot be understood without a law; nor a law be known, or supposed without a law-maker, or without rewards and punishment." *Essay Concerning Human Understanding*, Vol. I, Book I, Ch. 3, §12. See also Vol. I, Book II, Ch. 28, §6, where Locke says: "It would be in vain for one intelligent being to set a rule to the actions of another if he had it not in his power to reward the compliance with and punish deviation from his rule by some good and evil that is not the natural product and consequence of the action itself." In that case it "would operate of itself without a law. This . . . is the true nature of all law, properly so called."

law of worldly princes. But since natural law is literally law, it must be in some manner promulgated—that is, made public, or known—to those to whom it applies. Otherwise it is not law. This explains the propriety of the term "law" in the term "natural law."

(b) Now consider the propriety of the term "natural." One basis for this term is that, as stated above, natural law is made known to us, or at any rate can be, through the use of our natural faculties of reason to draw conclusions from the evident general facts and design of nature. Included among these general facts are such things as the natural needs, propensities and inclinations of human beings, the faculties and powers by which we differ from and are related to the animals and other parts of nature. Roughly, the idea is that, given the faith that God exists (or alternatively, that God's existence itself can be shown by reason), we are able to discern from the order of nature what God's intentions towards us must be, and that among these intentions is that we are to act from certain principles in our conduct toward one another. In view of God's authority, these principles discerned by natural reason as God's intentions are laws for us. Hence the term "natural" in the name "natural law."

From the preceding we see that natural law differs from divine law. For divine law is that part of the law of God which can only be known by revelation. To ascertain the requirements of divine law is beyond the powers of our natural reason. Moreover, natural law is also distinct from all human enactments and so from the actual law of states, or what Locke sometimes calls "municipal, or positive, law." The laws of states are to conform to the principles of natural law (when these are applicable). As Locke says (¶135), the obligations of the law of nature hold in society as well as in the state of nature, and the law of nature "stands as an Eternal Rule to all Men, Legislators as well as others." Thus the principles of natural law are fundamental principles of right and justice applicable to the laws of states and to political and social institutions. Here is another reason for the term "law" in the name "natural law": natural law applies to law and to legal institutions.

2. We should note finally that what Locke calls the Fundamental Law of Nature is not to be taken as the most fundamental principle of his philosophical theology as a whole; and the same is usually true for other views.

(a) The point is this: there must be some further and even more fundamental principle that accounts for God's legitimate authority. In the absence of this authority, God's enactments, however promulgated to us, will not be binding as laws for us. Different writers explain the grounds of God's authority in different ways. In ¶6 (which I will be quoting later, in §3), Locke explains God's authority over us by the right of creation. Since God has created us from nothing and must continually sustain our being if we are to go on existing, supreme authority over us resides in God.[11] Hobbes, on the other hand, seems content to trace God's authority to God's omnipotence: dominion belongs to God ". . . not as Creator, and Gracious; but as Omnipotent."[12]

(b) To conclude: even when the system of law is that of natural law, we must still distinguish between:

(i) Who has supreme authority in that system, and

(ii) Why that person has that authority, and

(iii) The principles that specify the content of the norms of the system. Thus the account of why God has legitimate authority over mankind is distinct from the account of the content of natural law itself and of the various norms and rules that are justified by reference to it.[13]

3. When I refer to natural law I understand it as just explained, namely, as the law of God as known by our natural reason. This is the traditional sense in which Locke uses it, and it is also central for him; so when he speaks of natural law or natural right, there is a reference, direct or indirect,

---

11. See *Essays on the Law of Nature,* pp. 151–157.

12. *Leviathan,* p. 187.

13. Locke says in the *Essays on the Law of Nature* that it is "the decree of the divine will discernible by the light of nature and indicating what is and what is not in conformity with rational nature, and for this very reason commanding or prohibiting" (p. 111). In the *Essay Concerning Human Understanding* (1690) he refers to the kinds of law we use to judge moral rectitude as the Divine Law: ". . . that law which God has set to the actions of men, whether promulgated to them by the light of nature, or the voice of revelation" (Vol. I, Book II, Ch. 28, §8). There is an incoherence in Locke's account of the basis of right and justice: namely, that he wants to account for them by maintaining that the relevant principles thereof are God's commands; on the other hand, that we are obligated to conform to God's commands presupposes that God has rightful authority over us, a right of creation, and that God is wise and beneficent. The right of creation of a wise and beneficent God, however, cannot itself be commanded by God, as the validity of any such command would presuppose that right. Locke never satisfactorily resolved this question and was effectively criticized on this point by Samuel Clarke. A clear discussion of these matters is found in Michael Ayres, *Locke: Epistemology-Ontology* (London: Routledge, 1991), Vol. 2, Chs. 15–16. Locke's doctrine is an example of the view Kant argues against in the *Grundlegung* in giving the third formula of the categorical imperative: Ak: IV: 431ff.

to the fundamental law of nature understood as the law of God as known by reason.

There is, however, at least one possible exception. It is not clear whether or how the connection with the law of nature is to be established with regard to the principle of fidelity (that promises and compacts are to be kept): this Locke seems to take as part of the law of nature (¶14), but the grounds of this principle he does not consider. However, in the cases we are concerned with, for example, the natural right of persons to the equal freedom to which we are all born (in view of our powers of reason) and the natural right of property, the connection with the fundamental law of nature is clear enough. I come back to this later when we examine how the natural rights just mentioned are derived from the fundamental law of nature.

Observe finally that Locke's conception of natural law provides us with an example of an independent order of moral and political values by reference to which our political judgments of justice and the common good are to be assessed. Correct or sound judgments are true of, or accurate with respect to, this order, the content of which is in large part specified by the fundamental law of nature as God's law. Thus Locke's view contains a conception of justification distinct from the conception of public justification in justice as fairness as a form of political liberalism.[14] However, justice as fairness neither asserts nor denies the idea of such an independent order, or justification as showing moral and political judgments to be true by reference to this order.

§3. The Fundamental Law of Nature

1. I shall now review the statement and description of the law of nature, its role, its content and several clauses, as well as some of the rights

---

14. John Rawls: *Justice as Fairness: A Restatement,* ed. Erin Kelly (Cambridge: Harvard University Press, 2001), §9.2: "An essential feature of a well-ordered society is that its public conception of political justice establishes a shared basis for citizens to justify to one another their political judgments: each cooperates, politically and socially, with the rest on terms all can endorse as just. This is the meaning of public justification."

that Locke thinks derive from it. First, let's note the very important statement of this law which reads as follows:

> The *State of Nature* has a Law of Nature to govern it, which obliges ev-
> ery one: And Reason, which is that Law, teaches all Mankind, who will
> but consult it, that being all equal and independent, no one ought to
> harm another in his Life, Health, Liberty, or Possessions. For Men be-
> ing all the Workmanship of one Omnipotent, and infinitely wise
> Maker; All the Servants of one Sovereign Master, sent into the World
> by his order and about his business, they are his Property, whose
> Workmanship they are, made to last during his, not one another's plea-
> sure. And being furnished with like Faculties, sharing all in one Com-
> munity of Nature, there cannot be supposed any such *Subordination*
> among us, that may Authorize us to destroy one another, as if we
> were made for one another's uses, as the inferior ranks of Creatures
> are for ours. Every one as he is *bound to preserve himself,* and not to quit
> his Station willfully; so by the like reason when his own Preservation
> comes not in competition, ought he, as much as he can, *to preserve the
> rest of Mankind,* and may not unless it be to do Justice on an Offender,
> take away, or impair the life, or what tends to the Preservation of the
> Life, the Liberty, Health, Limb, or Goods of another. (¶6)

The most basic law of nature, or what Locke calls "the *Fundamental Law
of Nature,*" is that "*Man [is] to be preserved,* as much as possible" (¶16); or, as
he puts it in ¶134, it is "*the preservation of the Society,* and (as far as will consist with the public good) of every person in it." Much the same is repeated
in ¶¶135, 159, and 183.

2. The statement that "The *State of Nature* has a Law of Nature to govern it," which opens the definition in ¶6, is supplemented by many passages
throughout the *Second Treatise* that describe that natural law: Thus:

(a) In agreement with what I have said earlier, the Law of Nature is described as a "Declaration" of "the Will of God" (¶135).

(b) Concerning the fundamental law of nature, Locke says "Reason,
which is that Law, teaches all Mankind" (¶6). Locke describes the fundamental law of nature as not only *known* by reason, but as the law "of *reason
and common Equity*"(¶8); as "the right Rule of Reason" (¶10); as "the
Common Law of Reason" (¶16), and as the *Law of Reason* (¶57).

(c) In ¶136 the fundamental law of nature is described as "unwritten, and so nowhere to be found but in the minds of Men." In ¶12, it is "as intelligible and plain to a rational Creature, and a Studier of that Law, as the positive Laws of Commonwealths, nay possibly plainer; As much as Reason is easier to be understood, than the . . . intricate Contrivances of Men." (See also ¶124.) All this fits with the idea that the Law of Nature is God's will, "being promulgated or made known by *Reason* only" (¶57).

3. Locke also writes on the role of the fundamental law of nature:

(a) First, from ¶6 we see that the fundamental law of nature associates all mankind into one great natural community with the law of nature to govern it. In ¶172 Locke speaks of a man who puts himself into a state of war with another as having "quitted Reason, which God hath given to be the Rule betwixt Man and Man, and the common bond whereby human kind is united into one fellowship and society." In ¶128 Locke says that the Law of Nature, common to us all, causes each of us and the rest of mankind to be *"one Community,* [making] up one Society distinct from all other Creatures."

The law of nature would suffice to govern us were it not for the corruption and viciousness of degenerate people. There would be no need for us to separate into civil societies each with its distinct political authority, and so to split up "this great and natural Community" (¶128). Thus, the fundamental law of nature is a law for the community of humankind in the state of nature. This state, while a state of liberty, is not a state of license: it is bound by a law of nature and reason (¶6).

(b) The fundamental law of nature is also the regulative principle for political and social institutions of the various civil societies into which the community of humankind divides. Municipal (i.e., civil) law is right and just only when it is founded on, or accords with it. The fundamental law of nature does not cease to apply in society, but stands as an eternal rule to all men, legislators as well as others. No human sanction is good, or valid, when contrary to it.[15]

(c) The law of nature is normative and directive: it is a law to guide free and rational persons for their good. See the important statement in ¶57,

15. "The Obligations of the Law of Nature, cease not in Society . . . [but] . . . [stand] as an Eternal Rule to all Men, *Legislators* as well as others. The *Rules* that they make . . . must . . . be conformable to the Law of Nature . . . and the *fundamental Law of Nature* being the *preservation of Mankind,* no Human Sanction can be good, or valid against it" (¶135; see also ¶171).

where Locke says: "For *Law*, in its true Notion, is not so much the Limitation as *the direction of a free and intelligent Agent* to his proper Interest, and prescribes no farther than is for the general Good of those under that Law. Could they be happier without it, the *Law*, as a useless thing would of itself vanish. . . . *the end of Law* is not to abolish or restrain, but *to preserve and enlarge Freedom*. . . . *where there is no Law, there is no Freedom*. For *Liberty* is to be free from restraint and violence from others which cannot be, where there is no Law."

For Locke, then, the ideas of reason and law, of freedom and the general good, are closely connected. The fundamental law of nature is known by reason; it prescribes only for our good; it seeks to enlarge and to preserve our freedom, that is, our security from the restraint and violence of others. Liberty abides by law and is distinct from license, which abides by no law. Here law is the law of reason given by the law of nature.

§4. The State of Nature as a State of Equality

1. From its role as just described we see that the fundamental law of nature is the basic law of both the state of nature and political society (applying to its political and social institutions). The state of nature is, for Locke, a state of perfect freedom and equality (¶4):

(i) It is a state of freedom because all are at liberty to order their actions and to dispose of their possessions and persons as they see fit, within the limits set by the law of nature. It is not necessary that they ask the permission of anyone else, nor are they dependent on another's will.

(ii) The state of nature is a state of equality, that is, a state of equal power and jurisdiction among persons, all being, as it were, equally sovereign over themselves: "all being Kings," as Locke says in ¶123. Clearly equal power means equal liberty and political authority over oneself. Power is not to be understood as strength, or control over resources, or much less as force, but as right and jurisdiction.

In ¶54 Locke makes the important point that this state of equal freedom is compatible with various kinds of inequalities, for example, inequalities arising from differences of age, merit, or virtue; and, as it turns out, differences in inherited or acquired (real) property. As we have noted, the equality Locke speaks of is a state of equal right to our natural freedom, a state of equal jurisdiction over ourselves under the law of nature. This free-dom we are born to in virtue of our capacity for reason, and it is rightfully ours when we attain the age of reason (¶57).

2. By starting with the state of nature as a state of equal freedom, Locke is flatly rejecting Robert Filmer's starting point, which was that we are born in a state of natural subordination.[16] Does Locke present an argu-ment for his starting point? Or is he rather, as I am inclined to think, elabo-rating a certain conception of human society under God? Locke's explana-tion of his view (¶4) is that God has not by a "manifest Declaration" designated any one person as having an undoubted right of (political) do-minion and sovereignty over the rest. God could do this but has not. Given the historical fact that God has not, nothing is more evident than that per-sons of the same natural kind and possessing all the same (relevant) advan-tages of nature are born to a state of equal freedom and political jurisdic-tion over themselves.

I think Locke's view here is this: No one could have political authority over others unless God had so designated by a manifest declaration, or un-less there were relevant difference(s) between that person and the rest. But given that God has not so declared, and given that we are of the same natu-ral kind and possess all the same (relevant) advantages of nature, we are born to a state of equality: that is, to a state of equal freedom and political jurisdiction over ourselves. Certainly inequalities of age, merit, and virtue, and of property, exist (¶54). But they are not, for Locke, relevant differences for establishing political authority, which is (to abbreviate) *"a Right of mak-ing Laws with Penalties of Death . . . and of employing the force of the Community, in the Execution of such Laws . . ., and all this only for the Public Good"* (¶3).

Perhaps it is not surprising, then, that for Locke political authority can arise only by the consent of those with equal jurisdiction over themselves. He simply elaborates a different conception of political society than Filmer. Ask yourself: Is this a fault in Locke, and if so, why?

16. All are born into natural political subordination, except for those few who are des-ignated by God to be dominant, and to be absolute rulers (through tracing their lines by the rule of primogeniture back to Noah, and thence to Adam). See Filmer, *Patriarcha.* Locke's *First Treatise* is devoted to refuting Filmer's argument that God gave ultimate power to Adam, and that all legitimate sovereigns inherit that power directly from Adam. Locke reiterates his major points in ¶1 of the *Second Treatise.*

§5. The Content of the Fundamental Law of Nature

1. This brings us finally to the content of the fundamental law of nature, namely, what it prescribes, including the several (natural) rights Locke takes it to imply. In talking about equality above, we have already said something about those rights. The term "Fundamental Law of Nature" is used in: ¶¶16, 134, 135, 159, 183; and there are also statements about the "Law of Nature" in: ¶¶4, 6, 7, 8, 16, 57, 134, 135, 159, 171, 172, and 181–183.

Two important clauses of the Fundamental Law of Nature are contained in the statement I quoted earlier from ¶6. These read as follows:

(a) The first clause: "being all equal and independent, no one ought to harm another in his Life, Health, Liberty, or Possessions."

(b) The second clause: "Every one as he is *bound to preserve himself,* and not to quit his Station willfully; so by like reason when his own Preservation comes not in competition, ought he, as much as he can, *to preserve the rest of Mankind,* and may not unless it be to do Justice on an Offender, take away, or impair the life, or what tends to the Preservation of the Life, the Liberty, Health, Limb, or Goods of another."

Note the force of "by like reason" in the second clause. I am bound to preserve myself because I am God's property; but others also are God's property, and so for the same reason I am bound to preserve them also, at least when their preservation is not in competition with mine. In ¶134 Locke says: "the *first and fundamental natural Law,* which is to govern even the Legislative itself, is *the preservation of Society* and (as far as will consist with the public good) of every person in it."

(c) A third clause, in ¶16, concerns a priority for the innocent:
"*Man being to be preserved,* as much as possible, when all cannot be preserved, the safety of the Innocent is to be preferred."

2. One application of this last clause is to self-defense: if I am wrongly attacked by another intending to take my life, then since I am innocent (let's assume), I have a right of self-defense.

Another application of the third, and also of the second clause is to protect the families (the wives and children) of those violent men who begin an unjust war, seeking conquest. Since their families are innocent—not involved in their guilt and destruction—enough property and goods must be left to them by the (just) victor so that they do not perish. (See ¶¶178–183.)

Locke says, in ¶183: ". . . the Fundamental Law of Nature being, that all, as much as may be, should be preserved, it follows, that if there be not enough fully to *satisfy* both, *viz.* for the *Conqueror's Losses,* and Children's Maintenance, he that hath, and to spare, must remit something of his full Satisfaction, and give way to the pressing and preferable Title of those, who are in danger to perish without it."

Locke also states that even the guilty are sometimes to be spared: "for the *end of Government* being the *preservation of all,* as much as may be, even the guilty are to be spared, where it can prove no prejudice to the innocent" (¶159). In this paragraph, Locke is stressing that all members of society are to be preserved and that the sovereign (the Crown), in those cases the law cannot foresee, may exercise its discretion (prerogative) in preserving "as much as may be," to use Locke's phrase.

§6. The Fundamental Law of Nature as the Basis of Natural Rights

1. The natural rights we shall review do not to derive from the fundamental law of nature alone (with the content just discussed), but from that law as supplemented by two premises:

(i) The fact of God's silence: that God has not designated anyone to exercise political authority over the rest of humankind; and

(ii) The fact of equality: that we are "Creatures of the same species and rank promiscuously born to all the same advantages of Nature [with respect to establishing political authority] and the use of the same faculties [powers of natural reason and will, and so on]" (¶4).

2. As Locke first discusses these rights in ¶¶7–11, they are:

(a) The executive right we each have to punish transgressors of the fundamental law of nature; for that law would be in vain if no one had the power to execute (enforce) it and thereby preserve the innocent and restrain offenders. Since the state of nature is a state of equality—equal (political) jurisdiction—all have this executive right equally: this right deriving from our right to preserve mankind.

(b) The right to seek reparation, which right derives from our right of self-preservation.

In the social compact we give up our personal right to preserve ourselves and the rest of mankind to be *regulated* by the laws of society, so far as the preservation of ourselves and society shall require. We *wholly* give up the right of punishing, and engage ourselves to assist the executive power of society as its laws may require (¶130; see also ¶¶128–130).

3. It is important to recognize that for Locke nearly all natural rights have a derivation. Aside from rights associated with the principle of fidelity, I believe he views them as following from the fundamental law of nature, together with the two premises (the two facts) noted above: the fact of God's silence, and the fact of equality, as well, of course, as from the fact of God's legitimate authority over us. An example will convey what is meant:

Locke wishes to argue, against Filmer, that in the state of nature man has a natural right of private property (to be discussed in the third lecture on Locke). This right does not depend on the express consent of the rest of humankind. In the state of nature man is at liberty to use what "he hath mixed his *Labor* with," provided first, that there is enough and as good left for others (¶27) and second, that we take no more than we can use, so that nothing we take spoils (¶31).

Now this rule (that we are at liberty to use what we have mixed our labor with, subject to these two provisos) is a law of nature, let's say. It expresses a natural right (a liberty of use) in the sense that it is a rule that is reasonable for the first stage of the state of nature; and under those circumstances it gives us a liberty of use. Note though that this right follows from the fundamental law of nature.

Locke supposes that (i) given that fundamental law—that all mankind is to be preserved, etc.—and (ii) given that the bounty of nature is for our use, and (iii) given that the (express) consent of the rest of mankind is impossible to obtain, it must be God's intention that we may appropriate from nature's bounty and make use of it subject to the two provisos. Otherwise, all mankind, and, so far as possible, every member of it, could not be preserved.

Thus, the natural right of property (the liberty to use) in the state of nature is the conclusion of an argument from the fundamental law of nature (supplemented by other premises). I think the same is true for other cases of natural rights, modulo the rights based on the principle of fidelity.

4. The significance of the preceding remarks is that Locke does not found his social contract doctrine on a list of natural rights and natural laws without any explanation of where they come from. While the idea of such a list is not as such implausible, it is not Locke's. He does say that even

while in a state of nature men must be bound by their promises for ". . . Truth and keeping Faith belongs to Men, as Men, and not as Members of society" (¶14). Telling the truth and keeping faith are presumably part of the fundamental law of nature, a further aspect included in it, as is the priority for the protection of the innocent. Perhaps it is part of the law of nature more generally conceived. God's right of creation is also treated as evident, but that is not, certainly, a natural right.

Thus, Locke starts from the principle of the fundamental law of nature and these two facts: the fact of equality, and the historical fact (as he argues in the *First Treatise*) that God has not designated anyone to have political authority over the rest. He then derives various natural rights from that basis.

We should be clear that our natural rights depend upon our prior duties, namely, duties imposed by the fundamental law of nature and by our duty to obey God, who has legitimate authority over us. So within Locke's view, understood as a theological doctrine, we are not self-authenticating sources of valid claims, as I have used that term in characterizing the conception of the person in justice as fairness.[17] This is because our claims are founded, within Locke's conception, on prior duties owed to God. However, within a political society that guarantees liberty of conscience, say (which Locke's affirms), these claims when made by citizens will be self-authenticating, in the sense that from that society's political point of view, these claims are self-imposed.

5. Finally, it is very important that the fundamental law of nature is a distributive, not an aggregative, principle. By this I mean that it does not direct us to strive for the greatest public good, say, to preserve the greatest number of persons. Rather, it expresses concern for each person: while mankind is to be preserved, in so far as is possible, so is every member of mankind (¶134). Moreover, as complemented by other premises (God's silence about *political* authority and the fact of equality), the law of nature assigns certain equal natural rights to all persons (who possess the powers of reason and are capable of being masters of themselves).

Moreover, these rights are to have very great weight. Locke will argue that, beginning from the state of nature as a state of equal political jurisdiction, legitimate political authority can arise only by consent. This provides

17. See John Rawls, *Justice as Fairness: A Restatement,* p. 23, where the term is used to describe persons' regarding themselves as being entitled to make claims on their institutions so as to advance their conceptions of the good.

the root of his argument against royal absolutism: his idea is that a political authority of that kind could never arise by consent.

6. I conclude by remarking that Locke's underlying thought throughout is that we belong to God as God's property; that our rights and duties derive from God's ownership of us, as well as from the purposes for which we are made, which purposes are for Locke clear and intelligible in the fundamental law of nature itself.

This deserves emphasis because Locke is often discussed apart from this religious background; and for much of the time I shall do the same. Today various views are called "Lockean" which actually have rather little connection with Locke. A view that stipulates various rights of property without the kind of derivation that Locke gives for them—as in Nozick's in *Anarchy, State and Utopia*[18]—is often so described. Yet for Locke and his contemporaries this religious background is fundamental, and to neglect it is to risk seriously misunderstanding their thought. So I call your attention to it here.

Locke seems to have thought that those who do not believe in God, and who have no fear of God's judgments and divine punishments, cannot be trusted: they are dangerous and liable to violate the laws of common reason that follow from the fundamental law of nature, and to take advantage of shifting circumstances as suits their interests.[19]

18. Robert Nozick, *Anarchy, State and Utopia* (New York: Basic Books, 1974).

19. See Locke's *A Letter Concerning Toleration,* ed. James H. Tully (Indianapolis: Hackett, 1983). Also on this point, see John Dunn, "The Concept of 'Trust' in the Politics of John Locke," in *Philosophy in History* (Cambridge: Cambridge University Press, 1984), p. 294.

LOCKE II

His Account of a Legitimate Regime

§1. Resistance under a Mixed Constitution

1. Recall that in Lecture I, Locke was contrasted with Hobbes. Hobbes is concerned with the problem of destructive civil war, and he uses the idea of the social contract as a point of view from which to argue that given our basic interests, including our transcendent religious interest in salvation, all have sufficient reasons (based on those interests) to support an effective and, in Hobbes's view, necessarily absolute sovereign, whenever such a sovereign exists (Locke Lecture I: §1.3).

Locke's aim is very different. He wants to defend the cause of the first Whigs in the Exclusion Crisis of 1679–81.[1] His problem is to formulate the right of resistance to the Crown under a mixed constitution, as the English Constitution was then regarded. Locke's argument is that Charles II, by his abuse of the prerogative[2] and other powers, has conducted himself as an absolute monarch and has thereby dissolved the regime, so that all of its powers, including those of Parliament, return to the people. Government is a fiduciary power, a power held on trust from the people under the social compact; and when that trust is violated, the people's constituent power (as I shall call it) once again comes into play.

2. To explain: let's define a mixed constitution as one in which two or more constitutional agents share in the legislative power; in the English case these agents are the Crown and Parliament. Neither is supreme: rather

---

1. For a long time, it was assumed that the *Second Treatise* was written after the revolution of 1688, as a justification of it. According to Laslett, however, the original part of the *Second Treatise* was written in 1679–80 and includes Chs. 2–7, 10–14, and 19, with other chapters added later, some in 1681 and 1683, and others later in 1689. See Laslett's Introduction to *Two Treatises of Government*, p. 65.

2. The power to act according to discretion, for the public good, without the prescription of the law, and sometimes even against it, is called the Prerogative. See ¶160.

they are coordinate powers. Legislation cannot be enacted without the Crown's consent, as the Crown must approve proposed statutes before they become law. On the other hand, the Crown cannot govern without Parliament, on whom it depends for tax monies to run the government bureaucracy, support the army, and so on. And it is the duty of the Crown to enforce the laws enacted by Parliament with its approval, as well as to conduct foreign affairs and defense. The Crown combines what Locke calls the executive and the federative powers.

Thus, we have two constitutional agents who, as coordinate powers, are equal in this sense: neither is subordinate to the other and when there is a conflict between them, there is no constitutional means, no legal framework within the constitution, for settling the conflict. Locke recognizes this clearly in ¶168, the important paragraph that ends Chapter 14. Here he asserts the right of resistance on the part of the people in such a situation.

The source of Locke's constitutional doctrine seems to be a work by George Lawson: *Politica sacra et civilis* (Religious and Civil Polity) of 1657 (published in 1660).[3] Lawson's view is that when in a mixed constitution there is a persistent conflict between Crown and Parliament, the government itself is dissolved and all of its powers return to the political community as a whole. The people are then free to exercise their constituent power and to take the necessary steps to eliminate the conflict and to restore the traditional constitution, or else to establish a new and different form of regime. Locke's first statement of Lawson's view is in ¶149, which must be read with the four paragraphs (¶¶150–153) that follow. Observe that Locke is very careful to say that the Crown is a coordinate power with a share in the legislative power and not subject to laws without its own consent. Thus in "a tolerable sense" the Crown may be called "supreme" (¶151). This was the Whig view then widely held, and differs from the later doctrine of parliamentary supremacy.

3. Locke uses the idea of the social compact (a term he often uses) as a point of view from which we can see how a mixed regime could legitimately arise. The original compact, or compact of society, unites the people into one society and at the same time establishes a form of regime with political authority.

Two points about this: first, the social compact is unanimous, for in vir-

3. On Lawson, an innovative figure, see the excellent study by Julian Franklin, *Locke's Theory of Sovereignty* (Cambridge: Cambridge University Press, 1978), Ch. 3. On this see esp. pp. 69–81.

tue of it all join into one civil society for the purpose of establishing a political regime; second, political power in the form determined by the majority is a fiduciary power entrusted for certain ends (¶149). The compact of society is, then, a compact of the people with each other to establish a government; it is not a compact between the people and the government or its agents. That the legislative power is a fiduciary power emphasizes that the constituent power of the people always exists and cannot be alienated. In the case of a conflict between constitutional powers, or between the government and the people, it is the people who are to judge (¶168). In doing so they exercise once again their constituent power. If the Crown or Parliament arouse the people to action, Locke says they have only themselves to blame (¶¶225–230).

§2. Locke's Fundamental Thesis concerning Legitimacy

1. I now turn to Locke's fundamental thesis about how the doctrine of the social compact imposes limits on the nature of legitimate regimes. The basic idea of this doctrine—that legitimate political power can only be founded on consent—is repeated throughout the *Second Treatise*. The statement in ¶95 is suitable for our purposes. It reads in part:

> Men being, as has been said, by Nature, all free, equal and independent, no one can be put out of this Estate, and subjected to the Political Power of another, without his own *Consent*. The only way whereby any one divests himself of his Natural Liberty, and *puts on the bonds of Civil Society* is by agreeing with other Men to join and unite into a Community for their comfortable, safe, and peaceable living one amongst another, in a secure Enjoyment of their Properties, and a greater Security against any that are not of it. This any number of Men may do, because it injures not the Freedom of the rest . . . When any number of men have so *consented to make one Community* or Government, they are thereby presently incorporated, and make *one Body Politic,* wherein the *Majority* have a Right to act and conclude the rest.

Note that in this passage Locke is describing what we may call "originating" as opposed to "joining" consent. Originating consent is that consent given by those who initially establish one body politic through a social compact; whereas joining consent is that given by individuals as they reach the age of reason and consent to join this or that existing political community. This distinction is important when we note Hume's criticism of Locke in "Of the Original Contract" (1752). Locke takes for granted that we can subject ourselves to political authority by our own consent. His thesis is rather that, regarding the state of nature as a state of equal freedom, we can become subject to political authority in no other way. Thus, as we shall see, absolute government is always illegitimate.

2. To develop Locke's view, recall his definition of political power: "*a Right* of making Laws with Penalties of Death, and consequently all less Penalties, for the Regulating and Preserving of Property, and of employing the force of the Community, in the Execution of such Laws, and in the defense of the Commonwealth from Foreign Injury, and all this only for the Public Good" (¶3).

As this definition shows, political power is not strength or force but a complex of rights possessed by a political regime. Of course, to be effective, such a regime must have coercive, or sanctioning power—that is, the right, suitably limited, to exercise force and to impose sanctions to enforce laws, and so on. But for Locke, political power is a form of legitimate authority appropriately related to the state of equal freedom and bounded by the fundamental law of nature.

3. Note that Locke's thesis that the only basis of legitimate government is consent applies only to political authority. He does not hold what we might call a consensual (or contractualist) account of duties and obligations generally.[4] Many of the duties and obligations he recognizes do not arise from consent:

(a) To start with the most obvious case: our duties to God arise from God's right of creation; it would be sacrilegious—indeed preposterous—to suppose they arise from consent. The same holds for our duty to comply with the laws of nature and all the duties and obligations that follow from it. More specifically:

(b) Our duty to honor and respect our parents (as discussed in Ch. 6 on Paternal Power) is not consensual; and moreover, this duty is perpetual.

---

4. An example of such a view, although it must be carefully interpreted, is T. M. Scanlon's contractualism. See his essay in *Utilitarianism and Beyond*, ed. Amartya Sen and Bernard Williams (Cambridge: Cambridge University Press, 1982); also his book *What We Owe to Each Other* (Cambridge, Mass.: Harvard University Press, 1998).

Not even a king is released from his duty to honor and respect his mother (¶¶66, 68). Thus, while our reaching the age of reason brings to an end our subjection to parental authority, it does not affect certain other duties and obligations we owe our parents.

(c) The duty to respect the (real) property of another in a state of nature—land, its fruits, etc.—does not arise from consent, but from the precepts of natural law that apply in that state in accordance with the laws of nature, as I discussed in the first lecture. Here we assume that these precepts are generally followed and that people's properties, for example real properties, are acquired legitimately, and that the various provisos (stated by Locke in Ch. 5) have been satisfied.

(d) Finally, the fundamental law of nature imposes a duty to give special weight to the safety of the innocent (the righteous or just) (¶16). In ¶183 Locke argues that a victor, even in a just war of self-defense in which the victor's actions are entirely justified, must recognize the claims of the wives and children of those who unjustly made war against him. They are among the innocent; and the victor must also recognize what Locke calls the "native right" of the defeated to be free in their own persons and to continue to own their own properties and to inherit their father's goods, assuming they did not wrongfully assist the loser (¶¶190–194). These rights the victor must recognize are rooted in the fundamental law of nature.

There are many duties and obligations, then, that do not arise from consent. With the exception of duties and obligations arising from the principle of fidelity (keeping one's promises and other commitments), all of them can, I believe, be seen as consequences of the fundamental law of nature under certain conditions. And, of course, as we have said, our being bound by that law does not arise from consent, nor of course does our duty to God.

4. At this point it may seem that Locke proceeds as though his fundamental thesis about consent as the origin of political power were obvious. Indeed, it does have an obvious ring about it: how else, we might ask, could free and equal persons—all being equally endowed with reason and having equal jurisdiction over themselves—become the subjects of such an authority unless by their free consent? Compare the case of free and equal sovereign nations: how can they become bound to some one of themselves unless, say by treaty, they give their free consent?

But however plausible Locke's thesis might be, he does not just say that it is obvious. His reasoning in the *Second Treatise* can be seen as an argument by cases as follows: the basic law is the fundamental law of nature, and we must justify every power and liberty, every right or duty, in our political relationships by reference to that law, together with the principle of fidelity.

The idea is that we enumerate the various powers and rights that we accept in everyday life, and that might offhand be the foundation of political authority. For example, the right of (real) property, parental power, and the right of a victor in a just war, each of which Locke discusses. Then it is plain, Locke thinks, that none of these powers and rights can be the foundation of political authority. Rather, each of these powers and rights is suited for certain ends of different forms of association under certain special conditions, conditions which sometimes hold in the state of nature, sometimes in society, and sometimes in both. His idea is that different forms of association have different forms of authority (see ¶83, last sentence). They give rise to other kinds of authority with different powers and rights. We must look for another way to establish legitimate political authority.

5. To illustrate, consider the case of parental authority. This is sufficiently comprehensive in scope to look in some ways like political power. Filmer, in *Patriarcha*, argued that all political authority has Adam's paternal authority, originally given by God, as its source. Against Filmer, Locke holds that the authority of parents over their children is temporary. We are all born to a state of perfect liberty and equality even if we are not born in it (¶55). Until we reach the age of reason some one must act as our guardian or trustee, and make the decisions required to secure our good and to prepare us for assuming our rightful freedom at the age of reason, at which time parental power ceases. The point of Locke's account of parental power is to show, against Filmer, how it arises from our immaturity and ends with our coming of age, and that it cannot give rise to political power.[5]

6. In the next lecture, I shall discuss Locke's account of the right of

---

5. A feature of Locke's view is that he sometimes treats women as equals with men, for example, as equals with their husbands, as in ¶65, *Second Treatise*. Susan Okin, in her *Women in Western Political Thought* (Princeton: Princeton University Press, 1979), pp. 199ff, argues that Locke does this only when it suits his case against Filmer's patriarchalism. Thus, within the family, when husband and wife disagree, it is the husband who has authority: ". . . it naturally falls to the Man's share, as the abler and stronger." *Two Treatises:* II: ¶82; see also I: ¶47. There is no idea of even considering whether women have equal political rights.

property in some detail, but note here that it is essential to Locke's view that, just as with parental power, the right of property cannot be the basis of political power. To show this, he does two things (among others) in Chapter 5:

(a) He maintains first, as opposed to Filmer, that even though originally the earth and its fruits were given in common, individuals and families could and did take (real) property in things without the consent of all humankind, beginning with the first ages of the world and long before political authority. (Real) property can exist prior to government. It was in part to render this property secure that people entered civil society. Contrary to the feudal tie between (real) property and political authority, Locke holds that property precedes government and is not the basis of it.

(b) Locke holds, second, that while the accumulation of real properties of different sizes, the introduction of money, the growth of population and the need for drawing boundary lines between tribes, and other changes, led to a stage of development in which organized political authority became necessary, real property does not of itself give rise to political authority, as in feudal societies. For political authority to come into existence, a social compact is required. Clearly, the terms of this compact are influenced by the existence and distribution of real property but that is another matter; property precedes government but is not the basis of it.

§3. Locke's Criterion for a Legitimate Political Regime

1. Locke's account of a legitimate political authority and of obligations to it has two parts.

(a) The first part is an account of legitimacy: it lays down when a political regime as a system of political and social institutions is legitimate.

(b) The second part lays down the conditions under which we are bound, as individuals, or citizens, to comply with an existing regime. It is an account of political duty and obligation.

These two parts should be carefully distinguished.

Let's turn to the first part, the criterion for a legitimate regime, which we can formulate as follows: A political regime is legitimate if and only if it is such that it *could* have been contracted into during a rightly-conducted process of historical change, a process that began with the state of nature as a state of perfect freedom and equality—a state of equal right, all being kings. We will call this process "ideal history." This formulation calls for considerable explanation and comment.

2. First, what is a rightly-conducted process of historical change (or ideal history)? It is a historical process that satisfies two rather different conditions:

(a) One condition is that all persons act rationally to advance their legitimate interests, that is, interests that are permissible within the bounds of the law of nature. These interests, in Locke's phrase, are their interests in their lives, liberties, and estates.[6]

(b) The other condition is that everyone acts reasonably, that is, in accordance with their duties and obligations under the law of nature.

In short, everyone acts both rationally and rightly, or reasonably.

This means that in ideal history institutional changes (for example, the introduction of money, or the fixing of tribal boundaries) are agreed to:

First, only if the individuals involved have good reasons for believing that, in view of their current and expected future circumstances, these changes are to their rational advantage, that is, that they advance their legitimate interests; and

Second, only if no one subjects any one else to coercion or to threats of violence, or fraud, all contrary to the fundamental law of nature, and moreover, only if all honor their duties to one another under that law.

The first condition is one of rationality, both individual and collective; the second condition is one of right, or reasonable, conduct accepting the bounds imposed on our natural freedom by the fundamental law of nature.

Here we should note explicitly that for Locke, force and threats of violence cannot be used to extract consent. Promises given under these conditions do not bind (¶¶176, 186). Further, one cannot grant or cede a right or power that one does not have (¶135). Thus, by compact we cannot sell ourselves into slavery (¶23; see also ¶141).

To sum up: for Locke, all agreements in ideal history are free, uncoerced, and unanimous as well as reasonable and rational from everyone's point of view.

---

6. Interests of this kind belong to Locke's standard view of persons in his contract doctrine. We have seen that a contract doctrine must contain a standard view of some kind. This view is part of its normalization of the parties to the contract in order to formulate a rational basis for unanimous consent.

3. Note above in §3.1 the use of the word "could" in stating the social contract criterion for a legitimate regime. It says that a political regime is legitimate if and only if it is a form of government that *could* be contracted into as part of a rightly-conducted process of historical change, or of what we have called "ideal history." Here it is assumed that ideal history may include a series of agreements over a long period of time. Their effect is cumulative and reflected in the institutional structure of society at any given moment.

Thus, we don't say, on Locke's view, that a political regime is legitimate if it *would* have been contracted into in ideal history. That is a far stronger statement, one that Locke need not make. He proceeds by imposing certain constraints on what is reasonable and rational in ideal history. Presumably different kinds of regimes could be contracted into, each consistent with these constraints.

But it meets Locke's aims to show that royal absolutism could not be thus contracted into: this form of regime is excluded. That Locke's aim is to argue against royal absolutism is shown by the numerous occasions on which he takes up this question and by the vehemence of what he says. For him, to put ourselves under an absolute monarch is contrary to our (natural) duties and irrational; for to do that is to put ourselves in a situation that is worse than the state of nature (¶¶13, 91ff, 137), something rational beings will not do.[7] On this, see the important statement in ¶131 where he says that when men give up the equality, liberty, and executive power they have in the state of nature in order to enter into society with its laws and restrictions, they do so "only with an intention in everyone the better to preserve himself his Liberty and Property; (For no rational Creature can be supposed to change his condition with an intention to be worse)." He goes on to say that whoever has power must govern by established standing laws, and not by extempory decrees, ". . . all this to be directed to no other *end*, but the *Peace, Safety,* and *public good* of the People." To understand the role of the rule of law for Locke, we must put it in this context.

On the other hand, a mixed constitution could be contracted into. For Locke, that the English Constitution is both mixed and legitimate is not in dispute. Thus, once his criterion is accepted, absolutism is illegitimate, and

---

7. Locke differs here from Hobbes, who views the state of nature as the worst condition of all.

so a king with absolutist pretensions may be resisted within the context of a mixed constitution.

4. It is implicit in what we have said that Locke's criterion for a legitimate regime is hypothetical. That is, we can tell whether a form of regime is legitimate by seeing whether it could have been contracted into in the course of ideal history. It need not actually have been contracted into; a regime may be legitimate even if it has arisen in some other fashion.

To illustrate: Locke recognizes that the Norman conquest did not establish the legitimacy, say by the right of conquest, of Norman rule (¶177). But various institutional changes since that time have transformed the original Norman regime into a mixed constitution (as Locke understands it); and so the existing regime now satisfies the social contract criterion. It is a form of regime that could be contracted into, and hence could be, and is, accepted as legitimate.

However, although Locke's criterion is hypothetical, it is not non-historical. That is, ideal history is a possible course of historical change, assuming that human beings can conduct themselves reasonably and rationally. This may be very unlikely, but it is not impossible. By contrast, I have supposed that in the political conception of justice that I have called "justice as fairness" the original position is non-historical; it is to be regarded as a device of representation that models our more general considered convictions.[8]

5. To conclude: Locke's criterion of a legitimate political regime is a negative one: that is, it excludes certain forms of regime as illegitimate: those that could not be contracted into by a series of agreements in ideal history. This criterion doesn't specify the best, or ideal, or even the better political regimes. To do this Locke would have to maintain that there is only one best regime, or a few equally good best regimes, one of which would be contracted into. To maintain this he would need a far more general doctrine. Moreover, it is far beyond what Locke requires for his political purposes. Very sensibly, he argues for what he needs and not more.

§4. The Political Obligation for Individuals

1. So far we have discussed Locke's criterion of legitimacy—the form a legitimate government may take. It is important to distinguish between an

8. See Rawls, *Justice as Fairness: A Restatement,* §§6.3–6.5.

account of legitimacy and an account of political duty and obligation of individual persons. I now turn to the second of these and ask: How do we—as individuals—become bound to a particular regime that may exist at any time, and to which we may be subject?

The contrast here with Filmer's view is sharp.[9] Filmer's starting point was the Bible as an inspired work. It disclosed God's will in all essential matters and contained the relevant truths about the nature of the world and human society. For Filmer, we are born under and must always be subject to some authority. This is the idea of natural subjection, which Locke mentions in ¶¶114, 116, and 117. The idea of nature as a state of equal right, all being equally sovereigns over themselves, and the idea that political authority must be seen to arise from consent are, for Filmer, completely false. For him, the Bible shows that human society originated in one man, Adam; and before Eve was created Adam owned the whole world, all the land and all the creatures in it. The world was his property, and he was subject only to God. Thus, it was the will of God that the world begin this way, with Adam alone, and not with two or more men, or with a multitude consisting of equal numbers of men and women.

Filmer thought, then, that all human beings were to be subordinate to the first man, Adam. By virtue of being the father, or patriarch, of his eventually very large family (he is supposed to have lived over 900 years), he was the ruler and all were subject to him. Upon his death, power over the family, or state, passed to his son by the rules of primogeniture. And since all persons have sprung from Adam, all are naturally and physiologically related to each other. Thus, God willed that human society is to be founded on natural and not on consensual bonds: its form is to be hierarchical and to rest on natural subordination.

2. In the important paragraphs ¶¶113–122, Locke argues against the idea of natural subjection. In regard to the political obligations of individuals, his view is that neither paternity nor place of birth or residence suffices to determine our political obligation. Fathers cannot bind their sons (¶116); and each person must, at the age of reason, give some form of consent. This consent we may think of as *joining consent*, a consent that, when it is what he calls *"express consent,"* incorporates us into an existing political soci-

9. Robert Filmer, *Patriarcha and Other Writings;* see also Lecture I, note 5 for further references.

ety. Locke remarks that as persons come of age, they do not give their consent "in a multitude together" (¶117), but do so singly. Therefore, we take no notice of their consent, and we conclude wrongly that they are naturally subjects. All of this Locke is directing against Filmer.

Now the question is: how do individuals give "joining consent"? At this point Locke introduces a distinction between "express" and "tacit" consent (¶¶119–122). Locke's text here is not very explicit; but some main points seem to be these:

(a) Express consent is given by "positive Engagement, and express Promise and Compact" (¶122), e.g. an oath of allegiance to the Crown,[10] (which is mentioned in ¶¶62, 151); whereas tacit consent is not so given.

(b) Express consent is given with the intention of incorporating our person into the commonwealth, and with the intention of making ourselves a member of that society, a subject of that government; whereas tacit consent is not given with this intention (¶¶119, 122).

(c) Express consent has the consequence of making us a perpetual member of society (¶121f), inalterably subject to it, and never again at liberty as in the state of nature (to which we are born), whereas tacit consent does not have this consequence (¶121f): it binds us only to honor the laws of the commonwealth so long as we dwell upon and enjoy the land (etc.) of the commonwealth.

(d) Express consent is like originating consent in that it incorporates our person into society; tacit consent does not.

To sum up, Locke's idea is that by express, joining consent (normally as a native-born Englishman) we become a full citizen of the commonwealth; whereas by tacit consent we undertake to comply with the laws of a regime so long as we reside in its territory (as resident aliens).

3. As we have seen, Locke's doctrine has two parts: one is an account of legitimacy, the other is an account of political duty and obligation of persons. Both parts are aimed at Filmer's account of the legitimacy of absolute monarchy as based on divine right and Adam's paternal power, with its idea of natural subjection.

The question now arises as to the relation between these two parts of Locke's view. From Locke's standpoint, one main point is that we can only become bound by express consent to a legitimate and not to an unjust re-

10. See John Dunn, *Political Thought of John Locke*, pp. 136–141.

gime. (Tacit consent is less important for Locke.) Thus, the legitimacy of a regime is a necessary condition of our having a political obligation to comply with its laws. In ¶20 Locke says that if the law is not justly administered, *"War is made* upon the Sufferers." This means that we do not (indeed cannot) have a political duty or obligation to a regime that is clearly unjust and violent. I say clearly unjust and violent, or at least sufficiently so, since it is unreasonable to expect any human regime to be perfectly just, and due allowance must be made for the normal faults, moral and otherwise, of those who exercise political power.

That the legitimacy of the regime is a necessary condition of political obligation fits the aim of Locke's doctrine: for keep in mind that Locke wants to justify resistance to the Crown under a mixed constitution. It accords with the idea of political authority as a fiduciary power; and with his view (stated in ¶225) that the people are loath to oppose an existing regime that exercises that power at all reasonably, and that does not threaten their essential rights and liberties. Locke also thinks that it is relatively easy for those who hold political authority to satisfy this necessary condition. Unjust rulers bring rebellions and revolutions on themselves (¶¶227–230).

Thus, so long as this condition is met, persons as they come of age will willingly give their free and express consent. Locke thinks it good for sovereigns to be fully aware that their reasonable conduct in exercising political authority is a necessary condition of their subjects being bound to accept their legitimacy: this awareness will serve as a constraint on their behavior. Nothing unleashes sovereigns so much as their false belief that their subjects owe them obedience, no matter what.

4. Observe, however, that the fact that we have no political obligation to an illegitimate regime does not imply that we are not bound to act in accordance with its laws, or to moderate our resistance to it, for other reasons. But these reasons will not derive from our political duty or obligation arising from our consent.

Rather, it may be that we should avoid resistance because it would not be effective; indeed, it might make the regime even more repressive, and bring undue harm to the innocent. The point is that there are various grounds in Locke's view for complying with a regime and its laws, and many of these are not based on political duty or obligation. Among these, I think, is a duty not to oppose a legitimate and just existing regime, whether in our own or in another country. But all things considered, there may be a right of resistance to an illegitimate and sufficiently unjust regime when the likelihood is great enough that resistance will be effective and that a legitimate regime will be established in its stead without great loss of innocent life.

Here, of course, we have to balance imponderables: How great must the likelihood be? How unjust the regime?—and much else. These questions have no precise answers and depend, as one says, on judgment. Political philosophy cannot formulate a precise procedure of judgment; and this should be expressly and repeatedly stated. What it may provide is a guiding framework for deliberation to be tested by reflection. Such a framework may include some fairly definite listing of the more relevant considerations as well as some indication of their relative weight when they conflict, as they are bound to do. There is no avoiding, then, having to reach a complex judgment weighing many imponderables, about which reasonable persons are bound to differ. This is a paradigm case of what I have called "the burdens of judgment": the sources of reasonable disagreement among reasonable persons.[11]

§5. Constituent Power and the Dissolution of Government

1. There are three potentially very radical ideas in Locke. One we have just surveyed, namely, the idea of the state of nature as a state of perfect freedom and equal political jurisdiction, and the incorporation of this idea in the criterion of a legitimate political regime.

The second idea is that of the constituent power of the people to establish the institutional form of the legislative power to which they entrust the regulation of their political life for the public good. Included in this idea is the further idea that, in a mixed constitution, whenever one of the coordinate constitutional agents—either the Crown or Parliament—violates its trust, the government is dissolved. In this case the people have the power to constitute a new frame of government and to depose those who have violated their trust.

---

11. On the idea of the burdens of judgment, see Rawls, *Justice as Fairness: A Restatement*, pp. 35–36; also Rawls, *Political Liberalism* (New York: Columbia University Press, 1993), pp. 54–58.

2. Let us now review some points about the idea of constituent power, as it is basic for the idea of constitutional government.

(a) Constitutional government makes the fundamental distinction between constituent and ordinary power (or as Lawson said in *Politica Sacra et Civilis,* between real and personal power). Constituent power is the power (the right) to determine the form of government, the constitution itself; ordinary power is the power (the right) exercised by officers of the government under the constitution in the everyday course of political affairs. Constitutional politics is the exercise of constituent power (say, mobilizing the electorate to amend the constitution); ordinary politics is the exercise of ordinary power (say, urging Parliament, or Congress, to enact laws; or judges deciding cases).[12]

(b) In this doctrine there is no contract of government, that is, a contract between the Crown and the legislative on the one side, and the people on the other. The social compact, for Locke, is an agreement entered into by the people as individuals with each other: they each make an agreement with the rest, and this agreement is unanimous. All agree to join into one society to be governed by a political regime. The form of this regime is whatever the majority of them shall determine is appropriate, given the present and foreseeable circumstances of society.

(c) The majority entrusts to this regime the exercise of ordinary political authority. Thus, it should be stressed that political power in Locke is a fiduciary power, a trust. If it is asked who is to decide whether those exercising ordinary power violate their trust, the answer must be that it is the people who must decide (¶¶149, 168, 240–243).

3. Finally, while Locke thought that Charles II had in effect dissolved the government by exceeding his prerogative and other powers, he says nothing about how the people (society as a whole) are to act, or through what institutions they are to exercise their constituent power. We might ask, "Who are the people and how can they act?" Locke gives no account of these matters.

---

12. On the distinction between constitutional and ordinary politics, see Bruce Ackerman's important work, *We the People* (Cambridge, Mass.: Harvard University Press, 1991); Vol. I, Chs. 1–3 give the general idea; the whole is good. In his view, the three main eras of American constitutional politics are the period of the Founding, the period of the Civil War amendments, and the period of the New Deal. Modulo matters of interpretation, there are these three different, though of course related, constitutions.

Lawson, again in *Politica Sacra et Civilis*, held that the community as a people—a nation—is not dissolved by civil war so long as there remains in it a sufficient will to reestablish a legitimate regime by the people's exercise of their constituent power. He seems to have thought of the community as acting through the county courts at the local level to organize a meeting of the people's representatives to act as a constitutional convention. Such a convention would, of course, make use of parliamentary forms and procedures, but it would not be a parliament. As a convention of the community's representatives, it would have constituent power to establish a new form of regime, which if accepted by the community, would be legitimate.[13]

Presumably Locke's views were similar to this, but in 1689 such views were rejected by his fellow Whigs as far too radical. I shall not pursue these matters here. The relevant point for our purposes is that the idea of the constituent power of the people and of the dissolution of government must remain indeterminate and indeed a rather unsettling idea until it is embodied in a definite way in institutions.

Thus, consider the distinction in our Constitution between the ordinary powers of elected and appointed officials, and the constituent powers exercised by the electorate in passing amendments to the Constitution and by a constitutional convention, and in the whole procedure to which such a convention belongs. These last arrangements are necessary to give institutional expression to the idea of the people's constituent power, and they are an essential part of a fully developed constitutional regime. But historically this comes later. The first constitutional convention seems to have been in Massachusetts in 1780. It is an American invention.[14]

There is a third potentially radical idea in Locke, the idea that the right of property is founded on labor. We touch on this in the next lecture.

13. Julian Franklin, *John Locke and the Theory of Sovereignty* (New York: Cambridge University Press, 1978), discusses this on pp. 73ff.

14. See Leonard Levy, editor with introduction: *Essays on the Making of the Constitution*, 2nd ed. (Oxford: Oxford University Press, 1987), p. xxi.

LOCKE III

Property and the Class State

§1. Problem Stated

1. I now take up Locke's account of property and the problem to which it gives rise. This problem can be stated as follows: Locke thought his social contract doctrine supported a constitutional state with the rule of law and a representative body sharing supreme legislative authority with the Crown. However, in this state only people who have a certain amount of property can vote. These owners of property are, let's say, active (vs. passive) citizens: they alone, among citizens, exercise political authority.

The problem now arises whether this constitutional though class state is consistent with Locke's social contract doctrine. On our interpretation, we ask whether a class state could arise by free consent in the course of ideal history. Recall that ideal history begins from the state of nature as a state of equal jurisdiction in which everyone acts reasonably and rationally. It has seemed to some, for example, to C. B. MacPherson,[1] that the class state is inconsistent with Locke's doctrine about how legitimate political authority can arise.

Before proceeding I should say that it is not Locke's concern to justify private property. This is because in the audience he is addressing there is no dispute about it. That ownership of property is justified is taken for granted. Locke's task is to explain how this widely accepted institution can be accounted for, shown to be right, within his social contract doctrine. Many of the details of Chapter 5 of the *Second Treatise* are to fill in this story; to demonstrate, as against Filmer, that the contract view accords with common opinion.

---

1. See C. B. MacPherson, *The Political Theory of Possessive Individualism* (Oxford: Oxford University Press, 1962).

2. A comment on MacPherson: he believes that unequal political rights arise in Locke only because Locke does not view those without property as parties to the original compact. He attributes to Locke the idea that those without property, being brutish and callous, are not capable of being reasonable and rational, and so they are not capable of giving their consent. Very little in the text of the *Two Treatises* supports this contention, so why does MacPherson hold it? The answer may be that he thinks it simply obvious that if those without property were parties to the original compact, they would not, assuming them to be reasonable and rational, consent to the unequal political rights of the class state. Thus he may think Locke must have excluded them as incompetent and incapable of reason.

Now, if this is MacPherson's reasoning, it overlooks a central point about all agreements, from social compacts to contracts in everyday life: namely, that in general, their specific terms depend on the relative bargaining positions of the parties outside the situation in which the terms of the contract are being discussed. The fact that the parties are equal in certain fundamental respects (with equal jurisdiction over themselves, equal sovereigns, as it were) does not imply that all the terms of the social compact must also be equal. Rather, these terms may be unequal, depending on the distribution of property among the parties, as well as on their aims and interests in entering the agreement.[2] This is precisely what seems to happen in Locke's form of the social contract view.

3. If we are unhappy with Locke's class state, and still want to affirm some form of contract doctrine, we must find a way to revise the doctrine so as to exclude the unwanted inequalities in basic rights and liberties. Justice as fairness has a way of doing this: it uses the original position as a device of representation. The veil of ignorance limits information about bargaining advantages outside that contractual situation.[3] Of course, other ways may be superior; or perhaps no revisions of the social contract view will prove satisfactory, once we have considered them thoroughly.

In these lectures I am trying to think through a few political conceptions, all the way through, if possible. This, and not the specific things we go over (though I hope they are not trivial) is the justification of our narrow focus. The idea of thinking political conceptions through is less famil-

2. These points are made by Joshua Cohen, "Structure, Choice and Legitimacy: Locke's Theory of the State," *Philosophy and Public Affairs,* Fall 1986, pp. 310f.

3. Rawls, *Justice as Fairness: A Restatement;* see §6.

iar to us than, say, thinking through conceptions in mathematics, physics, or economics. But perhaps it can be done. Why not? We can only find out by trying.

4. So much for preliminary comments on the problem of the class state in Locke. I first sketch some main points about his account of property, calling your attention to a few important points in the *Two Treatises,* stressing some sections in Chapter 4 of the first, and Chapter 5 of the second. With this done, I indicate how a constitutional class state might be thought to come about in the course of ideal history. The purpose in doing this is to show that such a state is consistent with Locke's basic ideas.

The thought here is not to criticize Locke, who was a great man—one who, while cautious, and some say even timid, nevertheless ran enormous risks to his life for many years to defend the cause of constitutional government against royal absolutism. He put his head where his mouth was. It would be indecent to take a lofty critical tone towards him because his view is not as democratic as we now would like.

Our aim, then, is one of clarification: if Locke's formulation of the social contract doctrine is not satisfactory—because, say, it is compatible with the class state—how then should it be revised? We examine how such a state could arise in ideal history in order to highlight certain basic features of Locke's view, hoping that getting a clear idea about them may show us how best to revise it.

§2. Background of the Question

1. The question of the franchise is not raised explicitly in the *Second Treatise.* Although there was controversy about redistricting during the Exclusion Crisis of 1679–81, the franchise as such was not the central issue. The basis for thinking that Locke accepts the class state is what he says in the *Second Treatise,* ¶¶140f, where he seems to accept as justified that the franchise be limited to those who met the 40 shilling freehold rule in existence at the time (in land terms, that is roughly 4.5 acres of arable land). Although not a large sum, various estimates indicate that it excluded a large part of the male population, possibly as large as 4/5 at the time of the Exclusion Crisis, though others think it was considerably less and closer to 3/5

or less.[4] These variations do not matter for our purpose of examining legitimacy of the class state in Locke's doctrine.

Locke's complaint against the Crown is that it resists redistricting to bring representation in Parliament in line with the appropriate principle. He says in ¶158: "If . . . the Executive, who has the power of Convoking the Legislative, observing rather the true proportion, than fashion of *Representation*, regulates, not by old custom, but true reason, the *number of Members*, in all places, that have a right to be distinctly represented, which no part of the People however incorporated can pretend to, but in proportion to the assistance, which it [that part of the people however incorporated] affords to the public, it [the executive] cannot be judged, to have set up a new Legislative, but . . . to have rectified the disorders, which succession of time had . . . inevitably introduced."

Now this passage, read together with the whole of ¶¶157–158 and 140, seems to mean by those "that have a right to be distinctly represented" (as opposed to those who have a right to be, say, virtually represented), those who have the right to vote. However, we should not read the passage as accepting property as the sole basis of redistricting. Rather, we should read

4. There are various estimates. J. H. Plumb, *The Growth of Political Stability in England, 1675–1725* (London: Macmillan, 1967), pp. 27ff, gives the estimate of 200,000 as conservative for the size of the electorate at the time of William II. This was perhaps as few as 1/30 of the nation including women, children, and the laboring poor, whom no one considered worthy of political rights (pp. 28f). J. R. Jones in *Country and Court* (Cambridge, Mass.: Harvard University Press, 1979) gives the size of the electorate in Queen Anne's reign as about 250,000 (p. 43). Richard Ashcraft in his *Revolutionary Politics and Locke's Two Treatises of Government* (Princeton: Princeton University Press, 1986) has an account of the electorate pointing out that it tended to increase for two reasons: one was the steady inflation of the time, which lowered the real value of the property qualification; the other was the tendency of Parliament to enlarge the franchise as a way of defending itself against the Crown (pp. 147f). The Whigs under Shaftesbury looked to an electorate of tradesmen, artisans, shopkeepers, and merchants, and most freeholders who prospered at the expense of middle-size landowners and the small gentry (p. 146). Also, the electorate varied from one part of the country to another; in London, for example, Ashcraft thinks there was virtually manhood suffrage in elections of parliamentary representatives and city officials (p. 148). Ashcraft cites Derek Hirst as thinking that in 1641 the electorate may have been as large as 2/5 of the male population (pp. 151f). In his *Authority and Conflict: England, 1603–1658* (Cambridge, Mass.: Harvard University Press, 1986), Hirst says that after Ireton's proposals of 1647–1649, representation was fairer than it was to be again until the later 19th century (p. 330).

¶¶157–158 together as saying that "fair and equal" representation (¶158) is based on both "wealth and inhabitants" (¶157), each given a weight in a manner Locke leaves unspecified.[5]

I assume, then, that Locke accepts the class state as consistent with his view. Our task, as I have said, is to find an explanation of how he could do so, and to reject MacPherson's explanation.

§3. Locke's Reply to Filmer: I: Chapter 4

1. I now turn to the *First Treatise* and to Locke's rejection there of property as a basis of political authority. I begin with a summary of Filmer's views, following Laslett, who in his introduction to his edition of Filmer's writings sums them up as follows:[6]

There is no legitimate government but monarchy only.
There is no legitimate monarchy but paternal only.
There is no paternal monarchy but absolute, that is, arbitrary.
There is no such thing as legitimate aristocracy or democracy.
No legitimate government can be a tyranny.
We are not free by nature but always born subject to obligation.

For our purposes here, perhaps the last statement is most important. And in *First Treatise*, ¶6, Locke would seem to agree. There he says that Filmer's ". . . great Position is, that *Men are not naturally free*. This is the Foundation on which his absolute Monarchy stands. . . . But if this Foundation fails, all his Fabric falls with it, and Governments must be left again to the old way of being made by contrivance, and the consent of Men . . . making use of their Reason to unite together in Society." Thus Locke states a basic foundational difference between himself and Filmer; and he claims that his view returns to an older social contract tradition.

2. Before discussing Locke's views on property, a comment about the idea of property. Property consists, it is often said, in a bundle of rights, with certain conditions imposed as to how those rights can be exercised.

5. On this point, see John Dunn, *Political Thought of John Locke.*
6. See the Introduction by Peter Laslett to his edition of *Patriarcha and Other Political Writings of Sir Robert Filmer* (Oxford: Blackwell, 1949), p. 20.

Different conceptions of property, private or otherwise, specify the bundle of rights in different ways.

For Locke, property—or "propriety in" (as he often says)—is a right to do something, or a right to use something, under certain conditions, a right that cannot be taken from us without our consent.[7] We should distinguish the right itself and its grounds, from the kind of action or thing we have a right to do or to use. Even when the right is the right to use and to have appropriate control over land and natural resources, property does not mean land or resources, even if Locke sometimes seems to talk that way. There is one meaning of property as a bundle of rights: the right (as a bundle) cannot be taken away without our consent. Different rights connect with the different kinds of actions and things we can have property in.

Also we should distinguish at least two uses—not meanings—of "property" according to the kinds of things connected with the bundle of rights in question.

(a) One is Locke's broad use, in which the rights involve lives, liberties, and estates, as found in ¶¶87, 123, 138, 173.

(b) The other is his narrow use, in which the rights involve such things as: fruits of the earth, ¶¶28–32; or land, ¶¶32–39, 47–50; or estates, ¶¶87, 123, 131, 138, 173; or fortunes, ¶¶135, 221.

(c) And then there are indeterminate uses: we cannot tell whether some of these are broad or narrow, for example, ¶94, where Locke declares that: ". . . Government has no other end but the preservation of Property." This is a very strong assertion of the purpose of government, but seems to cover both uses of "property." Others are quite clearly linked to other broad or narrow uses, given the larger context.

3. To proceed: recall that the aim of Locke's argument from cases is to show, against Filmer, that the right of property cannot be the basis of political authority. He does this by making two points.

(a) In the *First Treatise*, Chapter 4, he holds that property in land and resources alone cannot give rise to political authority: my having greater property than those without property gives me no political jurisdiction over them.

(b) In the *Second Treatise*, Chapter 5, he argues that property in land and

---

7. See James Tully, *A Discourse on Property* (Cambridge: Cambridge University Press, 1980), pp. 112–116, with definition on p. 116.

resources can, and did, arise before government; and indeed that one reason for establishing government is for the protection of already existing property.

Thus, for Locke, property neither establishes nor requires political authority, in contrast with Filmer's and the feudal view.

I begin with the first point. The clearest statement of it is in the *First Treatise:* Chapter 4, ¶¶39, 41–43. Filmer had claimed that God gave the world to Adam as Adam's property. Much in these chapters is, like much of the rest of the *First Treatise,* extremely tedious, but some passages are fundamental to Locke's view. After a long discussion Locke says in I: ¶39: ". . . for however, in respect of one another, Men may be allowed to have propriety in their distinct Portions of the Creatures; yet in respect of God the Maker of Heaven and Earth, who is the sole Lord and Proprietor of the whole World, Man's Propriety in Creatures is nothing but that *Liberty to use them,* which God has permitted, and so Man's property may be altered and enlarged, as we see it was here, after the Flood, when other uses of them are allowed, which before were not. From all [of] which I suppose, it is clear, that neither *Adam* nor *Noah,* had any *Private Dominion,* any Property in the Creatures, exclusive of his Posterity, as they should successively grow up into need of them, and come to be able to make use of them." This passage, along with the passage in I: ¶41, contains several central features of Locke's conception of property.

For one thing, property in something (here, "propriety in creatures") is a liberty to use that something for the satisfaction of our needs and requirements. God is always the lord and proprietor of the world itself, of living things and natural resources. But given the fundamental law of nature, which wills the preservation of mankind, and so far as possible, every member of it (including our own person), we have two natural duties: one, to preserve ourselves, the other, to preserve mankind.

4. In view of these two duties, we have two natural rights. These are *enabling rights:* that is, rights we have so that we can fulfill certain duties that are prior in the order of grounds. And from those duties, we also have a third natural right. This Locke describes here as a "liberty to use" inferior things and natural resources as essential means to preserve mankind and ourselves as members of it. From I: ¶41: ". . . it is more reasonable to think, that God who bid Mankind increase and multiply, should rather himself give them all a Right, to make use of the Food and Rayment, and other

Conveniences of Life, the Materials whereof he had so plentifully provided for them; than to make them depend upon the Will of a Man for their Subsistence, who should have Power [right] to destroy them all when he pleased."

Another feature of Locke's view of property is that this liberty of use is not an exclusive right: that is, it is not a right to which that we can appeal to restrict the liberty of use of those who succeed us, when they need to use, or to have access to, the bounty of nature for their legitimate interests. In short, no one can be excluded from the use of, or from the access to, the necessary means of life provided by the great common of the world, except from that which we have made our property subject to the two provisos. This third natural right to the means of preservation is our right, along with every one else, in the use of, or the access to, that great common.

These remarks prepare us for I: ¶¶41–42, in which Locke rejects altogether the idea that property can be the basis of political authority. This seems already clear from the passage in I: ¶41 quoted above. But Locke goes on to say that God has not left us to the mercy of others; nor given any one such property that excludes others, who are in need, from also having a right to the surplus of others' goods: "And therefore no Man could ever have a just Power over the Life of another, by Right of property in Land or Possessions; since it would always be a Sin in any Man of Estate, to let his Brother perish for want of affording him Relief out of his Plenty. As *Justice* gives every Man a Title to the product of his honest Industry, and the fair Acquisitions of his Ancestors descended to him; so *Charity* gives every Man a Title to so much out of another's Plenty, as will keep him from extreme want. . . . [A] Man can no more justly make use of another's necessity, to force him to become his Vassal, by withholding that Relief . . . than he that has more strength can seize upon a weaker, master him to his Obedience, and with a Dagger at his Throat offer him Death or Slavery" (I: ¶42).

This is a strong statement, and I: ¶43 makes the same point. It may seem at first that ¶43 says that even in such extreme situations consent is what establishes political authority. Locke says: "Should anyone make so perverse [a] use of God's Blessings poured on him with a liberal Hand; should any one be Cruel and Uncharitable to that extremity, yet all this would not prove that Propriety in Land, even in this Case, gave any Authority over the Persons of Men, but only that Compact might; since the Authority of the Rich Proprietor, and the Subjection of the Needy Beggar began not from the Possession of the Lord [ownership of property], but the Consent of the poor Man, who preferred being his Subject to starving."

That Locke describes the man of property as making a perverse use of his blessings, and as cruel and uncharitable, means, I think, that he denies the binding force of consent in such a case. Rather, he is saying that whatever political authority there might be (and there may be none) arises from compact: from the consent the poor man gives. As to how much authority there is, Locke goes on to say that if we count such consent as valid, we might as well say that when our stores of grain are full at a time of scarcity and with money in our pocket, when others are starving; or our being on a vessel at sea and able to swim when others are drowning and need our help; in all these and other such cases we could likewise properly demand others' consent to our political authority over them. But Locke believes no such thing; and concludes that no matter what private dominion God gave to Adam (and he says he has proved that God gave Adam no such private dominion), it could never give rise to sovereignty. Only free consent under certain conditions, violated in the cases described, can do that.

5. From the preceding, we may infer three further constraints on ideal history:

(a) Practices and custom, however primitive they may be, must allow for, or secure to, all persons a title to the product of their honest labor. This is *a principle of justice*. (So we have a precept of justice: *to each according to the product of their honest labor.*)

(b) Barring catastrophes, practices and custom must permit no one to fall into extreme want, or to become incompetent and unable to exercise their natural rights and to fulfill their duties in an intelligent manner. This is *a principle of charity*.

(c) The third natural right is to be respected: all have the liberty of use, or of access to, the great common of the world, so that in return for their honest industry they can earn the means of life. This is *a principle of reasonable opportunity*. Here we can't say equal, or fair, opportunity; these terms appear too strong for what Locke has in mind. Nevertheless, this reasonable opportunity is of great significance.

It would seem to follow from these constraints that, in ideal history, it simply cannot happen that the larger part of the adult male population (the fraction without the vote) can be so brutish and so callous as to be incompetent, and hence unfit—because not sufficiently reasonable or rational—to be a party to the social compact. For if we say this, we must also say either that political power can arise from great inequality in real property (land and natural resources) without consent, which Locke denies; or else that the constraints of ideal history are violated: the poor are denied sufficient means out of the surplus of the rest to be able to fulfill their duties to God and intelligently to exercise their natural rights.

To conclude: Locke's view in the *First Treatise* is that *the right of property is conditional*. It is not a right to do what we please with our own, just like that, no matter how the use of our own affects others. Our right—our liberty of use—presupposes that certain background conditions are satisfied. These conditions are indicated by the three principles of justice, charity, and reasonable opportunity. This last implies that those without property must have a reasonable opportunity of employment: the opportunity to earn by their honest labor the means of life and to rise in the world.

§4. Locke's Reply to Filmer: II: Chapter 5

1. Turning to the *Second Treatise,* Locke's argument against Filmer in Chapter 5 is roughly this: His aim (as he states in ¶25) is to show how we might in the first ages of the world, and before the existence of political authority, come to have legitimate property "in several parts of that which God gave to Mankind in common." Locke must answer Filmer here, since he must show how his view can account for, as opposed to justify, the right of property acknowledged on all sides.

Locke holds that God gave the world to all mankind in common, and not to Adam. But this grant of property is understood by Locke not as a grant of collective exclusive ownership—exclusive ownership by mankind as a collective body—but as a liberty that all persons have to use the necessary means of life provided by nature and the right to appropriate them by honest labor so as to satisfy our needs and requirements.[8] All this is done so as to fulfill our two natural duties to preserve mankind and ourselves as members of it.

8. See Richard Tuck, *Natural Rights Theories* (Cambridge: Cambridge University Press, 1979), pp. 166–172.

Two provisos are implicit in this conception:

(a) First proviso: enough, and as good left for others: ¶¶27, 33, 37.[9] This follows because the right of use is not an exclusive proprietorship. Others also have the same right.

(b) Second proviso: spoilage clause: ¶¶31, 36f, 46.[10] This follows because God is always sole proprietor of the earth and its resources. To take more fish, say, than we need as food is to waste and destroy part of God's property.

2. Next we come to *the great Foundation of Property*" (a phrase Locke uses in ¶44) (see ¶¶27, 32, 34, 37, 39, 44f, 51). This foundation is the property we have in our own person, which no one else has a right to (¶27). The labor of our body, the product (the work) of our hands, are properly ours. This too suggests a precept of justice: to each according to the product of his honest labor (¶27).

Again in ¶44: we are masters of ourselves and proprietors of our own person, and the actions and the labor of it, and so we have in ourselves "the great Foundation of Property." What we improve for ourselves is truly our own, and not common property. So labor, in the beginning, gave the right in things.

In ¶¶40–46 Locke presents a version of the labor cost theory of value, for example: that labor accounts for 90 to 99 percent of the value of land. The point of these sections is to argue that the institution of property in land, properly limited, is for everyone's benefit. Those without land need not be sufferers for it. In ¶41 Locke says that a king in a large and potentially fruitful territory in America, rich in land not yet improved by labor, is fed, housed, and clad worse than a day laborer in England. The institution of private property in land, when duly hedged by the constraints of ideal history, is both individually and collectively rational: he holds that it makes us all better off than we would be without it.

9. Locke says: "No man but he can have a right to what that [viz. his labor] is once joined to, at least where there is enough, and as good, left for others." *Second Treatise*, ¶27, p. 288.

10. "As much as any one can make use of to any advantage of life before it spoils; so much he may by his labour fix a Property in. Whatever is beyond this, is more than his share, and belongs to others. Nothing was made by God for Man to spoil or destroy." *Second Treatise*, ¶31, p. 290.

3. We come finally to the introduction of money and the transition to political authority. Locke discusses these matters in: ¶¶36f, 45, 47–50.

(a) A crucial point here is that the introduction of money in effect suspends the spoilage proviso, which says that we can take no more from the bounty of nature than we can use before it spoils. For now by industrious labor we can acquire more than we can use but exchange the surplus for money (or claims to valuable things of various kinds), and thereby accumulate larger and larger holdings in land and natural resources, or whatever. Money allows us to "fairly possess" more land, say, than we can use the product of, "by receiving in exchange for the overplus, Gold and Silver, which may be hoarded up without injury to anyone" (¶50).

(b) In tacitly (without a compact) consenting to the use of money, people "agreed to disproportionate and unequal Possession of the Earth" and did so by "a tacit and voluntary consent" (¶50).

(c) Both property and money come into being before political society and without social compact, and this only by "putting a value on gold and silver and tacitly agreeing in the use of Money" (¶50).[11]

4. Thus, Locke has, I think, a two-stage account of property. The first stage is that of the state of nature in its various phases before political society. Here we may distinguish three phases:

(a) the first ages of the world: ¶¶26–39, 94.
(b) the age of fixing tribal boundaries by consent: ¶¶38, 45.
(c) the age of money and trade arising by consent: ¶¶35, 45, 47–50.

The second stage is that of political authority, and has, it seems, two phases:

(a) the age of paternal monarchy: ¶¶74ff, 94, 105–110, 162.
(b) the age of government by social compact and the regulating of property: ¶¶38, 50, 72f.

In the second stage, it is the age of government by social compact that Locke is mainly concerned with. *In this stage property is conventional:* that is, it is specified and regulated by the positive laws of society. I assume these laws respect all the constraints of the fundamental law of nature we have discussed. They also respect what Locke calls the *"Fundamental Law of Prop-*

---

11. How is this tacit consent related, if at all, to that of ¶¶119–122? Presumably it is different, but how?

erty" in political society: that no one's property can be taken from them, even for the necessary support of the government, without their consent, or the consent of their representatives (¶140).

An important consequence of the conventional nature of (real) property in political society is that a liberal socialist regime[12] is not, I think, incompatible with what Locke says. Indeed, it may be unlikely that the Parliament (the representatives) in Locke's class state would ever enact the laws definitive of socialist institutions. Perhaps so, but that is another matter. The point is only that there need be no violation of the rights of (real) property, as Locke defines them, in such a regime.

Moreover, it is perfectly possible that once political parties form, they may compete with one another for votes, say by urging the expansion of the electorate by lowering, or eliminating, the property qualification. Indeed, this happened in Locke's time, as Parliament tended to look favorably on increases in the franchise, particularly in the cities and towns, in part as way of defending itself against the Crown.[13] Given evolving political and economic conditions within ideal history, there may be good reasons for enough of those with property to favor such legislation. This kind of legislation if passed would not violate, so far as I can see, anything in Locke's account of property. In time, then, there might develop from Locke's class state something like a modern constitutional democratic regime. Has something similar to this actually happened?

§5. Problem of the Class State

1. Finally we come to the problem of the class state in Locke. Recall that this is the problem of how it can happen, consistent with Locke's view, that beginning from the state of nature as a state of equal jurisdiction, all being equal sovereigns as it were, a social compact leading to a class state could be entered into.

One might want to reject this problem as not well posed. That is, one might say that Locke does not in fact accept the class state; at best he only appears to. We cannot fight every political war at once, so he takes them as they come, beginning with the most urgent. As the most urgent problem,

12. Such a regime was envisaged by the English Labor party and the German Social Democrats.

13. See note 4 above.

he opposes royal absolutism. So one ought not to say Locke accepts the class state. He is really not taking any stand on this question, nor on the equality of women.

Now, I sympathize with this reply. It may be correct. For our purposes I simply assume that he does accept the class state in the following weak sense: he thinks such a state could, and in fact did, come about and exist in the English mixed constitution of his day. I don't say that he accepts the class state if this means he fully endorses its values and is satisfied with it.

2. Again, one might reject the problem as not allowing Locke to appeal to reasons of necessity. That is, his thought in accepting the class state, so far as he appears to do so, might be that even in ideal history social conditions can be quite harsh and limiting, so that if a class state is justified, and could come about consistent with his view, that is only because of harsh and limiting conditions. As things get better over time, a class state will no longer be legitimate by Locke's own principles; only a regime founded on a more equal franchise and distribution of property will meet his requirements for legitimacy. Eventually a just constitutional state may come about that answers fully to the ideas of liberty and equality in his doctrine.

As before I am sympathetic to this objection. I don't deny Locke the plea of necessity, as political philosophy must recognize the limits of the possible. It cannot simply condemn the world. Nor do I deny that there are ideas of liberty and equality in Locke that can provide much of, though perhaps not all of, the basis of a conception of what we would regard as a just and equal democratic regime.

Rather, the point is this. For Locke to accept a class state, it is only required that there should exist, in ideal history, some conditions under which, consistent with his view, a class state could come about. To show this to be the case all we need do is to tell one plausible story about such conditions, a story that answers to all the enumerated constraints. We might then conjecture that such is the way Locke may have thought the English constitution could have come about, although of course it did not. (Recall what we said earlier about William the Conqueror.) What we are doing is testing Locke's account of legitimacy. Here it should be stressed that there can be other conditions in which not a class state, but only a state far closer to our present ideals, could come about.

We need to keep in mind the point of this exercise: namely, to illustrate how, in Locke's doctrine, the terms of the social compact and the form of regime depend on various contingencies, including people's bargaining advantages, external to the compact situation. This is because knowledge of these is not excluded. The parties who are to determine the basic principles of the social compact are not behind a "veil of ignorance," as in justice as fairness.[14] The result is that persons enter the compact situation not solely as free and equal, reasonable and rational, but also as in this or that situation with this or that amount of property. Their legitimate interests are shaped accordingly and may set them at odds. If we want to work out a political conception in which the terms of social cooperation and the form of regime are independent of such contingencies, we must find a way to revise the social contract view.

§6. A Just-So Story of the Origin of the Class State

1. I conclude with a brief sketch showing how a class state could arise in ideal history. We have seen that everyone is assumed to act both reasonably and rationally. No one violates their duties under the fundamental law of nature or fails to act rationally in advancing their legitimate interests. These interests are interests in their property in the broad sense, that is, their lives, liberties, and estates, however small their property in land (real property) may be.

Following Joshua Cohen, we say the social compact must satisfy three criteria:[15]

(a) Individual rationality: Each person must reasonably believe that he or she will be at least as well off in the society of the social compact as in the state of nature where each now is. The standard used to decide whether persons are better off is their legitimate interests, as defined above by reference to their property in the broad sense.

(b) Collective rationality: There must be no other alternative social compact (including the form of regime it establishes) such that everyone would prefer it to the agreement in question. Put another way, there is no other agreement that would make some of them better off without making any of the others worse off. (This is simply Pareto.)

(c) Coalition rationality: To cut through great complexities, we simply

14. John Rawls, *Justice as Fairness: A Restatement.* See §6: "The Idea of the Original Position."

15. See Joshua Cohen, "Structure, Choice and Legitimacy: Locke's Theory of the State," pp. 311–323. Together these conditions define the core of a cooperative game.

assume there are only two coalitions: one includes all those with enough property to meet the voting qualification (40 shilling freehold rule, say). Call these people those with (sufficient) property. The other coalition includes those who fail to meet that qualification, although they may have some property less than 40 shillings. Call these people those without (sufficient) property. Coalition rationality now means that both coalitions, and their individual members, think they will do better under the proposed social compact than under any other agreement mutually acceptable to both coalitions. The members of both coalitions must think the agreement better than their coalition's going off on its own, or splitting.

Again to cut through complexities, we assume there are only four alternatives:

(i) class state (with 40 shilling freehold voting qualification).

(ii) democratic state with universal suffrage.

(iii) Split into two states:

(a) a state of those with (sufficient) property.

(b) a state of those without (sufficient) property.

(iv) state of nature, or the status quo.

Once more to cut through complexities (we keep having to do this!), we assume that there are no preferences for the form of the state as such: regimes are judged by people solely by reference to the expected fulfillment of their legitimate interests (those compatible with their duties under the fundamental law of nature and specified in terms of their property in the broad sense).

2. Now, a bit of elaboration: Both the class state and the democratic state are constitutional states. That is, they both satisfy the rule of law, as Locke defines it in ¶¶124–126, 136f, 142. So even those who do not meet the property qualification can expect greater protection for their lives, liberties, and estates, however small, than in a state of nature. By individual rationality, then, the class state is to be preferred to the state of nature.

There is, however, an opposition of interests between the class state and the democratic state. Those with property prefer the class state, those without property prefer the democratic state. The propertied fear that those without property may use the democratic franchise to redistribute their real wealth.

(a) Let's assume that those with property will refuse to agree to the democratic state and prefer to split, or go off on their own, instead. This they can do under the law of nature, provided that the principle of charity is not violated. I understand Locke's view as permitting withholding cooperation in these circumstances (¶95).

(b) Those without property have to decide, then, whether to go it alone in a democratic state, or to join the class state with those who have property. If they decide that joining the class state is indeed rational for them, the class state is coalitional rational. Both coalitions prefer it to any other mutually acceptable alternative.

Now suppose, as Locke would require, that the class state meets the following principles:

(a) Everyone is a citizen with the protections of the rule of law (¶120), including, of course, passive citizens (those without sufficient property to vote).

(b) Citizenship carries with it a reasonable opportunity to acquire, with diligence and industry, sufficient property to meet the voting qualification. This means that opportunities for gainful employment must be guaranteed.

(c) Moreover, these opportunities are made secure by the principle of justice, which among other precepts, guarantees for all the product of their honest labor.

(d) Finally, by the principle of charity, the class state recognizes a claim on the surplus of society so as to keep everyone from extreme want.

These principles are among the terms those with property offer those without property. We assume that these terms, once accepted, will be honored: that is, strictly complied with and that everyone knows this. Those without property do not have to calculate how likely it is that the propertied are going to renege, and so on.

3. Given all these stipulations, we can see how the class state might arise as follows:

Conditions of Acceptance: Let X be the proposed social compact. X is agreed to when it meets the following three conditions:

(a) Individual Rationality: all individuals prefer X to the state of nature.

(b) Collective Rationality: there is no alternative Y such that all individuals prefer Y to X.

(c) Coalition Rationality: with two coalitions A and B, there is no alternative Y such that either A or B prefers Y to X, or such that either A or B can enforce Y by going off on its own, or by splitting.

Locke's conjectured social compact:

(a) the set of alternatives is: Class State, Democratic State, Split, State of Nature.

(b) Preferences of Propertied: Class, Split, Democratic, State of Nature.

(c) Preferences of Propertyless: Democratic, Class, Split, State of Nature. Both coalitions prefer a class state to a split, and since the propertied can enforce a split, the chosen social compact is the Class State; the propertyless cannot prevent a split, so they join the Class State.

4. If this story is sound and compatible with ideal history, Locke's mixed constitution with its forty shilling franchise can arise. Other stories, however, are also possible. It is an important aspect of Locke's view that many different forms of regime could come about. His view does not require a class state; it simply permits it. Cohen describes other conditions, like those of the nineteenth century, under which it is plausible to hold that democracy would be agreed to. Locke himself describes in ¶¶107–111 how monarchy came about in the early "golden age" when properties were small and roughly equal and before vain ambition corrupted men's minds.

What is important about this is that what is basic to Locke's view is the kind of justification it proposes for political institutions. When people agree to the social compact he views them as individuals who know their particular social and economic interests as well as their position and status in society. This means that the justifications citizens give to one another in arriving at the social compact take these interests into account.

One aim of our story about the class state was to defend Locke against MacPherson's misinterpretation. But in doing so we have uncovered a disturbing feature of his view. Not only does it make citizens' rights and liberties depend on historical contingencies in ways we would like to avoid, but it also raises the question of whether the constitutional settlement should not be reconsidered after each important shift in the distribution of political and economic power. It would seem that the basic freedoms and opportunities of a constitutional regime should be fixed far more solidly than that, and not be subject to such changes.

Hence, as I have said, we must find some way to revise Locke's contract doctrine. Both Rousseau and Kant make revisions, and justice as fairness follows their lead. In conclusion, I should stress that I am not criticizing Locke the man, who as I said was a great figure, and whose social compact view was well framed for his purposes at the time of the Exclusion Crisis. We are probing his view and finding it is not well framed for our purposes. That is not surprising, since as Collingwood would say, our problems are not his problems and they call for different solutions.

HUME

HUME I

"Of the Original Contract"

§1. Introductory Remarks

So far we've talked about Hobbes and Locke, and have gone over them rather quickly.[1] That is inevitable, given the scope and aim of these lectures, and I'm not going to apologize. I just hope you are aware that there is, of course, much more that we could talk about in each of them. The problem facing us today is to get some sort of natural transition from talking about Hobbes and Locke, who are two writers in the social contract tradition, to talking about Hume and Mill, who are two writers in the utilitarian tradition. We seek a point of view that highlights the main points of contrast between them and brings out the philosophical differences that divide them and concerning which the debate took place.

One might say that any main philosophical tradition, whether in political thought or elsewhere, often bases itself on certain intuitive ideas, and requires the elaboration and development of these ideas; and you find various authors over time doing that in different ways, and so different variants arise. The intuitive idea of the social contract tradition is the notion of agreement—agreement between equal persons who are at least rational, and their somehow agreeing to a certain way of being governed, either, as in Hobbes's case, to authorize a sovereign, or in Locke's case to join a community and then to organize somehow the will of the majority to set up the legislative power or the constitution. That notion of agreement is, I think, intuitively appealing. If I agree to something, then I am bound by the terms of the agreement, and that goes back, you might say, to the basic idea

1. [The two Hume lectures are derived from transcriptions of recording tapes of lectures delivered on March 4 and 11, 1983, for Rawls's class in Modern Political Philosophy at Harvard University. Relevant passages from Rawls's handwritten lecture notes have been added. —Ed.]

of consent, or promising. I think Locke takes the notion of promising as somehow given, as something that we all understand. There is not any attempt on his part to derive it from the fundamental laws of nature.

Of course, the social contract view will vary in many ways, depending on how the notion of agreement is spelled out in some sort of detail. What are the conditions of agreement? Who agrees to it? How are the persons who agree described? What are their intentions? What are their interests? A lot of other things have to be developed and worked out. We made a contrast between Hobbes and Locke when, in the case of Hobbes, I emphasized the point that he seems to be concerned with giving everyone compelling reasons, addressed to their own interests, for why it is rational for them to want an effective sovereign to continue to exist. That's a notion, then, that would try to base obligations on peoples' rational and fundamental interests. In Hobbes there is not, on the whole, an appeal to the past. If the sovereign exists now, then everyone has an interest in wanting the sovereign to continue to exist, and it does not matter how the sovereign power actually arose in the past. We are obliged, each of us, in terms of our fundamental interests, to support an effective sovereign now.

Locke's view is, of course, quite different. It begins with a condition of equal rights in the state of nature, and then imagining that through a series of agreements over time, each of these agreements having to satisfy certain conditions, a regime is established. For Locke, a legitimate regime will be one that could have been established in a certain way and that meets certain conditions. This is true whether or not any regime can be shown to have come about in this way historically. Therefore, in his case legitimacy depends on the *form of the regime,* and how it *could have come about,* and its actual protection of certain legitimate rights.

If you spell out the contrasts here between the Lockean and the Hobbesian arguments—the form that they would take, say, in public discussion in 1688 and 1699—a Hobbist would say, after William and Mary were securely established, that everyone had an obligation to comply with their regime because it was an effective sovereign. If a sovereign is effective then we are obliged to support that regime. Whereas a Lockean argument would actually be somewhat different. It would say, presuming that we apply Locke's argument to the same situation, that the previous regime had violated the rights of the people. Political power had then reverted to the people, and through the process of revolution and restoration a new regime had been set up that respected the rights of the people. "Respecting the rights of the people" means that it is a legitimate regime, one that could be contracted into from a state of equal rights. So, those arguments of Hobbes and Locke are rather different, although both do have a kind of social contract view involving the notion of agreement.

The utilitarian tradition has a different sort of intuitive idea. It involves the idea of the general interest, or general well being of society, of public good, public interest—all different phrases that you will find Hume uses. And utilitarian doctrine starts from the idea of producing the greatest social (or public) good. On this view we have a reason for supporting a government or supporting a regime if, very roughly, its continued existence and effectiveness promotes the welfare of the people, or would lead to a greater welfare or to greater well-being than any regime that could be set up as an alternative to it at the time. The utilitarian, then, will make arguments that will appeal to the general well-being or the general good of society. Again, there are many refinements that have to be made in the notion of well-being, and in going deeper into Hume and Mill we'll look into some of the problems involved in doing that. One ought to notice that the notion of promises, or of origins, or of contracts do not enter into the utilitarian view in any way. What the utilitarian does is to look to the present and future and simply ask whether the present form of regime, the present organization of social institutions, is such as to promote the general welfare in the best and most effective way.

The utilitarian view differs from Hobbes *inter alia* in these three ways: (a) Utilitarianism rejects psychological egoism [except for Bentham], and it insists on the significance of the sentiments of affection and benevolence. Although here, Hume's thesis of limited generosity is important in his account of justice and politics. (b) Utilitarianism rejects Hobbes's relativistic conventionalism regarding the distinction between right and wrong, and insists on the reasonableness and objectivity of the principle of utility. (c) Utilitarianism rejects Hobbes's view that political authority rests on force. It maintains that instead political authority is founded on governments' working to the good of society as a whole (for social welfare), as that is defined by the principle of utility, which different utilitarians will define in different ways.

Before I actually turn to Hume I might point out that he is one of a long line of utilitarian writers, only a few of whom we will be able to discuss. Utilitarianism was, and still is perhaps, the most influential and longest continuing tradition in English speaking moral philosophy. While it perhaps can claim no writer of the stature of Aristotle and Kant (their ethical works being in a class by themselves), taking the tradition as a whole, and viewing its extent and continuity and ever increasing refinement in certain parts of the view, utilitarianism is perhaps unique in its collective brilliance. It has run at least from the early part of the 18th century to the present time and has been marked by a long line of brilliant writers who have learned from each other. These include Frances Hutcheson, Hume, and Adam Smith; Jeremy Bentham, P. Y. Edgeworth, and Henry Sidgwick, the main classical utilitarians; and John Stuart Mill, whose views include many non-utilitarian features. As a result, having evolved continuously over nearly three centuries, it is probably the most impressive tradition in moral philosophy.

One must remember that utilitarianism is historically part of a doctrine of society, and is not simply a detached philosophical doctrine. The utilitarians were also political theorists and had a psychological theory. Also, utilitarianism has had considerable influence in certain parts of Economics. Part of the explanation for this is that if we look at the more important economists in the English tradition before 1900 and the well-known utilitarian philosophers, we'll find that they're the same people; only Ricardo is missing. Hume and Adam Smith were both utilitarian philosophers and economists, and the same is true of Bentham and James Mill, John Stuart Mill (though he is questionably a utilitarian, for reasons I shall discuss later) and Sidgwick; and Edgeworth, while he was known primarily as an economist, was something of a philosopher, at least a moral philosopher. It is not until 1900 that this overlap in the tradition stops. Sidgwick and the great economist Marshall were both in the same department at Cambridge when they decided to found a separate department of economics, I believe in about 1896. Since that time there has been a split, although utilitarianism still influences economics, and welfare economics has a close connection historically to the utilitarian tradition. Still, since 1900 the tradition has divided into two more or less mutually-ignoring groups, the economists and the philosophers, to the reciprocal disadvantage of both;

at least insofar as economists concern themselves with political economy and so-called welfare economics, and philosophers with moral and political philosophy. This division is not easy to rectify given the pressures of specialization, and much else. It is also very difficult nowadays to get a sufficient grasp of topics in both subjects for one person intelligently to discuss them.

Of course, I haven't time to cover all the important utilitarians, and therefore, I am just going to talk about Hume and Mill and attempt to give some of the flavor of this alternative view and the intuitive idea that underlies it. For Hume, I suggest that you read "Of the Original Contract," and the *Enquiry Concerning the Principles of Morals* (1751), with special attention to sections I–V, IX, and Appendix III (roughly 80 pages in the Oxford edition, and slightly over half of the whole).[2]

First, a word about Hume the man:

(a) His dates: 1711–1776.

(b) He was born into a Scottish gentry family in Berwick, not far south of Edinburgh.

(c) He attended University of Edinburgh beginning at age 11—for a few years.

(d) At age 18 (1729) he was seized with the idea of writing the *Treatise*.

(e) Some significant dates in Hume's life:

   (i) 1729–34: Hume read and reflected at home.

   (ii) 1734–37: Hume lived in France where he worked on the *Treatise*.

   (iii) 1739–40: *Treatise* published when Hume returned to England.

   (iv) 1748, 1751: Publication of *Enquiry Concerning Principles of Understanding* and of *Morals* (respectively).

   (v) 1748: "Of the Original Contract," which appeared in the third edition of Hume's *Essays Moral and Political* as a new essay in that edition.

2. [Rawls's 1979 lecture notes have the following paragraph here. The lectures on Sidgwick referred to below appear in the Appendix to this volume. —Ed.]
   "My aims here are limited: I shall focus entirely on what I shall call the *Historical Tradition,* and distinguish three variants of utilitarianism: (a) that of *Hume,* which I discuss today and next time . . .
   (b) Then I shall take up the *Classical* line of Bentham-Edgeworth and Sidgwick.
   (c) Finally, J. S. Mill.
   Our task is to relate these in some way as we proceed."

What was the guiding idea of the *Treatise* which seized Hume's imagination and led him to labor on it more or less in isolation for ten years? We can only surmise from the work itself.

(a) The key I think lies in the subtitle: *A Treatise of Human Nature: Being an Attempt to Introduce the Experimental Method of Reasoning into MORAL SUBJECTS.*

(b) A word on the *meaning* of "moral"—it is not the same as today, for it included *psychology* and topics concerned with *social theory.*

(c) "Experimental" has also changed in that it has become more *specific.* For Hume it meant *methods of science—an appeal to experience and observation,* and thought experiments and theory. *Newton* was the great exemplar, as becomes clear from the introduction to the *Treatise.* Hume aims to *apply* his methods to moral subjects: that is, the subjects related to understanding the first principles that account for (1st Bk.) human beliefs and knowledge; (2nd Bk.) human passions, that is, feelings and emotions, desires and sentiments, character and will; (3rd Bk.) the human phenomena of the *moral* sentiments (more narrowly speaking), including our capacity for making moral judgments and how we do this; how far we can be moved to act from these judgments, and so on.

(d) Hume approached these topics in a completely different way than Locke:

> (i) Locke is like a *constitutional lawyer* working within the system of law defined by the Fundamental Law of Nature; and Locke argues the case for resistance to the Crown within a mixed constitution within that framework. The argument proceeds within the moral system of the FLN; it is, as it were, *legal* and *historical.*
>
> (ii) Hume's view is that of a *naturalist* observing and studying the phenomena of human institutions and practices, and the role of moral concepts, judgments, and sentiments, in supporting these institutions and practices, and in regulating human conduct.
>
> (iii) Hume wants to ascertain the *first principles* that govern and explain these phenomena, the moral phenomena—judgments and approvals, etc.—included. Much as Newton ascertained the first principles of the laws of motion, Hume stressed certain *laws of association* as 1st principles re knowledge and belief; and he traced moral judgments in the *Treatise* as deriving importantly from our

capacity for sympathy—which is replaced in the *Enquiry* by the Principle of Humanity. Hume's account of the "judicious spectator" is one of the most important ideas in moral philosophy (discussed in Lecture II below).

(iv) These details we cannot cover here: the point to *stress* is that Hume's background and philosophical point of view are altogether different from Locke's. He approaches the subject of morality from the point of view of an observing naturalist. Even when Hume and Locke are discussing the same topic, they do so from a different point of view. They are not in general trying to answer the same questions.

§2. Hume's Critique of Locke's Social Contract

Now I will turn to Hume's critique of Locke's social contract view. It appears in at least one prominent place—in Hume's essay "Of the Original Contract," which appeared in 1748 in the third edition of his *Moral and Political Essays*. The essay is divided into four parts. I often find it helpful to count paragraphs: ¶¶1–19 is the first part; ¶¶20–31 is the second; and ¶¶32–45, the third part, presents Hume's philosophical argument contrary to Locke's social contract. And then ¶¶46–49 is the conclusion.

The way Hume organized the essay, it isn't clear where the breaks are, and I think it might be helpful to have some preliminary idea of what is in it. In part 1, Hume begins by granting that both the Tory view of the divine right of kings, and the Whig view that government rests on the consent of the people, have some truth in them—but not, of course, in the way in which they each intend. The truth that Hume concedes would hardly be the sort of truth that the proponents of each of those views would want. For example, he's most brief with the Tory view, and somewhat deliberately insulting, I would assume. He says that the Crown may rule by divine right, but no more so than does a thief who takes my purse, because all powers derive from the supreme being (¶3). This is obviously not intended seriously, but I suppose is intended to wake up the reader in the course of the argument.

Hume then mocks the Whig view, which, he says, supposes "that there is a kind of *original contract* by which the subjects have tacitly reserved the power of resisting their sovereign whenever they find themselves aggrieved by that authority with which they have . . . voluntarily entrusted him" (¶1). I assume Locke and his social contract view to be the target, or among the targets of Hume's argument here, although Locke is not actually mentioned when Hume says (¶4) that if by the original contract is meant the first origin of government, say in the woods and deserts when people first associated together, then it cannot be denied that all government at first is founded on contract. For at that time people were nearly equal in bodily force and mental powers, and culture and education having not yet given rise to inequality. In those circumstances, then, consent was necessary for political authority as well as for people's sense of the advantages that peace and social order would bring for them. Yet, he goes on to say that "this consent was very long imperfect, and could not be the basis of a regular administration" (¶5). That is to say, the idea of social compact, or the original compact, as Locke presents it, was beyond the comprehension of people at that time. And since that is the time when government first originated, he therefore thinks that Locke's doctrine—which he says affirms "that all men are still born equal and owe allegiance to no prince or government unless bound by the obligation and sanction of a promise" (¶6)—is hardly strictly applicable, or strictly accurate, even with regard to this first origin of government. Although it does have, as he says, some truth in it.

Hume then proceeds to enumerate a number of objections which he thinks show that consent can hardly count as a foundation of government and a basis of obligation at the present time. For example, he says that social contract doctrine is not recognized or even known by most parts of the world. "We find everywhere princes who claim their subjects as their property [that being an actual practice at the time] and assert their independent right of sovereignty from conquest or succession" (¶7). He adds that magistrates would imprison propounders of the theories of consent as dangerous and seditious people, "if our friends did not before shut you up as delirious for advancing such absurdities" (¶7). (This seems a somewhat extreme remark, but this is his view of the matter.) If such doctrines are not even accepted in most places, and if they're not now understood, how can consent be binding? His point is that in order for consent to have the kind of effects that Locke says it would, consent would have to be publicly recognized and understood to be the basis of political obligation. Hume is not offhand denying that possibility. He is just saying that those are not the present circumstances. So, consent cannot be the basis of government or authority. In any case, he goes on to say, the original consent being ancient, that is, "too old to fall under the knowledge of the present generation" (¶8), it cannot be binding now. For parents cannot bind their descendants down to remote generations (¶8).

Another objection Hume makes is that almost all governments that presently exist were founded on usurpation or conquest (he mentions William the Conqueror in 1066), and in any case they have arisen through force and violence "without any pretense of fair consent or voluntary subjection of the people" (¶9). In some cases they have arisen by marriage, by dynastic considerations and so forth, which treat the people of a country as part of a dowry or legacy (¶11). Still another objection is that elections do not carry any great weight for they are often controlled by a combination of a few great figures, and the social contract idea of consent, a particular originating consent, has no correspondence to the facts (¶12). Nor would the consent given in the Revolution of 1688 and 1689 be any different, on Hume's view. He says that a majority of about seven hundred people (members of Parliament), and not the nation of some ten million as a whole, determined where the political authority would lie at that time (¶15). So, in conclusion, consent has rarely taken place, and when it does take place, on Hume's view it is so irregular and limited to so few people that it can hardly have any such authority as Locke ascribes to it. Again, he doesn't mention Locke by name.

Beginning in part 2, ¶¶20–31, Hume says there must be some foundation of government other than consent. I now want to give a rough account of this argument. He does not deny that consent is "one just foundation of government," and when it does obtain he says that it is "surely the best and the most sacred of any" (¶20). But he argues that because it so seldom actually is the basis, it can't be the only one. He says that for consent to bind and to be a foundation of government certain conditions have to hold, and he gives a series of reasons why they do not. For one thing the social contract view presumes a state of knowledge of and regard for justice that people do not actually have. On Hume's view, it asks too much of human nature. It asks for a kind of state of perfection that is much superior to our past or present state.

Again, the social contract view presupposes that people believe their obligation to government depends on their consent. But, common sense nowhere supposes this. People think, actually, that their allegiance to a certain prince—who "from long possession has acquired a title independent of their choice or inclination" (¶22)—is decided by their place of birth. And it is absurd to hold that past consent is a significant basis of political obligation when the people who are alleged to consent do not themselves believe that allegiance depends on their agreements (¶23). Then in ¶24, an often quoted paragraph, and a very strong one, Hume says that to suppose that a poor peasant has a free choice to leave the country when he knows no foreign language and has no funds to depart and to make a fresh start abroad, is like supposing that someone, by remaining in a vessel at sea, freely consents to the domination of the captain, though he was carried aboard while asleep, and to leave, must jump overboard and drown. So, what Hume is saying is that to suppose that peasants or other working people—any but perhaps the few hundred who determine the form of regime—consent in any way that's binding, would be like saying that the person taken aboard the ship while asleep had given his consent to be aboard. The most plausible case of passive or tacit consent, Hume thinks, is that which binds a foreigner who settles in a country the government and the laws of which he is acquainted with ahead of time. In that case, in Hume's view, although the allegiance is more voluntary than that of a native subject, the government actually expects less of it and depends less on it (¶27).

Hume says in ¶28 that if one generation died all at once, and another took its place as a group all at once, suddenly arriving at the age of reason with sense enough to choose their government, they then might by general consent establish their form of civil polity without regard to precedent. But the conditions of human life are not like that, and from its circumstances, with "one man every hour going out of the world, another coming into it," we can see that a new consent for each generation is impossible in any effective way. In order to achieve stability (a necessity in government) "the new brood should conform themselves to the established constitution" and make no "violent innovations" (¶28).

Finally, Hume remarks that to say that "all lawful government arises from the consent of the people" is to "do them [governments] far more honor than they actually deserve or even expect and desire from us" (¶30).

Starting with ¶31, Hume introduces what I call the philosophical critique of Locke's view. He begins by distinguishing between natural duties, for example duties like love of children, gratitude toward our benefactors, etc., and duties that are founded on a sense of obligation—that is, duties that presuppose a recognition of the general interests and necessities of society and the impossibility of orderly social life if these duties are neglected. He calls these latter duties "artificial duties." The term "artificial" has of course changed since Hume's time. Then it was a term which meant artifice of reason, conveying a notion that such duties are in an important way rational. When Charles the Second first went into Saint Paul's Cathedral after it was rebuilt from Christopher Wren's design after the fire, Wren stood with him under the dome waiting with great apprehension to see what Charles would say. He was greatly relieved when Charles looked up and he said that it was "awful and artificial"—not very high praise today, but then it meant both awe inspiring and rational.

Among the artificial duties are (a) those of justice, a regard for the property of others; (b) fidelity, keeping one's promises; and (c) the civic duty of allegiance to government. Hume's philosophical argument against Locke here is that these duties, justice, fidelity, and allegiance, are explained and justified by the notion of *utility*, that is to say, by reference to "the general necessities and interests of society." (Particularly relevant here are ¶¶35–38 and ¶45.) If the duties of justice and fidelity were not generally recognized and honored by members of society, then on Hume's view orderly social life would be impossible. "Society cannot possibly be maintained without the authority of magistrates" (¶35). This is the basic philosophical explanation, he thinks, of these duties. Thus it is quite pointless, Hume thinks, to try to justify, or to explain our allegiance to government, by an appeal to the duty of fidelity, or keeping promises, that is, by reference to some presumed or actual social compact based on the consent of individuals. For if we ask why we should honor any compact or agreement that we have made, or to treat individual consent as binding, Hume claims that we have no alternative but to resort to the principle of utility as an explanation. Therefore, when asked for the grounds of our allegiance to government, instead of taking the extra step of appealing to the principle of fidelity to a presumed contract why not appeal directly to the principle of utility? Nothing is gained by way of a philosophical justification by founding the duty of allegiance on the duty of fidelity. In this sense, Hume regards Locke's social compact view, we might say, as an unnecessary shuffle, and moreover, one that tends to conceal that the justification for all duties must appeal to the general necessities of society, or what Hume in other contexts calls "utility."

Hume's conclusion, therefore, is that as a philosophical doctrine, the social contract is not only implausible, and contradictory to common sense in that it goes against all kinds of things that people actually believe, and it is against widespread political opinion, as he argued in the earlier parts of the essay. But it is also superficial in that it fails to bring out what has to be the real ground of political obligation, namely, the general necessities and interests of society.

Hume comments at the end of the essay, in ¶48, that in morals it is impossible to find anything that is new, and that opinions that are new are almost always false. He believes that in questions of morals, it is the general opinion and practice of mankind that is decisive when it exists. He says, "New discoveries are not to be expected in these matters." In other words, he regards Locke's view, which he finds to be historically inaccurate, as a newfound doctrine, and one that therefore goes against the general practice and opinion of humankind.

How are we to assess Hume's criticism of Locke? His critique is forceful and convincing, or at any rate highly plausible in many respects, but weaker in others. I think it may be said that Hume's essay (and Bentham's later essay, although Bentham says essentially the same thing that Hume does) was historically very influential in weakening the social contract view. There tend to be, at least in England, no successors to a doctrine like Locke's. On that evidence, Hume's essay was historically very effective.

Hume, however, seems to read Locke as saying that our allegiance to government as it exists *now* depends upon original consent, or an original compact, some generations in the past, and that it is this consent that binds us now. But Locke does not actually say this. He does not believe that the consent of the ancestors can bind the descendants, and he says this explicitly in ¶116 of the *Second Treatise:* "Whatever engagements or promises any one has made for himself, he is under obligation of them, but *cannot* by any *Compact* whatsoever, bind his children or posterity." Each person is born, Locke thinks, to natural freedom, even now. And this state we can only leave by our actions after we have attained the age of reason. So Hume overlooks in Locke the notion of what I call "joining consent," as opposed to "originating consent."

Again, Hume does not note the contrast in Locke between expressed consent and passive or tacit consent, another difference that is important. Locke says that anyone who has by actual agreement given consent to be a subject of a government must remain so; while those who submit to a government simply because they own and enjoy land under its protection (tacit consent), regain the liberty to join another government if they no longer possess and enjoy the land. They may obey the laws and receive the protection of the laws, but are not actually members of the commonwealth unless they have entered into it by express consent (¶¶119–122).

A more important and fundamental aspect of Locke's doctrine that Hume fails to see, or at least fails to take account of in his argument, is that it has two parts. In speaking about Locke's social contract criterion, I mentioned that one part, the first part, is that to be legitimate, a constitution must be such that each person could have contracted into it from a state of equal political jurisdiction. I discussed what is involved in that notion of contracting "into"—not, of course, a very precise notion, but an important element of Locke's view which cannot be put aside.

The other part of his social contract criterion addresses the question of when an existing, legitimate constitution binds particular individuals, who are then full citizens and subjects of the regime. Locke here discusses joining consent, and he makes the distinction, discussed above, between express consent and passive consent. But the important point is that if this joining consent is to be binding, it must be the case that the form of the regime is legitimate (according to the first part of the social contract criterion). Locke is careful to say that promises extorted by superior force are invalid. He says it in ¶¶176, 186, 189, and 196 of the *Second Treatise*. I presume he would say the same thing in the case of illegitimate regimes. Passive consent, or express consent even, if they are as it were forced, fall under the same comments that he makes in these paragraphs about promises.

One should add as a consistent part of Locke's view that individuals have a *natural duty* to support a legitimate regime when it does exist and when it is working effectively. This duty we might say arises from the fundamental law of nature and does not depend on anyone's consent. Locke says in his account of revolution, when he is explaining how one can oppose the Crown, that to overthrow or alter a just constitution is one of the great crimes one can perform. I assume that in order to justify that, there would be an implicit appeal to the fundamental law of nature. So I am supposing that in Locke, if one has a just regime, then there is a duty we *all* have, *regardless* whether we consent, to comply with its laws; this is a consequence of the fundamental law of nature.

So consider then Locke's account of how the English people at any given time could be bound to an existing regime, even if it originated in force and violence at some time in the past. He is able to give an account of that. His account would be that the present regime is legitimate if it has a form that *could* have been freely contracted into from a position of equal right, even if it *actually* reached its present form almost by accident or through various changes over time. If it now has the correct form—one that could be contracted into—then people are individually bound to it in virtue of their natural duty, arising from the fundamental law of nature, to support a legitimate regime.

If all this is right, then the really substantive issue of importance between Locke and Hume is whether Locke's social contract doctrine, applied to the form of a political regime, and being a criterion that is hypothetical, would select as right and just the very same family of political regimes or constitutions that would be selected by Hume's notion of the general necessities and interest of society, or, in other words, his notion of utility. Is Locke's social contract criterion, the first part of it, going to lead to the same forms of regime being considered legitimate as will Hume's principle of utility? Or will they be different? That is one way to understand the really substantive issue between them. And Hume never really discusses that issue. In fact he does not even seem to be aware of this fundamental matter. Hume is very effective in criticizing the notion of joining consent of individuals which is part of Locke's general account of political obligation. Or at least I think you should consider whether that is so. But Hume never really discusses whether Locke's criterion of agreement beginning from a state of equal right, and his own criteria of general advantage, are going to lead to the same form of regimes as being legitimate. These criteria offhand seem quite different. Certainly they don't mean the same thing, so one might assume that they would lead to different outcomes. You could at least assume they are different criteria in the absence of a lot of argument to the contrary and explanation of both of the views, including what the notion of utility is. We will consider this point in the next lecture. In the meantime, you should think about whether or not these two criteria for a legitimate regime are the same thing, or whether the notion of equal right is going to lead to a difference with Hume's view of utility.

HUME II

Utility, Justice, and the Judicious Spectator

§1. Remarks on the Principle of Utility

As I was saying in the last lecture, the really substantive question between Hume and Locke which comes to me as I read the essay "Of the Original Contract" is whether Locke's social contract doctrine, when applied as a criterion to the form of a political regime, will select the very same family of constitutions or regimes as legitimate or just that would be selected by Hume's principle of utility.[1] Hume, as I mentioned, never discusses, and in fact, never seems to be aware of this fundamental matter. Furthermore, his account of utility is extremely loose in that essay; it means simply the general interests and necessities of society.

Now, in some sense, Locke's criterion would include that principle. That is, if people proceed from the state of nature to political society by consent, with no coercion, etc., then one would suppose that those agreements, freely entered into, would include the general principle of Hume's and promote the general interests of society. Therefore, one might want to ask, "Well, what is the difference?"

Recall that in Locke's system of institutional change, beginning from the state of nature, there is a series of undertakings to which rational persons consent freely and voluntarily. Each of these changes, in Locke's view, would be collectively rational, barring accident and catastrophe and so on. So, we are assuming a sort of idealized process of such contractual agreements. Locke plainly is assuming that it was collectively rational for everyone to consent to, say, the introduction of money and the many other changes that take place. So, beginning with the state of nature, a well or-

---

1. [Transcription of March 11, 1983, lecture, with additions from Rawls's handwritten lecture notes. —Ed.]

dered commonwealth with a legitimate regime must then, in Locke's view, improve everyone's situation with respect first to the state of nature, and then to each of the subsequent stages. Therefore, Locke's regime would seem to satisfy Hume's condition of answering to the general interests and necessities of society. So, both principles, both Hume's and Locke's, are stated in a sufficiently loose and general way that its hard to tell whether and in what respects they are going to differ. Although, as I mentioned before, they surely don't mean the same thing, and you might say their basic foundation is very different.

Suppose we give a stricter sense to the principle of utility, and take it to mean that a regime is legitimate if, and only if, of all the forms of regime that might be possible, or that are available at some moment, or at some time historically, it is that regime which is most likely to lead to, or most likely to produce, the greatest net sum of social advantages (we might also use the term "social utility") at least in the long run.

We are imagining that you can in some way define the notion of the "sum of social advantages." Instead of talking about Hume's "general interest and necessities of society," we've introduced the notion of the greatest net sum of advantages, both now and in the future. Would this be the same as Locke's view or not? Again, it doesn't sound the same. Take the case that most concerns Locke in the *Second Treatise*, that is, the case of royal absolutism, or arbitrary rule of the Crown within a mixed monarchy. Locke intended always to exclude such a regime as legitimate, and his argument is set up for that purpose. He argues that that form of regime cannot be contracted into. Does the principle of utility as we have now stated it allow for royal absolutism or not? One might say that it may in fact do so, but it would require a lot of argument. It would depend on circumstances and various contingencies, and it is not at all obvious that royal absolutism would either be excluded or allowed.

I mentioned last time that in arguing against Locke towards the end of the essay "Of the Original Contract," and in assuming that Locke's appeal to promises is unnecessary, Hume simply denies what Locke asserts. He doesn't face up to the possibility of using the social contract as a test of the form of a regime. In much the same way, Locke in turn simply denies what Filmer asserts. (See Locke Lecture I on Filmer.) Locke is assuming that the notions of contract, promise, and other notions are not to be derived, or at least he doesn't make any attempt to derive them, from the notion of the fundamental law of nature. So, we get a case again where there is not really a confrontation of the two views at the most basic level.

Now, before saying more about Hume, I want to try to specify the utilitarian view in such a way as to make its principles appear at least to have more precision than Hume's general phrase, "the general interest and necessities of society." To do this I am going to think of utilitarianism in the classical sense of principles associated with Bentham and Edgeworth and Sidgwick.

The basic idea is that one is going to define a notion of the good that is independent from the notion of the right. That is, we introduce a notion of the good, say as pleasure, or absence of pain, or some sort of agreeable feeling, or as the satisfaction of desire, or the fulfillment of interests of individuals. If we care to, we can idealize that and say that the good is the satisfaction of the rational interests, or the rational preferences, of individuals. In saying that that is independent from the notion of the right, I mean that we can explain the notion of pleasure, or absence of pain, or agreeable feeling, or the notion of fulfillment or satisfaction of desire, or the notion of the fulfillment of rational preference—we can introduce and explain all those notions without saying anything about right and wrong. We can introduce them independently of any notions that intuitively would be characterized as having to do with right and wrong. So, if we say we are going to maximize the fulfillment of desires, then that means that we would include evil desires as well as the good ones. There would not be any constraint coming from the notion of right and wrong on what those desires might be.

The first step, then, would be to introduce independently the notion of the good; and the next step would be to define the right as that which maximizes the good. In order to get a traditional utilitarian view, the idea of the good would have to take the form I have indicated: that is, it would have to be pleasure, or the satisfaction of desires, or the satisfaction of rational preference. If we introduce another notion of the good, say that of human perfection, or human excellence, or something of that sort, then we would not get a traditional utilitarian view, but what we might call a perfectionist view.

If we take the principle of utility and apply it to social institutions, we would get something like this: that those institutions and constitutional forms are right and just provided that they maximize the good, understood in the utilitarian sense as either pleasure, or the fulfillment of desire, where we are summing the good of all individuals in society, both present and future. We are beginning from the present time, considering what existing institutions might be, and summing the good over all individuals in this way. Observe that, in this way of putting it, there isn't any principle of equality built in, and there isn't any principle of distribution included, so there are no constraints on how the good may be distributed, and there are no notions of right involved. One is simply trying to maximize that sum. That is how utilitarianism is understood in what I'm calling the "Bentham-Edgeworth-Sidgwick view" (although one can best describe their view further so that it includes a more hedonistic characterization of the notion of the good). When we later come to Mill, I want to see whether his principle of utility fits this view of utilitarianism, or whether he has some more complicated notion, as I believe he does.

§2. The Artificial Virtue of Justice

Let's now look very briefly at Hume's aims in *An Enquiry Concerning the Principles of Morals* (1751), as stated in Section I, and then turn to Hume's account of the artificial virtue of justice in Section III and Appendix III, and elsewhere. To outline Section I, in ¶¶1–2 Hume asserts that moral distinctions are real and are made by us in our judgments, and that this is a fact not to be seriously denied. In ¶¶3–7 he states three pairs of alternatives that explain this fact involved in present controversies, and then in ¶8 he foreshadows his own doctrine, which accepts the second alternative in each of the three pairs. Then in ¶9 he discusses his theory of morals as an experimental (or empirical) study (what we today would call a kind of psychology).

Hume's own view, as foreshadowed in ¶¶3–7 and 8, is as follows: (i) First, moral distinctions are not known and applied to things by *reason* alone (contra Cudworth and Clarke; cf. Hume's footnote 12 in Section III, ¶34). Rather, they depend upon a peculiar *sentiment*. (ii) More specifically, we recognize moral distinctions and have the ability to apply them, not via deductive or inductive or probabilistic arguments, but from an *internal sense*. Moral judgments express a response of our moral sensibility to the awareness of certain facts from a certain point of view. (iii) Moreover, we concur in our moral judgments, not because as rational and intelligent beings we grasp their truth, as we grasp the truth for example of the axioms of geometry (as Cudworth and Clarke held). Rather, we concur in our moral judgments because we share the same moral sensibility.

Now to comment on this: First, in the *Treatise of Human Nature* (1740), Hume explained the operations of our moral sensibility via a complicated theory of sympathy, set forth in Book II of that work. In the *Enquiry* he uses however instead the "principle of humanity." See his explanation of this in Section V, ¶17, the footnote. [We will discuss the principle of humanity later.] Second, in the first instance Hume's account of our moral sensibility is *epistemological*. It explains how we know and apply moral distinctions. The explanation of how we are *moved* to act from, or in compliance with, these distinctions is a separate question. So you need distinguish then the problem of knowledge and how we come to know moral distinctions, from the problem of motivation and what moves us to act on moral distinctions. Hume is mainly concerned with the former question.

Now I want to turn to Hume's account of justice and say a few things about that and contrast it with Locke's view. Hume discusses justice in the *Treatise of Human Nature*, Book III, Part II, "Of Justice and Injustice," as well as in his later book, *Enquiry Concerning the Principles of Morals*, Section III, "Of Justice." The way Hume uses the term "justice" must be carefully understood, because he isn't using it in a contemporary sense. He is talking about the basic order and structure of civil society, and, in particular, about the principles and rules which specify the right to property. What Hume calls "virtues" are qualities of human character and dispositions of people to behave and to conduct themselves in a certain way. Justice as a virtue is the disposition of persons to behave and to respect those rules which define property and the other rules surrounding the notion of property. He is using the term "justice" in a rather narrow way. It is only one of many virtues, many of them what he calls "natural virtues," which operate by instinct. Justice is perhaps the most important, along with fidelity and integrity, of what Hume calls the "artificial virtues": those which "produce pleasure and approbation by means of an artifice or contrivance, which arises from the circumstances and necessity of mankind."[2]

Hume's principles of justice are, in effect, largely principles for the regu-

---

2. Hume, *Treatise of Human Nature*, Book III: *Of Morals*, Part II: "Of Justice and Injustice," Sec. I.

lation of economic production and competition between the members of civil society, as they pursue their economic interests. The basic rules of competition, in Hume's view, turn out to be essentially three:

First is a principle about *private property*, and this requires very roughly that everyone be left undisturbed in the enjoyment of what they properly possess. In order to define "properly possess" we have to introduce a number of other rules which specify the rights of ownership. In the *Treatise*, Hume discusses a variety of such rules having to do with present possession, occupation, prescription (or long possession), accession and succession, and these rules come into play under certain circumstances.[3] For example, in case the owner of property dies, in order to avoid controversy about who is to come into possession, there have to be rules about inheritance and the like.

The second rule of justice has to do with *trade and exchanges* of property, and the idea is that there are rights over property that can be transferred under certain conditions.[4] The basic idea is that transfer can only take place by consent. Hume thinks of the second principle as necessary so that the holdings of property within society can be continually adjusted over time according to the various interests and abilities of individuals, and the various best uses that they are able to make of them. So we have to allow for the adjustment and transfer of holdings of property over time.

Hume's third main principle pertains to *contracts* and the performance of *promises*.[5] He thinks of it as more general and inclusive than the second, which has to do with trade and exchange, although it also covers that in a way. It covers agreements of all kinds, including agreements to future performances.

We now have these three principles, which Hume thinks of as principles of justice. The first one, you might say, views society in the form of an association of owners, the second one views society in the form of a market, and the third sanctions the general principle of contract and promises. Together, Hume thinks of these three principles as regulating and specifying the rules of economic competition and production between the members of society, and they constitute the basic norms of economic relations between the members of society. So, we can then say that a just person, on

3. Ibid., Book III, Part II, Sec. III.
4. Ibid., Book III, Part II, Sec. IV.
5. Ibid., Book III, Part II, Sec. V.

Hume's view (because he thinks of virtue as a quality of people—it transfers back, you might say, from the institutional structure to the person) is one who is disposed to honor these basic rules. Hume assumes throughout his discussion that social institutions actually satisfy his principle of utility, however broad and general that is. In other words, on the presumption that institutions do in fact fulfill that principle, then Hume thinks of the just person as one who is disposed to honor these basic rules. He goes on to say, "justice is an artificial virtue and based on convention" in a sense that I will explain later.

In Section III of *An Enquiry Concerning the Principles of Morals,* where Hume talks about justice, his thesis is that *public utility* (that's another term, I take it, for the general interests of society—he uses a lot of different terms, and his language is very loose)—public utility is the sole origin of justice, and reflection on its consequences is the sole basis of its merits. That is supposed to be put in contrast to the case of the natural virtues, where public utility is perhaps one basis of their merit, but certainly not the sole one.

What this thesis means to Hume is that the institutions of justice (I will abbreviate them as property, transfer, and contract) would not exist, or be adhered to, unless people recognized their public utility, and unless people had a sense that these institutions were in the general interest. I take Hume to be saying that we would not approve of these institutions unless we recognized that as general systems of rules publicly recognized and generally acted upon by all, or at any rate by most persons, these institutions have beneficial social consequences and serve the public good.

As I mentioned in the last lecture, Hume calls justice an "artificial virtue" because it is a disposition to adhere to a general system of rules recognized to be for the public good. This system of rules is itself, so to speak, an artifice of reason, and that's what the term "artificial" meant at that time. An artifice of reason was something that could be understood by reason and in no other way. Moreover, the recognition that this general system of rules has these consequences for the general good is itself something that requires the use of reason.

Let me make a further point, contrasting the artificial virtue of justice with a natural virtue like benevolence. The idea is that an individual act of benevolence—being kind to someone, being kind to children, say, or to people who need our help—does not require the conception of a general system of rules. It is something that we are prompted to do because we recognize that an individual person needs our help. It doesn't involve in the same way that the rules of property do some conception of social good, or depend on an idea of how general systems of rules are required to produce the social good.

A further point is that in contrast to the natural virtues like benevolence, the public good that results from rules regarding property, transfer and contract, all regarded as systems of public rules, depends essentially, in Hume's view, on their being adhered to even when, in an individual case, complying with the rules may seem to do more harm than good. This would not be so in the case of a natural virtue like benevolence. The rules of property are distinctive in that we are to adhere to them as public systems of rules even when, despite their being as well designed as they can be, they are still going to require us, in certain particular cases, to do things that may seem to us to be harmful. For example, rules of property may require that misers who are, perhaps, not able or willing to use their property productively, nevertheless have the right to keep it. Or in the case of inheritance, the rules specify who is going to inherit property, even though it may seem to us that that person who does inherit it cannot or will not use it productively; or perhaps we think that they're bad or unworthy and ought not to have it. Nevertheless, in Hume's view, the benefits of the system of property can be attained only if these general rules are mutually recognized as applying to everyone, and only if we adhere to them more or less inflexibly, even when, in particular cases, our actions seem to do more harm than good.

So, the general social background, in Hume's view, for an artificial virtue is roughly the following: *First,* that there exists a system of general institutional rules which define property transfer and contracts, which system of rules he regards as an artifice of reason. The *second feature* is that this system of rules is publicly recognized by the members of society as promoting the public good and the general interest and necessities of society, and that this recognition by the members of society is itself a work of reason. By "publicly recognize," I mean that each person recognizes that the system of rules is for the general benefit of society, and each recognizes that the other also recognizes that, and so on.

A *third* point is that the benefits of this general system of institutional rules depend, as I have just said, on its being inflexibly followed, even in particular cases where it may appear harmful to do so, or where there appear to be better alternatives than complying with the existing rules. I take it to be Hume's view that not to follow them, or to regard them in too flexible a fashion would undermine legitimate expectations—it would undermine the reliability of being able to count on what other people are going to do. For social behavior to be reliable and foreseeable, it is necessary to have certain general systems of rules that can be counted on to be inflexibly followed. One can allow for certain kinds of exceptions (e.g. to prevent imminent disaster) and allow for complicated rules to some degree. But, in Hume's view, there is a limit to the extent to which one can do that.

Finally, the *fourth* point is that the disposition to be just is a quality of character to adhere to these rules with the appropriate degree of inflexibility, *provided that others* in society have a manifest intention likewise to comply with them. And Hume believes that once we understand the background of these rules, then it is a normal fact about people, given the laws of human psychology and the like, that they will have this *disposition to be just.*

I call your attention to the fact that towards the end of the last section of the *Enquiry Concerning the Principles of Morals* (Section IX, Part II) Hume talks about a "sensible knave" who, for his own profit, may allow himself exceptions to these rules. Hume doesn't actually address any argument to him in terms of his own interests. He just regards such a person as one who is not motivated as most of us are, who isn't offended at the thought of himself, say, acting unfairly, or unjustly, or free-riding, as we might say, on this system of rules.

I would urge you to read Appendix III of the *Enquiry,* "Some Further Considerations With Regard To Justice." It is very instructive on what Hume's notion of artificial virtue is. Pay attention there to the sense in which he says that justice is based upon "convention," understood as "a sense of common interest."[6] He uses the example of two men rowing a boat, each relying on the other to pull his oar, without the need of promises or contract, to illustrate what he has in mind when he says that *justice is based on convention.* Now the four points I have just gone over touch all the things that Hume has in mind there.

---

6. See Hume, *Enquiries Concerning the Human Understanding and the Principles of Morals,* ed. L. A. Selby-Bigge (Oxford: Oxford University Press, 2nd ed., 1902), p. 306.

There are two further points I want to make in regard to this account. Hume talked as though the general interests of society alone account for the institution of property and transfer and contract, and also account for how these institutions provide a background for the artificial virtues of justice and fidelity and integrity and the like. But he does not seem to allow for the possibility that it may actually be the case that it's not the general interests of society that account for private property and this particular specification or arrangement of it. Rather, there may be some other interests involved that account for property—perhaps the interests of the more powerful, or maybe the interests of those who have the most property. He just does not seem to allow for that. Now I don't think that one should say that Hume is not aware of that possibility. One would have to assume that he is. I interpret him as giving a kind of idealized account of how the institution of property and the virtues of justice, integrity, and so forth could come about, and as setting out the general features and general factors that actually explain the natural roots, the psychological basis of our moral behavior.

In other words, I think it is important to understand about Hume that he is trying to give an account of why it is that we have the virtues that we have, and why it is that we are motivated to act in accordance with those virtues. And this is intended to be, for the most part, an actual psychological account. It is not like Locke's view, a normative doctrine beginning from the fundamental law of nature and other natural laws, and saying what our rights and duties are, and then giving an account of the form of regime that could legitimately come about. That is not what Hume is doing, or at least it is not what I take Hume to be doing. I see him as explaining why we have some virtues—why they exist, why they are praised, why we are motivated to act in accordance with them—as one might do in psychology, or, one might say more broadly, a science of human nature. So, for his purposes I think it's adequate for him to give this more or less idealized account, leaving aside certain other possible interests, and seeing how the institutions of property and the virtues that are associated with them might come about, and how they would be different from other virtues, for example, the natural virtues.

This would mean that on Locke's account, a system of property would appear to be derivative from the fundamental law of nature, and it would include certain rights to property which would have to be respected in certain ways. This is, as I have said, a normative account. One is working within a kind of system of natural law, with all its overtones. Whereas on Hume's view, any system of rights is just going to be a system of *institutional rules* that will be recognized in society and acted upon because of certain psychological forces that he has attempted to explain. It's a very different kind of view that Hume is presenting, in which any account of rights is going to be derivative from some notion of utility and on how it actually can be expected to operate in social institutions.

§3. The Judicious Spectator

Now I will end by saying something about Hume's principle of humanity and then his notion of the "judicious spectator," which is one of the most interesting and important ideas in the *Enquiry,* and which is also found in the *Treatise of Human Nature.*[7] You should think of this as a psychological account of how we make moral judgments. Hume is explaining the "mechanism" of moral judgments. How are they made and what accounts for their content? Hume aims to explain our moral judgments and feelings as natural phenomena. He wants to be the "Newton of the Passions." In contrast to Locke, he does not present a normative system of principles founded on the Laws of Nature as the laws of God known to reason. Instead he is investigating how morality comes about as a natural phenomena, the role it plays in social life and in establishing social unity and mutual understanding, and what natural human capacities make morality possible. In short, how does morality work, and what aspects of human psychology support it?

The "principle of humanity" is the psychological tendency we have to identify with the interests and concerns of others when our own interests do not come into competition with them. There are two main discussions of the principle of humanity in the *Enquiry,* in Sections V and IX, and also an important passage in Section VI.[8] These are Section V: especially ¶¶17,

7. [See Rawls, *Lectures on the History of Moral Philosophy,* Hume Lecture V, pp. 84–104, for an in-depth account of the role of Hume's idea of the "judicious spectator." —Ed.]

8. [In addition to "the principle of humanity" (p. 272), Hume refers in the *Enquiry Concerning the Principles of Morals* to "the principles of humanity and sympathy" (p. 231), also to "such principle in our nature as humanity or a concern for others" (p. 231), "the sentiment of humanity" (p. 272), and the "affection of humanity" (p. 273), and says "it alone can be the foundation of morals" (p. 273). —Ed.]

41–45, and then the footnotes to ¶¶3–4 (contra the argument that morals are an invention of politicians), and ¶¶14–16 (contra psychological egoism). In Section IX, see especially ¶¶4–8; and in Section VI, see ¶¶3–6. In Part II of Section IX, Hume considers the problem of moral motivation versus the epistemological problem, and perhaps most clearly in his answer to the "sensible knave" (¶¶22–25) he takes his stand with the "confederacy of humankind" (¶19), which is no doubt implicit in the *Enquiry* (even though it holds itself out as a psychological and social inquiry).

In its simplest form he is saying that, when we say qualities of character are virtuous or vicious, or actions are right or wrong, we are considering them from a suitably general or "common point of view,"[9] the point of view of the "judicious spectator,"[10] without any reference to our own interests; and we are *expressing,* by making the moral judgment, our *approval and disapproval.* The reason why we approve or disapprove of qualities of character or institutions is that, when we consider them from this general point of view, our judgments are guided by the tendency of these actions or qualities or institutions to affect the general interests of society, or the general happiness of society. What Hume is trying to do is explain the fact that we agree. How can there be a basis on which people can agree when they judge institutions? When looked at from each person's own standpoint, it is not possible to have agreement as to whether institutions or actions are good or bad. How then can there be a basis for people to agree about these things? On Hume's view there is only one possible basis, and that is one that appeals to our principle of humanity, which again is the psychological tendency we have to identify with the interests and concerns of others when our own interests do not come into competition with them.[11]

The point of view of the judicious spectator is one we take up towards others' qualities of character, or towards rules of institutions; it enables us to appraise them solely according to their tendency to affect the general in-

---

9. Hume, *Enquiries,* Sec. IX, Part I, p. 272.

10. ["Judicious spectator" is a term used only in the *Treatise of Human Nature,* Book III, Part 3, Sec. i (Oxford: Oxford University Press, 2nd ed., 1978), p. 581. In the next paragraph Hume distinguishes "his peculiar point of view" from "some steady and general points of view." Hume uses "common point of view" and "spectator" in conjunction in the *Treatise,* on p. 591. —Ed.]

11. [As Hume says: "If he mean, therefore, to express that this man possesses qualities, whose tendency is pernicious to society, he has chosen this common point of view, and has touched the principle of humanity, in which every man, in some degree, concurs." *Enquiries,* p. 272. —Ed.]

terests or general happiness of society. How is it that that brings us into agreement? It does so because the only factor in our, you might say, "sensible nature" that is brought into play when we take up the point of view of the judicious spectator is our *principle of humanity*, or fellow-feeling. When our own interests and the interests of our family are not involved or affected, the only motivational aspect of our character that is going to direct our judgment, and that we are going to express, is how an action or an institution or quality of character is going to affect the interests and concerns of those who are themselves involved. So, on Hume's view, then, what makes agreement on moral judgment possible is our being able to take up and to imagine ourselves into the point of view of the judicious spectator. We must be able to do that in such a way that we respond to and have, as it were, a kind of affinity with the effects of these institutions or qualities of character in virtue of their beneficial effects on the persons who are advantaged by them. We can then approve of virtuous persons, say, in other cultures and other countries and other times, because we are able by taking this point of view to identify with and sympathize with the people who are benefited by those institutions and characteristics.

That, then, will be what makes agreement in moral judgment possible, and it is by working out that idea that one can see why the principle of utility has the content it does. That is, the idea would be that the greater extent to which any institution were to satisfy that principle would correspond with the extent to which the person who takes the point of view of the judicious spectator would feel stronger approval of that institution. The more it satisfies the principle of utility, the stronger the effects on or the affinity with the person's moral sensibility.

I believe this is supposed to be, in Hume's view, a psychological account of how it is possible for us to make moral judgments and to come to agreement about moral judgments. It is his view that the only possible basis for agreement is via the principle of humanity. There is not any other aspect in human nature that, on his view, would make agreement possible. If we work that idea out, from the way in which he sets up the point of view of the judicious spectator, we can see why, I think, it is natural for him to have ended up with the criterion of right and wrong which he did, namely the principle of utility.

Just to conclude our discussion of Hume, the idea of the judicious spectator is one of the most important and interesting ideas in moral philosophy. It appears in Hume for the first time. Hume's whole view, including his account of property and the judicious spectator, should be understood as an attempt to give a psychological account of our moral thought. There is a contrast between Hume and Locke in that regard. Hume is trying to explain how we are able to make moral distinctions with the idea of the judicious spectator. Where does the distinction between right and wrong come from? He is not talking about moral motivation—about why we are moved to do what is right or what we believe to be right. Rather, he's interested in where the distinction between right and wrong comes from. He is asking, "How do we learn to make that distinction? How do we come to agree on what is right and wrong?" His answer is that we learn to take the point of view of the judicious spectator. All that is moving our judgments from that point of view is the principle of humanity. In this way, we all respond to things in the same way.

Finally, to repeat a point made earlier: If we contrast Hume's and Locke's accounts of property, we may think of Locke as a constitutional lawyer, where Locke is arguing within a constitution whose laws are set forth by God. He is arguing with Filmer. It is all a normative view, taking for granted certain fundamental ideas. The constitution is one of the universe of all humans. The basic law is the fundamental law of nature and the principle that God has supreme authority over all creation. His argument within that constitution is with Filmer. Hume is not working within this framework. Hume does not believe any of that. He hates religion. He is just trying to explain why there is property. Why does it exist? How did it come about? What sustains it? What social purpose does it serve? He is not answering the same question at all as Locke is—the normative question within the constitution of the universe—when he addresses the question of property. So for Hume, anything about past history of property or government does not count; it is not important for whether or not property or government is justifiable now. For Hume, let bygones be bygones. On a utilitarian view, what counts is how the institution operates now and into the future, and whether it is the case that the institutions we have now are more likely to serve the needs of society. Hume's aim is to view these issues from the standpoint of what we now call "social science." He is trying to give an empirical account of these matters.

ROUSSEAU

ROUSSEAU I

The Social Contract: Its Problem

§1. Introduction

1. Rousseau, unfortunately, we have to read in translation.[1] While a great deal is lost, something of Rousseau's marvelous style is nevertheless preserved.[2] Earlier I mentioned that Hobbes's *Leviathan* is the greatest work of political philosophy in English, or so I think. Perhaps we can say also that *On the Social Contract* is the greatest work in French. I say "perhaps" since the *Social Contract* does not display the range of Rousseau's thought as the *Leviathan* does of Hobbes's. But if we combine the *Social Contract* with the *Second Discourse (Discourse on the Origin and Foundations of Inequality)* and with *Emile* (on moral psychology and our education into society), the observation seems right. Montesquieu, Tocqueville, and Constant are of the first rank, and splendid writers; but in Rousseau the union of literary force and power of thought is unsurpassed.

I comment on this union of literary force and power of thought because it is so striking. One might wonder, however, whether the force and splendor of style is a good or a bad thing in a philosophical work. Does it add to or detract from the clarity of thought a writer hopes to convey? I

---

1. In the following lectures on Rousseau I shall refer to Jean-Jacques Rousseau, *The First and Second Discourses*, ed. Roger D. Masters, trans. Roger D. and Judith R. Masters (New York: St. Martin's Press, 1964), and *On the Social Contract, with Geneva Manuscript and Political Economy*, ed. Roger D. Masters, trans. Judith R. Masters (New York: St. Martin's Press, 1978). Citations within the text will be abbreviated as SD for the *Second Discourse*, and SC for the *Social Contract*. In the former, page numbers will be used; in the latter, references will be to book, chapter, and paragraph.

2. On the hazards of translation, recall that (in 1987, I think) a Soviet announcer on Moscow TV translated John Denver's "Rocky Mountain High" as "Drunk in the Mountains." And in the early days of trying to write programs for computer translation into Russian and back, the sentence "The spirit is willing but the flesh is weak" came back as: "The wine is good but the meat stinks."

shan't pursue this question except to say that style can be a danger, attracting attention to itself, as it does in Rousseau. We may be dazzled and distracted and so fail to note the intricacies of reasoning that call for our full concentration.[3] I say this because I believe that Rousseau's ideas are deep and consistent; there are shifts of mood and no doubt surface contradictions, but the whole structure of thought hangs together in one unified view.

Perhaps the best philosophical style is clear and lucid, aiming to present the thought itself, without side effects, yet with a certain grace and formal beauty of line. Frege and Wittgenstein often achieve this ideal. But the greatest German works in political philosophy—those of Kant, Hegel, and Marx—are not especially well written; indeed, they are often rather badly written. Nietzsche is a great stylist, but his works do not belong to political philosophy, though his views certainly bear on it.

2. We must now try to get a sense of the questions and problems that moved Rousseau in writing the *Social Contract*. His concerns are broader than those of Hobbes and Locke: Hobbes, we saw, was concerned with overcoming the problem of divisive civil war, while Locke's concern was with the justification of resistance to the Crown within a mixed constitution. Rousseau, by contrast, is a critic of culture and civilization: he seeks to diagnose what he sees as the deep-rooted evils of contemporary society and depicts the vices and miseries it arouses in its members. He hopes to explain why these evils and vices come about, and to describe the basic framework of a political and social world in which they would not be present.

Rousseau, like Hume, is of another century than Hobbes and Locke. He represents the generation that rejected the old order, though it was still in power during his lifetime, and that prepared the way for the coming French Revolution. Established traditions were being questioned, and the sciences were developing rapidly.

Much is known of Rousseau's life, because he wrote three autobiographical works. He was born in 1712 in Geneva, then a Protestant city-state. His mother, whose family was of the academic and social elite, and were therefore voting citizens, died soon after he was born, and for ten

3. His marvelous style is also liable to spoofs, as when de Maistre, on hearing Rousseau's famous sentence that opens Book I, Chapter I of *On The Social Contract*, "Man was born free and he is everywhere in chains," retorted: "You might as well say: 'Sheep were born carnivorous and everywhere eat grass.'" Or a recent book review in the *New York Times:* "Monkeys were born free and are everywhere in zoos."

years he was brought up and educated by his father, a watchmaker. In 1722 his father had to leave Geneva after a fight, and Rousseau was left for two years with his mother's brother, who put him in a pension with a Protestant minister. He then served as an apprentice in various trades. He left town on his own in 1728 at age sixteen, with no money, and made his way around Europe serving as a lackey of various sorts—a footman, a secretary, a tutor, a music teacher—sometimes working for, living with, and cultivating friendships with very influential people, all the while reading and educating himself, and taking financial help where he could find it. By 1742, when he settled in Paris, to stay there until 1762, he was a composer (he wrote two operas), poet, dramatist, essayist, philosopher, political scientist, novelist, chemist, botanist—a self-made man.

After 1749 Rousseau began to write the works for which he was later famous. *On the Social Contract* and *Emile,* published in 1762, were the cause of legal action against Rousseau in France and Geneva because it was felt they attacked revealed religion, and he was forced to leave Paris. Rousseau's later years were spent in trying to justify his writing; and the *Social Contract,* which was later quoted by Robespierre to justify the Revolution, was actually not much read until after 1789, the year the Bastille was stormed.[4]

3. One way to convey the sweep of Rousseau's thought is to note his various writings and to indicate how they fit together into a coherent body of thought. *The Second Discourse,* which concerns the whole of human history and the origin of inequality, political oppression, and the social vices, is dark and pessimistic; the *Social Contract* is sunnier and tries to set out the basis of a fully just and workable, yet at the same time stable and happy regime. In this sense, it is realistically utopian. Perhaps in view of its subject and aim, it is the least eloquent and impassioned of Rousseau's major works.

We can divide Rousseau's major writings into three groups as follows:

(a) First, three works of historical and cultural criticism in which he sets out what he sees as the evils of 18th-century French (European) civilization and offers a diagnosis of their cause and origin:

1750: *Discourse on the Sciences and the Arts (The First Discourse)*
1754: *Discourse on the Origin of Inequality (The Second Discourse)*
1758: *Letter to M. d'Alembert on the Theater*

4. Biographical material is taken, for the most part, from Roger Masters, ed., *On the Social Contract,* Introduction. See also Maurice Cranston, *Jean-Jacques: The Early Life and Work of Jean-Jacques Rousseau, 1712–1754* (London: Penguin Books, 1983).

In these works Rousseau appears as a critic of the Enlightenment, of its ideas of progress and of the benefit to human happiness of advances in the arts and sciences, and of the possibilities of social improvement through more widespread education. There is a conservative tendency in Rousseau, and his contemporaries Diderot, Voltaire, and d'Alembert saw him as different from themselves.[5]

(b) Second, the three constructive works in which Rousseau describes his ideal of a just, workable, and happy political society and considers how it might be established and made stable:

> 1761: *La Nouvelle Héloïse* (which contains much of his alpine idyll of Geneva as a rural democracy)
> 1762: *Du Contrat Social*
> 1762: *Emile*

(c) Third, three autobiographical works, which have had an enormous influence in literature and on the sensibility of romanticism:

> 1766: *Confessions:* first part completed on return to France after his stay in England with Hume, the whole published in 1781
> 1772–76: *Dialogues: Rousseau juge de Jean-Jacques*
> 1776–78: *Reveries of a Solitary Walker*

Indeed, these works are important for the modern emphasis on such values as integrity and authenticity, and for the effort to understand oneself, to overcome alienation, to live for oneself and not in the opinion of others; and much else. This is a significant part of some justifications for liberty of thought and conscience, as we shall later see in Mill.

§2. The Stages of History before Political Society

1. As a way to indicate the background of the problem Rousseau is concerned with in the *Social Contract,* I discuss first the *Second Discourse.* Rousseau tells us in one of the four autobiographical letters that he wrote to

---

5. This conservative tendency is illustrated by the contrast between the story of Rousseau's opera, *Devin du Village,* with that of Pergolesi's *La Serva Padrona.* See Maurice Cranston, *Jean-Jacques,* p. 279.

Malesherbes[6] in 1762 (there is a briefer account in *Confessions*, Bk. 8, 1749, trans. J. M. Cohen, 327f) that he had a sudden overwhelming illumination on the road to Vincennes (six miles from Paris) in 1749. He had set out to visit Diderot (there in prison), but it was a long walk and a hot day. He had brought along a copy of *Le Mercure de France* and therein he saw the question proposed by the Academy of Dijon—"Has the restoration of the sciences and the arts tended to purify morals?" Rousseau felt dizzy and overcome. Gasping for breath, he collapsed under a tree, weeping. He says:

> If anything ever resembled a sudden inspiration, it was what that advertisement stimulated in me: all at once I felt my mind dazzled by a thousand lights, a crowd of splendid ideas presented themselves to me with such force and in such confusion, that I was thrown into a state of indescribable bewilderment. I felt my head seized by a dizziness that resembled intoxication . . . Unable to breathe and walk at the same time, I sank down under a tree . . . if ever I could have written the quarter of what I saw and felt under that tree, with what clarity would I have revealed all the contradictions of the social system, with what force would I have exposed all the abuses of our institutions, with what simplicity would I have demonstrated that man is naturally good and that it is through these institutions alone that men become bad.[7]

Rousseau said that this one fleeting moment of ecstatic reverie provided the aims of his writings as a whole.[8]

2. This quotation nicely states the well-known theme of Rousseau's thought, namely: that man is naturally good and that it is through social institutions alone that men became bad. But the meaning of this theme is not obvious. Indeed, there is some difficulty knowing in what sense Rousseau can assert it, for it seems to conflict with much that he says in the *Second*

---

6. Malesherbes was the King's Directeur de la librairie, by law an official charged with supervising the book trade in France. He was a friend of the *philosophes* and often helped them to outwit the legal labyrinth of the regime. Rousseau was on good terms with him, and before the *Social Contract* came out had written him four autobiographical letters. See James Miller, *Rousseau: Dreamer of Democracy* (New Haven: Yale University Press, 1984), p. 76f.

7. See Cranston: *Jean-Jacques: 1712–1754*, p. 228.

8. See Miller, *Rousseau: Dreamer of Democracy*, p. 5.

Discourse. To explain this difficulty, and how it might be resolved, I look at the *Discourse* itself.

In two parts of about equal length, this work is an account of the history of mankind beginning with the earliest stage of the state of nature and ending with the beginning of political authority and civil society. It surveys the historical changes in culture and society and connects the hostilities and vices of civilization to increasing inequality in political power, in social position, and in wealth and property.

At the outset Rousseau distinguishes between natural inequality and moral or political inequality. The former is "established by nature and consists in the difference of ages, bodily strengths, and qualities of mind or soul." The latter, which he sometimes calls contrived inequality, is founded on convention and "is established, or at least authorized, by . . . consent" (SD, 101). But he thinks it obvious that in civilization, as we now see it, there is no essential link between these two inequalities. To think otherwise would be like asking ". . . whether those who command are necessarily worth more than those who obey, and whether strength of body or mind, wisdom or virtue, are always found in the same individuals in proportion to power and wealth: a question perhaps good for slaves to discuss in the hearing of their masters, but not suitable for reasonable and free men who seek the truth" (SD, 101–102). Rather, Rousseau wants to show how it came about that there is no essential link, as he thinks there ought to be, and how it is that, as things now are, ". . . a child (can) command an old man, an imbecile lead a wise man, and a handful of men be glutted with superfluities while the starving multitude lacks necessities" (SD, 181).

3. Now the idea of the state of nature can be understood in at least three ways:

(1) The juristic sense, as the absence of political authority. This is Locke's sense. Individuals are in a state of nature when they are not subject to any, or not to the same, political authority.

(2) The chronological sense, as the historically first condition of mankind, whatever its characteristics. In patristic thought (that of the early church fathers), the state of nature—that of Adam and Eve before the fall—was a state of moral perfection (so far as this is possible for human beings unaided by grace) and rationality. It was also a state of equality.

(3) The cultural sense, as a primitive state of culture, as a state in which the arts and sciences—civilization in its non-political elements—have barely begun.

Plainly these different forms of society and culture need not all be realized in the same period of time. The period preceding established political authority may be a very long one, as it seems to have been for Locke, and is explicitly said to be by Rousseau. For Rousseau divides the juristic state of nature into four distinct stages of culture, all of them of long duration; and in his terminology (in the *Second Discourse*), the term "state of nature" means not the pre-political stage as a whole but only the first and earliest of the four cultural stages.

4. This first stage of primitive man is not regarded by Rousseau as an ideal stage at all. It is the third stage, by which time considerable cultural development has occurred, that he thinks of as ideal in the *Second Discourse*, and is the one he regrets did not endure. In his account Rousseau draws on several previous writers: his first stage draws on Pufendorf; his third is similar to the state of nature of Montaigne; and his fourth stage—which is one of great conflict and disorder and eventually leads to the establishment of political authority under the domination of those with property—draws on Hobbes, although Rousseau differs from him in important ways, as I mention later.

The relevance of all this for us is in the following: Rousseau wants to say that man is naturally good and that it is through social institutions that we become bad. Yet when we look at the details of his account of the development of culture and social organization and the role that our various faculties play in it—particularly our reason, imagination and self-consciousness—it may seem inevitable that the social evils and individual vices Rousseau deplores will come about.

In the first stage our faculties are not developed. We are then moved by *amour de soi* (natural love of ourselves) and by simple desires such as the desires for food, shelter, sleep, and sex. And while we feel *compassion* (SD, 130–134) for others, which is the source of the social virtues (SD, 131f), this stage is still one of a brute. That is, it is the stage of a lazy, unreflective, though happy and fairly harmless animal, one not prone to inflict pain on others.

Yet even as animals, human beings are distinguished from other animals in two very important respects:

First, they possess the capacity for free will, and so the potentiality to act in the light of valid reasons; they are not, like animals, guided by instincts alone (SD, 113f).

Second, human beings are perfectible, that is, they have the potentiality for self-improvement through the development of their faculties and their expression in culture over time. An aspect of our perfectibility, which depends on language (SD, 124), is that we are historical beings. This means that perfectibility resides as much in the species as in the individual, and it is seen in the historical development of civilization. The particular realization of our nature depends on the culture of the society in which we live. By contrast, animals become all that they will be in a relatively few months, and are the same today as thousands of years ago (SD, 114–115).

5. When, however, we become distinguished from other animals through cultural development—by language and by simple forms of social organization (families and small groups)—we become concerned for two things: first, for our natural well-being and the means of sustaining life; and, second, for what others think of us and our relative standing in our social group. The first concerns are the object of *amour de soi* (the natural love of ourselves), which, as noted above, is the concern for one's good as given by certain natural needs common to man and other animals. The second are the object of *amour-propre,* a distinct form of self-concern that arises only in society. It is the natural concern for a secure standing in relation to others and involves a need for equal acceptance with them.[9]

I stress that *amour-propre* has a natural form along with its proper object, as well as an unnatural form, which has its perverted, or unnatural object. In its natural, or proper, form (its form appropriate to human nature), *amour-propre* is a need which directs us to secure for ourselves equal standing along with others and a position among our associates in which we are accepted as having needs and aspirations which must be taken into account on the same basis as those of everyone else. This means that on the basis of our needs and wants we can make claims which are endorsed by others as imposing rightful limits on their conduct. Needing and asking for this acceptance from others involves giving the same to them in return. For, moved by this natural *amour-propre,* we are ready to grant the very same standing to others, and to recognize the rightful limits that their needs and

---

9. My account of *amour-propre* follows that of N. J. H. Dent, *Rousseau* (Oxford: Blackwell, 1988), and that of Frederick Neuhouser in his "Freedom, Dependence, and the General Will," *Philosophical Review,* July 1993, pp. 376f. Dent gives a statement in his *A Rousseau Dictionary* (Oxford: Blackwell, 1992), pp. 33–36. I am indebted to Neuhouser for this account of how *amour-propre* is related to the principle of reciprocity.

rightful claims impose on us, provided—and this is essential—our equal status is accepted and made secure in social arrangements.

The question arises whether *amour-propre*, which expresses our social nature, contains within itself, as a natural disposition, a principle of reciprocity. I believe not. The principle of reciprocity is formulated and grasped by reason, imagination, and conscience, and not by *amour-propre*. So that principle is not known and followed by *amour-propre* alone. However, moved by *amour-propre* we are ready to accept and to act on a principle of reciprocity whenever our culture makes it available and intelligible to us, and society's basic arrangements establish our secure and equal standing along with others.

By contrast, unnatural, or perverted, *amour-propre* (often translated simply as "vanity") shows itself in such vices as vanity and arrogance, in the desire to be superior to and to dominate others, and to be admired by them. Its unnatural or perverted object is to be superior to others and to have them in positions beneath us.

I should mention, however, that the first interpretation I have given above of amour-propre is not widely accepted. Far more widely accepted is that amour-propre is simply what I have called unnatural or perverted *amour-propre*, and nothing more than that. Thus, whether it incorporates the principle of reciprocity never arises. I accept what we may call the wide view of *amour-propre* for two reasons (aside from the fact that the main idea is in N. J. H. Dent, whose book and dictionary are recommended).[10]

The first reason (and I must say it carries much weight with me) is that Kant endorses the wide view when he says in the *Religion:* Bk. I, Sec. 1, Ak: VI:27:

> The predisposition to humanity can be brought under the general title of self-love which is physical and yet compares . . . that is to say, we judge ourselves happy or unhappy only by making comparisons with others. Out of this self-love springs the inclination to acquire worth in the opinion of others. This is originally a desire merely for equality, to allow no one superiority above oneself, bound up with a constant care lest others strive to obtain such superiority; but from this arises gradually the unjustifiable craving to win it for oneself over others. Upon this twin stem of *jealousy* and *rivalry* may be grafted the very great vices of secret and open animosity against all whom we look upon as not belonging to us—vices, however, which really do not sprout from

10. N. J. H. Dent, *Rousseau*, and *A Rousseau Dictionary.*

nature as their root; rather they are inclinations aroused in us by the anxious endeavors of others to attain a hated superiority over us . . . the vices which are grafted upon this inclination might be termed the vices of *culture*, the highest form of malignancy, as, for example, in *envy, ingratitude, spitefulness,* and the like . . . they can be called the *diabolical* vices.

It was not until I connected the *Second Discourse* with Kant's remarks here that I felt I finally understood what either of them was saying. As so often, Kant is the best interpreter of Rousseau.[11]

The second reason for accepting the wide view of *amour-propre* is that it is required to make sense of Rousseau's great works as a coherent and consistent view. For reasons I shall try to make clear, the solution of the human predicament Rousseau offers in the *Social Contract* only coheres with the *Second Discourse* when we adopt the wide view of *amour-propre*. Without it, Rousseau's thought becomes all the more darkly pessimistic, and the kind of political society depicted in the *Social Contract* appears utterly utopian. The reason is that if *amour-propre* is not at first, as Kant says, a desire merely for equality, and if it is not ready, assured of that equality by society's institutions, to grant in reciprocity the same equality to others, what psychological basis is there in human nature, as Rousseau conceives it, to make such a society possible? Reason and conscience alone? That is hardly sufficient. Rousseau's overall scheme of thought becomes, indeed, unworkable. Lacking the wide view of *amour-propre* leads us to say foolish things about Rousseau, such as that he is a dazzling though confused and inconsistent writer. Don't believe it.

6. Above I remarked that the social evils founded on inequality and unnatural *amour-propre* seem, offhand, inevitable. This is because they are connected with our reason, imagination, and self-consciousness. Reflection, reason, and imagination can become the enemies of compassion and block its tendencies leading us to identify with the sufferings of others (SD, 132f). Rousseau says (SD, 132): "Reason engenders vanity and reflection fortifies it; reason turns man back upon himself, it separates him from all that bothers and afflicts him. Philosophy isolates him; because of it he says in secret, at the sight of a suffering man: Perish if you will, I am safe. No longer can anything except dangers to the entire society trouble the tranquil sleep of

11. See Ernst Cassirer, *The Question of Jean-Jacques Rousseau,* trans. Peter Gay (New York: Columbia University Press, 1954).

the philosopher and tear him from his bed. . . . Savage man does not have this admirable talent, and for want of wisdom and reason he is always seen heedlessly yielding to the first sentiment of humanity." And somewhat later (SD, 133): ". . . the human race would have perished long ago if its preservation had depended only on the reasonings of its members."

Here Rousseau is commenting on the effect of the development of culture and reason on the sentiment of humanity that moves simpler people. But this is just an example of a general tendency as human beings evolved from the:

First stage, of the lazy, unreflective, but free and potentially perfectible and happy animal who lives alone and is moved only by *amour de soi* and compassion. Here there are no moral problems and the passions are few and calm (SD, 142),

to the:

Second stage, of nascent society, a period covering centuries in the course of which we learned to use the simpler tools and weapons, developed crude language, united in groups for mutual protection, and developed the permanent family with very limited institutions of property; individuals owned their own weapons, each family had its own shelter; a sense of self develops, and sentiments of preference lead to love, which in turn brings jealousy in its train (SD, 142–148).

to the:

Third stage, which is the patriarchal stage of human society where the only government is that of the family. People live in loose village groups and gain their subsistence by hunting, fishing, and gathering from the bounty of nature; and amusement is found in spontaneous gatherings of song and dance, and so on. Men begin to appreciate one another and duties of civility follow. Public esteem has a value (SD, 149).

If we ask why these transitions to the next stage occur, Rousseau suggests the reasons are economic. Under the pressure of increasing numbers it became more effective to join together and hunt in groups and to engage in various cooperative activities. But already in this simple pastoral world the setting of inflamed *amour-propre* is in place. Permanent proximity generates enduring ties; the sentiments of love and jealousy (unknown to simpler beings) are now aroused. Rousseau says: "The one who sang or danced the best, the handsomest, the most adroit, or the most eloquent became the most highly considered; and that was the first step toward inequality and, at the same time, toward vice" (SD, 149).

It is this third, or patriarchal, stage, "at equal distances from the stupidity of brutes and the fatal enlightenment of civil man" (SD, 150), that Rousseau thinks must have been the best for man. He says:

> . . . although men had come to have less endurance and although natural pity had already undergone some alteration, this period of the development of human faculties, maintaining a golden mean between the indolence of the primitive state and the petulant activity of our vanity, must have been the happiest and most durable epoch . . . the least subject to revolutions, the best for man, and that he must have come out of it only by some fatal accident, which for the common good ought never to have happened. The example of savages, who have almost all been found at this point, seems to confirm that the human race was made to remain in it always; that this state is the veritable prime of the world; and that all subsequent progress has been in appearance so many steps toward the perfection of the individual, and in fact toward the decrepitude of the species. (SD, 150–151)

But this third stage was left behind with the transition to the fourth stage, with its first stage of inequality. This occurred with the development of metallurgy and agriculture, which led people more and more to need the help of others, and so to the division of labor, as well as to the establishment of private property in land and tools; and finally to the inequality among people originating at first from natural inequalities (those in strength, wit, ingenuity, etc.) (SD, 151–154).

Natural differences between us are part of the difficulty. For Rousseau suggests that a reasonably happy state might have persisted had talents been equal (SD, 154). But the stage of metallurgy and agriculture gradually develops into one of inequality, with the beginning of law and property and the distinction between rich and poor: "The stronger did more work; the cleverer turned his to better advantage; the more ingenious found ways to shorten his labor . . . working equally, the one earned a great deal while the other barely had enough to live" (SD, 154–155).

§3. The Stage of Civil Society and of Political Authority

1. For Rousseau, political authority is in part a trick of the rich. That is, it was not a case of the stronger over the weaker. Rather, the first social

compact was, in effect, fraudulent, the rich dominating and deceiving the poor. The central evil was economic inequality, with the rich having assured possessions, the poor having little or nothing. But the poor, not foreseeing the consequences, were ready to acquiesce in law and political authority as a remedy for the conflict and insecurity of an agricultural society without government (SD, 158ff).[12]

The actual form of government established reflects the greater or lesser inequalities among individuals at the time that political authority is instituted. If one person is preeminent in power and wealth, that person alone is elected magistrate and the state is a monarchy. If a number of roughly equal persons prevail over the rest, there is aristocracy; whereas if fortunes and talents of all persons are not too unequal, there is democracy. In each case, political authority added political inequality to the kinds of inequality that already existed (SD, 171f).

The last pages of the *Second Discourse* sketch "the progress of inequality," as Rousseau calls it, in three stages: "the establishment of the law and of the right of property was the first stage, the institution of the magistracy the second, and the third and last was the changing of legitimate power into arbitrary power. So that the status of rich and poor was authorized by the first epoch, that of powerful and weak by the second, and by the third that of master and slave, which is the last degree of inequality and the limit to which all the others finally lead, until new revolutions dissolve the government altogether or bring it closer to its legitimate institution" (SD, 172).

So things finally come full circle: humanity begins with the state of nature (the first of the four cultural stages before civil society) in which all are equal. It arrives finally at the ultimate stage of inequality where all become equals again because they are nothing, and there is no longer any law except the will of the master, who is ruled by his passions: "The notions of good and the principles of justice [which arose with the compact of government] vanish once again. Here everything is brought back to . . . a new state of nature different from the one with which we began, in that the one was the state of nature in its purity; and this last is the fruit of an excess of corruption" (SD, 177).

2. In the last paragraph of the *Second Discourse* Rousseau, referring to the vanities, vices, and miseries of contemporary civilization he has just de-

12. Other modes of origin of government—conquest, subjection to an absolute master (what Locke referred to as royal absolutism), paternal authority, subjection to tyranny—Rousseau rejects as very unlikely (SD, 161–168).

scribed, states his main conclusion as follows: ". . . this [state of society and culture, described above] is not the original state of man; and . . . it is the spirit of society alone, and the inequality it engenders, which thus change and alter all our natural inclinations" (SD, 180). And again: "It follows from this exposition that inequality, being almost null in the state of nature, draws its force and growth from the development of our faculties and the progress of the human mind, and finally becomes stable and legitimate by the establishment of property and laws" (SD, 180).

We can say that, for Rousseau, there are two connected processes going on throughout history.

One is the gradual realization of our perfectibility, that is, of our capacity for progressive achievements and refinements in the arts and sciences, and in the invention of institutions and cultural forms over time.

The other process is that of our increasing alienation from one another in a society divided by growing inequalities. These inequalities arouse in us the vices of inflamed *amour-propre,* the vices of pride and vanity along with the will to dominate, and lead to fawning and obsequiousness among the lower orders. These two processes combine to make possible the rule of arbitrary political power and keep the vast majority in servile dependence on the rich and powerful (SD, 175).

§4. The Relevance for the Social Contract

1. It is strange, I have suggested, that Rousseau should say that man is naturally good and that it is through social institutions that we become bad. For, as we have seen, primitive human beings are indolent, thoughtless, if happy brutes, who, it seems, once social groups are formed, become more and more vain and domineering, seeking to lord it over those who have less, or else to lapse into servility and obsequiousness towards those who have more.[13] Our reason expands and multiplies our desires without end; and as we come to live more and more in the opinions of others, our natural differences are occasions for vanity and shame. Why, then, isn't it human nature that is bad at root, with social life merely bringing out how bad our nature actually is? Yes, we are perfectible: our potentialities can be developed through culture over time without apparent limit, and institutions preserv-

13. As Kant once said unkindly about his fellow Prussians, scornful of all their titles: "They are so often undecided whether to try to dominate or to grovel."

ing these achievements can be duly prized and maintained. But if we are perfectible only at the price of misery and vice, how can our nature be good?

There are, I think, at least two reasons why Rousseau wants to say that our nature is good.[14] One is that he is rejecting certain aspects of Christian orthodoxy, and in particular, the Augustinian doctrine of original sin. One view of slavery and private property among the Patristic Fathers was that God sanctioned these institutions as remedies for our propensities to sin. These propensities began with the Fall and are now embedded in our sinful nature. Their effect can be mitigated only by God's grace; the role of law and social institutions is merely to contain them.

To this Augustinian doctrine Rousseau wants to say: to the contrary, slavery and private property are historical developments, the result of gradual changes in human propensities under the influence of social practices under certain conditions. This long development took a particular path. It is essential for Rousseau that this development might have been different; he refers to different accidents, and to chance combinations of foreign causes (SD, 140), which, I take it, is his way of saying that it was not inevitable.[15]

2. There is a second view Rousseau is rejecting: that of Hobbes. He is saying that the vices of pride and vanity, and the rest, which (on his reading of Hobbes) characterize Hobbes's state of nature, are not natural to man (SD, 128ff). These vices and the misery to which they lead are the result of unnatural or perverted *amour-propre*. They are the outcome of a particular course of history. What is natural to us, our natural *amour-propre*, as we saw earlier, is a deep concern for a secure social standing relative to others, consistent with mutual recognition and reciprocity. This is very different from vanity and pride and the will to dominate. Human nature as Hobbes depicts it is found only in Rousseau's last stage of culture (the state of nature in Locke's juristic sense). Recall that this stage arises only after the development of:

(1) metallurgy and agriculture;

(2) large inequalities in private property, including property in land;

(3) division of labor, with some under the direction of, and so dependent on, others;

(4) these inequalities made greater by differences in native endowments

14. Observe that Rousseau is careful about how he does this, as seen from his comments on methodology in SD, 103, 105, 180.

15. [See Appendix A at the end of this lecture for further elaboration of the Christian doctrine of original sin, from Rawls's 1981 lecture notes. —Ed.]

as these are trained and educated, with some more highly trained and educated than the rest.

It is these features which, in the absence of an effective public institutional commitment to preserving equality, lead people to see their relations as antagonistic. They view society as a rivalry, as a competitive scrabble of each against all. In Rousseau's view, Hobbes describes people whose character and aims have been fashioned by these social conditions.

A further point against Hobbes, as Rousseau reads him, is that the state of war Hobbes presents depends on the passions of pride and vanity. But for Rousseau, these passions presuppose a certain cultural and intellectual development, which in turn presupposes certain social institutions. In Rousseau, primitive man was not capable of pride and vanity and the other vices of civilization. Only *amour de soi* (shown in such desires as those for food, drink, and sleep [SD, 116]) and compassion are in this sense natural for Rousseau. Vanity and pride, and the vices of inflamed *amour-propre*, were not present in the first stages, but are found only much later.

3. The *Second Discourse* is one of Rousseau's most pessimistic works. By the time of *On the Social Contract* (when he wrote the statement to Malesherbes from *Dialogue I*, quoted earlier) he no longer thinks that there is a best age anywhere in the past and he looks more to the future, or perhaps better, to what is possible. He now believes that it is at least possible to describe a legitimate form of government and its system of institutions such that it would, with good fortune, be reasonably just, happy, and stable. Its members would be free from the more serious vices of inflamed *amour-propre* such as vanity and pretense, insincerity and greed. It is not inevitable that we grow worse and worse; it is possible for us to get better.

If, however, the *Social Contract* presents the principles of political right for a just and workable, stable society, there is not much leeway. Rousseau's belief that human nature is good, and that it is through social institutions that we become bad, comes to these two propositions:

(a) Social institutions and conditions of social life exercise a predominant influence over which human propensities will develop and express themselves over time. When realized, some of these propensities are good, some are bad.

(b) There exists at least one possible and reasonably workable scheme of legitimate political institutions that both satisfies the principles of political right and meets the requirements for institutional stability and human happiness.

Thus, that our nature is good means that it allows a scheme of just, stable, and happy political institutions. What this society is like and how it might arise Rousseau tells us in the *Social Contract*. The point of Rousseau's genealogy of vice in the *Second Discourse* is to show that we need not reject the idea of our natural goodness. The reason given is that the ideal of social cooperation (found in the *Social Contract*) is compatible with our nature if the idea of natural goodness is true. While the *Social Contract* modifies somewhat the pessimism of the *Second Discourse,* the earlier work provides the background for the problem Rousseau addresses in the later.

We conclude that human nature is good in the sense that just and stable political and social arrangements are at least possible. The remedy for our trouble consists in a social world properly arranged to cohere with our true nature and the natural state of our *amour-propre*. Thus the opening paragraph of Book I of the *Social Contract*: "I want to inquire whether there can be a legitimate and reliable rule of administration in the civil order, taking men as they are and laws as they can be. I shall try always to reconcile in this research what right permits with what interest prescribes, so that justice and utility are not at variance."

4. Now the question arises: how good does he think human nature really is? In asking this question, I assume that human nature can be represented (for the purposes of answering this question) by the most fundamental principles of human psychology, including principles of learning of all kinds. We have these principles right when, together with the principles of common-sense political sociology, we can give at least a plausible account of the kinds of virtues and vices, aims and aspirations, final ends and desires, and much else—in short, the kind of character—we come to have under different social and historical conditions. The principles of human nature are like a function: given social and historical conditions, they assign the kinds of character that will develop and be acquired in society.

Accepting this definition, then whether human nature is good depends, it seems, on two things:

(a) on the range and variety of historical conditions under which the society of the *Social Contract* can be realized, and

(b) on whether those conditions can be reached from most, or from many, other different conditions.

Suppose that we cannot reach the conditions for a just, happy, and stable society from where we are: we are too far along the path of vice and corruption, and cannot cooperate to solve our problems. Too bad for us.

But suppose further that we could not do so in most conditions likely to arise out of our long history? Then the pessimism of the *Second Discourse* is hardly mitigated.

Masters, in the introduction to his new edition of the *Second Discourse,* says the following: "Almost alone in his century, Rousseau seems to have viewed human nature as an animal species whose nature defines a good and healthy mode of life, but whose evolution has made a naturally good life inaccessible (at least for most of those living in civilized societies)."

I concur in this judgment, and nothing I have said conflicts with it. Also, it fits with the relation between the *Second Discourse* and the *Social Contract* I have suggested: namely, that the latter explains how to arrange the institutions of a social world so that the vices and miseries accounted for in the former, and which we now see in most all ages and in our culture and civilization, will not arise.

Rousseau's answer is: we must arrange our political and social institutions according to the terms of cooperation expressed by the social contract (SC, 1.6): it is these terms that, when effectively realized, ensure that those institutions secure our moral freedom, political and social equality, and independence. They also make possible our civic freedom and prevent the hostilities and vices that would otherwise plague us.

Rousseau Lecture I (1981): Appendix A

ROUSSEAU: THE DOCTRINE OF THE NATURAL GOODNESS OF HUMAN NATURE

§1. Contra Original Sin

Let's start by contrasting Rousseau's view with the orthodox doctrine of original sin, which includes these parts: (a) The original natural perfection of the first pair, Adam and Eve. (b) Their sin was their own fault, an act of free will, by a nature without defect. (c) It was motivated by pride and self-will. (d) The punishment and corruption of their sin is manifest in concupiscence and propagated in the sexual act. (e) All of us now are co-responsible and participate in their sin; so that now (f) our nature is scarred and subject to death and misery, (g) escape from which lies only in divine grace.

Keeping these points in mind, note that Rousseau rejects them one by one: (a) The natural state (State of Nature) is not one of natural perfection but a primitive state in which our potentialities for perfection and our reason and moral sensibilities are undeveloped. They are realized only in society via many changes over time. (b) Human misery and present vices and false values are not rooted in free choices but come about as the consequence of unfortunate historical accidents and social trends. (c) Rousseau denies the first pair could have acted from pride and self-will, for these motives are found only in society. (d) Vice and false values are propagated by social institutions as each generation responds to them. (e) The way out lies in our own hands.

Rousseau's account of historical and social development is secular and naturalistic, like the account of others in the Enlightenment: Diderot, Condorcet, d'Alembert, and so on. (Compare his account with Hume's.)

§2. Rousseau contra Hobbes: Further Meaning of Natural Goodness—as Premise of Social Theory

Although Rousseau is rejecting original sin (as did Hume and many others, with some heat), so is he also rejecting elements of Hobbes's view. In particular, he thought (whether correctly or not) that Hobbes held pride and vanity, and the will to dominate, to be basic and original impulses or psychological principles of human nature, which accounts in part for why the State of Nature is a State of War. Rousseau denies this, and attributes these propensities to society. In the primitive state of nature, people are moved only by their natural needs, guided by self-love *(amour de soi)*, and restrained by natural compassion.

Rousseau also rejected Hobbes's view that the ostensible forms of compassion and other like feelings could be reduced to self-love. He holds that compassion and self-love are distinct; indeed self-love guided by reason and moderated by compassion provides, under suitable social conditions and modes of education, the psychological basis of humane and moral conduct.

§3. The Possibilities of a Well-Regulated Society

Now let's ask what these disputes about an original human nature and its propensities are all about. Everyone agrees, let's say, that given people as they are, many are moved by pride and vanity and the will to dominate, at least on some occasions; and sufficiently many to be a major political factor. What difference does it make whether these propensities are original or derived? And do we know what we mean by this distinction; and could we tell in actual behavior which is which?

The matter at stake might be put this way: Suppose we assume (as Rousseau and the Enlightenment did) that human beings and their ends are the basic units of deliberation and action, as well as of responsibility (suitably understood), so that our deeds collectively are one of the main causes

Part 1 Introduction 1.1	Part 2
(1) 1.2–1.5 Rebuts false accounts of political authority based on kinds of [inequality] including force	(1) 3.1–3.9 Discusses government as subordinate to Sovereign, as executor of Sovereign's laws; as agent
(2) 1.6–1.9 Presents the correct account of legitimate political authority 2.1–2.6 Discusses Sovereign and the source of the law	(2) 3.10–3.18 Discusses what can be done to prevent government from usurping Sovereign's authority: the Sovereign as assembly of the people 4.1–4.4 Discusses how to order the general will as conduct of popular assemblies so that they may best express the general will and preserve freedom and equality
(3) 2.7–2.12 The legislator and the problem of stability	(3) 4.5–4.8 Institutions of stability: dictatorship, censorship, civil religion Conclusion 4.9

Figure 5. Outline of the *Social Contract*. Adapted from Hilail Gildin's discussion in *Rousseau's Social Contract* (Chicago: University of Chicago Press, 1983), pp. 12–17.

of historical and social change. Then to have a social theory is to have, among other things, a theory of these units of deliberation and action; and any such theory must attribute to them certain original principles which specify how they act given various social conditions.

Thus, what is really at stake in these disputes about an original human nature are the prospects of fundamental social change and the wisdom of adopting this or that means to it, given our present historical and social situation. Unless we are to act in the dark, we must be able to explain how a well-regulated free and humane society will operate, what it might look like; and why it will be stable and feasible, given a certain system of education when the suitable background obtains. Also, can we reach such a society from where we are without the use of means that cause psychological characteristics to come to dominate in us which themselves make such a society impossible?

In *Emile* Rousseau discusses the psychological theory which he thinks makes a well-regulated society both possible and stable. It requires that all coercive authority, public or otherwise, is to be based on principles persons can give to themselves as free moral persons, and which exclude personal dependence.

Rousseau: Appendix B

Comments on Figure 5:

1. Leaving aside 1.1 and 4.9 (first and last chapters of the *Social Contract*), each book falls into equal parts with the same number of chapters.

2. It is not until 3.10–3.18 (in 2nd part of Part II) that it becomes clear that the Sovereign must be an assembly of the people and that it must meet at fixed and periodic intervals (cf. 3.13.1).

List of Rousseau's Works

1750	*Discours sur les sciences et les arts* ("First Discourse") (written 1749)
1752	*Le Devin de Village* (opera)
1755	*Discours sur l'origine de l'inégalité* ("Second Discourse") "Economie Politique" (article in Diderot's *Encyclopédie*)

1756	*"Lettre sur la Providence"* (reply to Voltaire's *"Poème sur le désastre de Lisbonne"*)
1758	*Lettre à M. d'Alembert sur les spectacles*
1761	*La Nouvelle Héloïse*
1762	Writing of four biographical letters to Malesherbes
	Emile
	Contrat Social
	"Lettre à Christophe de Beaumont" (reply to the Archbishop of Paris on *Emile*)
1764	*Lettres écrites de la montagne* (reply to J. R. Tronchin's *Lettres écrites de la campagne*)
1765	*Projet de constitution pour la Corse*
1766	*Confessions* (1st part—completed on return to France) published 1781
1772	*Considérations sur le gouvernement de Pologne*
1772–76	*Dialogues: Rousseau juge de Jean-Jacques*
1776–78	*Les Rêveries du promeneur solitaire*

BIBLIOGRAPHY

Cassirer, Ernst, *The Question of Jean-Jacques Rousseau,* trans. Peter Gay (New York: Columbia University Press, 1954).

Cohen, Joshua, "Reflections on Rousseau: Autonomy and Democracy," *Philosophy and Public Affairs,* Summer 1986.

Cranston, Maurice, Introduction to his translation of the *Social Contract* (Penguin, 1968), pp. 9–25 (critical), pp. 25–43 (biographical); *The Early Life and Works of Jean-Jacques Rousseau, 1712–1754* (New York: Penguin, 1983).

Dent, N. J. H., *Rousseau* (Oxford: Blackwell, 1988); and *A Rousseau Dictionary* (Oxford: Blackwell, 1992).

Gay, Peter, *The Enlightenment: An Interpretation,* 2 vols. (Knopf, 1969); on Rousseau, pp. 529–552 (re *La Nouvelle Héloïse,* pp. 240f).

Gildin, Hilail, *Rousseau's Social Contract* (Chicago, 1983).

Green, F. C., *Jean-Jacques Rousseau: A Study of His Life and Writings* (Cambridge, 1955).

Grimsley, Ronald, *The Philosophy of Rousseau* (Oxford, 1973).

Lovejoy, Arthur O., *Essays in the History of Ideas* (Johns Hopkins, 1948). Contains "The Supposed Primitivism of Rousseau's Discourse on Inequality."

Masters, Roger, *Rousseau* (Princeton, 1968).

Miller, James, *Rousseau: Dreamer of Democracy* (Yale, 1984).

Neuhouser, Frederick, "Freedom, Dependence, and the General Will," *Philosophical Review,* July 1993.

Shklar, J. N., *Men and Citizens* (Cambridge UP, 1969).

ROUSSEAU II

The Social Contract: Assumptions and the General Will (I)

§1. Introduction

1. In the last lecture, we tried to get a sense of the questions and problems that moved Rousseau in writing the *Social Contract*. I said that his concerns are broader than those of Hobbes and Locke: Hobbes was concerned with overcoming the problem of divisive civil war, Locke with the justification of resistance to the Crown within a mixed constitution. Rousseau is a critic of culture and civilization: in the *Second Discourse* he diagnoses what he sees as the deep-rooted evils of society and depicts the vices and miseries it arouses in its members. He hopes to explain why these evils and vices come about, and to describe in the *Social Contract* the basic framework of a political and social world in which they would not be present.

The *Social Contract* sketches the principles of political right that must be realized in institutions if we are to have a just and workable, stable and reasonably happy society. I suggested that Rousseau's saying that human nature is good, and that it is through social institutions that we become bad, comes to these two propositions:

First, social institutions and conditions of social life exercise a predominant influence over which human propensities develop and express themselves over time. Some propensities are good, some are bad; and which ones are encouraged and manifest themselves depends on social conditions.

Second, there exists at least one possible and reasonably workable scheme of political institutions that both satisfies the principles of political right and meets the requirements for stability and human happiness. Thus, our nature is good in that it allows such a social world.

2. Consider once more the opening paragraph of the introduction to Book I of the *Social Contract*: "I want to inquire whether there can be a legitimate and reliable rule of administration in the civil order, taking men as

they are and laws as they can be. I shall try always to reconcile in this re-search what right permits with what interest prescribes, so that justice and utility are not at variance." That Rousseau views his reasoning as realistic and as aimed at what is possible is shown by his saying he means to take hu-man beings as they are and laws as they can be. To ensure both stability and happiness, a certain fit must be achieved between what right permits and interest prescribes. Otherwise the just and the useful will clash and a stable and legitimate regime is not possible.

Note that there is an ambiguity in Rousseau's saying he means to take human beings as they are. Surely he doesn't mean people as he sees them now, with all the vices and habits of a corrupt civilization (as described in the *Second Discourse*). Rather, he means human beings as they are according to the basic principles and propensities of human nature. These principles and propensities are those by reference to which we can account for the kinds of virtues and vices, aims and aspirations, final ends and desires—in short, the kind of character—people have under different social conditions. These principles and propensities include such things as the capacity for free will (to identify valid reasons and to act in the light of them) and per-fectibility (the potentiality for self-improvement through the historical de-velopment of our faculties through culture). Basic psychological aspects of our nature also include *amour de soi* and *amour-propre*, with this last under-stood on the wide view, following Kant.

3. In discussing any political conception with its conception of right and justice there are four questions we must distinguish: namely,

(1) What does the conception say are the reasonable or true principles of political right and justice; and how is the correctness of these principles established?

(2) What workable and practicable political and social institutions most effectively realize these principles and keep society stable over time?

(3) In what ways do people learn principles of right and acquire the mo-tivation to act from them and to affirm the political conception to which they belong?

(4) How might a society realizing these principles of right and justice come about; and how has it come about in some actual cases, if there are any?

Now, I shall interpret the idea of the social compact as addressed to the first two questions. In discussing it I begin from a hypothetical ongoing steady state in which the society of the social compact is fully realized and in equilibrium. Social institutions and laws may change from time to time, but its basic structure remains right and just. We then ask the first question: what are the principles of right in this society? The answer, in a phrase, is: they must express the terms of the social compact. We shall explore this phrase later.

We then ask the second question: what political and social institutions most effectively realize these principles and keep society stable over time? The answer to this is: certain general aspects of the basic structure of political society necessary to meet the terms of the social compact. An example is how the basic structure achieves three basic aspects of equality, to wit: how it upholds an equal standing and respect for all citizens; how it realizes the rule of law as applying to all and coming from all; and how it secures a sufficiently equal material equality.[1] We must say what these things mean.

The other two questions—the third about moral psychology, the fourth about historical origins—I put aside for the next lecture.

§2. The Social Compact

1. Let's turn to the idea of the social compact, which, as Rousseau puts it, is the act whereby people become a people (SC, 1:5.2). Later I connect it with the idea of the general will (and its various companion ideas, such as the common good and the common interest), and with the ideas of sovereignty and fundamental political laws. But before doing this, note that in Chapters 2–5 of Book I of *On the Social Contract* Rousseau argues from cases, much as Locke does, that political authority must be founded on a social compact. In parallel fashion, he argues that political right must be based on convention, and that neither paternal authority, nor right of the strongest, nor the right of the victor in war can suffice for political authority. As the heading of Chapter 5 says, "it is always necessary to go back to a first convention"—a social compact.

Implicit in these arguments by cases is the thought that all persons being, as Locke said, equal kings (*Second Treatise*, ¶123), we are bound to a po-

---

1. Frederick Neuhouser in his "Freedom, Dependence, and the General Will" cites these three aspects of equality. See pp. 386–391.

litical authority only if it has arisen, or could appropriately arise, from our consent as free and equal, and as reasonable and rational. Each alternative basis of authority, when examined, turns out to depend upon our lacking one or more of the three conditions essential for binding consent: that is, we lack either the ability, or the opportunity, or the proper will that binding consent requires. For example, as Rousseau explains in the *Social Contract:*

(a) Minors before the age of reason are not yet fully reasonable and rational, so parents or trustees must act in their behalf until they come of age (SC, 1:2.1f).

(b) Defeated subjects of a victor in war lack the opportunity to give their free consent; the signs of consent, even if given, in those circumstances are forced and cannot bind. Self-preservation moves them to obey, and they can again do as they please when the victor loses power. It is absurd to think right begins and ceases as force does (SC, 1:3).

(c) Slaves "lose everything in their chains, even the desire to be rid of them" (SC, 1:2.8), and so they lack both the ability and the will to give their free consent. But people are not slaves by nature: it is subjection to force that makes a man a slave, and it is the lack of will (the cowardice) resulting from slavery that holds the slave in bondage (SC, 1:4).

2. Now to our main topic: the social compact as Rousseau states it in SC, 1:6. This compact specifies the terms of social cooperation to be reflected in political and social institutions. I present Rousseau's account of the social compact as making four assumptions.[2] These are implicit in how he lays out the compact's general features and the conditions on which it rests.

First Assumption: those cooperating aim to advance their fundamental interests—their reasonable and rational good as they see it. Two of these interests connect with the love of self in both of its proper natural forms, *amour de soi* and *amour-propre.*

As *amour de soi* the love of self not only takes an interest in the means of well-being of various kinds, but also includes the interest in developing and exercising the two potentialities that we humans have in the state of nature that other animals do not have. One of these is the capacity to have a free will and thus the capacity to act in the light of valid reasons

---

2. These assumptions draw on Joshua Cohen, "Reflections on Rousseau: Autonomy and Democracy," *Philosophy and Public Affairs,* Summer 1986, pp. 276–279.

(SD, 113f); the other is the capacity of perfectibility and self-improvement through the development of our faculties and through our participation in culture as it develops over time (SD, 114f).

To these we could add our capacity for intellectual thought (not simply images) (SD, 119–126); our capacity for the moral attitudes and emotions (SD, 134–137); and our capacity for identification with others (pity and compassion as appropriate to the circumstances) (SD, 131f).

To recall what I said in the last lecture, the love of self, as *amour-propre* in its natural proper form, is the need we have to be recognized by others as having a secure standing, or status, as an equal member of our social group. This standing means that on the basis of our needs and wants we are viewed by others as entitled to make claims that they will recognize as imposing limits on their conduct, provided, of course, our claims meet certain conditions of reciprocity. Moved by this natural proper form of *amour-propre,* we are ready to grant the same standing to others in return, and hence to honor the limits that their needs and claims impose on us.

3. Second Assumption: the persons cooperating must advance their interests under the conditions of social interdependence with others. Here Rousseau supposes that people have reached the point historically where social cooperation in the form of political and social institutions is both necessary and mutually advantageous. Social interdependence is now part of our condition (SC, 1:6.1).

But this dependence must not to be mistaken for personal dependence on the will of others. This form of dependence, Rousseau thinks, as we know from the *Second Discourse,* is largely responsible for the development of unnatural, or perverted, *amour-propre* as it is displayed in the will to dominate and lord it over others, and in the other vices of civilization.

This second assumption deserves note: Rousseau never thinks that we can be independent of other human beings. He takes for granted that we are always bound to society in some form, and cannot live without it. He makes it equally clear both in the *Second Discourse* and in the *Social Contract* that it would not be good for us not to be in society: it is only in some appropriate social form that our nature can come to full expression and fruition (SC, 1:8.1). The social compact does not make us independent of society. Rather it will make us completely dependent on society as a whole, as a corporate body. We are independent of all other particular citizens as individuals, but we are dependent entirely on the City (polis), as he says (SC, 2:12.3).

It is not merely that a life outside of society is not feasible for us; or that we cannot return to the stage of primitive human beings before society came about—to that of a lazy, indolent, and harmless brute. It is rather that that life is not appropriate to our nature as having free will and being perfectible, and much else (SD, 102). Voltaire said that when he read the *Second Discourse* he was tempted to walk on all fours. A pleasant witticism, but he should have read the book more carefully.

4. Third Assumption: all persons have an equal capacity for and interest in their freedom, that is, a capacity both for having a free will and for acting in the light of valid reasons, as well as an interest in acting on their own judgments as to what they think is best in the light of the particular aims and interests that most move them. In short, we have both an equal capacity for judging what best advances our good as we see it, and an equal desire to act on this judgment. This assumption makes explicit what we said above about what falls under *amour de soi*.

Fourth Assumption: all persons have both an equal capacity for a political sense of justice and an interest in acting accordingly. This sense of justice is viewed as a capacity to understand, to apply, and to act from the principles of the social compact. This follows from the third assumption above, given what Rousseau says in SC, 1:8.1, about the passage from the state of nature to a civil state producing "a remarkable change in man, by substituting justice for instinct in his behavior and giving his actions the morality they previously lacked."

From what we said under the Second Assumption about social interdependence, clearly Rousseau is not thinking of the social compact as being made in a state of nature, or even in a state of early society. It is partly for this reason that we take the compact to address only the first two questions distinguished above in §1.3.

5. With these four assumptions, the fundamental problem becomes, as Rousseau puts it (SC, 1:6.4):

(i) How to "find a form of association that defends and protects the person and goods of each associate with all the common force."

And yet at the same time in this form of association:

(ii) ". . . each one, uniting with all, nevertheless obeys only himself and remains as free as before."

This is the problem to which the social contract is to be the solution.

The problem is how, then, without sacrificing our freedom, to unite with others to secure the fulfillment of our fundamental interests, and to guarantee the conditions for the development and exercise of our capacities (SC, 1:8.1). Rousseau answers the problem roughly as follows: given the fact of social interdependence, and the necessity for and the possibility of mutually advantageous social cooperation, the form of association is to be such that it would be reasonable and rational for equal persons, moved by both forms of love of self, to agree to it.

Given all the preceding assumptions, Rousseau thinks that the articles of the social compact are: "So completely determined by the nature of the act [the conditions and point of the social contract] that the slightest modification would render them [those articles] null and void" (SC, 1:6.5).

I think Rousseau means by this that once we state clearly the problem of the social compact, it is also clear what the general political and social form of association must be. Since he thinks the articles of the social compact are everywhere the same, and everywhere tacitly admitted and recognized, he must also think that the problem of the social compact is understood by our common human reason.

Rousseau says further that the articles of association when rightly understood reduce to a single clause: "the total alienation of each associate, with all his rights, to the whole community" (SC, 1:6.6).

6. On this statement, Rousseau makes three comments:

First (SC, 1:6.6): he says we give ourselves to society as a whole absolutely (without qualification), and the conditions to which we commit ourselves are the same for all. For this reason "no one has an interest in making [those conditions] burdensome for the others." Though we are committed absolutely to the articles agreed to, the scope of those articles is not all-encompassing: they do not involve an all-inclusive regulation of social life. Our love of self (in both its forms) prevents this, as does our interest in our freedom to advance our particular ends as we judge best, all the while being personally independent, in the sense of not being dependent on any particular person. Thus the general laws specifying the social compact must order restrictions on civil freedom as needed to advance the common good so as to preserve a proper scope for individual liberty (SC, 1:6.4).

In SC, 1:8.2, Rousseau mentions three forms of freedom: natural, civil, and moral, in that order. Natural freedom, the right to anything we want and can get, limited only by the force of the individual, we lose by the social compact. In return we gain "civil freedom and the proprietorship of everything he [man] possesses," which is limited only by the general will. And in return we also gain moral freedom. This alone makes us master of ourselves: "For the impulse of appetite alone is slavery, and obedience to the law one has prescribed to oneself is freedom" (SC, 1:8.3).

The point to be made here is that the institutions of the society of the social compact must order our relations of dependence upon society as a whole and our relations with one another so that both our moral and our civil freedom are, if possible, fully achieved.

7. Rousseau's second comment is made in elaborating the articles of association. He says that since the alienation of ourselves to the whole society is unconditional, the social union is as perfect as it can be. His point is that as parties to the social compact we no longer have any rights valid against society itself, provided the compact is properly formed and fully honored. There is no higher authority to which we can appeal to judge between ourselves and the political society of the social compact. To claim this would be to see ourselves as still in the state of nature, as still outside the legitimate political society the compact establishes. The terms of that compact properly made and fully honored constitute the final court of appeal (SC, 1:6.7).

Here it is essential to remember that the social compact is an answer to the first question we noted earlier, namely: what are the correct principles of political right? There is no paradox, then, in saying, as I interpret Rousseau to say, that there is no higher authority to which we may appeal than the terms of the social compact itself, provided, as always, it is properly formed and fully honored.

Rousseau's third (and final) comment is that: "as each gives himself to all, he gives himself to no one; and since there is no associate over whom one does not acquire the same right one grants him over oneself, one gains the equivalent of everything one loses." Indeed, we do even better: for now our life and our means of life are protected by the united force of the whole community (SC, 1:6.8).

Now, this establishes our personal independence. Why? Well, we gain the same rights over others as they gain over us, and this we have done by agreeing to an exchange of rights, for reasons rooted in our fundamental interests, including the interest in our freedom. We are no longer dependent on the particular and arbitrary wills of other specific persons. From the *Second Discourse* we know that Rousseau thinks this kind of dependence must be avoided: it corrupts our perfectibility and arouses the unnatural forms of *amour-propre*—the will to dominate or the fawning servility found in a society marked by unjustified inequalities.

Each of us is, of course, dependent on political society as a whole. But in the society of the social compact each is an equal citizen and not subject to anyone's arbitrary will or authority. Moreover, as we shall see, there is a public commitment to establishing an equality of conditions among citizens that ensures their personal independence. It is part of Rousseau's moral psychology that our natural and proper *amour-propre* requires that we be personally independent, and that there be a public commitment to an equality of conditions that guarantees that independence.

8. Finally, Rousseau gives another definition of the social compact reduced to its essentials: "Each of us puts his person and all his power in common under the supreme direction of the general will; and in a body we receive each member as an indivisible part of the whole" (SC, 1:6.9).

This is the first occurrence in the *Social Contract* of the term "the general will" *(la volonté générale)*. It is essential to understand its meaning and how it connects with Rousseau's other basic ideas. So I turn to this idea.

First, however, let's look at some of the terms defined in SC, 1:6.10: With the social contract there comes into being a *public person,* in classical times called a *city* (the polis), now a *republic,* or *body politic.* This body is an artificial and collective body with as many members as voters in the assembly. The assembly includes the whole people, all citizens.[3]

In its active role (e.g., that of enacting a basic law), the body politic is called the *Sovereign;* in its passive role, the *State;* when spoken of in connection with other similar bodies, it is called a *Power;* as when we say "the great powers of Europe," meaning the leading European states.

Those persons associated together by the social contract, when taken collectively, are *the people.* When taken individually as those who share (equally) in the sovereign power, they are *citizens;* while they are *subjects* insofar as they put themselves under the laws of the state. Above I have said that citizens share equally in sovereign power. Although Rousseau doesn't say this in SC, 1:6.10, it's plainly his view, and it's worth emphasizing since it distinguishes his view from Locke's.

---

3. Note here, however, that for Rousseau the assembly did not include women. They are not regarded as active citizens; for Rousseau, their place is in the home.

§3. The General Will

1. What we have said so far about the social compact is extremely general and rather unclear. In order to get a clearer view, let's look at the nature of the association that Rousseau thinks would be entered into given the conditions he imposes on the compact. A way to do this is to figure out how he understands the general will.[4]

This term occurs about seventy times in the *Social Contract* (including references via pronouns). The first occurrence is the one noted above. To repeat it: "Each of us puts [into the community] his person and all his power in common under the supreme direction of the general will; and in a body we receive each member as an indivisible part of the whole" (SC, 1.6.9).

Thus, what provides the justification of political authority in society on matters of political justice—an authority exercised through a vote of the assembly of the people—is *bona fide* expressions of the general will. This will is properly expressed in fundamental political laws concerning constitutional essentials and basic justice, or in laws suitably related thereto. Fundamental laws are legitimate in virtue of their being *bona fide* expressions of the general will. How are we to understand this idea?

2. To begin: Each individual incorporated into political society has particular interests (SC, 1:7.7). Within the limits of civil freedom (established by the social compact), these interests are the basis of valid reasons for action. Each of us has, then, a private, or particular, will. Here, by will, I take Rousseau to mean a capacity for deliberative reason: this is the capacity for free will of the *Second Discourse*. One aspect of this capacity is shown in our making decisions in the light of reasons connected with our particular interests. These decisions are expressions of our particular will.

Observe that the existence of particular interests is taken for granted. The society of the social contract is not one in which people have no inter-

---

4. The idea of the general will has a long history. See Judith Shklar, *Men and Citizens* (Cambridge: Cambridge University Press, 1969), pp. 168–169 and 184–197. See also her article on the general will in *Dictionary of the History of Ideas*, ed. P. Weiner (New York: Scribner's, 1973), Vol. 2, pp. 275–281; and Patrick Riley, *The General Will Before Rousseau* (Princeton: Princeton University Press, 1986).

ests separate from those of the political society, or no interests distinct from and often contrary to the general will and the common good.

3. For Rousseau the society of the social compact is not a mere aggregation of people. Rather, an essential condition of that society is that its members have what Rousseau calls a general will. About this, I shall now ask five questions:

(1) What is the general will the will of?
(2) What does the general will will?
(3) What makes the common good possible?
(4) What makes common interests possible?
(5) What determines our fundamental interests?

In answer to the first question: What is the general will the will of?: it is the will all citizens have as members of the political society of the social compact. It is a will distinct from the private will each also has as a particular person (SC, 1:7.7).

To answer the second question: what does the general will will?: we say that, as members of the political society, citizens share a conception of their common good (SC, 4:1.1). That they share such a conception is itself public knowledge between them. We might say: when all citizens conduct themselves in their thought and action reasonably and rationally as the social compact requires, the general will of each citizen wills the common good, as specified by their shared conception of that common good.

Let's note that the general will is not, certainly, the will of an entity that in some way transcends the members of society. It is not, say, the will of the society as a whole as such (SC, 1:7.5; 2:4.1). It is individual citizens who have a general will: that is, each has a capacity for deliberative reason which, on appropriate occasions, leads them to decide what to do—how to vote, say—on the basis of what they each think will best advance their common interest in what is necessary for their common preservation and general welfare, i.e. the common good (SC, 1:7.7). In other words, the general will is a form of deliberative reason that each citizen shares with all other citizens in virtue of their sharing a conception of their common good.

What citizens think best advances this common good identifies what they view as good reasons for their political decisions. Every form of deliberative reason and will must have its own way of identifying valid reasons. Thus, as members of the assembly, as citizens, we are not to vote our particular, private interests as we might like to, but to express our opinion as to which of the general measures presented as alternatives best advances the common good (SC, 4:1.6; 4:2.8).

This brings us to the third question: What makes the common good possible? As stated, the general will wills the common good, but the common good is specified by our common interest. Here the common good is social conditions that make possible, or assist, citizens' attaining their common interests. Thus, without common interests, there would be no common good, and so, no general will. Consider SC, 2:1.1: "The first and most important consequence of the principles established above is that the general will alone can guide the forces of the State according to the end for which it was instituted, which is the common good. For if the opposition of private interests made the establishment of societies necessary, it is the agreement of these same interests that made it possible. It is what these different interests have in common that forms the social bond, and if there were not some point at which all the interests are in agreement, no society could exist. Now it is uniquely on the basis of this common interest that society ought to be governed."

Note that it is our common interests that yield the social bond and make possible our general will. This confirms what we said above: namely, that the general will is not the will of an entity that transcends citizens as individuals. For the general will ceases or dies when citizens' interests change so that they no longer have fundamental interests in common. The general will depends on such interests.

The fourth question is: What makes possible the common interests that specify the common good? The answer to this is our fundamental interests as we have described them under our initial assumptions; for example, the first assumption where we grouped them under *amour de soi* and *amour-propre*. There are also fundamental interests given our common and enduring social situation: for example, the fact that our situation is one of social interdependence, and that mutually advantageous social cooperation is both necessary and possible.

This brings us to the fifth question: What determines our (common) fundamental interests? To this the answer is Rousseau's conception of human nature and of the fundamental interests and capacities essential and appropriate to it. Or we could say: it is his conception of the person regarded in its most essential aspects. This conception is, I believe, a normative conception and from it the enumeration of our fundamental interests is derived. As stated earlier, Rousseau doesn't look to people as they actually are in a society marked by extremes of inequality between rich and poor, powerful and weak, with the resulting evil of domination and subjection. He is looking to human beings as they are by nature, understood in the light of his conception thereof. That nature determines our fundamental interests.

Notice here what is common to social contract doctrines, namely, a normalization of interests attributed to the parties to the contracts. In Hobbes, it is our fundamental interests in self-preservation, conjugal affections, and "riches and the means of commodious living." In Locke it is lives, liberties, and estates. In Rousseau it is the fundamental interests we have surveyed. Everyone is assumed to have these interests in roughly the same form, and, as reasonable and rational, to order them in the same way.

4. Perhaps this interpretation of Rousseau's thought is borne out by what he says about the general will in SC, 2:3:

2:3.1. The general will is always right and always tends to the public good.

2:3.2. There is often a great difference between the will of all and the general will.

2:3.2. The general will considers only the common interest, while the will of all considers private interest, and is but the sum of private wills.

2:3.2. The general will is what remains after taking away from private wills the pluses and minuses that cancel each other out and taking the sum of these wills as modified by those subtractions.

2:3.3. The great number of small differences will converge on the general will and the decision will always be good, provided that the people are properly informed and have no communication among themselves.

2:3.3. When one group dominates in society, there is no longer a general will.

2:3.4. For the general will to be well expressed, there should be no sectional associations in the state and each citizen should decide for himself.

2:3.4. If sectional associations exist, then to enlighten the general will it is necessary to multiply their number and to prevent inequality among them.

These statements can be interpreted in various ways. I read them as saying that our particular interests are likely to bias our vote, and this is so even when, with the best intentions, we try to ignore them and to vote our opinion as to what best advances the common good. This is a very different conception of voting than the one we are perhaps more familiar with: that we can always vote our particular interests. But accepting Rousseau's view, particular interests are obstacles to conscientious voting; they get in the way of a reasoned view of the common good, for this good is specified as meeting the fundamental interests which all citizens share.

Hence we see why Rousseau says such things as these: The general will considers only the common interest. The general will is what remains after taking away from the private wills the pluses and minuses that cancel each other out. These pluses and minuses I read as the various private and particular interests that cause the biases that incline us this way or that. Even when we are conscientious and intend to vote our opinion as to what best advances the common good, we may miss the mark swayed by particular interests in ways unnoticed by us.

Rousseau says the great number of small differences, that is, the great number of small biases, will most likely converge on the general will. So if the people are properly informed and vote their own opinion, the overall vote will most likely be correct. What he may have in mind here is that each informed and conscientious vote can be seen as a sample of the truth with a considerably greater than 50/50 chance of being correct. Therefore, as the number of such samples increases (as more well-informed citizens vote conscientiously) the probability increases that the outcome of the vote converges on what really does advance the common good.[5]

5. To briefly recap the answers to the five questions:

(1) The general will is a form of deliberative reason shared and exercised by each citizen as a member of the corporate body, or the public person (the body politic), that comes into being with the social compact (SC, 1:6.10);

(2) The general will wills the common good, understood as the social conditions that make it possible for citizens to realize their common interests;

---

5. Of course, for this interpretation to work, it must be assumed that the samples are independent of one another. Otherwise the Bernoulli law of large numbers will not apply. Perhaps this is why Rousseau says that there should be no communication among citizens. But in any case, the analogy seems rather far-fetched. It is discussed by K. J. Arrow, *Social Choice and Individual Values*, 2nd ed. (New Haven: Yale University Press, 1986), pp. 85f.

(3) What makes the common good possible is our common interests;

(4) What makes our common interests possible is our shared fundamental interests;

(5) What determines our fundamental interests is our common human nature (as Rousseau conceives of it) and the fundamental interests and capacities appropriate to it; or alternatively, Rousseau's conception of the person as a normative idea.

Once we have answered this fifth question, we have pushed the formal account of the general will and what makes it possible as far as we can. By formal account, I mean that the account concerns the general will's relation to such formal ideas as the common good, common interests, fundamental interests, and a conception of human nature.[6]

Next time I shall go over five other questions concerning the general will. Being able to answer these is a good test of whether we understand the idea of the general will. While some references to the general will in the *Social Contract* are obscure, I believe the idea itself can be made clear, and the main things Rousseau says about it are consistent and make good sense.

6. By way of comment, I have no objection to calling our human nature with its fundamental interests appropriate to it "the essence of human nature." This is objectionable only when we think that by saying it, we are giving some further grounding, or some deeper (or metaphysical) justification of what we have already said. I would say instead that if Rousseau's view covers all that we think on clear reflection we may reasonably judge and can claim, then it stands by itself. That is all that one can do. Not of course that his view actually does that.

ROUSSEAU III

The General Will (II) and the Question of Stability

§1. The Point of View of the General Will

1. The five questions about the general will we have gone over so far have, as I've indicated, an abstract, formal quality. Missing so far is the content of the general will: that is, the specific political principles and values, and the social conditions that the general will wills and requires to be realized in the basic structure.

Answers to the next five questions will shed some light on these things:

(6) What is the point of view of the general will?
(7) Why must the general will, to be rightful, spring from all and apply to all?
(8) What is the relation between the general will and justice?
(9) Why does the general will tend to equality?
(10) How is the general will related to civil and moral freedom?

Answers to these questions tell us much about the content of the general will. The last question is especially important, as we shall see. A proper understanding of it holds the key to understanding the full power of Rousseau's thought.

2. We begin with the sixth question: What is the point of view of the general will? For Rousseau the common good (which is specified by the social conditions needed for us to attain our common interests) is not to be accounted for in utilitarian terms. That is, in willing the common good the general will does not will the social conditions required to attain the greatest happiness (the greatest fulfillment of all the various interests of individuals) summed over all members of society. In *Political Economy* Rousseau says that the maxim that the government "is allowed to sacrifice an innocent man for the safety of the multitude" is "one of the most execrable that

tyranny ever invented, the most false that might be proposed, the most dangerous that might be accepted, and the most directly opposed to the fundamental laws of society." He continues: "Rather than that one ought to perish for all, all have engaged their goods and their lives for the defense of each one among them, in order that private weakness always be protected by public force, and each member by the whole State."[1]

Here Rousseau is emphatic that the fundamental laws of the society of the social compact are not to be founded on an aggregative principle. The general will does not will maximizing the fulfillment of the sum of all the interests of all kinds that individuals have. Rather, the fundamental laws of society are to be based solely on common interests. (Recall SC, 2:1.1.)

We have seen that our common interests are given in terms of certain fundamental interests. These include the interests expressed by the two natural forms of self-love (*amour de soi* and *amour-propre*) as well as our interests in the security of our person and property. Security of property, rather than mere possession, is one of the advantages of civil society (SC, 1:8.2). There are also our interests in the general social conditions for the development of our potentialities (for free will and perfectibility) and our freedom to advance our aims as we see fit within the limits of civil freedom.

3. It is these fundamental interests secured for each citizen—and not the greatest satisfaction of our various interests of all kinds both fundamental and particular—that specify our good from the point of view of the general will. These fundamental interests everyone shares. The appropriate grounds for basic laws is that they secure through social cooperation, on terms all would agree to, the social conditions necessary to realize those interests.

To express this idea from the point of view of the general will, we say that only reasons based on the fundamental interests we share as citizens should count as reasons when we are acting as members of the assembly in enacting constitutional norms or basic laws. From that point of view, those fundamental interests take absolute priority over our particular interests in the order of reasons there appropriate. When we vote on fundamental laws, we are to give our opinion as to which laws best establish the political

---

1. See Jean-Jacques Rousseau, *On the Social Contract, with Geneva Manuscript and Political Economy*, p. 220.

and social conditions enabling everyone equally to advance their fundamental interests.

Note that the idea of a point of view, as used in these remarks, is an idea of deliberative reason, and as such it has a certain rough structure: that is, it is framed to consider certain kinds of questions—those about which constitutional norms or basic laws best advance the common good—and it admits only certain kinds of reasons as having any weight. Thus, it is clear from this that Rousseau's view contains an idea of what I have called public reason.[2] So far as I know the idea originates with him, though versions of it are certainly found later in Kant, who is also important in this connection.

§2. The General Will: The Rule of Law, Justice, and Equality

1. We can proceed more easily by taking the next three questions together:

(7) Why must the general will, to be rightful, spring from all and apply to all?

(8) What is the relation between the general will and justice?

(9) Why does the general will tend to equality?

The point of view of the general will connects these three questions and shows how they are related.[3] It shows why, to be rightful, it must spring from all and apply to all; it shows how it is related to justice and why it inclines towards equality, as Rousseau says in SC, 2:1.3. A central part of the answer is in SC, 2:4.5, which reads:

> The engagements that bind us to the social body are obligatory only because they are mutual, and their nature is such that in fulfilling them

2. John Rawls, *Justice as Fairness: A Restatement*, ed. Erin Kelly (Cambridge, Mass.: Harvard University Press, 2001), pp. 91f. Public reason is the form of reasoning appropriate to equal citizens who as a corporate body impose rules on one another backed by the sanctions of state power. Shared guidelines for inquiry and methods of reasoning make that reason public, while freedom of speech and thought in a constitutional regime make that reason free.

3. Keep in mind throughout the following comments that the public acts in which the general will is most characteristically expressed are the enactments of basic political or fundamental laws (SC, 2:12.2) in which citizens have voted their opinion as to which such enactments best secure the common good.

one cannot work for someone else without also working for oneself. Why is the general will always right and why do all constantly want the happiness of each, if not because there is no one who does not apply that word "each" to himself, and does not think of himself as he votes for all? Which proves that the equality of right, and the concept of justice it produces, are derived from each man's preference for himself and consequently from the nature of man; that the general will, to be truly such, should be general in its object as well as in its essence; that it should come from all to apply to all; and that it loses its natural rectitude when it is directed towards any individual, determinate object. Because then, judging what is foreign to us, we have no true principle of equity to guide us.

2. This is a marvelous paragraph. Be sure to read it carefully. It is impossible to summarize briefly. Rousseau holds that when we exercise our general will in a vote on the fundamental laws of society, we are to consider basic political and social institutions. These fundamental laws will, in effect, specify—render determinate—the terms of social cooperation and give definite content to the social compact.

This being so, we are in effect voting for all members of society, and in doing so we think of ourselves and our fundamental interests. Since we are voting on a fundamental law, the general will is general in its object. That is, fundamental laws mention no individuals or associations by name, and must apply to all. This answers the second part of the seventh question.

Moreover, we are each guided by our fundamental interests, which we all have in common. Thus, the general will is always rightful and, in virtue of their general will, citizens want the happiness of each. For in voting they take the "each" to be themselves as they vote for all. The general will springs from all in that everyone by adopting the point of view of the general will is guided by the same fundamental interests as everyone else. This answers the first part of the seventh question.

We also see why the general will wills justice. In the passage quoted above Rousseau says (or so I interpret him) that the idea of justice, which the general will produces, derives from a predilection we each have for ourselves, and thus derives from human nature as such. Here it is essential to note that this predilection yields the idea of justice only when it is expressed from the point of view of the general will. When not made subordinate to that point of view—the point of view of our deliberative reason with the structure sketched previously—our predilection for ourselves may, of course, produce injustice and violations of right.

3. We see also why the general will wills equality: it does so first, because of the features of the point of view peculiar to the general will, and second, from the nature of our fundamental interests, including our interest in avoiding the social conditions of personal dependence. These conditions must be avoided if our *amour-propre* and perfectibility are not to be corrupted, and if we are not to be subject to the arbitrary will and authority of particular others. Knowing the nature of these fundamental interests, citizens, in voting their opinion as to what best promotes the common good, vote for fundamental laws that secure the wanted equality of conditions.

Rousseau addresses these considerations about equality in SC, 2:11.1–3. Here he says (2:11.1) that freedom and equality are: "the greatest good of all, which ought to be the end of every system of legislation . . . Freedom because all private dependence *(dépendance particulière)* is that much force subtracted from the body of the State; equality because freedom cannot last without it."

For Rousseau, in the society of the social compact, freedom and equality, when properly understood and suitably related, are not in conflict. This is because equality is necessary for freedom. Lack of personal independence means a loss of freedom, and that independence requires equality. Rousseau views equality as essential for freedom and that, in large part, is what makes it essential. Equality is not, however, strict equality: "With regard to equality, this word must not be understood to mean that degrees of power and wealth should be exactly the same [for all], but rather that with regard to power, it should be incapable of all violence and never exerted except by virtue of status [authority] and the laws; and with regard to wealth, no citizen should be so opulent that he can buy another, and none so poor that he is constrained to sell himself" (SC, 2:11.2).

Rousseau denies that this moderated degree of inequality, which is not so great as to lead to personal dependence, and yet not so restrictive as to lose the benefits of civil freedom, is a fantasy that cannot be achieved in practice. Granted some abuse and error is inevitable. But, he says: ". . . does it follow that it [inequality] must not at least be regulated? It is precisely because the force of things always tends to destroy equality that the force of legislation should always tend to maintain it" (SC, 2:11.3). Also: "The private will tends by its nature towards preferences, and the general will toward equality" (SC, 2:1.3).

This remark of Rousseau's is an ancestor of the first reason why, in justice as fairness, the basic structure is taken as the primary subject of justice.[4]

4. To pull together these remarks about the general will: The point of view of the general will is a point of view we are to take up when we vote our opinion as to what fundamental laws best advance the common interests that establish the bonds of society. Since these laws are general and apply to all citizens, we are to reason about those laws in light of the fundamental interests we share with others. These interests specify our common interests, and the social conditions for achieving these interests specify the common good.

Accepted facts, or reasonable beliefs, about what best advances the common good provide the basis for the reasons that properly have weight in our deliberations from the point of view of the general will. The general will results from our capacity to take up this appropriate point of view. It calls upon our shared capacity for deliberative reason in the case of political society. As such, the general will is one form of the potentiality for free will of the *Second Discourse:* it is realized as citizens in society pursue the common good as it directs. One corollary of this is that the achievement of our freedom—as the full exercise of our capacity for free will—is possible only in society of a certain kind, one that meets certain conditions in its basic structure. This is a very important point, and we will come back to it below.

We can now see why Rousseau thinks our wills tend to coincide and become the general will when we ask ourselves the right question. Of course, this is only a tendency, and not a certainty, since our knowledge is incomplete and our beliefs about appropriate means may reasonably differ. Moreover, there may be reasonable differences of opinion in matters of interpre-

---

4. Rawls, *Justice as Fairness,* §§3, 4, 15. The basic structure of society is the way in which the main political and social institutions of society fit together into one system of social cooperation, and the way they assign basic rights and duties and regulate the division of advantages that arises from social cooperation over time. A just basic structure secures what we may call background justice. To ensure that fair background conditions (for free and fair agreements) are maintained over time, it is essential that the basic structure be the primary subject of justice.

tation—for example, about the level of poverty at which people are so poor as to sell themselves and thus lose their personal independence.

§3. The General Will and Moral and Civil Freedom

1. This brings us to the tenth question: How is the general will related to civil and moral freedom? Rousseau believes that the society of the social compact achieves in its basic political and social institutions both civil and moral freedom. The social compact provides the essential social background conditions for civil freedom. Assuming that fundamental laws are properly based on what is required for the common good, citizens are free to pursue their aims within the limits laid down by the general will (SC, 1:8.2). This is quite straightforward.

The deeper question concerns moral freedom. In his accounting of what we gain from the society of the social compact, he says the following: "To the foregoing acquisitions of the civil state could be added moral freedom, which alone makes man truly the master of himself. For the impulse of appetite alone is slavery, and obedience to the law one has prescribed for oneself is freedom" (SC, 1:8.3).

Similarly, moral freedom consists in obeying the law one has prescribed for oneself. And we know that that law is the fundamental law of the society of the social compact: namely, the laws enacted from the point of view of the general will and properly based on citizens' fundamental shared interests. So far so good, but there seems more to it than this.

2. Perhaps we have only to pull together what we have said. I assume that all the requisite conditions are satisfied for the society of the social compact to obtain. Obviously Rousseau is not talking about the case when they do not. With this granted, in that society citizens achieve their moral freedom in these respects:

One respect is that, in obeying the law and conducting our civil freedom within the limits that the general will has laid down, we are acting not only in accordance with the general will, but from our own will. The reason is that we have freely voted along with others in laying down those limits, and this holds whether we were in the majority or not (again assuming the requisite conditions). (On this see SC, 4:2.8–9.)

Another respect is that the law we give to ourselves satisfies the conditions of the social compact, and the terms of this compact issue from our nature as we now are. That is, those terms depend on our fundamental interests, and these are always our fundamental interests, given by our nature in Rousseau's sense. This is so even if, when we look at disfigured and distorted members of corrupt societies, it may appear that they are not, although those cases are not relevant here. In those societies people may be mistaken about what their fundamental interests really are, though they surely know from their vices and misery that something is grievously wrong.

3. Again, we might worry about the terms of the social compact because of our social interdependence. Recall that this interdependence is one of our basic assumptions in setting up the compact situation. Doesn't this weigh down and constrict our freedom? Yet for Rousseau this interdependence is also part of our nature. This is shown in some of the attributes he says are necessary to the legislator, as the person who "dares to undertake the founding of a people" (SC, 2:7.3). Integral to his view is that our fundamental interests and our capacities for freedom and perfectibility can come to their fullest fruition only in society, or more specifically, in the society of the social compact. So much is clear even from the *Second Discourse*.

Another matter that may cause difficulty is the thought that the social compact is an event that happened some time in the past. However, in the case of Rousseau, I do not think he views it—or perhaps better, that we need not view it—that way in interpreting him. Rather, I take a present time, ongoing, interpretation: this means that the terms of the social compact arise out of the conditions that always obtain in a society well-ordered in Rousseau's sense. Thus, citizens are always socially interdependent in such a society. They always have the same fundamental interests. They always have the same capacity for free will and to achieve moral and civil freedom under appropriate conditions. They are always moved by *amour de soi* and *amour-propre*, and so on. This follows this present time interpretation, once the situation of the social compact is set up in Rousseau's way.

The terms of the social compact, then, simply issue from the way citizens fundamentally are now, at any time, in a society realizing those terms. So following and acting from laws satisfying those terms, citizens act from a law they give to themselves. They achieve their moral freedom.

In conclusion: moral freedom, then, once properly understood, is simply not possible outside of society. This is because that freedom is the capacity to fully exercise and to be guided by the form of deliberative reason appropriate to the situation at hand. That, for Rousseau, is what moral freedom is. And it cannot be realized without attaining skills attainable only within a social context: all the skills necessary for language in which to express thought, and beyond that the ideas and conceptions required to deliberate correctly and much else. It is also not possible without significant social occasions in which to exercise the requisite powers to their fullest.

§4. The General Will and Stability

1. There are still questions about the general will we haven't discussed, and indeed we can't cover them all. This is because almost everything in the *Social Contract* bears on the idea of the general will in some way. We should consider two other questions, so I turn to them briefly.

Recall that in the last lecture I listed four questions that must be distinguished in considering any political conception of right and justice, including Rousseau's: namely,

(1) What does the conception say are the reasonable or true principles of political right and justice; and how is the correctness of these principles established?

(2) What workable and practicable political and social institutions most effectively realize these principles?

(3) In what ways do people learn principles of right and acquire the motivation to act from them so as to preserve stability over time?

(4) How might a society realizing the principles of right and justice come about; and how has it in some actual cases, if any such exist, come about?

We have interpreted the idea of the social compact as addressed to the first two questions. For Rousseau the principles of political right are those that meet the terms of that compact, and these terms require that certain principles and values be realized in that society's basic structure. The third question is about the psychological forces that help to maintain stability and how they are acquired and learned. The fourth question is about origins and the process whereby the society of the social compact might arise.

In SC, 2:7–12, of the *Social Contract* we find the curious figure of the legislator (or law-giver), the founder of the state who gives the people their fundamental laws. The law-giver is not the government or the sovereign, and because it is his role to set up the constitution, he has no role in that constitution. Nor does he have a role as a ruler, "For . . . one who has authority over laws should also not have authority over men" (SC, 2:7.4). He has no right to impose his will on the people. While he is viewed as having extraordinary wisdom and knowledge, he has no authority for his work as a law-maker, and yet he must somehow persuade the people to accept his laws. Historically, this has often been done by persuading the people that the laws are given to them, through him, by the gods. Religion and persuasion, it seems, are required at the founding of a just state.

2. What is the role of the law-giver in Rousseau's doctrine? I believe this figure is Rousseau's way of addressing the last two of the questions just listed. If we look at SC, 2:6.10, we find passages that bear on each of those questions. Thus, Rousseau says:

> Laws are properly speaking only the conditions of the civil association. The people that is subject to the laws ought to be their author. Only those who are forming an association have the right to regulate the conditions of society. But how will they regulate these conditions? Will it be in common accord, by sudden inspiration? . . . Who will give it the necessary foresight to formulate acts and publish them in advance? . . . How will a blind multitude, which often does not know what it wants because it rarely knows what is good for it, carry out by itself an undertaking as vast and as difficult as a system of legislation? . . . The general will is always right, but the judgment that guides it is not always enlightened. . . . Private individuals see the good they reject; the public wants the good it does not see. All are equally in need of guides. The former must be obligated to make their wills conform to their reason. The latter must be taught to know what it wants. . . . From this arises the necessity for a legislator.

Here Rousseau has in mind the fourth question, that of origins and transition: he is asking how, given the great obstacles that must have obtained in the absence of a free, equal, and just social world, how a society of the social compact could ever have come about. Surely, Rousseau suggests, it requires a kind of rare good fortune in the person of a law-giver. Lycurgus of ancient Greece is mentioned as an example of a historical figure who played this role, abdicating his throne to give his homeland laws

(SC, 2:7.5). Only such a law-giver will know enough about human nature to know how laws and institutions need to be arranged in order to transform people's characters and interests so that, given historical conditions, their actions accord with what those arrangements enjoin. And only such a law-giver would be able to persuade people to follow those laws in the first place.

3. That Rousseau is also concerned with the question of stability is shown in other things he says. Thus, in SC, 2:7.2, he says: "If it is true that a great prince [Rousseau's term for government as a collective body] is a rare man, what about a great legislator? The former only has to follow the model that the latter should propose. The latter is the mechanic who invents the machine; the former is only the workman who puts it together and starts it running." He adds: "At the birth of societies, says Montesquieu, the leaders of republics create the institutions; thereafter, it is the institutions that form the leaders of republics."

Later in SC, 2:7.9, Rousseau says: "In order for an emerging people to appreciate the healthy maxims of politics, and follow the fundamental rules of statecraft, the effect would have to become the cause; the social spirit, which should be the result of the institution, would have to preside over the founding of the institution itself; and men would have to be prior to laws what they ought to become by means of laws."

And so it is that: "This is what has always forced the fathers of nations to have recourse to the intervention of heaven and to attribute their own wisdom to the Gods" (SC, 2:7.10).

That Rousseau is talking about the third question of stability is clear once we put it in the form suggested by the above: namely, how does it happen that political institutions come to generate the social spirit that would be necessary, at the founding, to enact laws establishing those institutions. For if institutions do generate the spirit that would enact them, they will be enduring and stable.

How far-reaching is the change from the state of nature (the early stage of history of the *Second Discourse*) that is brought about by the legislator's work is evident from what Rousseau says earlier in SC, 2:7.3:

One who dares to undertake the founding of a people should feel that he is capable of changing human nature, so to speak; of transforming each individual, who by himself is a perfect and solitary whole, into a part of a larger whole from which the individual receives, in a sense, his life and his being; of altering man's constitution in order to strengthen it; of substituting a partial and moral existence for the physical and independent existence we have all received from nature. He must in short take away man's own forces in order to give him forces that are foreign to him and that he cannot make use of without the help of others. . . . So that if each citizen is nothing, and can do nothing, except with all the others, and if the force acquired by the whole is equal or superior to the sum of the natural forces of all the individuals, it may be said that legislation has reached its highest possible point of perfection.

This is an extraordinary paragraph. It illustrates the extent to which Rousseau views us as socially dependent on the society of the social compact even though we are personally independent (that is, not dependent on any other particular persons). The powers we acquire in society are powers we can only use in society and then only in cooperation with the complimentary powers of other persons. Think of how the trained powers of musicians reach their fullest fruition only when exercised with other musicians in chamber music and orchestras.

4. What Rousseau says about the law-giver is clear enough once we grasp the two questions he is addressing, admittedly in an unusual way. There is nothing mysterious about the role of the law-giver, however rare such a figure may be.

Taking the question of historical origins first, it is evident that the society of the social compact might come about in many ways. For example, it could happen that gradually over several centuries, through a series of violent religious wars, people eventually came to think it no longer practicable to use force in such struggles and reluctantly came to accept as a *modus vivendi* the principles of liberty and equality. Religious toleration seems to have come about in some such way. All thought the division of Christendom was a terrible disaster, nevertheless toleration seemed better than unending civil war and the destruction of society.

So later generations may come to endorse certain principles on their merits, much as after the wars of religion ceased, the principles of religious liberty were gradually accepted as basic constitutional liberties. It is a commonplace that early generations may introduce principles and institutions for different reasons than the reasons that those coming later, who have grown up under them, have for accepting them. Could society advance otherwise?

It is clear from the way Rousseau introduces the law-giver that he never supposes that people's entering into an agreement of any kind could be the transition from a pre-political stage to a society whose basic institutions conformed to the requisite terms of the social compact. It could not be in that way that a people of the early stage of history of the *Second Discourse,* the free, equal, and just society of the state of nature, could be transformed into citizens with a general will. The institutions that fashion a general will are designed by the law-giver who persuades the people that his authority is of a higher order and so they accept the laws he proposes. In due course later generations come to have and to perpetuate a general will. Once society is set up and running, it is in stable equilibrium: its institutions generate in those who live under them the general will needed to maintain it in subsequent generations as they come on the stage. Rousseau's reference to Montesquieu (quoted above) states this point perfectly.

Rousseau's legislator/law-giver should be seen, then, as in effect a fictional figure—a *deus ex machina*—introduced to take up the second pair of questions: that of moral learning and stability, and the other of historical origins. This device causes no problems for the unity and coherence of Rousseau's view, as is sometimes alleged. We see this once we distinguish the four questions and recognize that there are different ways in which the society of the social compact might come about.

§5. Freedom and the Social Compact

1. We have still to discuss the second part of the problem of the social compact. Recall Rousseau's statement of that problem as finding a form of association such that while uniting ourselves with others, we obey only ourselves and remain as free as before (SC, 1:6.4). How it is possible to remain as free as before seems highly puzzling when Rousseau emphasizes that we give ourselves with all our powers to the community, under the supreme direction of the general will, and we claim no rights in reserve against it. Some have found an implicit totalitarianism in his doctrine and have found particularly ominous his remark about our being forced to be free.

Let's consider this remark and see if there is a way to read it consistent with our obeying only ourselves and with our now being as free as before the social compact. The relevant passage is: ". . . in order for the social compact not to be an ineffectual formula, it tacitly includes the following engagement, which alone can give force to the others [the other commitments]: that whosoever refuses to obey the general will shall be constrained to do so by the entire body; which means only that he shall be forced to be free" (SC, 1:7.8).

We get a start on Rousseau's meaning here by looking at the next chapter on civil society. This chapter illustrates his change of view and mood from the *Second Discourse*. Here the transition from the state of nature is favorably described, although with an important proviso regarding our not suffering too greatly from the abuse of political authority. He says: "This passage from the state of nature to the civil state produces a remarkable change in man, by substituting justice for instinct in his behavior and giving his actions the morality they previously lacked. . . . Although in this state he deprives himself of several advantages given him by nature, he gains such great ones, his faculties are exercised and developed, his ideas broadened, his feelings ennobled, and his whole soul elevated to such a point that if the abuses of this new condition did not often degrade him beneath the condition he left, he ought ceaselessly to bless the happy moment that tore him away from it forever, and that changed him from a stupid, limited animal into an intelligent being and a man" (SC, 1:8.1).

From this it is clear that our human nature, with our fundamental interest in developing and exercising our two potentialities under conditions of personal independence, is only realized in political society, or rather, only in the political society of the social compact. In the next paragraph Rousseau distinguishes the natural liberty, which we lose on joining civil society, from the civil liberty and the legal right of property, which we gain. He goes on to say that man also acquires with civil society: "moral freedom, which alone makes man truly the master of himself. For the impulse of appetite alone is slavery, and obedience to the law one has prescribed for oneself is freedom" (SC, 1:8.3).

Now Rousseau's thought here is surely not that obedience to just any law we might prescribe to ourselves is freedom: in a fit of absent-mindedness I might prescribe to myself some crazy law! No. He clearly has in mind the laws we prescribe to ourselves as subjects when we vote on fundamental laws as citizens, from the point of view of our general will, and give our opinion, which we think all citizens could endorse (given our beliefs and information), on the question of which laws are best framed to advance the common good.

But as we have seen, when we do this we are moved by our fundamental interests in our freedom and in maintaining our personal independence, and so on. These fundamental interests have priority over our other interests: as fundamental, they aim at the essential conditions of our freedom and equality, which realize the conditions of our capacity for free will and for our perfectibility without personal dependence. In obeying fundamental laws properly enacted in accordance with the general will—a form of deliberative reason—we realize our moral freedom. With this capacity of reason fully developed, we have free will: we are in a position to understand and to be guided by the most appropriate reasons.

2. After this background, let's return to the remark about being forced to be free. The language is provocative, granted; but we look for the thought behind it. In the immediately preceding paragraph (SC, 1:7.7) he contrasts the private will we have as a separate individual (our "naturally independent existence") with the general will we have as a citizen. He says: "His [the citizen's] private interest can speak to him quite differently from the common interest. His absolute and naturally independent existence can bring him to view what he owes the common cause as a free contribution, the loss of which will harm others less than its payment burdens him . . . he might wish to enjoy the rights of the citizen without wanting to fulfill the duties of a subject" (SC, 1:7.7).

It is clear that Rousseau has in mind a case of what today we call free-riding on collectively advantageous schemes of cooperation. (Rousseau speaks to this problem in SC, 2:6.2, where he says that "there must be conventions and laws to combine rights with duties.")

As a familiar kind of example, consider the installation of pollution-control devices on cars. Suppose that from each device, everyone gains $7 worth of benefit from clean air ($7 of benefit to each citizen), yet a device costs each person $10. In a society of 1,000 citizens, each device contributes $7,000 worth of benefit; if all install the device, each citizen's net gain is $7n-10$ (n = number of citizens); this is large for $n > 1$. Nevertheless, each citizen taking the actions of the others as given, can gain by defecting.[5]

Rousseau assumes, I think, that the individual in question voted in the

---

5. Example from Peter C. Ordeshook, *Game Theory and Political Theory* (Cambridge: Cambridge University Press, 1986), p. 201f.

assembly to require the devices and to ensure their installation by inspection (defraying the cost of inspection from taxes or fees). In being forced by fines to comply with the law we gave ourselves, and voted for with the best of reasons, we are subjected to rules we ourselves endorse from the point of view of our general will. Now, that point of view is that of our moral freedom, and being able to act from laws so enacted raises us from the level of instinct and makes us truly a master of ourselves. Moreover, no one supposes that in being required to pay the fine we could still reasonably complain. On Rousseau's view, our fundamental interests are our regulative interests; in the social compact we agree to advance our private interests within the bounds of fundamental political laws endorsed by the general will, a will guided by the fundamental interests we share with others.

But of course Rousseau misspeaks in saying we remain as free as before. Actually, we are no longer naturally free at all. We are morally free, but not as free as before. We are free in a better and far different way.

§6. Rousseau's Ideas on Equality: In What Way Distinctive?

1. In §2.3 of this lecture, we saw that Rousseau said that freedom and equality are the "greatest good of all, which ought to be the end of every system of legislation," and that freedom cannot last without equality. In the first Rousseau lecture we discussed what he had to say about the types and sources of inequality, and about its destructive consequences. We should now consider what is distinctive about Rousseau's ideas on equality. Let's review several of the reasons we might have for wanting to regulate inequalities so as to keep them from getting out of line.

(a) One reason is the alleviation of suffering. In the absence of special circumstances, it is wrong that some, or much of society, should be amply provided for, while a few, or even many, are deprived and suffer hardships, not to mention treatable illnesses and starvation. More generally, one can view such situations as cases of misallocation of resources. For example, from a utilitarian standpoint (as stated by Pigou in his *Economics of Welfare*), when the distribution of income is unequal, the social product is being used inefficiently. That is, more urgent needs and wants go unfulfilled, while the less urgent ones of the wealthy, and even their idle pleasures and whims, are indulged. On this view, leaving aside effects on future production, income should be distributed so that the most urgent wants and needs that go unfulfilled are equally urgent among all persons. (This assumes people have similar utility functions as well as some way of making interpersonal comparisons.)

Note that in this case it is not inequality that bothers us. Nor are we even troubled by the effects of inequality, except insofar as these effects cause suffering, or deprivation, or else involve what we view as inefficient and wasteful allocation of goods.

(b) A second reason for controlling political and economic inequalities is to prevent a part of society from dominating the rest. When those two kinds of inequalities are large, they tend to go hand in hand. As Mill said, the bases of political power are (educated) intelligence, property, and the power of combination, by which he meant the ability to cooperate in pursuing one's political interests. This power allows the few, in virtue of their control over the political process, to enact a system of law and property ensuring their dominant position, not only in politics, but throughout the economy. This enables them to decide what gets produced, to control working conditions and the terms of employment offered, as well as to shape both the direction and volume of real saving (investment) and the pace of innovation, all of which in good part determines what society becomes over time.

If we view being dominated by others as a bad thing, and as making our life not as good, or as happy, as it might be, we must be concerned with the effects of political and economic inequality. Our employment opportunities are less good; we would prefer more control over the workplace and the general direction of the economy. So far, though, it's not clear that inequality in itself is either unjust or bad.

(c) A third reason seems to bring us closer to what might be wrong with inequality in itself. I refer to the fact that significant political and economic inequalities are often associated with inequalities of social status that may lead those of lower status to being viewed, by themselves and by others, as inferior. This may foster widespread attitudes of deference and servility on one side and arrogance and contempt on the other. For how people view themselves depends on how they are viewed by others—their sense of self-respect, their self-esteem, their confidence in themselves rests on other people's judgments and assessments.

With these effects of political and economic inequalities, and with the possible evils of status, we are much closer to Rousseau's concerns. Certainly these evils are serious, and the attitudes status rankings may generate can be great vices. But have we arrived yet at the conclusion that inequality is wrong or unjust in itself, rather than its having wrong or unjust effects on those who suffer from it?

It is closer to being wrong or unjust in itself in this sense: in a system of statuses not everyone can have the highest status. It is a positional good, as sometimes said, as high status depends on there being other positions beneath it; so if we value high status as such, we are also valuing something that necessarily involves others having lesser status. This may be wrong or unjust when the status positions are of great social importance, and certainly when status is attributed to us by birth, or by natural features of gender or race, and is not in an appropriate way earned or achieved. So a system of statuses is unjust when its ranks are endowed with more importance than their social role in service of the general good can justify.

(d) This suggests Rousseau's solution: namely that in political society everyone should be an equal citizen. But before elaborating this, I mention briefly that inequality can be wrong or unjust in itself whenever the basic structure of society makes important use of fair procedures.

Two examples of fair procedures are: fair, that is, open and workably competitive markets in the economy; and fair political elections. In these cases a certain equality, or a well-moderated inequality, is an essential condition of political justice. Here monopoly and its kindred are to be avoided, not simply for their bad effects, among them inefficiency, but also because without a special justification, they lead to markets that are unfair. The same kind of observation holds for unfair elections resulting from the dominance of a wealthy few in politics.[6]

2. For Rousseau the idea of equality is most significant at the highest level: that is, at the level of how political society itself is to be understood. And the social compact, its terms and conditions, tells us about this. From it we know that everyone is to have the same basic status of an equal citizen; that the general will is to will the common good (as the conditions which secure that each can advance their fundamental interests when personally

6. In the preceding paragraphs (a)–(d) I've drawn in part on "Notes on Equality" by T. M. Scanlon, dated November 1988. [See also T. M. Scanlon, "The Diversity of Objections to Inequality," in Scanlon, *The Difficulty of Tolerance* (Cambridge: Cambridge University Press, 2003). —Ed.]

independent of others, and within the limits of civil freedom). Moreover, economic and social inequalities are to be moderated so that the conditions of this independence are assured. In a note to SC, 2:11.1, Rousseau says, "Do you then want to give stability to the State? Bring the extremes as close together as possible: tolerate neither opulent people nor beggars." And as we observed earlier, in SC, 2:11.2, he goes on to say, "Equality . . . must not be understood to mean that degrees of power and wealth should be exactly the same, but rather that with regard to power, it should be incapable of all violence and never exerted except by virtue of status and the laws; and with regard to wealth, no citizen should be so opulent that he can buy another, and none so poor that he is constrained to sell himself."

All this enables us to say that in the society of the social compact, citizens—as persons—are equal at the highest level and in the most fundamental respects. Thus they all have the same fundamental interests in their freedom and in pursuing their ends within the limits of civil freedom. They all have a similar capacity for moral freedom—that is, the capacity to act in accordance with general laws they give to themselves as well as others for the sake of the common good. These laws each sees as founded on the appropriate form of deliberative reason for political society, this reason being the general will each citizen has as a member of that society.

But how, more exactly, is equality itself present at the highest level? Perhaps in this way: the social compact articulates, and when realized, achieves, a political relation between citizens as equals. They have capacities and interests that make them equal members in all fundamental matters. They recognize and view one another as being related as equal citizens; and their being what they are—citizens—includes their being related as equals. So being related as equals is part of what they are, of what they are recognized to be by others, and there is a public political commitment to preserve the conditions this equal relation between persons requires.

Now as we know from the *Second Discourse*, Rousseau is keenly aware of the significance of feelings of self-respect and self-worth, and the vices and miseries of self-love are aroused by political and economic inequalities that exceed the limits required for personal independence. Rousseau believes, I think, that all of us must, for our happiness, respect ourselves and maintain a lively sense of our self-worth. So for our feelings to be compatible with others' feelings we must respect ourselves and others as equals, and at the highest level; and this includes the level of how society is conceived and the level at which fundamental political laws are enacted. Thus, as equal citizens we can all, by way of the respect of others, bring into harmony our need for self-respect. Given our needs as persons and our natural indignation at being subject to the arbitrary power of others (a power that makes us do what they want, and not what we both can will as equals) the clear answer to the problem of inequality is equality at the highest level, as formulated in the social compact.

From the point of view of this equality, citizens can moderate lower-level inequalities by general laws in order to preserve conditions of personal independence so that no one is subject to arbitrary power, and no one experiences the wounds and indignities that arouse self-love.

3. Is this view of equality distinctive of Rousseau? Was he the first to see it? I am not sure of the answer to this question. Ideas of equality have been around from the beginning of political philosophy. But I suspect that the family of ideas that combine to give his idea of equality—the idea of equality at the highest level in how society is conceived, of citizens as equals at this highest level in virtue of their fundamental interests and their capacities for both moral and civil freedom, of self-love and its connection with the inequalities connected with arbitrary power—are, as a family, distinctive. That is, it is in combining this family of ideas in this particular and powerful way that the originality of Rousseau's idea of equality may lie.

MILL

MILL I

His Conception of Utility

§1. Introductory Remarks: J. S. Mill (1806–1873)

1. Mill was the eldest child of the utilitarian philosopher and economist James Mill, who, along with Bentham, was among the leaders of the Philosophical Radicals. Mill was educated entirely by his father and never attended a school or university. His father made him tutor his younger siblings, and Mill was kept so occupied that he was deprived of a normal childhood.

Under his father's tutelage, he gained at an early age full mastery of the utilitarian theory of politics and society as well as of its associationist psychology of human nature. He also mastered all his father could teach him about Ricardian economics, and by the age of sixteen Mill was a formidable intellectual figure in his own right.

2. Recall what we have said before: that in studying the works of the leading writers in the philosophical tradition, one guiding precept is to identify correctly the problems they were facing, and to understand how they viewed them and what questions they were asking. Once we do this, their answers will most likely seem much deeper, even if not always entirely sound. Writers who, at first, strike us as archaic and without interest, may become illuminating and repay serious study.

Thus, as with all political philosophers, we must ask what Mill took as his questions and what he was trying to accomplish through his writings. In particular, we should note Mill's choice of vocation. He did not aim to be a scholar, or, as Kant did, to write original and systematic works in philosophy, economics, or political theory, however original and systematic his works may in fact be. Nor did Mill wish to become a political figure or a man of party.

3. Instead Mill saw himself as an educator of enlightened and advanced

opinion. His aim was to explain and defend what he took to be the appropriate fundamental philosophical, moral, and political principles in accordance with which modern society should be organized. Otherwise he thought the society of the future would not achieve the requisite harmony and stability of an organic age, that is, an age unified by generally acknowledged political and social first principles.

The idea of an organic age (as opposed to a critical age) Mill took from the Saint-Simonians.[1] Mill thought modern society would be democratic and industrial and secular, that is, one without a state religion: a non-confessional state. This was the kind of society he thought he saw coming into being in England and elsewhere in Europe. He hoped to formulate the fundamental principles for such a society so they would be intelligible to the enlightened opinion of those who had influence in political and social life.

4. I have said that it was not part of Mill's chosen vocation that his writings should be significant works of scholarship, or original contributions to philosophical or social thought. In fact, however, I believe that Mill was a deep and original thinker, but his originality is always repressed, and this for two reasons:

First, it is required by his choice of vocation: in order to address those who have influence in political life—those who (as he says in his review of Tocqueville's *Democracy in America*) have property, intelligence, and the power of combination (the ability to combine with other people to get things done, especially in government)[2]—his writings cannot appear too original, too scholarly, or too difficult. Otherwise, he loses his audience.

Second, Mill's originality was repressed by his complicated psychological relation to his father. It was, I think, impossible for him to make an open public break with the utilitarianism of his father and Bentham. Doing so would have given comfort to those Mill regarded as his political opponents, the Tories who held the intuitionist conservative doctrine which he consistently opposed.[3] However, Mill did publicly express serious reservations about Bentham's doctrine in two essays, "Bentham" (1838) and "Coleridge"

1. A French sect, followers of Saint-Simon, who believed that historically organic periods are followed by critical periods, or periods characterized by doubt and skepticism.

2. John Stuart Mill, *Collected Works* (CW) (Toronto: University of Toronto Press, 1963–1991), Vol. XVIII, p. 163.

3. See Mill, *Whewell on Moral Philosophy* (1852). CW, X.

(1840); but not surprisingly he was more critical still in his anonymous "Remarks on Bentham's Philosophy" (1833).[4]

5. In his chosen vocation Mill surely succeeded to an extraordinary degree. He became one of the most influential political and social writers of the Victorian Age. For our purposes, understanding his vocation helps us to understand the defects of his works: their often loose and ambiguous terminology, and their almost incessant lofty style and sermonizing tone untroubled by self-doubt, even when the most intricate questions are being discussed. Those who disliked him said he sought to convince, and when that failed, to convict.

These defects are most disturbing in the later essays (after 1850, say), which are widely read, and three of which we will be discussing: *Utilitarianism*, *On Liberty*, and *The Subjection of Women*. By this time Mill had England's ear. He knew it and meant to keep it. But the most creative period of Mill's life is roughly 1827–1848. Anyone who doubts Mill's extraordinary gifts has only to consider the works of this period, beginning with the *Essays on Some Unsettled Questions of Political Economy* (late 1830–31, the 5th essay partially rewritten in 1833, but not published until 1844), then the many brilliant essays of the 1830s and *A System of Logic* in 1843, and on to *The Principles of Political Economy* in 1848.

Despite his defects, it is a great mistake to assume a superior manner in reading Mill. He is a great figure and deserves our attention and respect.

J. S. Mill: Biographical Data

1806 Born May 20, in London.

1809–1820 Period of intensive education at home by his father.

1820–1821 Year in France in the household of Sir Samuel Bentham.

1822 Studied law. First publication in newspapers.

1823 Begins his career in East India Company.

1823–1829 Period of study with friends in "Utilitarian Society" and at Grote's house.

1824 Founding of *Westminster Review*, for which he wrote until 1828.

1826–1827 Mental crisis.

1830 Met Harriet Taylor. In Paris during the Revolution of 1830.

1832 Death of Bentham; first Reform Bill.

4. This appeared first anonymously as Appendix B in Edward Lytton Bulwer's *England and the English* (London: Richard Bentley, 1833), in CW, X.

1833 Publication of "Remarks on Bentham's Philosophy."

1836 Death of Mill's father.

1838 Publication of "Bentham" and "Coleridge" (1840).

1843 Publication of *A System of Logic*. Eight editions in his life.

1844 Publication of *Essays on Some Unsettled Questions of Political Economy*, written 1831–32.

1848 Publication of *Principles of Political Economy*. Seven editions.

1851 Married Harriet Taylor, whose husband John Taylor had died in 1849.

1856 Became Chief Examiner of East India Company.

1858 Retired from East India Company. Death of Harriet Taylor.

1859 Publication of *On Liberty*.

1861 Publication of *Utilitarianism* and *On Representative Government*.

1865 Elected Member of Parliament for Westminster. Defeated in 1868.

1869 Publication of *The Subjection of Women*.

1871 Died May 7, in Avignon.

1873 Publication of *Autobiography*.

1879 Publication of *Chapters on Socialism*.

§2. One Way to Read Mill's Utilitarianism

1. I want to propose a way to read the essay *Utilitarianism* that connects it with Mill's earlier criticisms of Bentham, first in his "Remarks on Bentham's Philosophy" (1833), and then later in his essay "Bentham" (1838), written two years after his father's death in 1836. This essay along with his essay "Coleridge" (1840) marks the most open break Mill was to make with the utilitarianism of Bentham and his father. I say open break because I think the form of utilitarianism he developed, as will become clear in due course, was very a different doctrine from theirs. This, however, is a matter of interpretation and not widely shared.

In "Remarks on Bentham's Philosophy" (which I shall refer to as RB in textual citations), Mill first defines Bentham's philosophy, saying, "The first principles . . . are these;—that happiness, meaning by that term pleasure and exemption from pain, is the only thing desirable in itself; that all other things are desirable solely as a means to that end: That the production, therefore, of the greatest possible happiness, is the only fit purpose of all human thought and action, and consequently of all morality and government; and moreover, that pleasure and pain are the sole agencies by which the conduct of mankind is governed."(RB, ¶2). He then makes these objections, among others, to Bentham's view. First, he objects that Bentham nowhere attempts to give a serious philosophical justification of the principle of utility, and that Bentham displays a curt and dismissive tone with his opponents. Mill argues that those who hold other philosophical and moral doctrines deserve better than this (RB, ¶¶3–6).

2. Second, he objects that Bentham interprets the principle of utility in the narrow sense of what Mill calls the principle of specific consequences, which approves or disapproves of an action solely from a calculation of the consequences to which that kind of action, if generally practiced, would lead. Mill grants that this principle is appropriate in many cases, for example, from the point of view of a legislator who is concerned to encourage or to deter certain kinds of conduct by legal inducements or penalties; and Mill grants the merit of Bentham's work in advancing the study of jurisprudence and legislation (RB, ¶¶8–9).

Mill's objection is that this interpretation of the principle of utility is much too narrow for dealing with the fundamental political and social questions of the age; for these questions concern human character as a whole. Here we must not be concerned primarily with how to provide legal incentives for good conduct, or how to deter people from committing crimes, but with how to arrange basic social institutions so that the members of society come to have a character—with aims, desires, and sentiments—such that they are incapable of committing crimes, or are already inclined to engage in the desired conduct. These broader questions force us to go beyond the principles of specific consequences and to take into account the relation of actions to the formation of character, and from this to consider the guidance of conduct in general by means of political and social institutions. Legislation must be seen in the greater historical context and connected with "the theory of organic institutions and general forms of polity . . . [which] must be viewed as the great instruments of forming national character, of carrying forward the members of the community to perfection, or preserving them from degeneracy" (RB, ¶12; see generally RB, ¶¶7–12).

3. Mill says, third, that Bentham is not to be ranked high as an analyst

of human nature, that he wrongly supposed that we are moved entirely by a balance of desires concerning future pleasures and pains, and that he mistakenly tried to enumerate motives (human desires and aversions), which are in principle innumerable both in number and kind. He also ignored some of the most important social motives, such as conscience, or the feeling of duty, with the result that his view is psychologically egoistic in tone (RB, ¶¶23–30).

Mill further objects that Bentham fails to see that the greatest hope for human improvement lies in a change in our character and in our regulative and predominant desires. This failure on Bentham's part is connected with his failure to see political and social institutions as a means for social education of a people and as a way to adjust the conditions of social life to their stage of civilization (RB, ¶35).

4. Finally, Mill says that Bentham's prevailing error is to fix on only a part of the motives that actually move people and to regard them as "much cooler and more thoughtful calculators than they really are." This tendency, which is connected with his idea of the artificial, or reasoned, identification of interests, leads Bentham to think of legislation as achieving its effect through citizens' rational calculation of rewards and penalties, leading to laws and governments providing the necessary legal protections. He underestimates the role and effects of habit and imagination, and the central importance of people's attachment to institutions, which depends on the continuity of their existence and their identity in their outward form. It is this continuity and identity that adapt them to a people's historical recollections and helps their institutions to sustain their authority (RB, ¶¶36–37). Bentham overlooks the way in which long-standing institutions and traditions make possible the innumerable compromises and adjustments without which no government, Mill believes, can long be carried on. For Mill, Bentham is a "half-thinker" who said much of great merit, but, while presenting it as the whole truth, actually left it to others to supply half of the truth (RB, ¶¶36–37).

5. Keeping in mind this critique of Bentham, we can, I suggest, regard each chapter of *Utilitarianism* as Mill's attempt to reformulate part of the doctrine of Bentham and of his own father so as to meet his own objections to it, as he had stated them in the "Remarks" of 1833. Mill always professes to be a utilitarian and to be revising the doctrine, as it were, from within. One controversy about these revisions is whether they are really

consistent with utilitarianism, given a reasonably general characterization of it, or whether they amount to a substantially different doctrine; and if so, what this doctrine is. I put this question aside for the time being.

Chapter I of *Utilitarianism* addresses the first criticism of Bentham: that is, Mill says that he will address the question of the justification of the principle of utility, and he sketches what is needed in I: ¶¶3–5. This chapter together with Chapters IV and V complete his justification. (The whole argument is found in I: ¶¶3–5; IV: ¶¶1–4, 8–9, 12; V: ¶¶26–31, 32–38.) (In textual references, chapter numerals are followed by paragraph numbers. As usual, you will have to number your own paragraphs.)

Mill's argument here foreshadows the argument that Henry Sidgwick develops in great detail later in his *Methods of Ethics* (1st edition 1874; 7th and last edition 1907). Roughly, this argument is that everyone, including those who belong to the intuitionist school (this covers conservative writers like Sedgwick and Whewell who are among Mill's opponents), concedes that one major ground of right conduct is that it tends to promote human happiness. Hence, if there is some other first principle that may conflict with the principle of utility, we must have some way of deciding, in cases of conflict, which principle is to take priority and to settle the case. Both Mill and Sidgwick argue that there is no principle except the principle of utility that is sufficiently general, and that has all the features required to serve as a regulative first principle.

Mill and Sidgwick both argue further that the principle of utility is the principle we tend to use in practice, and that our use of it gives whatever order and coherence our considered moral judgments actually possess. They maintain that common sense morality when people do reflect and balance is secondary and is implicitly utilitarian. As I shall note next time, Mill presses this kind of argument in V: ¶¶26–31 in connection with the various precepts of justice.

6. Chapter II contains in its initial paragraphs Mill's reformulation of the idea of utility. I focus on ¶¶1–18, which, for our purposes, are the most relevant. They may be divided as follows.

¶1: Introduction.

¶2: States the principle of utility in roughly the form Bentham gave it, which Mill is going to revise.

¶¶3–10: Addresses the objection that utilitarianism is a doctrine fit only for swine. In the course of meeting this objection Mill presents his account of happiness as the ultimate end (which I take up below). These paragraphs form a unit. They are further elaborated in IV: ¶¶4–9.

¶¶11–18: These paragraphs also form a unit and discuss two objections: first, that utilitarianism is impracticable because happiness is unattainable; and second, that human beings can do without happiness, and forming our character so that we can do without it is the condition of achieving the nobility of virtue.

The rest of Chapter II takes up various other objections. I should mention, though, II: ¶¶24–25, which are important in sketching Mill's view of the relation between moral precepts and principles and the principle of utility itself as the supreme regulative standard. These paragraphs bear on recent discussions as to whether Mill is an act utilitarian or a rule utilitarian or something else. I touch on this question briefly in the next lecture.

7. Chapter III contains Mill's account of how we may naturally acquire a firm regulative desire to act from the principle of utility, that is, to act from this principle independent of external legal or social sanctions of various kinds, including public opinion viewed as coercive social pressure. Just as Chapter II develops the idea of utility that looks beyond Bentham's principle of specific consequences and is meant to apply to the basic institutions that shape and educate national character, so Chapter III goes beyond what Mill regards as Bentham's rational and calculating egoistic psychology. Here III: ¶¶8–11 are especially important, and I shall discuss them later.

Chapter IV contains an essential part of Mill's justification of the principle of utility (the so-called proof), while Chapter V takes up the utilitarian basis of the various principles and precepts of justice, and how they support moral and legal rights. This question Mill thinks Bentham did not treat satisfactorily, and Mill's discussion of it is impressive and one of the strongest parts of the essay. It will be our topic for the next lecture.

§3. Happiness as the Ultimate End

1. I now turn to Chapter II. Let's start straightaway by looking at Mill's summary statement at II: ¶10. Here he says that: "According to the Greatest Happiness Principle . . . the ultimate end, with reference to and for the sake of which all other things are desirable, (whether we are considering our own good or that of other people), is an existence exempt as far as

possible from pain, and as rich as possible in enjoyments, both in quantity and quality."

2. Note that Mill speaks of the ultimate end (the greatest happiness) as an existence (II: ¶10); or as a mode, or manner, of existence (II: ¶¶8 and 6 respectively). Happiness is not merely pleasurable or agreeable feelings, or a series of such feelings, whether simple or complex. It is a mode, or one might say, a way of life, as experienced and lived by the person whose life it is. Here I assume that a mode of life is happy only when it is more or less successful in achieving its aims.

Mill does not talk about pleasures and pains as merely feelings, or as sensory experiences of a certain kind. Rather, he speaks of them, especially pleasures, as enjoyable activities that are distinguished by their source (II: ¶4): that is, by the faculties, the exercise of which is involved in the enjoyable activity. It is in this connection that Mill mentions the higher vs. the lower faculties:

(a) the higher faculties are those of intellect, of feeling and imagination, and of the moral sentiments, while:

(b) the lower faculties are those associated with our bodily needs and requirements, the exercise of which gives rise to pleasures of mere sensation (II: ¶4).

3. Thus, by way of summary, happiness as the ultimate end is a mode (or manner) of existence—a way of life—which includes in due degree and variety a suitable place for both the higher and the lower pleasures, that is, a suitable place for the exercise of both the higher and the lower faculties in an appropriate ordering of enjoyable activities.

§4. The Decided Preference Criterion

1. The test of quality is said to be the following. One pleasure is higher in quality than another when:

(a) Those who have experience of two pleasures have a decided preference for the activity connected with one over the activity connected with the other, and this preference is independent both from any feeling of moral obligation to prefer that pleasure, and also from any consideration of its circumstantial advantages (II: ¶4).

(b) A decided preference for one pleasure over another (for instance, for the pleasures associated with having "faculties more elevated than the animal appetites" [II: ¶4]), means that the enjoyment of that pleasure will not be given up, or abandoned, for any amount of the enjoyment of the other pleasure that our nature is capable of, even when it is known that the preferred pleasure involves "a greater amount of discontent" (II: ¶5).

(c) A decided preference is one held by persons who have acquired habits of self-consciousness and self-observation (II: ¶10).

2. The decided preference criterion includes four elements:

(a) The persons making the comparison between the two pleasures (enjoyable activities) must be competently acquainted with both, and this normally involves experiencing both.

(b) These persons must have settled habits of self-consciousness and self-observation.

(c) The decided preference arrived at must not be influenced by a sense of moral obligation.

(d) It must not be formed on the basis of the circumstantial advantages of the pleasures in question (like permanence, safety, price, etc.), or their consequences (rewards and punishments), but in view of their intrinsic nature as pleasures.

It is (c) and (d) together that provide a foothold for speaking of the quality vs. the quantity of pleasure. We shall come back to this.

3. When he says that in comparing pleasures we are not to consider circumstantial advantages, Mill has in mind the kinds of reasons Bentham gave for preferring the higher pleasures (as Mill describes them). Bentham says, "Quantity of pleasure being equal, pushpin [a game of darts] is as good as poetry."[5] Here, think of a mode, or a way, of life as our living according to a plan of life, this plan consisting of various activities engaged in according to a certain schedule. With this thought in mind, what Bentham means is that in drawing up the schedule of activities that specifies our mode of life, there comes a point at which the marginal utility of pushpin (per unit of time) is just equal to the marginal utility of poetry (per unit of time). He grants that normally the total time and energy we give to poetry (or to the activities exercising the higher faculties) is greater than the time and energy we give to pushpin (or to other similar games and amuse-

---

5. In Jeremy Bentham, *Rationale of Reward*, in *The Works of Jeremy Bentham* (London: Simpkin, Marshall, 1843–1859), Vol. II, p. 253.

ments). The explanation is that, given human psychology, we can devote more time and energy to poetry before we become tired, or bored, and lose interest.

Bentham's view is that the source of pleasure (the activity that gives rise to it) is irrelevant: intensity and duration being the same, a pleasure is a pleasure is a pleasure. When Bentham says that at the margin, pushpin is as good as poetry, he is not expressing a low opinion of poetry (although he did indeed have such an opinion)[6] but rather stating his hedonistic doctrine.

4. Now, however, there is a difficulty, which arises as follows. Mill grants in II: ¶8 that differences in the quantity and the intensity of pleasure are also shown in, and known by, our preferences. That is, that in our decisions and choices we also disclose our estimates of the intensity and quantity of different pleasures. But if this is so, how can the decided preference criterion distinguish between the quality and quantity of different pleasures?

The answer lies, I think, in the special structure of the schedule of activities that specifies our preferred mode of existence as well as in the priorities we reveal in drawing up that schedule and in revising it as circumstances change.

Thus, what shows that a pleasure (as an activity) is of a higher quality than another is that we won't abandon it altogether (eliminate it from the schedule, from our way of life) in return for any amount of fulfillment of the lower pleasures which our nature is capable of. In arranging our way of life (or in scheduling our activities) there comes a point at which the rate of exchange of the lower for the higher pleasures is, practically speaking, infinite. This refusal to abandon the higher pleasures for any amount of the lower shows the special priority of the higher (II: ¶¶5–6).

5. Yet one question still remains. For surely in drawing up our schedule of activities there must come a point at which the opposite rate of exchange of the higher for the lower pleasures is also infinite, practically

---

6. On this, see Mill's comments in his essay "Bentham" in CW, Vol. X, pp. 113f, where he speaks of "Bentham's peculiar opinions on poetry." He says that Bentham enjoyed music, painting, and sculpture, but "towards poetry . . . that which employs the language of words, he entertained no favors. Words, he thought, were perverted from their proper office when they were employed in uttering anything but precise logical truth." Mill says that even so, Bentham's pushpin/poetry quote "is only a paradoxical way of stating what he would equally have said of the things which he most valued and admired."

speaking. The reason is that we must reserve a certain minimum of time and energy to keeping ourselves well and healthy, and in good spirits. This is necessary if we are to carry out effectively our other activities, particularly the higher ones. To express Mill's distinction between quantity and quality of pleasure we must say, then, that the explanation of why the two rates of exchange become infinite, practically speaking, are different. In the case of securing the necessary minimum needed to keep us well and healthy, and in good spirits, the explanation is physiological and psychological: it concerns our fitness and morale. Whereas with the other rate of exchange, the explanation lies in features intrinsic to the activities that involve the exercise of the higher faculties.

6. In summary: Mill's distinction between the quantity and quality of pleasures (activities) is this. He holds that when we look at the ways of life that we decidedly prefer, then the schedules of activities (over an appropriate period of time, say a year) which specify these ways of life have several characteristic features:

(a) There are essentially two different kinds of activities to be distinguished in these schedules, namely, those involving the exercise of the higher faculties vs. those involving the exercise of the lower faculties. These two kinds of faculties are regarded as sources of qualitatively distinct kinds of pleasures in the sense explained.

(b) In scheduling our activities we must, of course, give a significant place to the activities giving rise to the lower pleasures: this is required for normal health and vigor and psychological well-being. Once this minimum is secured, a greater fulfillment of the lower pleasures rapidly becomes of far less importance and soon approaches zero.

(c) On the other hand, above this minimum, the higher pleasures quickly take over and become the focus and center of our way of life, as shown in our schedule of activities over the appropriate unit of time. Above this minimum, we will never freely give up, or resign (as Mill says in II: ¶5), the activities giving rise to the higher pleasures, no matter how great the compensating fulfillment of the lower pleasures may be.

(d) Finally, in the evaluations made in (c) above, no account is taken of circumstantial advantages, or of the consequences, of the higher activities as a group, except insofar as this is necessary to be sure that the schedule of activities is practicable and feasible.

It is all these features taken together that give force to the term "quality" vs. "quantity" of pleasure. When Mill talks about this distinction, he has in mind the special structure of the overall schedule of activities which specifies our way of life and the priority we give to the activities involving the exercise of our higher faculties. Our conception of happiness, then, is that of a way of life more or less successfully lived, given reasonable expectations of what life can provide (II: ¶12). To say that there are higher vs. lower pleasures is just to say that we decidedly prefer a way of life the special structure of which gives the central focus and priority to those activities that call upon the higher faculties.

§5. Further Comments on the Decided Preference Criterion

(a) First, for Mill's purposes I don't think it necessary to make any fine-grained distinctions within the class of higher pleasures or within the class of lower pleasures. Mill is concerned to rebut the objection made by Carlyle and others that utilitarianism is a doctrine fit only for swine. He rebuts this charge as presuming a low view of human nature and he counters with his distinction between the higher and lower pleasures. Once this distinction is made and the decided preference for the higher pleasures established, Mill has made his case. Given his whole doctrine, further refinements within the higher and the lower pleasures are not essential.

(b) Mill comments (II: ¶8) that "neither pains nor pleasures are homogeneous, and pain is always heterogeneous with pleasure." He goes on to say that all distinctions within both pleasures and pains, and between pleasures and pains, are reflected in our judgments, resulting in our actual decisions and choices. This further emphasizes the fact that the distinction between the quality and the quantity of pleasures rests on special structural features and priorities embedded in the preferred schedule of activities specifying our way of life.

(c) It follows that it is a bad mistake to take Mill's distinction between the quality and quantity of pleasures as resting on differences between the introspectable qualities of pleasures and pains as kinds of sensory feelings or experiences. All the distinctions that Mill makes, and needs to make, are reflected in our actual decisions and choices. I take him to say that all these distinctions depend on matters open to view in the special structure and priorities of the way of life we decidedly prefer.

§6. Mill's Underlying Psychology

1. I now discuss some aspects of the moral psychology that underlies Mill's conception of utility as stated in *Utilitarianism*. This psychology consists of several important psychological principles. One principle—the principle of dignity—supports the idea of happiness that we have just discussed. Another principle, considered in III: ¶¶6–11, that the general happiness is recognized as the ethical standard, and that mankind has a desire to be in unity with his fellow creatures, supports Mill's idea of the ultimate sanction of the principle of utility regarded as the basic principle of morality. I start with the principle of dignity.

We have seen how meaning can be given to the idea of differences in the quality of pleasures by referring to the structure and priorities embedded in the ways of life that we, as normal human beings, decidedly prefer. But Mill doesn't stop with this criterion. He says (II: ¶¶4 and 6) that we also think a life not focused around the activities that call upon our higher faculties is a degrading form of existence.

He says that we may attribute the unwillingness to lead such a life to pride, or to the love of liberty and personal independence, or even to a love of power. But Mill thinks that the most appropriate explanation lies in a sense of dignity that all human beings possess in proportion to the development of their higher faculties (II: ¶6). By this last I take him to mean: in proportion to the degree to which our higher faculties have been realized by suitable training and education, and their development has not been stunted by impoverished conditions or lack of opportunity, not to speak of hostile circumstances.

2. Mill believes that our sense of dignity is so important to us that no mode of existence that violates it could be desired by us, without a special explanation (II: ¶7). To think that the desire to maintain our dignity is fulfilled at the sacrifice of happiness is, Mill thinks, to mistake happiness for contentment. The question arises as to how Mill's idea of dignity is related to what he says about the higher and the lower pleasures. Is it another way of making the same distinction, or does it add a further element? And is it consistent with his utilitarianism?

The text seems unclear on this point. I shall suppose that the idea of dignity does add a new element. One question is whether it can be interpreted in a way consistent with Mill's view as I have presented it; and I shall consider this later when we come to discuss *On Liberty*. The new element is this: not only do we have a decided preference for the higher over the lower pleasures, but we also have a higher-order desire to have desires cultivated by a way of life suitably focused on the higher activities and sufficient to sustain them.

This higher-order desire is a desire first, that as a human being with the higher faculties, these faculties be realized and cultivated, and second, that we have desires appropriate to set our higher faculties in motion and to enjoy their exercise, and that we do not have desires interfering with this.

3. It is important to note that in connection with the sense of dignity, Mill uses the language of ideals and human perfection (II: ¶6). He speaks of self-respect, rank, and status, and of certain ways of life seen by us as degrading and unworthy. He introduces, in effect, another form of value besides the enjoyable and the pleasing, namely, the admirable and the worthy along with their opposites, the degrading and the contemptible.[7]

Our sense of dignity is tied, then, to our recognition that some ways of life are admirable and worthy of our nature, while others are beneath us and unfitting. It is essential to add that the sense of dignity is not derived from a sense of moral obligation. To say this would conflict with one of the conditions of the decided preference criterion as well as with the sense of dignity as a different form of value.

7. Mill discusses these values in "Bentham," CW, X, pp. 95f, 112f; and in *On Liberty*, IV: ¶¶4–12 passim.

MILL II

His Account of Justice

§1. Our Approach to Mill

1. This is a good time to explain our approach to Mill, and to relate it to our approach to Locke and Rousseau.

With Locke we mainly discussed two things. First, we considered his account of legitimacy, that is, his criterion of a legitimate regime as one that can arise in ideal history. We saw that this means a regime that can be contracted into by rational persons without violating any duties imposed on them by the fundamental law of nature. And second, we considered Locke's account of property and how it was compatible with unequal basic political liberties (the property-qualification for the franchise), and so with a class-state.

With Rousseau we also considered mainly two things; first, his account of inequality in regard both to its historical origins and to its political and social consequences in giving rise to the vices and evils of civilization. This set the stage for the question whether there are any principles of right and justice such that when society realizes those principles in its institutions, those vices and evils are kept in check, if not eliminated altogether. *The Social Contract* answers this question. Rousseau sees the social compact as specifying the desired principles as norms of political and social cooperation between citizens as free and equal; and we tried to understand his idea of the general will.

We saw that Rousseau takes the idea of the social compact further than Locke. His view of the role and significance of equality (and inequality) is deeper and more central. Justice as fairness[1] follows Rousseau more closely in both of these respects.

1. The name of the political conception of justice developed in Rawls, *A Theory of Justice* (Cambridge, Mass.: Harvard University Press, 1971; rev. ed. 1999) and in *Justice as Fair-*

2. I begin by stating a problem about understanding Mill. In many of his writings, Mill states certain principles which he sometimes calls "the principles of the modern world." These principles we can think of as principles of political and social justice for the basic structure of society.[2] I will be discussing these principles in some detail in the next two lectures, when we take up the essays *On Liberty* and *The Subjection of Women;* but suffice it to say here that Mill thinks them necessary to protect the rights of individuals and minorities against the possible oppression of modern democratic majorities (*On Liberty,* Chapter I).

Now I believe that the content of Mill's principles of political and social justice is very close to the content of the two principles of justice as fairness.[3] This content is, I assume, close enough so that, for our present purposes, we may regard their substantive content as roughly the same. The problem that now arises is this:

How does it happen that an apparently utilitarian view leads to the same substantive content (the same principles of justice) as justice as fairness? Here there are at least two possible answers:

(a) Perhaps these principles of political justice can be justified—or arrived at—within both views, so that both support these principles much as they would in an overlapping consensus.[4] In the *Restatement,* I said that the parties in the original position, selecting principles for the basic structure, might be viewed as using what I called a utility function based on the fundamental needs and requirements of citizens conceived as free and equal

---

ness: *A Restatement,* ed. Erin Kelly (Cambridge, Mass.: Harvard University Press, 2001), hereafter cited as *Restatement.*

2. A society's basic structure consists of its main political and social institutions and the way they hang together in one system of cooperation (*Restatement,* pp. 8f).

3. The two principles of justice as fairness are: (a) each person has the same indefeasible claim to a fully adequate scheme of equal basic liberties, which scheme is compatible with the same scheme of liberties for all; and (b) social and economic inequalities are to satisfy two conditions: first, they are to be attached to offices and positions open to all under conditions of fair equality of opportunity; and second, they are to be to the greatest benefit of the least-advantaged members of society. This last is called "the difference principle." Some writers prefer the term "maximin principle," but I prefer the difference principle, to distinguish it from the maximin rule for decision under uncertainty (*Restatement,* pp. 42f).

4. An overlapping consensus is a consensus in which the same political conception of justice is endorsed by the reasonable, though opposing, religious, philosophical, and moral doctrines that gain a significant body of adherents and endure from one generation to the next (*Restatement,* p. 32 and p. 184).

persons, and characterized by the two moral powers, a capacity for a sense of justice, and a capacity for a conception of the good. It is not based on people's actual preferences and interests. Using this suitably constructed utility function, they would adopt the two principles of justice.[5] Mill's conception of utility might have much the same result. This is one thing we want to explore.

(b) On the other hand, Mill may be mistaken in thinking his doctrine leads to his principles of the modern world. While he might think his conception of utility does that, perhaps it does not actually do so.

3. I shall assume that the second answer is not correct. I assume instead that someone with Mill's enormous gifts can't be mistaken about something so basic to his whole doctrine. Little mistakes and slips, yes—they don't matter and we can fix them up. But fundamental errors at the very bottom level: no. That we should regard as very implausible, unless it turns out to our dismay that there is no other alternative.

I note that this is a precept of method. It guides us in how we are to approach and to interpret the texts we read. We must have confidence in the author, especially a gifted one. If we see that something is wrong when we take the text in a certain way, then we assume the author would have seen it too. So our interpretation is likely to be wrong. We then ask: How can we read the text so as to avoid the difficulty?

For the present, then, I suppose that the first alternative is the correct one; and therefore, that Mill's conception of utility, together with the fundamental principles of his moral psychology and his social theory, leads him to think correctly that his principles of the modern world would do better than the other principles he considers in maximizing utility—that is, in maximizing human happiness understood as a mode of existence (way of life) as described in the important II: ¶3–10 of *Utilitarianism*.

4. To check this understanding of Mill's doctrine, we must look at its details as found in the essays we read, *Utilitarianism*, *On Liberty*, and *The Subjection of Women*. We need to see how he treats several important political questions and to examine the way the conception of utility is connected with the principles of the modern world, and in particular with the principles of justice and the principle of liberty.

To this end, I shall try to show that one plausible rendering of Mill's view—I don't claim it is the most plausible—can be seen as utilitarian,

5. *Restatement*, p. 107.

when it is understood in terms of his conception of utility.[6] Although I read him as allowing an important role for perfectionist values, his view is still utilitarian in that it does not give perfectionist values a certain kind of weight as reasons in political questions, in particular questions of liberty. I will explain this in the next two lectures.

A special feature of Mill's view is that it rests on a particular psychological account of human nature, as expressed by certain quite specific psychological first principles. In one place Mill refers to them as: "the general laws of our emotional constitution" (*Utilitarianism*, V: ¶3). Among these principles are the following, the first two of which we discussed in the last lecture:

   (a) The decided preference criterion: *Utilitarianism*, II: ¶¶5–8.
   (b) The principle of dignity: *Utilitarianism*, II: ¶¶4, 6–7; *Liberty*, III: ¶6.
   (c) The principle of living in unity with others: *Utilitarianism*, III: ¶¶8–11.
   (d) The principle of individuality: *Liberty*, III: ¶1.
   (e) The Aristotelian principle: *Utilitarianism*, II: ¶8.

Clearly these principles are related in various ways, as some would seem to support or to underlie others; for example, (b) might be thought to underlie (a), or at least to support it. But I leave these matters aside for now.

5. I shall not argue that these principles are correct or incorrect, although many may find them implausible. They do make Mill's doctrine depend on a quite specific human psychology. We may think it better for a political conception of justice to be more robust in its principles and to depend, so far as possible, only on psychological features of human nature more evident to common sense. But still, if Mill's psychological principles are correct, then so far his doctrine is sound.

Here there is a range of possibilities. A political conception can depend on a quite specific human psychology; or else on a more general psychology together with a quite specific normative conception of person and society. Take, as an example of such a normative conception, that used in justice as fairness.[7] I would conjecture that political conceptions differ in how

6. Whether his conception of utility is itself utilitarian is an altogether different question. I believe it is not, but I put this aside for now.

7. A normative conception of the person and society is given by our moral and political thought and practice, and not by biological or psychological traits. In justice as fairness, in specifying society as a fair system of cooperation, we use the companion idea of free

they conceive of the division of labor between normative political conceptions on the one hand and basic psychological principles on the other. With a principle so general and abstract as that of utility, even as Mill understands it, a rather specific psychology seems required to get definite conclusions. Whereas it seems that the psychology of justice as fairness can perhaps be more general in ways to be explained later.

§2. Mill's Account of Justice

1. In Chapter V, "On the Connection between Justice and Utility," the long final chapter of *Utilitarianism*—it constitutes over a third of the essay—Mill gives his account of justice. He has saved this topic for a full treatment, as he thinks the apparent inconsistency between the principle of utility and our convictions and sentiments of justice is the only real difficulty in the utilitarian theory of morals (V: ¶38). As is evident at times from his replies, he thinks that the many other objections he examines are based on misunderstandings and worse. He now comes to what for him must have been a real problem. His wonderful discussion of this question must be the fruit of his own searching inquiries.

---

and equal persons as those who can play the role of fully cooperating members over a complete life. The normative and political conception of the person in justice as fairness is tied to persons' capacities as citizens. They are free and equal, and have the two moral powers: (1) a capacity for a sense of justice (the ability to understand, apply, and act from the principles of political justice that specify the fair terms of cooperation); and (2) a capacity for a conception of the good (to have, revise, and rationally to pursue an ordered family of final ends and aims that specifies a person's conception of what is of value in human life—normally set within a comprehensive religious, philosophical, or moral doctrine). They also have the powers of reason, inference, and judgment required to exercise the two moral powers.

They are *equal* in that they are all regarded as having, to the essential minimum degree, the moral powers necessary to engage in social cooperation over a complete life, and to take part in society as equal citizens. They are *free* in that they conceive of themselves and of one another as having the moral power to have a conception of the good, and the ability to revise and change it on reasonable and rational grounds if they so desire. There is no loss of their identity if they choose to do so. They are *free* also in that they consider themselves as self-authenticating sources of valid claims—as being entitled to make claims on their institutions so as to advance their conceptions of the good (*Restatement*, pp. 18–23).

My outline of Mill's argument in Chapter V on justice is as follows:

First part: ¶¶1–3: Statement of the problem.

Second part: ¶¶4–10: Six kinds of just and unjust conduct.

Third part: ¶¶11–15: Analysis of the Concept of Justice.

Fourth part: ¶¶16–25: (a) Sentiment of justice; and (b) Basis of rights in (latter in ¶¶24–25).

Fifth part: ¶¶26–31: Conflict of precepts of justice settled only by the principle of utility.

Sixth part: ¶¶32–38: Justice defined as the rules necessary for the essentials of human well-being.

2. Two general comments:

(a) In the first part of the argument, Mill states the problem for Chapter V as a whole as follows: The sentiment, or sense, of justice has great psychological intensity and it is also in apparent conflict with the principle of utility. So the question is: Can this sentiment nevertheless be accounted for in ways consistent with the principle of utility? What Mill wants to show is that it can. He argues that (a) given the kinds of things that we consider to be just and unjust (second part), and (b) given our psychological makeup, we can explain how our sense of justice arises and why it has the psychological intensity it does (fourth part). Mill states what he hopes to show in V: ¶3: "If, in everything which men are accustomed to characterize as just or unjust, some one common attribute or collection of attributes is always present, we may judge whether this particular attribute or combination of attributes would be capable of gathering around it a sentiment of that peculiar character and intensity by virtue of the general laws of our emotional constitution, or whether the sentiment is inexplicable, and requires to be regarded as a special provision of Nature."

Mill will try to show, of course, that the first is true and that the intensity of the sense of injustice can be accounted for consistent both with the principle of utility and with our moral psychology. Mill sums up his argument in V: ¶23: ". . . the sentiment of justice appears to me to be the animal desire to repel or retaliate a hurt or damage to oneself, or to those with whom one sympathizes, widened so as to include all persons, by the human capacity of enlarged sympathy, and the human conception of intelligent self-interest. From the latter elements [enlarged sympathy and intelligent self-interest] the feeling derives its morality; from the former [the animal desire to repel hurt to oneself], its peculiar impressiveness, and energy of self-assertion."

Thus, the sense of justice does not support an intuitionist view that justice is something *sui generis*. Rather, Mill holds that it fits perfectly with a utilitarian account of justice and a plausible psychological account of how that sentiment arises. Justice is not an independent and separate standard along side of and possibly having great weight contrary to the principle of utility. Instead, it is derivative from it.

(b) The last two parts of the argument, the fifth and sixth, exemplify the kind of justification Mill tried to give the principle of utility: namely, that although there are precepts and standards that apparently conflict with that principle, careful reflection shows that such is not the case. This supports the idea we noted before: namely, that in his justification of the principle of utility Mill claimed it is the only moral principle with sufficient generality and the appropriate content to serve as the first principle of a moral and political doctrine.

This form of argument is nicely displayed in the fifth part: ¶¶26–31, in which he argues that the conflict between the various precepts of justice can be resolved only by an appeal to a higher principle than any of those precepts. He thinks only the principle of utility can, in the end, serve this purpose. Thus, he says, for example, at V: ¶28 the following about those who agree that an action is unjust, but disagree with each other about their reasons for doing so: ". . . so long as the question is argued as one of justice simply, without going down to the principles which lie under justice and are the source of its authority, I am unable to see how any of these reasoners can be refuted." The final ¶¶32 to 38 give the remaining parts of Mill's justification for his principle of utility.

§3. The Place of Justice in Morality

1. In the third part of Chapter V, Mill surveys various kinds of actions and institutions that general moral opinion regards as just and unjust. Here he is, so to speak, describing the data: his account of justice as derived from utility and the principles of moral psychology must fit the points he makes in this survey.

Mill makes six points, summarized briefly as follows:

(a) It is commonly thought unjust to violate, and just to respect, people's legal rights (V: ¶5). (Here it is implicitly assumed that the law is not unjust.)

(b) But since some laws may be unjust, people sometimes have been given legal rights they ought not to have; and they are sometimes denied legal rights they ought to have. Thus a second kind of injustice is taking or withholding from people that to which they have a moral right (V: ¶6).

(c) It is just that people should have that which they deserve, whether it be good or evil, and unjust that they have what they don't deserve—again, good or evil (V: ¶7).

(d) It is unjust to break faith or to violate agreements; as well as to disappoint legitimate expectations (V: ¶8).

(e) When rights are concerned, it is unjust to be partial, that is, to be influenced by considerations that ought not to bear on the case at hand. Impartiality—being influenced exclusively by the relevant considerations—is an obligation of justice on persons such as judges, preceptors, and parents who have a judicial capacity (V: ¶9).

(f) Closely allied to impartiality is equality in the sense of natural justice: that is, of giving equal protection to the rights of all (V: ¶10).

2. Following this survey of the data, Mill locates where the concept of justice falls within his doctrine of utilitarianism as a whole. Consider the schema in Figure 6.

The evaluative point of view is my term—not Mill's—for the most general concept of value: all forms of value that Mill recognizes, moral and non-moral, fall under it. Mill's classification is not carefully presented. Still it serves his purpose of distinguishing morality (right and wrong) from the enjoyable and the admirable and the opportune, or expedient; and then, under morality, of distinguishing justice from charity and benevolence.

Mill's definition of morality, of right and wrong, goes like this. Right ac-

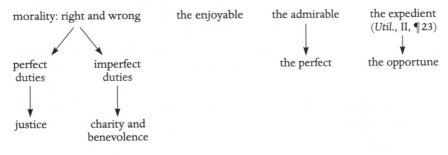

Figure 6. Mill: The evaluative point of view.

tions are actions that ought to be done, and wrong actions are actions that ought not to be done, and regarding which the failure to act appropriately ought to be punished in some way. They may be punished either by law, or by public disapprobation (moral opinion), or by reproaches of conscience. Here there are three very different kinds of sanctions. Considerations of utility settle whether an action ought to be done or ought not to be done. They also settle which sanction it is best to apply in different kinds of cases. Here "reproaches of conscience" refers indirectly to moral education. Some actions are best sanctioned by educating people so that their consciences reproach them for doing those actions.

Thus to summarize Mill's idea: an action is wrong, say, if it is a kind of action that not only has bad consequences when generally done, but its consequences are so bad that it increases overall social utility to establish the appropriate sanctions to ensure a certain degree of compliance (not necessarily perfect compliance, as this might require draconian measures). Now setting up these sanctions is always costly in utility terms. It involves the costs of the police, law courts, and prisons. The sanctions of public moral opinion and of conscience also involve disutilities, although less obvious ones. Nevertheless, the gain, on balance, in the case of wrong actions is judged sufficient to justify imposing them.

3. Mill thinks that what distinguishes the just and the unjust within the wider category of rights and wrongs, e.g. from charity or beneficence and the lack of it, is the idea of a personal right. He says: "Justice implies something which it is not only right to do, and wrong not to do, but which some individual [some assignable] person can claim from us as his *moral* right" (V: ¶15). By contrast, no individual, assignable person has a moral right to our beneficence or charity. The "perfect" duties of justice have correlative rights in some assignable persons; and these persons have a valid claim against society that their rights be guaranteed. Mill says later: "When we call anything a person's right, we mean that he has a valid claim on society to protect him in the possession of it, either by the force of law, or by that of education and opinion. If he has what we consider a sufficient claim, on whatever account, to have something guaranteed to him by society, we say that he has a right to it" (V: ¶24). "To have a right, then, is, I conceive, to have something which society ought to defend me in the possession of. If the objector goes on to ask why it ought, I can give him no other reason than general utility" (V: ¶25).

4. As I interpret Mill,[8] the possession of rights is specified by the rules of right and justice that are generally applicable. Often, but not always, these are legal rules that have an appropriate justification. But, for Mill, having a right does not depend on the utilities (costs and benefits) in a particular case. Although rights in a particular case may be overridden, this can happen only in very unusual circumstances; this is especially the case with the basic rights of justice.

Indeed, the instituting of rights is designed to inhibit, indeed to make unnecessary, our calculating utilities in particular cases. The security that basic rights provide would be endangered if the belief were widespread that a right could be violated for the sake of small gains that such calculations might reveal.

To sum up: Having a right does not depend on the balance of utilities of particular cases, but rather on the rules (legal or otherwise) of justice and on their utility as rules when generally enforced. A right may be overridden, however, but only in very exceptional circumstances when the utility gains and losses one way or the other are clearly very great. In these exceptional circumstances, the rule against being guided by utilities in the particular case is suspended.

§4. Features of Moral Rights in Mill

1. For Mill, moral rights have, it seems, three features. This is especially true of the political and social rights that Mill regards as essential for the institutions of the modern world, which I shall describe in the next two lectures. Here I draw on his account in V: ¶¶16–25, 32–33.

One feature is this: in order for there to be moral rights, say the rights of justice, there must be reasons of special weight to support them. These reasons must be weighty enough to justify demanding that other people respect those rights, by the force of law if necessary. Therefore these reasons must be of sufficient urgency to justify setting up the requisite institutional machinery to secure that end.

As Mill puts it: these reasons connect with "the essentials of human

---

8. Here I follow Fred Berger in *Happiness, Justice, and Freedom* (Berkeley: University of California Press, 1984), p. 132.

well-being" (V: ¶32), with "the very groundwork of our existence" (V: ¶25). Again, these reasons are founded on the kinds of utility that are "extraordinarily important and impressive" (V: ¶25).

2. A second feature of these moral rights is their peremptory character: by this I mean that for Mill, to have such a right is to have a moral (as opposed to a merely legal) justification for demanding something: for example, that our liberty be respected by others, and this by legal sanctions, or by general moral opinion, whichever is appropriate. Although these rights are not absolute—that is, they can sometimes be overridden, and then often by other such rights, as rights may conflict with each other—they cannot, as we have seen, be overridden except by reasons of very special weight and urgency.

Thus, for example, Mill suggests that the rights of justice cannot be overridden by reasons of policy, or the best way of managing some department of human affairs. See V: ¶¶32–33: here he says that we are not deluded in thinking "that justice is a more sacred thing than policy, and that the latter ought only to be listened to after the former has been satisfied" (V: ¶32). This remark seems to state something like the priority of basic justice. So also does the remark Mill adds a bit later: "Justice is a name for certain classes of moral rules, which concern the essentials of human well-being more nearly, and are therefore of more absolute obligation, than any other rules for the guidance of life" (V: ¶32). Mill goes on to say that the essence of justice is that of a right residing in an individual, and this testifies to and implies this more binding obligation. The moral rules of justice which forbid us to interfere wrongly with one another's freedom are: ". . . more vital to human well-being than any maxims, however important, which only point out the best mode of managing some department of human affairs" (V: ¶33). All this foreshadows Dworkin's well-known distinction between questions of principle and questions of policy, as well as his idea of rights as trumps.[9]

A third feature of the moral rights, especially those of justice, is that the claims they validate have force against existing law and institutions. When these arrangements deny those claims, the reform of law and institutions should be considered and, depending on circumstances, may be justified.

---

9. See Ronald Dworkin, *Taking Rights Seriously* (Cambridge, Mass.: Harvard University Press, 1978), pp. xi, 184–205.

3. Now we have the following problem: there are two ways in which legal rights, the rights recognized by law and institutions, may be justified:[10]

(a) By an appeal to a suitable principle of policy, or to a principle of the common good, and perhaps also to the principle of efficient or effective organization. Or:

(b) By an appeal to moral rights, say, to those of political and social justice. These moral rights we think of as identifiable prior to and independent of the specific nature of the existing legal institutions. Rather, we ascertain what these rights are by considering the basic needs and requirements of individuals. These needs and requirements ground people's claims to the rights of justice. They are referred to by Mill when he appeals to "the very groundwork of our existence" (V: ¶25), the "essentials of human well-being" (V: ¶32), and by other similar locutions.

Now these two kinds of justification are quite different: consider the case of Congress thinking about setting up a price support system for certain crops, to encourage their production, to smooth price changes, and the like. This is a matter of policy. No one supposes that farmers have a basic moral right to a system of price supports. Contrast this with the basic rights, e.g. liberty of conscience and rights of suffrage. Matters of policy may be the right or the best thing to do in certain circumstances; but legally protecting the rights of justice is a different matter.

The point is this: the policy of price supports (in the example above) is justified by the appeal to the well-being of society as a whole, or by an appeal to the common good; whereas the justification of laws by reference to the rights of justice offhand is not. Rather, Mill's view refers to the independently identifiable essential requirements of individuals on which those rights are grounded.

In specifying the rights of justice there is no apparent reference to aggregate social well-being. When Mill identifies the essentials of human well-being, or the elements of the groundwork of our existence, he does not do so via the idea of maximizing total utility. He looks to individuals' basic needs and to what constitutes the very framework of their existence. Yet, Mill also says that if he is asked why we ought legally to protect the rights of justice, he can give "no other reason than general utility" (V: ¶25).

10. This distinction is found in H. L. A. Hart in "Natural Rights: Bentham and John Stuart Mill," in his *Essays on Bentham* (Oxford: Clarendon Press, 1982), pp. 94f. I am much indebted to this essay.

§5. Mill's Two-Part Criterion

1. Mill seems committed to a two-part criterion[11] for identifying the basic rights of individuals, which I interpret here as the basic rights of political and social justice. The two parts are:

(i) First part: we look to the essentials of human well-being, to the groundwork of our existence: these essentials and groundwork (apparently) justify moral rights apart from aggregative considerations. And:

(ii) Second part: we look to those general rules the enforcement of which is especially productive of social utility in the aggregative sense, and hence tend to maximize that utility.

If Mill's account of rights is to avoid contradiction, it must be the case that the two parts of Mill's criterion always happen to converge (barring freakish cases).[12] This means that: Looking at least to the long run, maximizing social utility in the aggregative sense normally, if not always, requires setting up political and social institutions so that legal rules specify and enforce the protection of the basic rights of justice. These rights are identified by what constitutes the very groundwork of our individual existence. And the enforcement of these rules secures and protects for all persons equally the essential elements of human well-being, which elements ground the rights of justice.

2. But how can we know that the two parts of Mill's criterion always coincide? Mill does not try to show in Chapter V that maximizing general social utility requires that all persons be secured the same equal rights of justice. Why can't it happen that greater social utility is achieved by denying a small minority certain of the equal rights? They need not be denied the moral rights of justice entirely; but why must everyone enjoy the equal protection of all the moral rights of justice? On what basis is Mill so confident that everyone should have the same equal rights, which are to be secured equally?

Observe that Mill says that common opinion held the view that the just, while "generically distinct from . . . the expedient [or aggregate social utility: II: ¶23], and in idea opposed to it" always coincides with it in the long

11. Hart, "Natural Rights," p. 96.
12. We don't require that they necessarily converge.

run. On this see his remarks in V: ¶¶1–2. This suggests that in Chapter V he is mainly concerned with two things:

One is to give an account of the psychological intensity (or strength) of our sense of injustice consistent with the principle of utility; and

The other to explain how it is that, on a utilitarian view, there can be certain moral rights and rights of justice that society must protect, permitting violations only in the most exceptional cases.

My problem, however, and Hart's, is: we don't see how, from what has been said, we could know that in general, enforcing equal rights for all maximizes utility as Mill understands utility. To assure this, mustn't we always make rather special assumptions? If so, what are these assumptions? And in particular, which special assumptions is Mill making? Identifying these defines part of our task in understanding Mill. I shall come back to this.

3. Incidentally, it is no help to appeal to Bentham's maxim "everybody is to count for one, and nobody for more than one." The reason is that:

(a) Taken one way, it is simply a rule that follows from how utility is to be measured: namely, the equal utility of different people is to be weighed equally in arriving at the total sum of social utility. The social utility function is simply a linear sum of utilities (one for each person) with identical weights for all persons. On this, see the footnote to V: ¶36. H. S. Maine's Brahmin contradicts this rule when he says that the utility of a Brahmin is to be weighed 20 times that of those who are not Brahmins.[13]

This interpretation of "everybody [each] to count for one" is simply a truism about measuring and summing social utility. It says pleasures are pleasures; they are to be weighed the same no matter in whose consciousness they occur. It is equal justice to equal pleasures: but that is just what measuring is! Compare this to measuring an amount of water: a quart in one reservoir is equal to a quart in another. But this doesn't address the question of why equal rights must be secured for everyone. Mill's answer here seems oddly unaware of this question. I don't know why.

(b) Taken in another way, "everybody to count for one" means that everyone has "an equal claim to all the means of happiness"; or that "all persons have a right to equality of treatment"; but Mill adds, "except when some recognized social expediency requires the reverse" (V: ¶36). Injustice,

13. See H. S. Maine, *Lectures on the Early History of Institutions* (London: Murray, 1897), pp. 399f.

then, consists in part of those inequalities that are not justified by social expediency, by what is necessary to maximize social utility in the long run. This second interpretation leaves us where we were.

4. We are left with two questions we must try to answer.

First, why is Mill so confident that the two parts of his criterion for identifying the basic rights of justice do not diverge? Or, alternatively, why is he so confident that the political and social institutions that realize the principles of the modern world—principles with a content somewhat similar to the two principles of justice as fairness—are necessary to maximize social utility (in the long run), given the historical conditions of that world? And how does his answer rely on his conception of utility as spelled out in *Utilitarianism*, II: ¶¶3–10?

Second, if our conjecture that Mill's confidence rests on certain rather specific psychological principles of human nature is correct, then what are these more specific principles, and how does Mill think they work in tandem with his conception of utility to justify his principles of the modern world? Once Mill's doctrine is fully set out, we will have to ask whether it is utilitarian in an appropriate sense. But for the time being I leave that aside. Our first aim must be to understand his view.

§6. The Desire to Be in Unity with Others

1. In the last lecture we considered the sense of dignity as a psychological principle that supports Mill's view of happiness as a way of life giving a special place and priority to activities involving the exercise of the higher faculties. We now turn to another principle in his psychology, the desire to be in unity with others. This desire is taken up in III: ¶¶8–11 in connection with what Mill calls the ultimate sanction of utilitarian morality. This includes the desire, or willingness, to act justly, and so is appropriately discussed at this point.

As I have said, Chapter III presents part of Mill's moral psychology and his account of how we can be moved to act from (and not merely in accordance with) the principle of utility and the requirements of justice. In some places this chapter is not very clear; but I think that we can make satisfactory sense of it for our purposes.

One of Mill's main points is that whatever our philosophical account of moral judgments may be, whether we think moral distinctions have a tran-scendental or an objective foundation, or whether our view is naturalistic or even subjective, it is still true that as moral agents we do not act from moral principles unless we are moved by our conscience, or by moral con-viction, or some other form of moral motivation. Right conduct must have some basis in our nature and character. Thus, a transcendentalist or an intuitionist doctrine, as much as the utilitarian or any other doctrine, must include a moral psychology.

Another of Mill's main points is that historical experience shows that we can be educated to act from the principle of utility as well as from other moral principles. He contends that the principle of utility has a foothold in our moral psychology at least as secure and natural as that of any other principle.

2. I focus now on ¶¶8–11, which conclude Chapter III. ¶¶8–9 form a unit, as do ¶¶10–11. Let's begin with 8–9. Here Mill states several general theses of his moral psychology, as follows.

(a) Our moral feelings and attitudes are not, to be sure, innate in the sense that they are spontaneously present in everyone without training and education; but like the educated capacities to speak and to reason, to build cities and to engage in agriculture, they are a natural outgrowth of our na-ture. Moral feelings and attitudes are capable of springing up, to some small degree, spontaneously, and they are also susceptible of being brought to a high level of cultivation and development.

(b) Mill grants that by an extensive enough use of external sanctions and of early moral training guided by the laws of association, our moral faculty can be cultivated in almost any direction. But there is this difference: early associations which are entirely artificial creations, and which have no support in our nature, yield by degrees to the dissolving force of intellec-tual analysis. Unless the feeling of duty is associated with a principle conge-nial to our nature and harmonious with its natural sentiments, it will upon intellectual analysis gradually lose its power to move us. This is part of Mill's criterion of the natural as opposed to the artificial.

(c) Hence Mill needs to show that given the content of the principle of utility, the feelings of duty and moral obligation associated with it meet this essential condition. For if they did not, they would be artificial and there-fore would dissolve in the face of reflection and analysis.

3. Mill tries to show this in ¶¶10–11. He begins by saying that there is a

powerful natural sentiment in human nature that supports the principle of utility, namely, the desire to be in unity with others. This desire is such that, even apart from learning based on the laws of association, it tends to become stronger from the influences of advancing civilization. Let's consider first, the content of this desire to be in unity with others, and second, the influences which make it stronger as civilization advances:

(a) The content of this desire Mill describes in ¶11 as the desire that we should not be rivals with others for the means of happiness. It is also the desire that there should be a harmony between our feelings and aims and the feelings and aims of others, so that the objectives of our conduct and theirs are not in conflict but complementary. What Mill has in mind is that the desire to be in unity with others is the desire to act from a principle of reciprocity. For he says in ¶10 that the feeling of unity with others, when perfect, would never make us desire any beneficial condition for ourselves, in the benefits of which others are not also included.[14]

(b) Why is this desire a natural outgrowth of our nature? Mill thinks that the social state itself is not only natural to us, but necessary and habitual. Any features of society that are essential to it we tend to regard as equally essential to us. Society is our natural habitat, as it were, and so what is essential to it must be harmonious with our nature. But how have the features essential to modern society been affected by the advances of civilization? The desire to be in unity with others is increasingly characteristic of the present age; so Mill must think there are special features of an advancing society that more and more sustain that desire.

(c) Mill gives a brief account of these features in the long paragraph 10 of Chapter III. They are not sharply enumerated, but his main idea seems to be that numerous changes are making modern society increasingly a society in which people recognize that they must, of course, pay due regard to the feelings and interests of others. The increasing equality of modern civilization, and the large scale of cooperation with other people and of proposing to them collective purposes, have made us aware that we must work together for shared and not for individual ends.

(d) The increasing equality of modern society comes about in this way: Mill thinks that all society among human beings, except for that between

14. The fact that Mill says this leads us to ask whether the difference principle (see *Restatement*, pp. 42f) is a better expression of Mill's view about equality and distributive justice than the principle of utility. However, I shan't pursue this here.

master and slave, is impossible unless the interests of all are to be consulted; and a society between persons who regard one another as equals can only exist on the understanding that the interests of all are to be regarded equally. In every stage of society, everyone "except an absolute monarch lives on equal terms with somebody; and in every age some advance is made towards a state in which it will be impossible to live permanently on other terms [than equality] with anybody." So the advance of civilization towards greater equality strengthens the desire to be in unity with others.

Moreover, this desire is congenial to and harmonious with our nature and is not artificial. Why? Because the condition of equality is natural to society. It is the result of removing historical barriers and inequalities of power and property originating from force and conquest, and long maintained by dominion, ignorance, and the generally impoverished state of earlier society.

4. Aside, then, from the principle of dignity, what is the ultimate sanction of the principle of utility with its concern for equal justice? In Mill's description it would appear to have two components. The first component is the desire to be in unity with others, as supported and strengthened by the conditions of modern equality; while the second component is certain convictions about, and attitudes related to, that desire.

This second component needs to be clarified. I take Mill to mean that to those who have this desire, it seems as natural a desire as are the feelings that accompany it. That is, it does not strike them on reflection and analysis as a desire imposed by education guided by the laws of association, or by laws relying on the intimidating power of society, and such that, once they understand this, the desire tends to disappear. To the contrary, this desire they think to be an attribute that it would not be good for them to be without.

Thus, by Mill's criterion of the artificial vs. the natural, the desire to live in unity with others is natural and not undermined by analysis. And it is this conviction (indeed all these convictions and attitudes together) about the desire to be in unity with others that Mill says is the ultimate sanction of the principle of utility, and so the ultimate basis of our willingness to give justice.

The question now arises: how solid is the answer or explanation Mill gives here? Can we really make it out? Do we need to do better? How might we try?

MILL III

The Principle of Liberty

§1. The Problem of *On Liberty* (1859)

1. I begin with stating the problem of *On Liberty* as Mill formulates it in Chapter I. This problem is not the philosophical problem of freedom of the will, but that of civil or social liberty. It is the problem concerning "the nature and limits of the power that can be legitimately exercised by society over the individual." This is an ancient problem but one which, Mill believes, in the state of society of the England of his day, assumes a different form under new conditions. It requires, therefore, a different and, in Mill's view, more fundamental treatment (I: ¶1). What Mill has in mind is that the problem of liberty, as he anticipates it, will arise in the new organic age in which society will be democratic, secular, and industrial.

The problem is not that of protecting society from the tyranny of monarchs, or rulers generally, for this problem has been settled by the establishment of various constitutional checks on government power and by political immunities and rights. The problem concerns the abuses of democratic government itself, in particular the abuse by majorities of their power over minorities. Mill says: "The will of the people . . . practically means the will of the most numerous or the most active part of the people—the majority, or those who succeed in making themselves accepted as the majority; the people, consequently, may desire to oppress a part of their number; and precautions are as much needed against this as against any other abuse of power" (I: ¶4). Thus Mill's concern is the so-called "tyranny of the majority," to which Tocqueville had previously drawn attention.[1]

2. Note, however, that Mill is equally concerned with "the tyranny of the prevailing opinion and feeling, . . . the tendency of society to impose,

---

1. See Alexis de Tocqueville, *Democracy in America* (1st ed., 1835).

by other means than civil penalties, its own ideas and practices as rules of conduct on those who dissent from them; to fetter the development . . . of any individuality not in harmony with its ways . . . There is a limit to the legitimate interference of collective opinion with individual independence; and to find that limit, and maintain it against encroachment, is as indispensable to a good condition of human affairs, as protection against political despotism" (I: ¶5). Moreover, Mill foresees that this problem will occur under the new conditions of the imminent democratic society in which the newly enfranchised laboring class—the most numerous class—will have the vote.

The problem, then, is to determine what, under these new circumstances, is the "fitting adjustment between individual independence and social control" (I: ¶6). Some rules of conduct, legal and moral, are plainly necessary. No two ages resolve this question in the same way, and yet each age thinks its own way is "self-evident and self-justifying" (I: ¶6).

3. At this point Mill stresses a number of characteristic faults of prevailing moral opinion. Thus, this opinion is usually unreflective, the effect of custom and tradition. People are likely to think that no reasons at all are required to support their moral convictions. And indeed some philosophers (perhaps Mill refers to the conservative intuitionists here) encourage us to think that our feelings are "better than reasons and render reasons unnecessary" (I: ¶6). Then Mill states one of the main principles he wants to attack: "The practical principle which guides them to their opinions on the regulation of human conduct is the feeling in each person's mind that everybody should be required to act as he, and those with whom he sympathizes, would like them to act" (I: ¶6). Of course, no one "acknowledges to himself that his standard of judgment is his own liking"; but Mill maintains that it is true nonetheless, because: "an opinion on a point of conduct, not supported by reasons, can only count as one person's preference; and if the reasons, when given, are a mere appeal to a similar preference felt by other people, it is still only many people's liking instead of one" (I: ¶6). But to most people, their own preferences supported by the preferences of others are perfectly satisfactory reasons, and in fact, the only reasons they usually have for their moral convictions. [See also IV: ¶12.]

4. The prevailing moral opinion in society tends, Mill believes, to be a grouping of unreasoned and unreflective, mutually supporting shared preferences; yet these opinions are influenced by many kinds of causes:

(a) For instance, where there is an ascendant social class, a large portion of the morality of a country reflects the interests of that class and its feelings of class superiority.

(b) But also, the general and obvious interests of society have a share, and a large one, in influencing moral opinion; so the role of utility (in Hume's loose sense of an appeal to these interests) is not unimportant. These general interests, however, have their effect less from being recognized by reason than as a consequence of the sympathies and dislikes that grow out of them.

Thus, to sum up Mill's argument, the unreasoned likings and dislikings of society, or of some dominant portion of society, are the main elements which have, up to now, determined the rules for general observance, which have been enforced by the sanctions of law and prevailing opinion. And "wherever the sentiment of the majority is still genuine and intense, it is found to have abated little of its claim to be obeyed" (I: ¶7).

5. I have gone into these details since they help us recognize how Mill views the problem of liberty and what he sees the Principle of Liberty—first stated in I: ¶9—as doing. Mill wants to change not only the adjustment between social rules and individual independence, as actually determined up to now, but also how the public—the educated opinion he wants to address—reasons about those adjustments. He is presenting his Principle of Liberty as a principle of public reason in the coming democratic age: he views it as a principle to guide the public's political decisions on those questions. For he fears that the sway of prevailing and unreasoned opinion could be far worse in the new democratic society to come than it has been in the past.

Note that Mill thinks that the time for making changes is "now" but the situation is not hopeless. [Cf. III: ¶19 esp.] "The majority have not yet learnt to feel the power of government [as] their power, or its opinions their opinions" (I: ¶8). When those in the majority, including the new laboring class, come to feel this way, individual liberty will be as exposed to invasion from government as it has long been from public opinion.

On the other hand, Mill thinks there is much latent resistance to such invasions. But the situation, as he sees it, is in a state of flux and can go perhaps one way or the other. "There is . . . no recognized principle by which the propriety or impropriety of government interference is customarily tested. People decide according to their personal preferences" (I: ¶8).

They rarely decide in accordance with any principle, "to which they consistently adhere, as to what things are fit to be done by government." It is because of this lack of principle (in this state of flux) that when government does intervene, it is as likely to be wrong as right (I: ¶8).

6. Putting this together with I: ¶15, where Mill speaks of the present tendency to increase the power of society while reducing the power of the individual, we can say that he hoped to do the following:

(a) He aimed to state a principle of liberty appropriate for the new democratic age to come. This principle would govern the public political discussion of the adjustment of social rules and individual independence. And:

(b) By convincing arguments, Mill wanted to build up support of this principle ". . . a strong barrier of moral conviction" (I: ¶15). The disposition of people to impose their own opinions can only be restrained by an opposing power; in this case Mill thinks it must be at least in part the power of moral conviction. And:

(c) These arguments are to be based on reason, because only in this case do they appeal to genuinely moral convictions as opposed to widely shared and mutually supporting preferences. Here it becomes plain that by reasoned arguments Mill means arguments founded on the Principle of Liberty (as he explains it in Chapter I, ¶¶9–13), and as it is connected with his conception of Utility (I: ¶11). This principle meets, he thinks, all the requirements of a reasoned principle, whereas no other principle does so.

The Principle of Liberty is presented, then, as a public political principle framed to regulate free public discussion concerning the appropriate adjustment between individual independence and social control (I: ¶6). As such, it will be instrumental in shaping national character to have the aims, aspirations, and ideals required in the age to come.

I comment here that Mill's chosen vocation is evident: he sees himself as an educator of influential opinion. That is his aim. He thinks the situation is not hopeless: the future is still open. It is not unreasonable, or merely visionary, to try to forestall the possible tyranny of democratic majorities in the coming age. Plainly Mill attributes significant efficacy to moral convictions and to intellectual discussion about political and social matters. (Here he would seem to differ from Marx. But there is a question how to put this more exactly: for Marx too asserts that his *Das Kapital* has a social role.) Attempts to convince by reason and argument can have an important bearing, at least in those circumstances where things are in flux and can still go one way or the other. I wouldn't say that Mill's tone is particularly optimistic. He is doing what he thinks he can best do in the present circumstances.

The parts of Mill's *On Liberty* to read particularly carefully:

I: entire
II: ¶¶1–11; and the last 5 paragraphs, 37–41
III: ¶¶1–9; 14; 19; and an important passage in ¶13
IV: ¶¶1–12
V: ¶¶1–4; and the last 8 paragraphs, 16–23 (re government and state socialism and bureaucracy).

§2. Some Preliminary Points about Mill's Principle

1. Before taking up the meaning and force of Mill's Principle of Liberty, I consider a few preliminary points relating to it. Note first that he thinks of it as covering certain enumerated liberties. They are given by a list and not by a definition of liberty in general, or as such. (This procedure was used in justice as fairness, where Mill is followed in this respect.) It is these listed liberties which receive special protection and which are defined by certain legal and moral rights of justice.

(a) First (covering the inward domain of consciousness), liberty of conscience, liberty of thought and feeling; absolute freedom of opinion and sentiment on all subjects, practical and speculative, scientific, moral or theological. Freedom of speech and press is practically inseparable from the preceding.

(b) Second, liberty of tastes and pursuits; of framing the "plan of our life to suit our own character," without restraint so long as we do not injure the legitimate interests (or moral rights) of others, and even though they think our conduct foolish, degrading, or wrong.

(c) Third, liberty to combine with others for any purposes that do not injure the (legitimate) interests of others; freedom of association. (For a, b, c, see: I: ¶12.) Mill adds that "No society in which these liberties are not, on the whole, respected, is free, whatever may be its form of government; and none is completely free in which they do not exist absolute and unqualified" (I: ¶13). Thus, for the most part, Mill presents his argument by defending these specific liberties. He focuses primarily on the first two in Chapters II and III, respectively.

2. Next, observe the scope and the conditions under which Mill says the Principle of Liberty applies:

(a) It does not apply to children and immature adults; or to the mentally disturbed (I: ¶10).

(b) It does not apply to backward societies: he says: "Liberty, as a principle, has no application to any state of things anterior to the time when mankind have become capable of being improved by free and equal discussion" (I: ¶10). Mill notes that the nations with which he is concerned in the essay are nations that have long since reached this stage.

(c) Later Mill adds that the Principle does not apply to a people surrounded by external enemies, and always liable to hostile attack. Nor does it apply to a people beset by internal commotion and strife, in either of which a relaxation of self-command might be fatal (I: ¶14).

3. From these remarks it is clear that the Principle of Liberty is not a first or supreme principle: it is subordinate to the Principle of Utility and to be justified in terms of it. Rather, the Principle of Liberty is a kind of mediate axiom (*Utilitarianism*, II: ¶¶24–25). But nevertheless one of great importance: it is a principle of public reason—a political principle to guide the public's discussion in a democratic society.

That the Principle of Liberty is viewed by Mill as a mediate axiom, a subordinate principle (II: ¶24), is confirmed by what he says in I: ¶11: he writes: ". . . I forego any advantage which could be derived to my argument from the idea of abstract right, as a thing independent of utility. I regard utility as the ultimate appeal on all ethical questions." He adds the very crucial rider: ". . . but it must be utility in the largest sense, grounded on the permanent interests of man as a progressive being."

In the next lecture, I shall discuss these permanent interests and try to connect them with the psychological principles that underlie Mill's view. For now I note that among them are interests in the firm guarantee of the moral rights of justice, which establish the "very groundwork of our existence" (*Utilitarianism*, V: ¶25). Another permanent interest is an interest in the conditions of free individuality, which conditions are an essential part of the engine of progressive change.

Mill's idea is that only if a democratic society follows the Principle of

Liberty in regulating its public discussion of the rules bearing on the relation of individuals and society, and only if it adjusts its attitudes and laws accordingly, can its political and social institutions fulfill their role of shaping national character so that its citizens can realize the permanent interests of man as a progressive being.

§3. Mill's Principle of Liberty Stated

1. Mill states the Principle of Liberty in I: ¶¶9–13; IV: ¶¶3, 6; V: ¶2, with further explanation in ¶¶3 and 4. In the first statement it reads as follows (I: ¶9): ". . . the sole end for which mankind are warranted, individually or collectively, in interfering with the liberty of action of any of their number, is self-protection." He adds that: ". . . the only purpose for which power can be rightfully exercised over any member of a civilized community, against his will, is to prevent harm to others. His own good, either physical or moral, is not a sufficient warrant." Someone's own good is a good reason for: "remonstrating with him, or reasoning with him, or persuading him, or entreating him, but not for compelling him, or visiting him with any evil in case he do otherwise." To justify such coercion requires that the conduct in question is likely to produce evil to some one else. Regarding the part of a person's conduct which concerns himself alone, Mill says: "his independence is, of right, absolute. Over himself, over his own body and mind, the individual is sovereign" (I: ¶9).

2. This principle is, of course, intended by Mill to apply to restraints on liberty that are the result of what Mill calls the "moral coercion of public opinion," as well as to the restraints of law and other institutions enforced by sanctions of the state. We can formulate the principle of liberty in the form of three clauses as follows:

(a) First Clause: Society through its laws and the moral pressure of common opinion should never interfere with individuals' beliefs and conduct unless those beliefs and conduct injure the legitimate interests, or the (moral) rights, of others. In particular, only reasons of right and wrong should be appealed to in public discussions. This excludes three kinds of reasons: *Liberty*, III: ¶9; IV: ¶3.

(i) Paternalistic reasons, which invoke reasons founded on other persons' good—defined in terms of what is wise and prudent from their individual point of view.

(ii) Reasons of excellence and ideals of human perfection, specified by reference to our, or to society's, ideals of excellence and perfection. (*Utilitarianism*, II: ¶6; *On Liberty*, IV: ¶¶5, 7. All of IV: ¶¶3–12 is important.)

(iii) Reasons of dislike or disgust, or of preference, where the disliking, disgust, or preference cannot be supported by reasons of right and wrong, as defined in *Utilitarianism*, V: ¶¶14–15.

Thus, one way to read Mill's Principle of Liberty as a principle of public reason is to see it as excluding certain kinds of reasons from being taken into account in legislation, or in guiding the moral coercion of public opinion (as a social sanction). In the case of public reason, the three kinds of reasons given above count for zero.

I call your attention here to a question of interpretation. I have read the first clause of the Principle of Liberty as saying that society should never interfere with an individual's belief and conduct unless that person's beliefs and conduct injure the legitimate interests, or the moral rights, of others. This doesn't always fit with Mill's own way of stating the principle. He says in I: ¶9: ". . . the sole end for which mankind are warranted . . . in interfering with the liberty of action of any of their number is self-protection." Or: ". . . to prevent harm to others." Or: "the conduct . . . must be calculated to produce evil to some one else." Or: "the only part of the conduct of anyone for which he is amenable to society, is that which concerns others." And in I: ¶11 he speaks of conduct "hurtful to others," and in IV: ¶3, of conduct that "affects prejudicially the interests of others."

Obviously much that others do concerns us, but that is not to say that what they do produces evil to us. As Mill says in IV: ¶3, "The acts of an individual may be hurtful to others . . . without going the length of violating any of their constituted rights." "Concern" and "affect" are general terms covering much. We must decide, then, how to resolve this implicit ambiguity and vagueness of Mill's language and to do so in a way that makes sense of his text. To this end I read the leading text as given by III: ¶9 and supported by IV: ¶3. So we say the following, drawing on IV: ¶3:

First Clause: Society should never interfere with the individual's beliefs and conduct by law or punishment, or by moral opinion as coercive, unless the individual's beliefs and conduct injure—that is, wrong or violate—the legitimate interests of others, either in express legal provisions (assumed to be justified), or by tacit understanding ought to be considered as (moral) rights.

This still needs some commentary and interpretation, but we are now getting a definite doctrine. Now let's take bits at the start of III: ¶9 and later parts of the paragraph to render it more exact: Society is to allow the cultivation of individuality "within the limits imposed by the (moral) rights and the (legitimate) interests of others." Hence, individuals are "to be held to rigid rules of justice for the sake of others" and within these limits they are to give fair play to the nature of different persons, allowing them to lead different lives as they choose, because "whatever crushes individuality is despotism."

Accepting this for the moment, I continue the exposition.

Now, Mill is not denying that in other contexts—say in the context of personal life, or in the internal life of various associations—considerations that fall short of violating the (moral) rights of others can be sound reasons. Of course they can be. Nor is he denying that our dislike of and our annoyance with the beliefs and conduct of others is painful to us, even when it does not affect our rights or legitimate interests. Of course it is painful! And so it is a disutility, to use the general term.

His view is that to advance the permanent interests of humankind as a progressive being, society does better if it resolutely adheres to the Principle of Liberty which directs it to exclude the three kinds of reasons noted above. Thus, Mill's principle imposes a strategic constraint on the reasons admissible in public political discussion and thereby specifies an idea of public reason. (Compare this to the idea of public reason in *Restatement*.)[2]

3. Second Clause: If certain kinds of individual belief and conduct do injure the legitimate interests and moral rights of others, as shown by the considerations of right and wrong admissible by the first clause, then public discussion may properly take up the question whether those beliefs and conduct should be in some way restricted. The question may then be discussed on its merits, but of course excluding the three kinds of reasons noted above.

Observe that because injury to the legitimate interests or moral rights of others (as currently understood, or specified) can alone justify the interference of law and moral opinion, it does not follow that it always does justify it. The question remains to be discussed on its merits in terms of admissible reasons.

2. To publicly justify our political judgments to others is to convince them by public reason, that is, by ways of reasoning and inference appropriate to fundamental political questions, and by appealing to beliefs, grounds, and political values it is reasonable for others also to acknowledge and endorse. Rawls, *Restatement*, p. 27. See also §26.

Third Clause: The question must be settled by those merits.

4. In conclusion, the substantive force of Mill's principle of liberty is given by the three kinds of reasons excluded by the first clause, with the last two clauses saying in effect that reasons of right and wrong, as defined in *Utilitarianism*, Chapter V: ¶¶14–15, especially reasons of moral rights and justice, must settle the case. The result is that only certain kinds of reasons—only certain kinds of utilities—are appropriate to invoke in Mill's form of public reason.

§4. On Natural (Abstract) Right

1. Let's ask why Mill said (in I: ¶11) that he would forgo any advantage to his argument which could be derived from the idea of abstract right as a thing independent from utility.

One obvious reason, certainly, is simply to inform the reader of his philosophical position and to reaffirm his official utilitarian view that all rights, whether moral, legal, or institutional, are founded on utility (*Utilitarianism*, V: ¶25).

Utilitarians generally recognized the various rights of private property, for example. They held that these rights are justified because they promote the general welfare. But it is also possible, in principle at least, to argue that restrictions on the right of private property, or its abolition altogether, might be even more favorable to the general welfare, in view of present or future social conditions.

Mill accepts the general form of this argument. The special features of his view arise from his interpretation of utility in terms of the permanent interests of man as a progressive being. The idea that rights have a philosophical justification apart from utility, whether utility is understood in Bentham's or in Mill's way, or in some other way, all utilitarians rejected. This was one of their objections to the idea of natural rights, which Bentham described as "nonsense on stilts."[3]

2. But a second reason why Mill mentions his disavowal of abstract

---

3. Bentham said in *Anarchical Fallacies*: "Natural rights is simple nonsense: natural and imprescriptible rights, rhetorical nonsense,—nonsense on stilts." See *Nonsense upon Stilts*, ed. Jeremy Waldron (London: Methuen, 1987), p. 53. This book contains the text of three historically important critiques of the rights of man, those of Bentham, Burke, and Marx.

right is that his formulation of the principle of liberty may seem to presuppose it. This he wants to deny.

But if the overwhelming majority of society wants very much to interfere with the self-regarding conduct of but a few others—and Mill, in his strong chapter on "Liberty of Thought and Discussion," says they have no right to do so *(On Liberty,* II: ¶1)—we want to ask why shouldn't they? On some ways of understanding utility, the sum of utility would certainly seem to increase.

Mill also says at the same place (II: ¶1) that the principle of liberty of thought and discussion is to govern absolutely the dealings of society with the individual when the question of compulsion and control arises. I assume here that Mill means by "absolutely" that the principle of liberty admits of no exceptions, that it always holds under the normal conditions of the democratic age (at least barring very special circumstances). One is led to ask how the principle of liberty could always hold and allow of no exceptions, even in the case of a single individual, unless the principle invoked some natural right which could not be overridden.

Here we have to keep in mind Mill's statement in II: ¶1, where he says that even a whole people lack the power (right) to silence political discussion, even against a single person. This power, whether exercised by the people or by their government, is illegitimate. He says: "If all mankind minus one, were of one opinion, and only one person were of the contrary opinion, mankind would be no more justified in silencing that one person, than he, if he had the power, would be justified in silencing mankind." Once again, this prompts us to ask: how can the number of persons fail to make any difference as to the justification of silencing discussion unless some doctrine of natural, or abstract, right lies in the background? Is Mill simply indulging in a rhetorical flourish?

3. I interpret the passages that suggest a doctrine of abstract right as Mill's way of saying that it is better for the advancement of the permanent interests of man as a progressive being that the public political conception of the coming democratic society always affirm the principle of liberty without exception, even when applied to the case of a single individual dissenter.

Keep in mind that what Mill is doing is advocating the principle of liberty as a principle subordinate to the principle of utility to govern the public political discussions as to how to regulate basic political and social institutions. Recall that he regards these institutions as ways to form and to educate a national character suitable for the democratic age. He is saying that when we understand the role of the principle of liberty and the present and future conditions of its application, we will see that there are no good reasons founded on utility for making any exceptions when utility is properly understood as the permanent interests of man as a progressive being.

This interpretation is confirmed by what Mill says in II: ¶1. He writes: "Were an opinion a personal possession of no value except to the owner; if to be obstructed in the enjoyment of it were simply a private injury, it would make some difference whether the injury was inflicted only on a few persons or on many. But the peculiar evil of silencing the expression of an opinion is, that it is robbing the human race; posterity as well as the existing generation; those who dissent from the opinion, still more than those who hold it. If the opinion is right, they are deprived of the opportunity of exchanging error for truth: if wrong, they lose what is almost as great a benefit, the clearer perception . . . of truth, produced by its collision with error."

Of course, Mill has in mind opinion on general matters of doctrine, political and social, moral, philosophical and religious. He believes it is in the permanent interests (security and individuality) of man as a progressive being to know which of these general doctrines are true, or most reasonable; and he believes also that the necessary condition of reasonable belief on these questions is complete freedom of discussion and inquiry. "The beliefs which we have most warrant for have no safeguard to rest on, but a standing invitation to the whole world to prove them unfounded" (II: ¶8).

Thus by silencing one person in expressing an opinion, we do injury to the public process of free discussion. And this free process of discussion is necessary for advancing the permanent interests of man as a progressive being in the present age. Moreover, the injury done to free discussion is done without any compensating advantage. Not only does the silencing of discussion educate to the wrong kind of national character, but it tends to deprive society and its members of the benefits of truth. This last point is made in *On Liberty*, II: ¶¶3–11, the "infallibility argument," in which Mill argues that no human, regardless of his convictions, is infallible; and if all who express contrary opinions are suppressed, those who are wrong will lose the chance to discover the truth.

Conclusion

As we have discussed it, the idea of public reason involves the idea of admissible reasons vs. those reasons that are not admissible. But grounds must be given for why all reasons are not admissible, since it is easy to think that surely all reasons should be tallied up. Different political conceptions of justice may, of course, hold different reasons as admissible and offer different grounds for doing so.

In justice as fairness, the grounds for limiting the reasons admissible in public reason are the liberal principle of legitimacy—the principle that the collective political power of citizens on matters of constitutional essentials and basic questions of distributive justice should turn on the appeal to political values that all citizens may reasonably be expected to endorse, and so rest on a shared public understanding. Given the fact of reasonable pluralism, which free institutions lead and sustain, citizens have a duty to one another to exercise their power in accordance with this principle. A democratic society in which this is done realizes an ideal of civility.[4]

Mill's grounds for his idea of public reason are different, of course, but hardly antithetical. His principle of liberty along with his principles of moral right and justice, and the other principles of the modern world, are all principles subordinate to the supreme principle of utility. The principle of liberty is to be strictly followed in public discussion. This is part of society's basic institutions educating citizens to a certain national character: one that, of course, takes the equal liberties for granted, and promotes in the most effective way the permanent interests of humankind.

4. See *Restatement*, pp. 40–41 and 90–91, on the liberal principle of legitimacy and the fact of reasonable pluralism. See also Rawls, *Political Liberalism* (New York: Columbia University Press, 1993; paperback ed., 1996), pp. 137, 217.

MILL IV

His Doctrine as a Whole

§1. Introduction

1. Once again, I state the question we want to consider about Mill's doctrine. I have supposed that his principles of the modern world, as he calls them, his principles of justice and liberty, have roughly the same content as the two principles of justice. Hence Mill's well-ordered society would have, I think, basic institutions quite similar to those of the well-ordered society of justice as fairness.

The name "the principles of the modern world" is taken from *The Subjection of Women,* IV: ¶2, where Mill says that "the law of servitude in marriage is a monstrous contradiction to all the principles of the modern world." Elsewhere in *Subjection,* Mill uses other designations such as "the principles involved in modern society" in I: ¶23; "the principle(s) of the modern movement in morals and politics" in IV: ¶5. He speaks also of "the peculiar character of the modern world," which is followed by a statement of the nature of modern institutions and social ideas, and the principles of an open society allowing freedom of movement and unfettered choice of individuals, and securing equality of opportunity, as opposed to the aristocratic orders of the past in which all were born to a fixed social position (I: ¶13).

2. The main principles of the modern world would seem to be the following, although Mill does not discuss their relative importance. All references are to *The Subjection of Women.*[1]

(a) The principle of equal justice and equality of (basic) rights.

II: ¶¶11–12, 16; IV: ¶¶3, 5, 9, 18 (see also *Utilitarianism,* V: ¶¶4–10)

---

1. As before, because there is no standard, readily available text, I have referred to paragraphs within each chapter. This necessitates numbering those paragraphs by hand.

(b) The principle of liberty.

I: ¶13; IV: ¶¶9–20 (see also *On Liberty,* I: ¶¶9–12)

(c) Principles of open society and free choice of occupation and mode of life.

I: ¶¶13–15

(d) Equality of opportunity.

I: ¶¶23–24

(e) The principle of free and fair competition, economic and social.

I: ¶¶14–16

(f) The principle of (social) cooperation as among equals.

II: ¶¶7–12

(g) Principle of modern marriage as equality between husband and wife.

I: ¶25; II: ¶¶12, 16; IV: ¶¶2, 15–16, 18

(h) True principle of public charity: to help people to help themselves.

IV: ¶11

3. I comment that Mill's feminism, as we might call it, is different from much of the more radical feminism of the present day. His feminism simply means full justice and equality for women, and doing away with the subordination to which women had for so long been subject. The position of women in marriage Mill saw as intolerable. He had in mind, for example, the fact that at law, their property became their husband's, and that they owed obedience to their husband. Leaving royalty aside, the social subordination of women stood out, for Mill, as "an isolated fact in modern social institutions, a solitary breach of what has become their fundamental law; a single relic of an old world of thought and practice exploded in everything else, but retained in the one thing of most universal interest" (I: ¶16).

Although this seems clear and perhaps even obvious to many today, it was not so in Mill's time. His contemporaries thought him a fanatic on two subjects. One was the increase of population, which he thought depressed the well-being of the working classes; the other was the subordination of women. He was viewed as simply unbalanced on these topics; people shook their heads and stopped listening.

But Mill saw these topics as related. The well-being of the working classes required limiting the size of families; yet this was also required for the equality of women. Moreover, equality between husband and wife before the law was necessary if the family were not to be a school for despotism, "while the family, justly constituted, would be the real school of the virtues of freedom," as he put it in II: ¶12. So long as the family is a school for despotism, the character of men is gravely corrupted and this weakens the desirable tendencies to equality in all the institutions of society. So while Mill's feminism was certainly rooted in his conviction of the grave wrong of women's subordination, it was also supported in his mind by the far-reaching social good of realizing equal justice for women.

§2. The Framework of Mill's Doctrine

1. We now look at the framework of Mill's doctrine—its basic moral and psychological assumptions—in order to see how it is that his utilitarianism, presented initially as that of Bentham and Mill's father, should turn out to lead to his principles of the modern world.

In approaching this question we first examined his conception of utility with its decided preference criterion. Next we discussed his idea of the moral rights of justice and his apparent two-part criterion for identifying the basic rights of individuals. Then we considered his principle of liberty as a principle to govern public reason and its status as a principle subordinate to that of utility. All this leads us to ask:

First, why is Mill so confident that his principles of the modern world, his principles of justice and of liberty with the others listed above, are principles that would, if realized in basic institutions, maximize utility in the long run as defined by the permanent interests of humankind as a progressive being. Here, of course, utility is understood in the light of *Utilitarianism*, II: ¶¶3–10, and the idea of the permanent interests of humankind is from *On Liberty*, I: ¶11.

We need to know also how Mill's doctrine deals with values other than happiness and in what specific ways his doctrine relies on a psychological account of human nature. This leads us to ask:

Second, whether Mill's doctrine includes and gives weight to certain perfectionist values and ideals, falling under the admirable and the excellent, which are ideas he recognizes; or whether, once the conception of utility as happiness is granted, his doctrine rests solely on psychological principles that describe human nature at its deepest level.

2. Without being fully confident that this latter alternative is correct, I

conclude our study of Mill by sketching (I can't do more than that) a psychological reading of his utilitarianism as a whole formulated as a political and social doctrine to apply to the basic structure. This still allows that in other situations his view might take a different, though in general a subordinate form. The political and social permanent interests would normally override more particular and subordinate considerations.

This reading starts from the idea that happiness (as defined in *Utilitarianism*, II: ¶¶3–10) alone is good, and that happiness is to be maximized by political and social arrangements always looking to the long run. This gives the principle of utility in one of its political and social meanings. It is, I suggest, the supreme moral principle in Mill's political doctrine. Or more safely, it is the supreme principle of his account of moral right and wrong, and of political and social justice.

3. As I have said, to get his more definite conclusions Mill relies on a quite specific psychological conception of human nature. He thinks this conception is determinate enough to yield his principles of basic justice and essential liberties given his conception of utility as the permanent interests of humankind (I abbreviate the phrase) and given the conditions of the modern world with its present tendencies. Our problem, then, is to indicate his psychological first principles and sketch how Mill might have thought they lead to that conclusion when combined with his other assumptions.

The main psychological principles seem to be these:

(a) The decided preference criterion: *Utilitarianism*, II: ¶¶5–8.
(b) The principle of dignity: ibid., II: ¶¶4, 6–7; *Liberty*, III: ¶6.
(c) The principle of living in unity with others: *Utilitarianism*, III: ¶¶8–11.
(d) The Aristotelian principle: ibid., II: ¶8 (see TJ, sec. 65).
(e) The principle of individuality: *On Liberty*, III: ¶¶1–9.
(f) The recognition of our natural good: *Utilitarianism*, III: ¶¶10–11.

The first three we have discussed in lectures I and II.

The last principle is described as the capacity we have to recognize our natural good and to distinguish it from our apparent good as a mere artifact of social and associationist learning, often by some kind of reward and punishment. No doubt there are better ways to state these principles, but for the moment this list suffices.

My basic idea is that the role of these psychological principles in Mill's doctrine is this: along with the normative principle of utility and other considerations, such as the historical and social conditions of the modern world and its tendencies for change, those principles identify the four permanent interests of human beings.

This leaves us with the problem of explaining how Mill's frequent references to perfectionist values are to be understood. This question I leave to the end, when his whole view is before us.

§3. The First Two Permanent Interests of Humankind

1. So we now ask: how are we to understand the sense in which these interests are permanent? In what way are they tied to the idea that a human being is a progressive being? Mill does not discuss these questions so we must figure them out.

I assume that the idea of humankind as a progressive being implies the possibility of a more or less continual improvement in human civilization, arriving finally at the normal and natural state of society as one of full equality described in *Utilitarianism*, III: ¶¶10–11. In this state, society fully answers to Mill's principles of equal basic justice and liberty. So for Mill progress is an advance over time to, or in the direction of, the practically best, though normal and natural, state of society.

Now, for progress to be possible, certain necessary conditions must obtain. So following *Utilitarianism*, Chapter V, let's say that one of the permanent interests is the interest in being guaranteed the basic moral rights of equal justice. This means that the interest we have in society, through its laws and institutions, and its common moral opinion, is an interest in its securing for us "the essentials of our well-being" and "making safe for us the very groundwork of our existence" (V: ¶32, ¶25).

Next consider the permanent interests that arise from the idea of man as a progressive being. There seem to be two conditions any such interest must meet:

(i) An interest in the social conditions that are necessary for the continual progress or advance of civilization until the practically best state of society (morally speaking) is reached.

(ii) An interest in social conditions that themselves are conditions of the best state itself and required for its operation. These conditions are necessary if it is to remain the best state.

The permanent interests are, then, permanent in two ways. They are permanent as interests in the necessary conditions of continual progress to the best and also natural state of society; they are also permanent as interests in the conditions required to remain in that best state, once it is reached. Implicit in Mill's idea of the best state of society is the idea that such a society best realizes our nature as social beings. It most fully calls forth and exercises our higher faculties and satisfies our most important wants and aspirations, all this in ways consistent with the basic rights of equal justice and the legitimate interests of others. On this last, see *On Liberty*, III: ¶9.

To sum up: the first permanent interest is that in the basic rights of equal justice: it is an interest in conditions necessary for continual progress to the best state of society as a state of equality, as well as necessary to remain that state once reached.

2. From *On Liberty*, II we can, I think, identify a second permanent interest. Recall that this chapter discusses the liberties protecting the inward domain of consciousness, as Mill calls it. These liberties are liberty of conscience, freedom of thought and feeling, and absolute freedom of opinion and sentiment on all subjects, practical and speculative, scientific, moral, and theological.

Mill is concerned here with belief and discussion concerning general doctrines in religion and philosophy, morals and science, and all general political and social questions and matters of policy. He is not talking about speech as incitement likely to disrupt the peace or to arouse a crowd to violence; or about speech revealing troop movements in time of war, and many other such cases. He mentions this kind of case in *On Liberty*, III: ¶1, and grants that such speech can be restricted (footnote to II: ¶1).

Thus the second permanent interest is one in the social conditions relating to law, institutions, and the public attitudes that guarantee freedom of thought and liberty of conscience. Mill's argument in *On Liberty*, II is that these conditions are necessary for the discovery of truth on all subjects. Moreover, he also supposes that we have a permanent interest in knowing the truth. He doesn't entertain the dark thought that one finds in Russian novelists such as Dostoyevsky: witness Ivan's tale of the Grand Inquisitor in the *Brothers Karamazov*, that knowing the truth would be horrible, making us disconsolate and ready to support a dictatorial regime to preserve our comforting and necessary illusions. St. Augustine and Dostoyevsky are the two dark minds in Western thought, and the former has shaped it profoundly.

3. Mill's much-criticized argument from infallibility in II: ¶¶3–11 makes these points, and it can be set out roughly as follows: When society, through its laws and institutions, forbids the discussion of certain general doctrines, it implicitly assumes that the truth about those matters is already known with certainty. Put another way: it supposes that there is no possibility that accepted doctrines are not true and fully correct, that is, infallible. Why does Mill say this?

I surmise his argument rests on these premises:

(a) Knowing the truth about general doctrines is always beneficial: it is a great good, at least when the general doctrines are significant.

(b) Free discussion of these doctrines is a necessary condition for the correction of errors.

(c) Free discussion is also a necessary condition for our having any rational assurance that the general doctrines we believe are correct. Beyond this,

(d) Free discussion is a necessary condition for a full and proper understanding and appreciation of our own beliefs, and in that way making them our own. See *On Liberty*, III: ¶¶2–8.

(e) Existing society is in a state that allows it to learn from and to advance by free discussion of general doctrines.

With all these assumptions, Mill holds that for society to silence general discussion is irrational, unless it views itself as infallible: that is, unless society sees itself as already possessing the truth and supposes there is no possibility that it is mistaken. His argument assumes this conclusion to be a reductio: all reject it. For if society thinks it may not already possess the truth, or that there is indeed some real possibility that it is mistaken, or may fail to appreciate some aspect of the truth, then it jeopardizes without reason one of the permanent interests of human beings as progressive. This is our interest in knowing the truth and also in maintaining the necessary conditions of discovering and appreciating it on all significant matters.

§4. Two Other Permanent Interests

1. We now take up two further permanent interests. The first of these we can connect with the liberties Mill discusses in *On Liberty*, Chapter III, which are:

Liberty of tastes and pursuits; and the liberty of framing our mode of life to suit our character without restraint, so long as we do not injure the legitimate interests of others protected by the equal rights of justice and the precepts of right and wrong. In those ways we are at liberty even though others may find our mode of life foolish and imprudent, in no way admirable and even contemptible. Along with these liberties goes that of freedom of association to make them effective.

Let's call the interest in a firm guarantee of these liberties the permanent interest in the conditions of individuality, understanding that this includes individuality in association with other like-minded people. Now in III: ¶¶10–19 Mill argues that these liberties are an essential condition for the progress of civilization. In III: ¶17 he says that "the only unfailing and permanent source of improvement is liberty itself." So this permanent interest, along with the permanent interest in freedom of thought and liberty of conscience, is an interest we have as progressive beings.

Of course these liberties are essential not only now, but also in the best state of society once reached. They are fundamental for Mill in a less obvious way, which can be put thus: only where these liberties are fully respected can the decided preference criterion be properly applied. The significance of this is hard to exaggerate: it amounts to saying that only under conditions of free institutions can people acquire sufficient self-understanding to know, or make reasonable decisions about, what mode of life offers them the best chance of happiness (in Mill's sense). I shall come back to this basic point in a moment.

2. Finally, we come to a fourth and last permanent interest. This permanent interest I connect with Mill's belief (stated in *Utilitarianism*, III: ¶¶8–11) that the normal state of society, the state fully adapted to our deepest nature, is a society in which the equal rights of justice and liberty (surveyed above) are firmly guaranteed.

In this normal (and natural) state of society it is impossible to associate with others except on the condition that the interests of all are to be considered equally. This state in turn gives rise to the desire, which Mill views as natural to us, to live in unity with others. This offhand unclear phrase he explains as meaning the desire not to benefit from any social condition unless others are also included in its benefits. We have a principle of reciprocity. *Utilitarianism*, III: ¶10: "In an improving state of the human mind, the influences are constantly on the increase, which tend to generate in each individual a feeling of unity with all the rest; which feeling, if perfect, would make him never think of, or desire, any beneficial condition for himself, in the benefits of which they are not included."

So our fourth permanent interest is our interest in the social conditions and institutions that specify the natural state of society as a state of equality, and make this state one of possible steady equilibrium.

3. To sum up: the four permanent interests are these:

(a) First, the permanent interest in the institutions that guarantee the basic rights of equal justice (as these are discussed in *Utilitarianism,* V). These rights protect the "essentials of our well-being" and "make safe for us the very groundwork of our existence," and they are necessary for progress. This interest we have in all stages of civilization.

(b) Second, the permanent interest in the free institutions and in public attitudes of moral opinion that affirm freedom of thought and liberty of conscience. These institutions and attitudes are necessary for progress to the natural state of society as one of equality, as well as necessary to maintain that state.

(c) Third, the permanent interest in the free institutions and public attitudes that allow for individuality, and so protect and encourage the liberty of tastes and our choice of a mode of life suitable to our character, all of which enables us to make our mode of life our own. And paired with this, freedom of association to give individuality effect.

(d) Fourth, the permanent interest in just and free institutions and the attitudes required to realize the natural and normal state of society as a state of equality.

§5. Relation to the Decided Preference Criterion

1. This completes our survey of four permanent interests of man as a progressive being. I don't claim that the survey is complete; there may be other permanent interests in Mill's view, and admittedly the distinctions drawn are somewhat artificial. But they are useful, I think, in setting out how his doctrine fits together.

Mill wants to hold, as I have said, that once we adopt his conception of utility (*Utilitarianism,* II: 3–10), then his principles of justice and of liberty, complemented by common moral opinion that endorses those principles, specify the political and social order most effective in fulfilling our permanent interests. Given the conditions of the modern world and the principles of human psychology, there is no better way to arrange political and social institutions. But why, on Mill's assumptions, should this be true? How does he see the details?

2. Crucial to Mill's entire doctrine is the idea that only under just and free social arrangements can the decided preference criterion be properly applied. Keep in mind that this criterion involves making a judgment that one pleasure, or activity, is higher than another in terms of quality and more appropriate (and in this sense better) for a being with the higher faculties. This latter makes the connection with the principle of dignity. This has the striking consequence that in the absence of just and free arrangements, there is simply no way for society to acquire the specific knowledge and information it would need to maximize utility in Mill's sense. And this for two reasons:

(i) First, it is only under those institutions that individuals, either singly or together with others, can educate and develop their faculties in ways that best suit their character and inclination. Thus those institutions are needed for us to know which activities would be endorsed by people's decided preferences. And:

(ii) Second, there is no central agency in society—no central information office or planning board—that could possess the information required to maximize utility and therefore could know what more specific and detailed laws and regulations might advance the four permanent interests.

3. Consider an analogy: Mill assumes, let's say, that each person is somewhat like a firm in a perfectly competitive market. In such a market the firm decides what to produce given the prices of its inputs and outputs. There is no central planning agency that tells it what to do. Under certain conditions, which economic theory lays out, when each firm maximizes its profits, the total social product is efficiently produced (in the sense of Pareto).

The analogy is this: it is only under the conditions of a competitive market that firms are assumed to know best what to produce and how. The prices set on competitive markets contain the needed information for a firm's decisions to be efficient. Hence, they are left free to make their production decisions independently of one another.

In Mill's view, it is only when properly educated and given the opportunity to develop their faculties under conditions of equal justice and free institutions, that individuals can know which higher activities best answer to their nature and character.

The upshot is that to maximize utility in Mill's sense, it is necessary to set up just and free institutions, and to educate people's abilities. This establishes the background conditions under which the decided preference criterion can work. If society uses institutions other than these, hoping to maximize utility, it simply operates in the dark. Only persons raised and educated under the social conditions of free institutions can have, each in that person's own case, the necessary information.

4. Here let me make a few remarks in comment. First, I believe, as we noted already, that Mill does not make a fine-grained distinction within the class of higher pleasures or within the class of lower pleasures. Baseball is a higher activity, and why not? He is in part concerned to rebut Carlyle's doctrine that utilitarianism is a "doctrine worthy only of swine" (*Utilitarianism*, II: ¶3) and to stress that the distinction between the higher and the lower pleasures, and the higher and lower faculties, can be made—this by the decided preference criterion. For his purposes a rough distinction suffices.

A second remark is that this lack of fine-grained distinctions means that Mill holds all normal persons to be equally capable of enjoying and exercising their higher faculties, even granting that some are more talented than others. We might put this more precisely by saying: for each normal person (properly educated, and the rest) there is a range of higher activities they would want to make central to their life. He holds also that given decent opportunities, they will actually do so, barring special explanations. (Of course, these ranges of activities differ from person to person.) All this is borne out by the kind of explanations Mill mentions in *Utilitarianism*, II: ¶7, when he explains the apparent deviations from the principle of dignity, the basic psychological principle supporting the decided preference criterion. The idea that the higher activities and faculties are exclusively intellectual, aesthetic, and academic is just rubbish.

A third remark is that the higher pleasures of the more talented (granting there are such people) are not greater in value than the higher pleasures of the less talented. All activities decidedly preferred by normal people, properly educated and living under just and free institutions, count the same. Indeed, I think it will turn out that there is no occasion when as a matter of practice they need to be compared in value at all. But this would need to be shown. Offhand it seems the differences in quality of pleasures may, and indeed should, affect social policies. Can we admit this without the necessity of making a fine-grained distinction? Here we come to cases.[2]

Finally, a fourth remark: for Mill there is no general psychological theory of human nature that can be used by society, or by a central planning agency, to tell us, say by the use of certain psychological tests, which particular mode of life is best for this or that particular individual. The best information we can obtain is to look at the decisions of free individuals: we let them decide on their mode of life for themselves under the requisite free conditions. They are to determine which family of higher activities it is best to make the focus of their life. There exists no general psychological theory that could give us this information in advance.

5. To conclude: the equal rights of justice and the three kinds of liberties specify the institutional conditions necessary for equal citizens in a democratic society of the present age to be in the best position for each of them to find the mode of life that is most suitable. This helps to explain why Mill thinks—as it seems he does—that these just and free institutions are necessary to maximize utility understood in terms of our permanent interest as a progressive beings.

§6. Relation to Individuality

1. We have seen that the principle of individuality is connected with the decided preference criterion. So we need to consider the meaning of this principle as a basic psychological principle. In On Liberty, III: ¶1, Mill says the following: "It is desirable . . . that in things which do not primarily concern others, individuality should assert itself. Where, not a person's own character, but the traditions or customs of other people are the rule of conduct, there is wanting one of the principal ingredients of happiness, and quite the chief ingredient of individual and social progress." That this is a psychological principle is shown by individuality being one of the ingredients of happiness. (All of On Liberty, III: ¶¶1–9 is important on this.)

Mill thinks of individuality as having two components:

(a) One is the Greek ideal of self-development of our various natural powers, including the development and exercise of our higher faculties (III: ¶8).

2. This question was pressed by Jeffrey Cohen of Columbia.

(b) The second is the Christian ideal of self-government, and this includes, among other things (as I read Mill), the recognition of the limits on our conduct imposed by the basic rights of justice (III: ¶¶8–9).

2. Mill says in III: ¶8 that if it is any part of religion to think we were created by a good being, it is consistent with religion to believe that we have higher faculties in order that these faculties may be cultivated and unfolded, and not rooted out and consumed. It is also consistent with religion that God delights in our approaching the realization of the ideal conception embodied in our faculties. Mill rejects here what he calls the "Calvinistic conception of humanity," in which "all the good of which humanity is capable, is comprised in obedience" and the human faculties, capacities, and susceptibilities are to be crushed out (III: ¶7).

Mill's view seems presented as a perfectionist ideal. Later we consider how far it is to be read it as a psychological doctrine. For now I merely comment that Mill talks about ideals here because he views them as characterizing ways of life that would be adopted and followed by people under the conditions required for the decided preference criterion to work with the principle of dignity. These ideals characterize ways of life that most accord with our free and fully developed nature.

3. One feature of Mill's idea of individuality comes out when we compare it to an older view. When Locke discusses toleration in his "Letter on Toleration" (1689), he is concerned in large part with the problem of how to overcome the wars of religion. He proposes the solution of the church as a voluntary association within the state, while the state is to respect liberty of conscience within certain limits. During the wars of religion it was taken for granted that the content of belief was above all important. One must believe the truth, the true doctrine, otherwise one put one's salvation in jeopardy. Religious error was feared as a terrible thing; and those who spread error aroused dread.

By Mill's time, however, the view of the question has obviously changed. The struggle over the principle of toleration has long since been settled. And while the content of belief is not, of course, unimportant, it is also important how we believe. It now matters to what extent we have made our beliefs our own; how far we have tried to understand them, sought to ascertain their deeper meaning; and to give our beliefs a central role in our lives, and not, as it were, simply to mouth them.

This attitude is modern, though it arose in the course of the wars of religion. It is not, of course, original with Mill, who explicitly acknowledges it in William Humboldt (1792); and Milton had already said in *Areopagitica*, §49: ". . . if a man believes things only because his pastor says so, or the assembly so determines, without knowing other reason, though his belief be true, yet the very truth he holds becomes heresy." Rousseau was a major influence on this way of thought as well, with his emphasis on the self and the intrinsic value of one's interior life cultivated by self-observation. Whatever its origins, Mill gives an important statement of it in *On Liberty*, III: ¶¶1–9.

Part of this modern attitude is that belief in error is no longer feared in the same way. Feared certainly, because error can do great harm; but not feared as leading inevitably to damnation. Sincerity and conscientiousness are also significant. Clearly Mill doesn't entertain the possibility that those who have mistaken religious beliefs will thereby, for that reason, be damned. He takes for granted that error will not have that consequence. This belief is required, I surmise, for the value of individuality to become a central one, as it does in Mill. The idea of the significance of making our beliefs and aspirations our own would seem simply irrational if error, as such, might well mean damnation.

4. I have noted that part of Mill's idea of individuality is the idea of making what we believe our own beliefs. This is an aspect of free self-development. But other aspects which Mill emphasizes are: making our plan of life our own; making our desires our own; and bringing our desires and impulses into balance and setting an order of priorities that is also our own.

I don't think Mill means that we are to make ourselves different from other people for the sake of being different. Rather, he means that however similar or different our plan of life may be from the plans of others, we should have made our plan our own: that is, we understand its meaning and have appropriated it in our thought and character. We need not choose our life at all, as a so-called chooser of ends. We may rather affirm our way of life after due reflection, and do not follow it simply as custom. We have come to see the point of it, penetrated to its deeper meaning by the full and free use of our powers of thought, imagination, and feeling. In that way we have made our way of life our own, even if that way of life itself is of long standing, and in that sense traditional.

I mention this matter because Mill is sometimes said to put emphasis on eccentricity, on doing one's own thing. This I think a misreading. Certainly he expects that free institutions will lead to greater cultural diversity, and this he thinks desirable. But his emphasis is on free self-development and self-government; the latter implies self-discipline, and neither, alone or together, should be confused with eccentricity. The basic idea is our interest in individuality understood as the free and reflective formation of our thought and character within the strict limits set by the equal rights of justice for all.

In regard to this last, one must note the very important paragraph on the limits of justice in III: 9:

> It is not by wearing down into uniformity all that is individual in them-
> selves, but by cultivating it and calling it forth, within the limits im-
> posed by the rights and interests of others, that human beings become
> a noble and beautiful object of contemplation; . . . In proportion to the
> development of his individuality, each person becomes more valuable
> to himself, and is therefore more capable of being valuable to others.
> . . . To be held to rigid rules of justice for the sake of others, develops
> the feelings and capacities which have the good of others for their ob-
> ject. But to be restrained in things not affecting their good, by their
> mere displeasure, develops nothing valuable, except such force of char-
> acter as may unfold itself in resisting the restraint. . . . To give any fair
> play to the nature of each, it is essential that different persons should
> be allowed to lead different lives.

Mill's thought here suggests the further idea which unhappily we do not have time to discuss, namely: the greater overall value achieved under free institutions by human diversity when it is the outcome of the self-de-velopment of individuality within the limits of self-government, which in-clude respecting the rights of justice. This is an important theme of Mill's and of other modern liberalisms. It would not have occurred to Locke: he wouldn't have supposed that religious diversity itself was good, although he might have thought that it had its compensations by making possible the acceptance of the principle of free faith and toleration.

§7. The Place of Perfectionist Values

1. I conclude with two points. The first concerns the place in Mill of perfectionist values, which he often mentions. Plainly these have a role in

connection with the principle of dignity and of individuality. But how is this role best understood? In what sense is Mill advocating or endorsing perfectionist values? What political and social institutions, if any, do they justify?

Now Mill certainly recognizes the existence of the perfectionist values of the admirable and the excellent and their opposites, the degrading and the contemptible. And for him, these are significant values. Moreover, he takes it for granted that these values are recognized by us, since in the form of the principle of dignity they underlie his central idea of the decided preference criterion which always involves a judgment of what is appropriate for us. Thus, our recognizing the existence of these values and their great significance for us is a fundamental part of his normative doctrine and is supported by his basic human psychology.

However, in view of the content of the principle of liberty—its exclusion of perfectionist grounds for limiting individual liberty—these values cannot be imposed by the sanctions of law and common moral opinion as coercive social pressure. It is up to each of us together with our friends and associates to settle this for ourselves. In this sense, his doctrine is not perfectionist.

2. The fundamental values of Mill's political and social doctrine are those of justice and liberty as spelled out in his principles of the modern world. If one were to object that he has left out the perfectionist values, he would reply, I suggest, that he has not left them out. Rather, he would say that he has taken them into account as they should be, namely, by setting out principles that, when realized in social arrangements, will be most effective in leading people freely—and in accordance with their own nature and the advice and urgings of friends and other associates, as best suits them—to give those values a central place in their life.

It is not necessary, I think he would say, to coerce people to pursue activities that realize these values, and trying to do so when the institutions of justice and liberty are not in place does more injury than good. On the other hand, once these institutions are fully in place, the values of perfection will be realized in the most appropriate way in free lives and associations within the bounds of just and free institutions. The values of justice and liberty have a fundamental background role and in that sense a certain priority. Mill would say that he gives perfectionist values their due.

3. As for the second point—the role of Mill's psychological principles—I

make the following observation: All moral doctrines contain normative concepts and principles combined with elements of human psychology and political sociology, together with other institutional and historical assumptions. Mill's view is no exception. Still, it contains but one main normative assumption—the principle of utility, with its associated concepts and values. The essential role of this principle is seen everywhere, and reigns supreme as a doctrine of teleology in the chapter on the logic of practice, or art, at the end of his *System of Logic* (1843).

The first principles of Mill's psychology play an essential role, and if they fail or strike us as implausible, then his view fails or seems insecure. In his answer, I have suggested, much depends on them. Yet all moral doctrines depend on their underlying moral psychology. Mill's doctrine is not peculiar in this respect either.

I have not been much concerned with the overall success of Mill's view. Instead my object has been to explain how, given his apparently Benthamite beginning, he managed to end up with principles of justice, liberty, and equality not all that far away from justice as fairness, so that his political and social doctrine—lifted from his overall moral view—could give us the principles of a modern and comprehensive liberalism.

Appendix: Remarks on Mill's Social Theory [c. 1980]

A. Preliminary Remarks: The Background of Social Theory:

1. It is essential for the understanding of Mill that one understands *both* his own conception of his *vocation* (as an *educator* of public elite opinion with the aim of establishing sufficient consensus on first principles of the modern world for the organic age to come) and the background social theory in the light of which he saw historical development. The essays *Utilitarianism* (1861), *On Liberty* (1859), *On Representative Government* (1861), and *Subjection of Women* (1869) must all be read in this light.

2. But they are not sufficient by themselves: other writings present the social theory in more detail, especially *Principles of Political Economy* (1st edition, 1848; 3rd edition, 1852) and *A System of Logic* (1843). In the former, especially Book II, Chapters 1–2 (on property); Book IV, Chapters 1, 6–7 (on the Stationary State and the future of the laboring classes); and Book V, Chapters 1–2, 8–11 (on the role of government); and in the latter Book VI (on the method of the social sciences), which book is also the culminating set-piece of his *Logic*. In addition, see *Chapters on Socialism* (1879) and the earlier background of the origins of his views, e.g. *Autobiography* (1873), etc.

B. *Representative Government:* as the *ideally best polity and aim of progressive advance:*

1. The first three chapters of this work present Mill's background social theory and are worthy of careful attention, although other chapters fill out many details: e.g. Chapters 7–8 give Mill's arguments for some of his controversial proposals regarding proportional *representation* of minorities and plural voting for those more educated (what is instructive is Mill's *reasons* for these proposals and how they fit his overall view). Basic themes are illustrated by the discussion of local government, nationalism, federalism, and government of dependencies in Chapters 15–18.

2. Chapter I takes up the fundamental issue of how far the form of government is a matter amenable to rational choice. In paragraphs 4–11 Mill rejects the view (of Bentham) that government is a *means* to an *end* (and can be adopted as such) and (of Coleridge) that it is an *organic growth* not subject to human direction. His conclusion is that within certain conditions (stated in paragraphs 8–9) our institutions are a matter of choice (paragraph 11).

3. Paragraphs 12–14 discuss a fundamental objection to this conclusion: namely, that the form of government is fixed already in all essentials by the *distribution* of the elements of social power and that the strongest power holds governmental authority: thus any change must be *preceded* by a *change* in the distribution of social power. In reply Mill says this doctrine is too imprecise to be assessed; to make it more exact he enumerates six main elements of social power: (i) *physical strength* (numbers), (ii) *property*, (iii) *intelligence*, (iv) *organization*, (v) *possession of governmental authority*, (vi) *active* social power as guided by unified and effective *public opinion* (and degrees thereof: e.g. to passive and disunited [opinion]). This is a *general equilibrium* view of social power: it depends on the changing configuration of these elements.

4. Observe that in this chapter and the next two, Mill's argument supports the realism and practicality of his adopted vocation as public educator: he contends that given the configuration of social elements of power in his day (in the age of transition) the sixth element of power may have considerable weight and those who try to affect it may therefore achieve something. *Now* it can possibly be done, *later* perhaps not. Recall *On Liberty*, III: 19. Mill has, then, a *theory* that explains the rationality of his vocation.

5. This theory is discussed earlier in the important Book VI of *Logic*, especially Chapter 10: here Mill contends that the laws which govern the succession of social states must yield the apparent historical fact that *major* cultural and social changes have been preceded by *intellectual* changes that have issued from *previous* states of *intellectual* development. Since intellectual change is in part *autonomous*, social change cannot be solely in changes in the other elements of social power.

6. Finally, note that Chapters II–III of *On Representative Government* help to give sense to Mill's idea of utility in the broadest sense, that is, as advancing "the *permanent interests* of man as a *progressive* being" (*On Liberty*, I: 11): namely, that the best form of polity for realizing these interests is *Represen-*

tative Government (cf. *Utilitarianism,* II: 3–9, 11–18; III, especially 8–11; *On Liberty,* III: 2–9), and the tendency historically is towards the conditions that make such government possible. So the broad test of utility is: how well do institutions favor this historical trend and how suited are they to representative government, etc.

C. *Principles of Political Economy:*
  subtitled *with some of their applications to social philosophy:*

1. The idea that Mill is a defender of what we call *laissez-faire* capitalism is, I believe, an utter distortion, as can be seen by reading the parts listed in A: 2 above in *Political Economy:* Mill proposes in Book II rules regarding the holding of property, inheritance, and bequest, etc. that are aimed not, to be sure, at equality of property, but at preventing large concentrations and spreading property not too unequally over all classes over time. These rules are based on utilitarianism as defined in its broadest sense (B: 6 above). Book V, 1–2 and 8–11, especially discusses when government must be active and how.

2. In Book IV Mill actually presents a *reinterpretation* of the Ricardian notion of a Stationary State, which greatly alters its political and social implications: he sees this state not as a *doomsday* to be *avoided* by continual capital accumulation and innovation, but as a desirable state to be welcomed. This shift undercuts the ethos of a modern capitalist society as one of perpetual growth of capital and wealth: see Chapters 1, 5–6.

3. Mill favored what today is often called worker self-management in industry on the grounds, congruent with much of his view, that it encouraged participation and so active and vigorous people. While rejecting state command socialism as bureaucratic, he thought self-management [among workers] in privately owned firms would win out if markets were competitive. His feminism was an important part of this vision. See *Subjection of Women,* especially Ch. 2.

MARX

MARX I

His View of Capitalism as a Social System

§1. Preliminary Remarks

Karl Marx's dates, 1818–1883, make him a near contemporary of J. S. Mill, who was 12 years older (1806–1873). He was born into a century that was already becoming seriously interested in Socialism, including the work of the Saint-Simonians, with whom Mill associated in his early years.

One of the most remarkable achievements of Marx is that starting with an academic background in jurisprudence and philosophy, which he studied at the University of Berlin in the late 1830s, he turned to economics to clarify and to deepen his ideas only after he was about 28 years old. It is testimony to his marvelous gifts that he succeeded in becoming one of the great 19th-century figures of that subject, to be ranked along with Ricardo and Mill, Walras and Marshall. He was a self-taught, isolated scholar. While Ricardo and Mill knew other economists of the classical school, who formed a kind of working group, Marx had no such colleagues. Friedrich Engels, who was a close associate and collaborator after the early 1840s, and who was in some ways indispensable to Marx, was not an original thinker of Marx's caliber, and could not really give him the kind of intellectual help he could have used. Engels himself says, "What I contributed . . . Marx could have very well done without me. What Marx accomplished, I would have not have achieved. . . . Marx was a genius; we others were at best talented."[1] Given the circumstances of Marx's life, his achievement as an economic theorist and political sociologist of capitalism is extraordinary, indeed heroic.

1. Friedrich Engels, *Ludwig Feuerbach and the End of Classical German Philosophy*, p. 386. Tucker (see note 2) gives Engels more credit than he gives himself, saying, "His gifts and Marx's were in large measure complementary. Classical Marxism is an amalgam in which Engel's work constitutes an inalienable part." Introduction to the *Marx-Engels Reader*, §4.

1. The works of Marx that we will read can be divided as follows: First, the early and more philosophical writings of the 1840s: *On the Jewish Question* (1843) and *The German Ideology* (1845–1846).[2] Important but not assigned are: *Economic and Philosophic Manuscripts* (1844) and *Theses on Feuerbach* (1845).

Second, parts of the economic writings: *Capital*, Vol. I (1867) (first draft, 1861–63); Vol. II (1885) (worked on: 1868–70, 75–78); Vol. III (1894) (first draft, 1864–65). Important but not assigned is *Grundrisse* (1857–58).[3]

Third: one of Marx's political writings: *Critique of the Gotha Program* (1875).[4]

2. The objectives of our discussion of Marx are extremely modest, even more so than with our discussion of Mill. I will consider Marx solely as a critic of liberalism. With that in mind, I focus on his ideas about right and justice, particularly as they apply to the question of the justice of capitalism as a social system based on private property in the means of production. Marx's thought is enormous in scope, and it presents tremendous difficulties. To understand, much less to master, the ideas of *Capital*—all three volumes—is itself a forbidding task. Still, it is much better to discuss Marx, if only briefly, than not to discuss him at all. I hope you will be encouraged to come back to his thought and to pursue it more deeply at a later time.

When I say that we focus on Marx's critique of liberalism, I mean that we examine his criticisms of capitalism as a social system, criticisms that might seem offhand to apply as well to property-owning democracy, or equally to liberal socialism. We try to meet those of his criticisms that most clearly require an answer. For example:

(a) To Marx's objection that some of the basic rights and liberties—those he connects with the rights of man (and which we have labeled the

---

2. All the assigned works are in Robert C. Tucker, ed., *The Marx-Engels Reader*, 2nd ed. (New York: W. W. Norton, 1978). In Tucker these two essays are on pp. 26–52, 147–200. This latter selection is only the first part of the *German Ideology*, which is in the *Collected Works of Marx and Engels*, Vol. 5 (London: Lawrence and Wishart, 1976), and is over 500 pages.

3. From *Capital*, Vol. I, we will read the following: Ch. 1, Commodities, Secs. 1, 2, 4; Ch. 4, General Formula for Capital, entire; Ch. 6, The Buying and Selling of Labor Power, entire; Ch. 7, The Labor Process and the Process of Producing Surplus Value, Sec. 2, pp. 357–361; Ch. 10, The Working Day, Secs. 1, 2. All these selections are in Tucker, *Marx-Engels Reader*. From *Capital*, Vol. III, the selection in Tucker, pp. 439–441.

4. In this we will read only Sec. 1, in Tucker, *Marx-Engels Reader*, pp. 525–534.

liberties of the moderns)—express and protect the mutual egoisms of citizens in the civil society of a capitalist world, we reply that in a well-ordered property-owning democracy those rights and liberties, properly specified, suitably express and protect free and equal citizens' higher-order interests. While property in productive assets is permitted, that right is not a basic right, but subject to the requirement that, in existing conditions, it is the most effective way to meet the principles of justice.

(b) To the objection that the political rights and liberties of a constitutional regime are merely formal, we reply that by the fair value of the political liberties (together with the operation of the other principles of justice) all citizens, whatever their social position, may be assured a fair opportunity to exert political influence. This is one of the essential egalitarian features of justice as fairness.

(c) To Marx's objection that a constitutional regime with private property secures only the so-called negative liberties (those involving freedom to act unobstructed by others), we reply that the background institutions of a property-owning democracy, together with fair equality of opportunity and the difference principle, or some other analogous principle, give adequate protection to the so-called positive liberties (those involving the absence of obstacles to possible choices and activities, leading to self-realization).[5]

(d) To the objection against the division of labor under capitalism, we reply that the narrowing and demeaning features of the division should be largely overcome once the institutions of a property-owning democracy are realized.[6]

But while the idea of property-owning democracy tries to meet legitimate objections of the socialist tradition, the idea of the well-ordered society of justice as fairness is quite distinct from Marx's idea of a full communist society. This society seems to be one beyond justice in the sense that the circumstances that give rise to the problem of distributive justice are surpassed, and citizens need not, and are not, concerned with it in everyday life. Whereas justice as fairness assumes that, given the general facts of the political sociology of democratic regimes (e.g. the fact of reasonable pluralism), the principles and political virtues falling under justice of vari-

5. See Isaiah Berlin, *Four Essays on Liberty* (Oxford: Oxford University Press, 1969), Introduction, §2; and the Essay "Two Concepts of Liberty."

6. John Rawls, *A Theory of Justice* (Cambridge, Mass.: Harvard University Press, 1971), p. 529; revised edition (1999), p. 463f.

ous kinds will always play a role in public political life. The evanescence of justice, even of distributive justice, is not possible, nor, it seems, is it desirable. This is an intriguing question, and though tempted, I shan't discuss it further.

3. Today I review the aims of Marx's economic theory and his account of capitalism as a social system. We can, of course, treat these matters only in an elementary and simplified way. If we keep in mind that our objectives are modest, perhaps no harm is done. Giving special attention to Marx's economics is justified not only because he assigned it a central place, but because his economics is central to his account of capitalism as a system of domination and exploitation, and hence to capitalism an unjust social system. To understand Marx as a critic of liberalism, we must try to see why he views capitalism as unjust. For while most liberalisms are not, as libertarianism is,[7] committed to the right of private property in the means of production, many liberals, as Mill did, have defended private property in those means, not in general, but as justified under certain conditions.

Guided by these considerations, in the three lectures on Marx I shall try to cover these topics:

In the first, I consider how Marx viewed capitalism as a social system, and I note all too briefly what I take to be the point of his labor theory of value and what was its underlying intention.

In the second, I consider how Marx viewed the ideas of rights and justice and survey briefly the question—much discussed in recent years—whether he thought capitalism as a social system was unjust, or to be condemned only in the light of values other than, and not tied to, justice. It is clear that Marx condemns capitalism. The basic values he appeals to in doing so have seemed less clear.

In the third lecture, I discuss briefly Marx's conception of a full communist society as a society of freely associated producers in which ideological (or false) consciousness, as well as alienation and exploitation, have been overcome. I shall raise the question whether, for Marx, a full communist society is a society beyond justice, and whether the idea of rights has an essential role any longer.

It is evident that, as with Mill, we can cover but a fragment of Marx's thought. This perhaps is a reason for viewing his work from but one per-

7. For a libertarian view, see Robert Nozick, *Anarchy, State and Utopia* (New York: Basic Books, 1974).

spective: namely, as a criticism of liberalism. Doing this provides an instructive way to glimpse the great force of his doctrine.

4. Let me make a brief comment about the importance of Marx before proceeding. It may be thought that with the recent collapse of the Soviet Union, Marx's socialist philosophy and economics are of no significance today. I believe this would be a serious mistake for two reasons at least.

The first reason is that while central command socialism, such as reigned in the Soviet Union, is discredited—indeed, it was never a plausible doctrine—the same is not true of liberal socialism. This illuminating and worthwhile view has four elements:

(a) A constitutional democratic political regime, with the fair value of the political liberties.
(b) A system of free competitive markets, ensured by law as necessary.
(c) A scheme of worker-owned business, or, in part, also public-owned through stock shares, and managed by elected or firm-chosen managers.
(d) A property system establishing a widespread and a more or less even distribution of the means of production and natural resources.[8]

Of course, all this requires much more complicated elaboration. I simply remind you of the few essentials here.

The other reason for viewing Marx's socialist thought as significant is that laissez-faire capitalism has grave drawbacks, and these should be noted and reformed in fundamental ways. Liberal socialism, as well as other views, can help clear our minds as to how these changes are best done.

§2. Features of Capitalism as a Social System

1. The societies Marx studied were ones he called class societies. These are societies in which the social surplus—the total product of surplus labor, or unpaid labor[9]—is appropriated by one class of persons in virtue of their position in the social system. For example, in slave societies such as the an-

8. On these features, see John Roemer, *Liberal Socialism* (Cambridge, Mass.: Harvard University Press, 1994).

9. Surplus or unpaid labor is labor that the laborer is required to do beyond what is needed to produce the commodities necessary to support himself and his family. It does

tebellum South, the labor of the slave is at the disposal of the master as owner; and the slave's surplus or unpaid labor—I shall come back to this definition and other details later—and the product it produces is the property of the master. In feudal society the surplus labor of the serf was appropriated by the lord to whom the serf was bound and on whose fields the serf was required to work a certain number of days each year. This was forced labor: what the serf produced on the lord's fields was the lord's.

These are two examples clearly illustrating institutional setups that enable a certain class of people—slave-owners and lords—to appropriate as their own property the surplus labor of others. This they can do in virtue of their position in the social system. For Marx, among the fundamental basic units of analysis are classes, defined with respect to the whole social system as a mode of production in which they have a well-defined position and play an economic role.

2. Marx studies capitalism as a class society in the sense defined. This means that for him there is some class of persons in capitalist society who in virtue of their position in the institutional setup are able to appropriate the surplus labor of others. For him, like slavery and feudalism, capitalism is a system of domination and exploitation.

What makes capitalism distinctive is that to those who make their decisions and guide their actions according to its norms, it does not appear to be a system of domination and exploitation. How can this be? How can exploitation and domination go unrecognized? This question poses a difficulty: Marx thinks we need a theory to explain why these features of the system go unrecognized and how they are hidden from view. But I am getting ahead.

3. Now for the details of capitalism as a social system as Marx sees it:

First, capitalism is a social system divided into two mutually exclusive and exhaustive classes, the capitalists and the workers. This, of course, is a simplified conception. It can be suitably complicated by adding other classes—landlords, petty bourgeoisie—as the inquiry shifts. Here let's go with the simple conception.

(a) The capitalists own and have control over all the means (instruments) of production, as well as all natural resources (land, minerals, etc.).

---

not add to his own consumption and sustenance; it is others—feudal lords, slave-owners, or capitalists—who gain instead.

But in capitalism there is no slavery. The one factor of production the capitalists do not own is other people's labor-power, the capacity of people to labor. This factor of production is owned by the workers themselves, individually.

(b) In order to exercise and apply their labor-power, which is the only factor of production the workers own, the workers must have access to and be able to use the means of production owned by the capitalists. Without those means, their labor is not productive.

4. The second feature of capitalism is that a system of free competitive markets exists. The output of the production of consumption-good industries is sold to households on markets for consumption goods. There are also markets for the factors of production on which these factors can be bought from other capitalists, or landowners if we add a landowning class. There is finally a labor market where capitalists can hire labor-power from the workers. Factors of production and capital funds move freely within these markets. In particular, capital funds flow into industries with the highest rate of profit and this tends to establish a uniform rate of profit in all industries.

(a) In the *Grundrisse* Marx refers to capitalism as a system of personal independence, as opposed to feudalism which was a system of personal dependence.[10] The institutions of serfdom and slavery illustrate what is meant by a system of personal dependence. As we saw above, serfs and slaves are in various ways the property of the lord or the slave-owner. For example, serfs are not free to move but are tied to the lord's land, and they must work so many days a year on the lord's behalf, the product of their work being owned by the lord. In this case, Marx says the fact and rate of unpaid (surplus) labor is visible and open to view.

What he means is that both lord and serf know how many days the serf is required to work in the lord's fields, and both know the rate of exploitation, as given by the ratio of the days serfs work for the lord to the days serfs work for themselves. If serfs can count they know the rate of exploitation: it is open to view.

Call this ratio s/v. It equals surplus labor/necessary labor. It also equals the hours the serf works for the lord/the hours the serf works for himself

10. *Grundrisse*: Pelican ed., pp. 156–165, cf. 158. See also *Capital*, Vol. I, Ch. 1: §4. (Tucker, *Marx-Engels Reader*, p. 325; also p. 365.)

and his family. It also turns out often to equal the rate of exploitation. More on this later.

(b) By contrast, capitalism is a system of personal independence since the workers are free to assume other employment, and the wage agreement struck on the market is ostensibly a contract between free and independent economic agents. All such agents are viewed as protected by a legal system that guarantees freedom of contract and regulates the conditions of binding agreements.

For Marx, the striking feature of capitalism was that despite the fact that it is a social system with personal independence and free competitive markets with freedom of contract, it is still a system in which there is surplus or unpaid labor (or surplus value, the value of what is produced by surplus labor). The problem for him was: how was this possible? And how does it take place somehow hidden beneath the surface of the day to day transactions of the economic system?

A simple example illustrates what Marx means. In capitalism workers are paid, say, a standard (twelve-hour) day's wage. The capitalist hires (or rents) the worker's labor-power (*Arbeitskraft*), which then may be used more or less intensively, or longer if the standard day is lengthened. Now a unique feature, Marx thought, of labor-power, was that it was the only factor of production that, in the time it could work, it produced more value than it took to sustain itself over time. Other factors simply added the same value it took to fashion them in the first place. We might say: human labor alone is creative, and plainly there must be at least one such factor. Otherwise the economic system cannot grow over time.

All this is made obvious under feudalism, with its days of forced work on the lord's land, and it is obvious also in slavery. But workers in capitalism have no way of telling how many of their hours worked are necessary to sustain them, and how many are surplus labor for the benefit of the capitalist. Institutional arrangements conceal this fact. Thus, the distinctive feature of capitalism is that in it, as opposed to slavery and feudalism, the extraction of surplus or unpaid labor of workers is not open to view. People are unaware of its taking place and have no idea of its rate.[11]

Thus, one of the aims of Marx's *labor theory of value* is to try to explain

11. On this see the passage from *Capital*, Vol. I, Ch. 10: §2; in Tucker, *Marx-Engels Reader*: p. 365.

how surplus labor can exist in a system of personal independence, and how this surplus labor and its rate is hidden from view.

5. A third feature of capitalism is that the two kinds of economic agents—the capitalists and the workers—have different roles and aims in the social system as a mode of production:

(a) The capitalists' role and aim is represented by the cycle M-C-M^* (with $M < M^*$ and where M = money and C = commodities). This represents the fact that the capitalists invest liquid capital funds valued at M in machines and materials and in advances to labor (in the form of food, supplies, and equipment and the like) in order to produce a stock of commodities (output) to be sold at a profit. ($M < M^*$, normally.)

(b) The workers' role and aim is represented by the cycle C-M-C^* where the value of C normally equals the value of C^*. This represents the fact that the workers agree to work, and so produce, for use. That is, workers labor in order to purchase with their wages the commodities required to sustain themselves—to maintain their labor-power—and to reproduce themselves by supporting their families and children.

6. A fourth feature of capitalism is a consequence of the preceding differences in the social roles and aims of capitalists and workers. This feature is that the social role of the capitalists is to save: that is, to accumulate real capital and to build up society's productive forces—its plant, machinery, etc.—over time.

(a) $M < M^*$ in the capitalists' cycle expresses the fact that the capitalists are in a position to accumulate and to build up their real capital. It is the capitalists who save. The aggregate real net saving owned by all capitalists is society's accumulated means of production: machinery, plant, improved land (again allowing for landowners), etc. Thus, in a capitalist social system, it is the capitalists who, individually and in competition with one another, make society's decisions regarding both the amount of real saving (investment) in each period of time and its direction. All this determines which industries and which ways of production will be expanded, and which ones will be allowed to decline.

(b) The subjective aim of capitalists—that is, what they aim for and have in mind—in investing their capital funds is not simply profit, but the maximum profit. While the level of consumption of the capitalists is considerably higher than that of the workers, the capitalists do not—in the high period of capitalism when it is fulfilling its historical role—strive toward a higher and higher level of consumption.

(c) The reason they do not is that the competitive situation of the capitalists versus other capitalists (firms versus firms) forces the capitalists to save and to innovate. Otherwise their firms will fail and they will cease to be capitalists. So capitalists as individuals are not in general idle: often they manage and superintend their firms and help run them. For this they receive the wages of management, which does not count as profit. Marx is concerned with the origin and source of pure profit as what the capitalists receive merely for being owners of the means of production.

(d) The capitalists can perform the social role of building up real capital because of their position as owners of the means of production and natural resources, etc., other than labor-power. Their social position enables them to control the direction of investment, the organization of production, and the labor process generally, and to own the produced output, which they can then sell at a profit, and so on continually, as accumulation proceeds.

The exercise of all these prerogatives of ownership of the means of production is an essential part of the capitalists' dominant role, not only in the firm, but in society as a whole (e.g. in determining the direction of investment).

(e) Finally, it remains to add that workers do not save over their life as a whole; their saving is deferred consumption (saving, e.g., for their old age). Summing over the workers as a whole, net saving is zero: what the younger workers save the older workers spend. (This supposes the working population is constant.)

5. A fifth feature of capitalism, which is obvious from the preceding features, is that the two classes (in the simple model) have opposed interests, as well as distinctive roles in the social system. In the last phases of capitalism when its high period is past, these classes become increasingly antagonistic and social conflict becomes more visible and chronic. This leads to Marx's breakdown theory.

§3. The Labor Theory of Value

1. So far I have said hardly anything about the labor theory of value. This no doubt strikes you as rather strange, since that theory is associated with Marx's name. However, I think it is best, or at least instructive, first to review the main features of capitalism as a social order as Marx saw them,

and to give some idea of why it might have seemed to him a system of domination and exploitation. It is in that context, I believe, that the point of his labor theory of value is most easily understood.

We can think of the labor theory of value as saying several things. It says first, the total value added in a commodity-producing society is the total social labor time expended. Second, it says that total surplus value corresponds to the total unpaid labor time. Here unpaid labor is unnecessary labor,[12] the proceeds of which are not received by the laborer.

Marx's thought is that from the point of view of society as a whole, the potential human labor of all of its members is a factor of production of special social significance. It is special in that it is not to be regarded in the same way as other non-human factors of production, such as land and natural resources, the powers of nature, and tools and machinery and the rest. These last are the result of past labor. Human labor is special also in that it is a factor of production peculiarly characteristic of society. From the most basic point of view, a human society is organized so that human beings can produce and reproduce themselves over time by means of their collective human labor, all the while making use of the resources and forces of nature under society's control.

Now, it is a fact about class societies that the total value added is not shared solely by those who produce it, but large shares are also received by people who either perform no labor at all, or else their shares are far in excess of what their labor time would warrant. How this happens in a slave or feudal society is open to view. But, as we have said, Marx thinks it is hidden from view under capitalism; and so we need a theory, he thinks, of how this happens in a system of personal independence in which contracts are agreed to between ostensibly free and equal economic agents.

2. The point of the labor theory of value is to penetrate beneath the surface appearances of the capitalist order and to enable us to keep track of the expenditure of labor time and to discern the various institutional devices by which surplus or unpaid labor is extracted from the working class, and in what amounts. Marx's concern is not only with how non-wage incomes originate and how they get redistributed and hidden from view. He

---

12. [Unpaid labor is "unnecessary" insofar as workers do not need to be (and therefore are not) paid wages for it in order to purchase, as Rawls says above, "the commodities required to sustain themselves—to maintain their labor-power—and to reproduce themselves by supporting their families and children." —Ed.]

also wants to know the details of these hidden processes and whether the flows of labor-time may be quantified.

Marx's answer to how non-wage incomes originate is found in *Capital,* Vol. I. He thinks that since capitalists, as a class, own the means of production as their private property, they can extract a certain total of surplus or unpaid labor. Workers must, as it were, pay a fee—their surplus labor—for their use of those productive instruments. In *Capital,* Vol. III, he explains how the total surplus extracted is then redistributed as profit, interest, and rent among various claimants: to landowners in the form of rent and to money-lenders in the form of interest. In this case also, property-ownership is crucial. Those who own fertile pieces of land or natural resources, or who have liquid funds, may be able to get capitalists to give up part of their profit in the form of rent for the use of land, or in the form of interest payments for a loan. The capitalists extract unpaid labor from the workers, while landowners and money-lenders extract from the capitalists part of their profits. The exploiters are exploited in their turn. Cannibals All! as Fitzhugh's title proclaims.[13]

3. If this is right (here I follow Baumol),[14] Marx's concern is not with price theory. He knows perfectly well that prices can be explained in terms of supply and demand on a system of competitive markets and without the use of labor values.

Nor is Marx's labor theory of value a theory of just price like the price theory of the late scholastics, who were concerned with the idea of a just (or fair) price. They concluded that the just (or fair) price was the competitive price under certain suitable market conditions, for example, the absence of monopoly, or of a famine or drought.

Marx says that "the utility of a thing makes it a use-value." But, "Use-values become a reality only by use or consumption: they also constitute the substance of all wealth" (Tucker, *Marx-Engels Reader,* p. 303). Now Marx does not hold that labor is the source of all material wealth—of the use-values produced by labor. He rejects this idea explicitly, saying: "The use-values . . . are combinations of two elements—matter and labor. If we take away the useful labor expended on them, a material substratum is always

13. This is the title of George Fitzhugh's famous pro-slavery tract of 1856, in which he argues that the black slaves of the South are the freest people in the world.

14. W. J. Baumol, "The Transformation of Values: What Marx 'Really' Meant (An Interpretation)," *Journal of Economic Literature* (1974).

left, which is furnished by Nature without the help of man." Man works "as Nature does, that is by changing the form of matter" (Tucker, p. 309).

Finally, Marx does not see exploitation as arising from market imperfections or from the presence of oligopolistic elements.[15] His labor theory of value is meant to show, among other things, that even under a system of perfect competition, exploitation exists in a capitalist society. He wants to bring to light—to make clear for all to see—the way in which the capitalist order, even when it is fully competitive, and even when it fully satisfies the conception of justice most adequate to it, is still an unjust social system of domination and exploitation. This last is crucial. Marx wants to say that even a perfectly just capitalist system, one just by its own lights and the conception of justice most adequate to it, is a system of exploitation. It replaces feudal exploitation with capitalist exploitation.[16] At bottom, both are the same. That is what the labor theory of value is supposed to show.

4. I should now say that I do not think the labor theory of value is successful. Indeed, I think that Marx's views can better be stated without using this theory at all. In saying this I accept the view of Marglin, and of many other present day Marxist economists, who do not regard the labor theory of value either as sound or as essential. Sometimes it is insufficient; at other times, even when sufficient, it is superfluous.[17]

The real point of the labor theory of value concerns the fundamental controversy about the nature of capitalist product. Contrary to the dominant neo-orthodox view, which stresses the parity of the claims of land, capital, and labor, and therefore the parity of the claims of landlords, capitalists, and laborers, Marx puts forward the central and basic role of the working class under the capitalist mode of production as under previous such modes. The aim of the theory is to highlight the main features of capitalism as a mode of production that are hidden from view by the parity of the capitalists in market relations of exchange. All this is by way of providing what Marx thought was a truly scientific basis for condemning capitalism as a system of domination and exploitation.[18] We come back to this in the next lecture in discussing Marx and justice.

---

15. Such a view is found in A. C. Pigou, *The Economics of Welfare* (London: Macmillan, 1920).

16. *Capital*, I, Ch. XXVI: ¶¶5–7, in Tucker, *Marx-Engels Reader*, p. 433.

17. See Stephen A. Marglin, *Growth, Distribution, and Prices* (Cambridge, Mass.: Harvard University Press, 1984), pp. 462f.

18. See Marglin, *Growth, Distribution, and Prices*, pp. 463, 468.

5. With this said, I conclude with a comment about labor-power: Marx was proud of the distinction he drew between labor-power and labor, or the use of labor-power. He thought this distinction helped him to explain how profit could arise in a free market system of non-coercive exchanges in which, in every market, equal values exchange for equal values.

He holds that (under the assumptions of Vol. I) the capitalist, in hiring the worker, pays the worker the full value of the worker's labor-power. This means, as we have seen, that a worker is paid wages that equal the socially necessary labor time required for the production of his labor-power. During a day, this is the amount to cover the worker's maintenance and to make good wear and tear, and other losses. In short, a worker's wages cover what is socially necessary to enable workers to produce, and to reproduce themselves over time.

The distinction between labor-power and the use of labor-power is analogous to the distinction between a machine (as a piece of capital equipment) and the use of the machine (for a certain purpose for a certain period of time). Capitalists, in hiring workers, are renting human machines. Walras called the human being viewed as a machine, "personal capital." Education and training are often called investment in "human capital." How much a capitalist can use the human machine, what a capitalist can get the worker to do in the work process during a working day, may vary. In any case, the capitalist has paid a full day's value for the machine. Hiring the worker is worthwhile because labor-power has the capacity to produce more value than it takes to produce the labor-power itself. This is the crucial point.[19]

Appendix: Marx Lecture I

1. Now for a few definitions and remarks to clarify the labor theory of value. From *Capital*, Vol. I, we read the following. (All these selections are in Tucker, *Marx-Engels Reader*.)

    Ch. 1: Commodities, Secs. 1, 2, 4;

    Ch. 4: General Formula for Capital, entire;

---

19. There is a difficulty here: if labor alone is creative, why don't the capitalists bid up the price of labor until there are only zero profits? On this see Joseph A. Schumpeter, *History of Economic Analysis* (Oxford: Oxford University Press, 1954), pp. 650f. There are other answers.

Ch. 6: The Buying and Selling of Labor-Power, entire;

Ch. 7: The Labor Process and the Process of Producing Surplus Value, Sec. 2, pp. 357–361;

Ch. 10: The Working Day, Secs. 1, 2.

From *Capital*, Vol. III, the selection in Tucker, pp. 439–441.

2. References: (in Tucker) to definitions involved in the labor theory of value: commodity defined: 306f.

the value of a commodity is equal to the total socially necessary labor time required for its production: 305–307.

socially necessary labor time: 306.

abstract vs. concrete labor: 310.

simple labor: 310.

simple labor as unskilled labor: 311.

skilled labor as simple labor multiplied: 310.

labor-power defined: 336.

value of labor-power defined: 339.

3. A schema: in connection with Ch. 10, Sec. 1, pp. 361–364 (see Figure 7).

Necessary vs. surplus labor: 361–364.

Surplus value: 351.

Absolute and relative surplus value: 418.

4. A Definition:

The value of a mass of commodities = the value added by: $C + V + S$, where C = constant capital (machinery, raw materials, etc.).

V = variable capital (wages or paid labor).

S = surplus labor (unpaid labor).

Since machinery and raw materials add no value, and wages are paid

Paid Labor Time	Unpaid Labor Time
Wages	Profits
(Variable Capital)	(Surplus Value)
Necessary Labor	Surplus Labor
The Working Day	

Figure 7. Schema, Marx's *Capital*, Vol. I, Ch. 10, Sec. 1.

out for necessary labor, total surplus value is the product of total surplus labor.

This means that Marx's labor theory of value attributes the whole social surplus in any period time to surplus (unpaid) labor.

5. Some Ratios:

The ratio s/v = ratio of surplus labor / necessary labor.

= the rate of exploitation (the rate of surplus value).

The ratio $s/c + v$ = rate of profit.

The ratio $c/c + v$ = the organic composition of capital.

6. A Remark

The rate of profit depends only on s/v and $c/c + v$; that is, only on the rate of surplus value (exploitation) and the organic composition of capital.

This relation holds because:

$$s/c + v = (s/v)(1 - (c/c + v)),$$

which says that the rate of profit equals the rate of exploitation multiplied by one minus the organic composition of capital ($= c/c + v$).

Thus, the greater the rate of exploitation, the higher the rate of profit; and the greater the organic composition of capital, the lower the rate of profit.

MARX II

His Conception of Right and Justice

§1. A Paradox in Marx's Views of Justice

1. Let me begin with some discussion about Marx's ideas about exploitation: Marx's definition of exploitation in his labor theory of value is a purely descriptive definition: it is given by the ratio of surplus (or unpaid) labor over necessary labor, or s/v. But this cannot be all there is to the concept of exploitation. The reason is that a just socialist society, like any other society, needs a social surplus, let's assume, to provide for public goods such as public health, education and welfare, environmental protection, and much else. This means that people must work for more time than it takes to produce the goods they receive as wages. This is true in any society one cares to live in. Thus, while the ratio s/v is defined as the rate of exploitation, and while this is a purely descriptive definition, there must be more to exploitation than this. For certainly, exploitation is a moral concept, and implicitly appeals to principles of justice of some kind. Otherwise, it would not have the interest for us that it does.

For Marx it is the institutional background within which the ratio s/v occurs that makes this ratio a measure of exploitation. Whether s/v is exploitation depends on the nature of the basic structure that gives rise to it, and on who has the institutional control of s. Marx must have a way of judging that structure as just or unjust. In the next lecture, I remark that he views exploitation as arising once the basic structure rests on a basic inequality in alienable productive assets owned by the two main classes of capitalist society. In the capitalist case, surplus labor is in no way controlled by workers collectively, say through their democratic votes, nor is it in general to their good; whereas in socialist society the total of non-consumption goods (which replaces s in the socialist case) is both. We must look at the basic structure of society to see how what is produced by s is used. If it is used for such things as the average worker's public health, education, and welfare, it is no longer treated as surplus labor.[1]

The upshot is that the concept of exploitation presupposes a conception of right and justice in the light of which basic structures are judged. Or if not a conception of right and justice, certainly some kind of normative view is required. This raises the question: What kind of normative view did Marx hold? There has been considerable controversy about this among students of Marx, whether they are Marxists or not. For example, did he condemn capitalism as unjust? There are those who think he did, and those who think he did not.

Of course, both sides take for granted that he condemned capitalism. This is obvious and leaps off the pages of *Capital*. The question concerns the particular values in terms of which he did so: whether those values include a conception of right and justice, or are expressed in terms of other values, for example, those of freedom, self-realization, and humanity.

2. The answer I suggest (and here I follow Norman Geras and G. A. Cohen) is that Marx did condemn capitalism as unjust. On the other hand, he did not see himself as doing so.[2] What explains this seeming paradox is that Marx's explicit comments about justice interpret the concept in a narrow way, and this in two respects:

(a) He thinks of justice as the prevailing legal and judicial norms internal to the social and economic order; and when appropriate, those norms are adequate to that order's fulfilling its historical role.

(b) Marx also thinks of justice as relating to exchanges in the market and beyond that to the distribution of income and of consumption goods that results. In this aspect justice is commutative and distributive justice, both narrowly construed.

But once we think of a conception of political justice in a broad fashion as applying to the basic structure of society and thus to the institutions of background justice, then Marx might have had, at least implicitly, a conception of political justice in the broad sense. If this proves to be the case, it may remove the paradox. Whether he does have such a political conception turns, as I have said, on the specific values he appeals to in condemning capitalism.

1. See Tucker, *Marx-Engels Reader*, p. 440, from *Capital*, Vol. 3.
2. See Norman Geras, "The Controversy about Marx and Justice," in *Literature of Revolution: Essays on Marxism* (London: Verso, 1986), p. 36.

3. I shall proceed as follows: I first sketch some reasons for saying Marx does not condemn capitalism as unjust. And then I sketch some reasons for saying he does, at least implicitly. By this I mean that what he says implies that capitalism is unjust although he does not say so in so many words.

Later I will sketch his conception of a full communist society—the ideal in light of which he judges capitalism and all preceding historical forms of society—to see whether that ideal contains elements that make it include a conception of political justice and in what sense, if any, it is a society beyond justice.

It must be admitted, however, that this question may not be conclusively decidable. Marx did not think carefully or systematically about it. While he was a scholar by nature and temperament, given his aims, he didn't believe it was important to do so. Other things he thought more urgent. In this he may have been quite mistaken, since his seemingly dismissive attitude to ideas of right and justice may have had serious long-run consequences for socialism. Who knows? But leaving that aside, the result is that we have to piece together what he says, and ask ourselves what overall view best accounts for and connects the more significant and clearly formulated aspects of his thought.

§2. Justice as a Juridical Conception

1. I begin with the view suggested by Allen Wood and others.[3] The main thoughts seem to be these, and then I will give a few details.

(a) Marx holds in *Capital* that the wage relation, as an exchange of equivalent values (labor power for wages) involves no injustice to the worker.

(b) In his *Critique of the Gotha Program*, Marx attacks socialist ideas of fair or just distribution as seriously in error and moving the wrong way.

(c) Marx regards norms of right and justice as internal to—that is, as essential elements of—specific modes of production; and in this sense, they are relative to the particular historical period in which they are in force.

(d) Marx thinks of morality in general as ideological and thus as belonging to the superstructure of society; morality, and with it justice, changes

---

3. Allen Wood, *Karl Marx* (London: Routledge, 1981).

when that superstructure adjusts to the historical sequence of specific modes of production.

(e) To insist that Marx has a concern for justice is mistakenly to cast his views in a narrow, reformist direction of distributive concerns, such as wage levels and differences of income; whereas his aims were clearly more fundamental and more revolutionary, concerned as they were with the transformation of the private property and wage system itself.

(f) Also, to say that Marx was concerned with justice is to detract from his main effort, which was to uncover the real, active historical forces that were, he thought, leading to the overthrow and collapse of capitalism. To say this would substitute instead moral arguments of various kinds, which Marx viewed as idealistic, and of which he was highly suspicious.

(g) Besides, he thought that justice, since it was a juridical value, could not be put into effect in a full communist society, which Marx is alleged to have conceived as without juridical institutions of law and the state.

(h) Marx conceived of full communist society as one beyond the circumstances of scarcity and conflict. It is these circumstances that render the norms of justice necessary, all of which looks forward to the higher distributive standard: "From each according to their ability, to each according to their needs."[4]

(i) Marx did, of course, condemn capitalism, but he did so in the name of other values, such as freedom and self-realization.

2. Now for a few details about this first view. Wood, for example, thinks that Marx does not criticize capitalism as unjust, and that he even appears to say that it is just.[5] His explanation for this is the following:

Marx thinks of a conception of justice as a political and juridical conception that goes with the institutional separation between the state and society. This institutional separation presupposes the need for the state, and hence the existence of a dominating class and a dominated class. When such a state exists, exploitation (in Marx's sense) also exists. Political and legal institutions belong to what Marx sometimes calls the superstructure: these institutions have a regulatory role and are adjusted to the requirements of the mode and relations of production. Each social form, each kind of political organization and its associated mode of production, has a

---

4. See *Critique of the Gotha Program*, I, Tucker, p. 531.
5. Wood, *Karl Marx*.

distinctive conception of justice that is adequate for it as a social system. When these institutions are properly adjusted to the underlying mode of production, they serve its operative requirements in an effective way.

So, for Marx, the properly adjusted institutions of the superstructure include a conception of justice which serves the historical role of the underlying economic mode of production. Capitalism, like any other historical mode of production, has a properly adjusted superstructure and a conception of justice adequate to it. This conception is the one that best serves capitalism's historical role of building up the means of production at a rapid rate compared to earlier social forms. But then: "The modern laborer . . . instead of rising with the progress of industry, sinks deeper and deeper below the conditions of existence of its own class. He becomes a pauper" (*Communist Manifesto,* Tucker, p. 483).

Thus, capitalism's fulfillment of its role is what makes possible the full communist society of the not too distant future. Indeed, in the *Communist Manifesto,* the capitalist as the personification of capital is the great hero of history who transforms the world and prepares the way for the "victory of the proletariat" and the society Marx envisions.[6]

3. Thus, on this view, capitalism, especially in its high period, the period when it is effectively carrying out its historical role of building up the means of production, is not unjust. There is a conception of justice appropriate to it, and by this conception, it is just so long as its norms are respected. Other conceptions of justice are simply irrelevant; they may apply to other economic modes of production that have existed in previous times, or that will exist the future, but they do not apply in the particular historical conditions of capitalism.

There is no conception of justice, then, that is always applicable or that applies to all social forms. In this sense there are for Marx no universally valid principles of justice. Whether a conception of justice applies to a particular political and social system is settled by whether it is adequate to the existing mode of production in view of its historical role.

One passage in *Capital,* Vol. III, suggests this kind of view. Marx writes:

> To speak here of natural justice, as Gilbart does, . . . is nonsense. The justice of the transactions between agents of production rests on the fact that these [transactions] arise as natural consequences out of the

6. See "Manifesto of the Communist Party," Section I, Tucker, pp. 473–483.

production relationships. The juristic forms in which these economic transactions appear as willful [voluntary] acts of the parties concerned, as expressions of their common will and as contracts that may be enforced by law against some individual party, cannot, being mere forms, determine this content. They [these juristic forms] merely *express* it. This content is *just* whenever it corresponds, is appropriate, to the mode of production. It is unjust whenever it contradicts that mode. Slavery, on the basis of the capitalist production, is *unjust;* likewise *fraud* in the quality of commodities. (*Capital,* Vol. III, International Publishers edition, pp. 339–340. Chapter 21, ¶5; italics added)

This passage occurs when Marx is discussing interest-bearing capital. In a footnote to it he quotes Gilbart, *The History and Principles of Banking* (London, 1834), as saying: "That a man who borrows money with a view of making a profit by it, should give some portion of his profit to the lender, is a self-evident principle of natural justice." Marx replies that the payment of interest is not a matter of a self-evident principle of natural justice. The payment of interest arises as the natural consequence of the supply and demand for funds on the money market, as this market exists within the framework of capitalism. A loan is a valid contract, and the legal system under capitalism will enforce it.

4. This passage is not by itself an account of a conception of justice under capitalism, but it does suggest several points. First, there is the distinction Marx makes between juridical forms—for example, the juridical form of a (valid) contract (as, say, an agreement to make a loan, or a purchase)—and the content of these forms. The same juridical forms may be found in many different legal systems and may apply to economic transactions under widely different modes of production. I assume that the content of the juridical form of contract, say, refers to the specific kinds of contracts that can be legally made and that will be enforced. Thus, under capitalism, a contract into slavery, or for the buying and selling of slaves, is void, and therefore unjust under the capitalist conception of justice. I assume also that the content of the juridical form of contract covers the various conditions under which valid agreements are made. Thus, under capitalism, fraud and deception in reaching agreement is ruled out as unjust, as is everything else plainly incompatible with a regime of free contract.

Second, it seems that whether slavery or fraud, etc., is unjust under some mode of production is settled by whether or not permitting slavery and fraudulent practices specifies a content for the law of contracts which is most adequate to the existing mode of production, and is well adapted to the operation of this mode in fulfilling its historical role. Recall that this role is the rapid accumulation of (real) capital and the development of the technology to use it in innovative ways.

Hence, the juridical form of the law of contract under capitalism is most adequate when its content is adjusted so as to enable this mode of production to accumulate capital in the most effective way. Slavery is incompatible with this, and so with the requirements of capitalism as a mode of production. As a system of personal dependence, it is unjust under a capitalist conception of justice. One essential feature of capitalism is a system of free competitive markets, including a free market for the hire of free labor-power.

In this connection, it is said to be Marx's view that the competitive wage relation, as an essential feature of capitalism, is not unjust, provided that the workers are paid the full value of their labor-power, that is, the equivalent of the socially necessary labor time that it takes to produce and to reproduce the workers' labor-power. In discussing the labor contract in *Capital*, Marx says:

> What really influenced him [the capitalist] was the specific use-value which this commodity [labor-power] possesses of being *a source not only of value, but of more value than it has itself* [Marx's italics]. This is the special service that the capitalist expects from labor-power, and in this transaction he acts in accordance with the "eternal laws" of the exchange of commodities. The seller of labor-power, like the seller of any other commodity, realizes its exchange value, and parts with its use-value. . . . The owner of the money has paid the value of a day's labor-power; his, therefore, is the use of it for a day; a day's labor belongs to him. The circumstance, that on the one hand the daily sustenance of labor-power costs only half a day's labor, while on the other hand the very same labor-power can work during a whole day, that consequently the value which its use during one day creates, is double what he pays for that use, this circumstance is, without doubt, a piece of good luck for the buyer, but by no means an injury to the seller. (*Capital*, Vol. I, Chapter 7, §2, ¶21; or see Tucker, 357–358)

That is, it is not an injury, or an injustice under the conception of justice adequate to capitalism. As Marx says some lines below: "Equivalent has been exchanged for equivalent." And so the conception of justice appropriate to capitalism is satisfied. Paying workers less than the value of their labor-power would be unjust; and this is a far more relevant example of injustice than slavery. It may appear, then, that Marx thinks that capitalism with its free competitive market is perfectly just! Or at least not unjust.

5. Of course, this idea of the capitalist conception of justice as adequate to the capitalist mode of production does not belong to the capitalist conception of justice itself. On this interpretation, it belongs to Marx's idea of the historical role of conceptions of justice as part of the ideological consciousness of capitalist society. The capitalist conception of justice, as presented in its own terms, speaks of the freedom and equality and the equal rights of man. It is on these principles that the regime of free contract and the system of personal independence rests.

I shall come back later to the idea of ideological consciousness, only commenting here that it is always a form of false consciousness, and one of two kinds: either an illusion or a delusion. But this is getting ahead.

§3. That Marx Condemns Capitalism as Unjust

1. Contrary to the view we have just discussed, other writers (among them Norman Geras and G. A. Cohen)[7] hold that Marx does think that capitalism is unjust, and that he says things that strictly imply that it is. Therefore, they argue, he has and uses a conception of right and justice whether he knows that or not.

Among some main points of this second view are these:

(a) Marx's insistence that the wage relation is an exchange relation, where equivalent is exchanged for equivalent, was made from a partial, provisional point of view, seeing that relation as part of the system of circulation in capitalist society. It was supplemented by an account of the mode of production as a whole that showed it to be not an exchange relation at all, but clearly exploitive: it was simply the capitalist expropriation of unpaid labor.

7. See Cohen's review of Allen Wood's *Karl Marx* in *Mind*, July 1983.

(b) Although Marx did engage in polemics against what he saw as moralistic and ineffective criticism, he presented exploitation in his theory of capitalism as wrongful and unjust, often calling it "robbery" and "theft." These expressions imply that what was being done is wrong and unjust.

(c) By his discussion in the *Critique of the Gotha Program,* Marx ranked the principle of distribution according to need above the principle of distribution according to work of socialism (the first stage of communist society), as well as above the norms of capitalism. In doing this Marx, in effect, assumed an objective, non-historical standard of justice, according to which modes of production and the paired societies may be judged by their approximation to it.

(d) Marx's apparent statements of moral relativism are actually statements of the fact that certain material conditions are, in fact, necessary if certain principles of justice and fairness, and other important values, are to be realized. Just and fair social institutions presuppose certain background material circumstances and to ignore this fact is to show a lack of realism and understanding.

(e) A concern with distributive questions is not in the pejorative sense reformist, once we have a properly and broadly conceived conception of justice which covers the distribution of basic rights of all kinds, and so includes the rights of property and other fundamental matters. This certainly allows Marx a revolutionary doctrine and in no way inhibits it.

(f) Also, while Marx did not think that moral criticism founded on justice and other conceptions was sufficient, all the same it had a place in his thought and went along with his analysis of the historical forces for change.

(g) Classifying conceptions of right and justice as juridical is, in general, much too restricted. They can be conceived independently of state institutions of coercion and their systems of law; and indeed, this is done whenever they are used in judging the basic structure of society and its fundamental arrangements.

(h) In fact, the principle, "From each according to their ability, and to each according to their needs," is of this kind. Actually, it aims at an equal right of self-realization for all, even though Marx imagines it as occurring with the disappearance of the state and its coercive institutions of law.

(i) Finally, the alleged distinction between kinds of values and principles—values and principles of right and justice vs. values and principles of freedom and self-realization—is shown to be completely arbitrary by Marx's principle for a full communist society. This principle does grant a basic equal right of self-realization, if you prefer that language. And surely we can speak of the just distribution of basic freedoms as we can speak of the distribution of anything else. Perhaps Marx supposes other equal basic rights as well, as we shall see.

2. So much then for the more general points briefly stated. Now as before, I give a few details. Contrary to the first view, these writers hold that when we examine, say, how Marx sees the exchange relation between capitalists and workers as it really is beneath the surface appearances of capitalist society, then it is clear that he thinks it is no exchange at all, but a mere pretense—forced labor.[8]

> The exchange of equivalents, the original operation with which we started, has now become turned round in such a way that there is only an apparent exchange. This is owing to the fact, first, that the capital which is exchanged for labor-power is itself but a portion of the product of others' labor appropriated without an equivalent; and, secondly, that this capital must not only be replaced by its producer [the laborer], but replaced together with an added surplus. The relation of exchange subsisting between capitalist and laborer becomes a mere semblance appertaining to the process of circulation, a mere form. . . . The ever repeated purchase and sale of labor-power is now the mere form; what really takes place is this—the capitalist again and again appropriates, without equivalent, a portion of the previously materialized labor of others, and exchanges it for a greater quantity of living labor.[9]

Marx goes on to say that this process continues in accordance with the laws of property and exchange in capitalist society and is not a violation but an application of those laws. Under these laws it turns out to be the right of the capitalist to appropriate the unpaid labor of others or its product. He says (p. 584, at the end of the same paragraph): "The separation of property from labor has become the necessary consequence of a law that apparently originated in their identity." He comments in a footnote to this that the original principle that the laborer could appropriate the product of his

8. In *Capital*, Vol. I, Ch. 24: "The Conversion of Surplus-Value into Capital" (New York: International Publishers, 1967), pp. 583f.
9. Ibid., p. 583.

own labor has undergone "dialectical reversal." This has happened beneath the surface appearances of capitalist institutions.

3. This does not sound like a man describing a system of basic institutions that he can approve of and accept as just. So the question arises whether Marx says things that would normally be taken to imply that he thinks the capitalist system unjust. Those who take the view we are now considering maintain that he does, namely, when he speaks of the capitalist appropriation of surplus value in terms of robbery and theft and the like. To say this, they maintain, implies that the capitalist has no right to appropriate the surplus value, and his doing so is therefore wrongful or unjust. We might say instead that it is not the capitalist who is unjust, but the system itself.

Thus, referring in one place to the surplus product as "the tribute annually exacted from the working class by the capitalist class," Marx goes on: "Even if the latter uses a portion of the tribute to purchase the additional labor-power at its full price, so that the equivalent is exchanged for equivalent, the whole thing still remains the age-old activity of the conqueror, who buys commodities from the conquered with the money he has stolen from them."[10]

This not an isolated passage. There are many others, as when Marx speaks of the annual surplus product as "embezzled from English workers without any equivalent being given in return." He says that "all progress in capitalist agriculture is a progress in the art, not only of robbing the worker, but robbing the soil." The prospective abolition of capitalist property he describes as "the expropriation of a few usurpers."[11] And so on in numerous other passages.

Elsewhere Marx says that the worker may appear to enter the labor contract voluntarily; the sphere of circulation appears as "a very Eden of the innate rights of man . . . There alone rule Freedom, Equality, Property and Bentham" (*Capital*, Vol. I, International Publishers ed., p. 176; Tucker, p. 343). But the reality again is different: the free worker makes a voluntary agreement, that is, he "is compelled by social conditions, to sell the whole of his active life, his very capacity for work" (Tucker, p. 376). Again: "capital

10. Geras, *Literature of Revolution*, p. 17, quoting from *Capital*, Vol. I (Penguin edition), p. 728. There are many other such passages in *Capital*, Vol. I. Thus: I: 638, 728, 743, 761, 874, 875, 885, 889, 895, 930. Vol. II: 31. *Grundrisse*, 705.

11. Geras, *Literature of Revolution*, p. 17.

... pumps a definite quantity of surplus labor out of the direct producers, or laborers; capital obtains this surplus labor without an equivalent, and in essence it always remains forced labor—no matter how much it may seem to result from free contractual agreement" (*Capital*, Vol. III, Tucker, p. 440).

Now on the view we are examining, since Marx did not think that the capitalists rob the worker according to the capitalist conception of justice, he must have meant that they rob the workers in some other sense. Moreover, since Marx condemned slavery and feudalism in much the same terms, this other sense presumably belongs to a conception of justice that holds generally. That is, it must be one that applies to the basic structure of most if not all societies, and so it is in this sense non-relativist.

Thus those (e.g. G. A. Cohen) arguing that Marx did condemn capitalism as unjust saw that: since Marx did not think that, by the conception of justice adequate to capitalism, capitalists steal or rob, he must have meant that they steal or rob on some other, non-capitalist conception of justice: for to steal or to rob is to take what rightly belongs to another; and hence to act unjustly. Any economic system said to be based on theft must be viewed as unjust (on Cohen's view).

§4. Relation to Marginal Productivity Theory of Distribution

1. I think this view, that of Geras and Cohen and others, is correct. I try suggesting a particular form of it. One way to begin doing this, and to illustrate the aim of Marx's labor theory of value, is to conjecture how Marx would have replied to the marginal productivity theory of distribution. To be sure, although this theory was being developed at the time of his death (1883), he wouldn't have known of it; but what he would have thought of it is clear from many things he says.

This theory has sometimes been used to argue that under free competitive conditions, the distribution of wealth and income under capitalism is just. Such an argument, seldom heard now,[12] was not uncommon in the late 19th century, soon after the marginal productivity theory was developed by the neoclassical economists. They introduced the ideas of marginal utility

12. [This part of the lecture was written in the early 1980s, when the assumptions behind political and academic discussions regarding distributive justice were quite different than they are today. —Ed.]

and marginal productivity into the theory of price. Very roughly, the idea is that each factor of production—labor, land, and capital—contributes its share in producing society's total output. In accordance with the precept, to each person according to that person's contribution, it is just that those who contribute their land and capital should share in the output along with labor. Adam Smith said: ". . . rent may be considered as the produce of those powers of nature, the use of which the landlord lends to the farmer. . . . It [rent] is the work of nature which remains, after deducting or compensating everything which can be regarded as the work of man."[13] To which Marx in effect replies: since Mother Nature is not around to collect her share, the landlord comes to claim it in her stead.

2. Marx says the following (*Capital*, Vol. III, International Publishers, p. 824): "These means of production are in themselves capital by nature; capital is merely an 'economic appellation' for these means of production; and so, in itself land is by nature the earth monopolized by a certain number of landowners. Just as products confront the producer as an independent force in capital and capitalists—who actually are but the personification of capital,—so land becomes personified in the landlord and likewise gets on its hind legs to demand, as an independent force, its share of the product created with its help. Thus, not the land receives its due portion of the product for the restoration and improvement of its productivity, but instead the landlord takes a share of this product to chaffer away or squander."

Of course, the last words here, "to chaffer away or squander," are a distraction and they obscure, as Marx's expressions of contempt often do, his main point. This point is not that the landlord may be a spendthrift and lead a life of idleness and luxury; for many landlords are conscientious and take care of their estates. (Recall Levin in Tolstoy's *Anna Karenina*.) Rather, the point is that the landlord receives a return solely as an owner; that is, the landlord receives a rent from the land that measures the marginal contribution of the land: a unit of land receives a price according to what it is worth to a producer of grain, say. Marx is not talking about what a landlord receives in return for the management of the estate: what capitalists and land-

13. Adam Smith, *Wealth of Nations* (New York: Random House, 1937), Bk. II, Ch. V, pp. 344f.

lords receive as the wages of management is not counted as the extraction of surplus value.

What counts as extracted surplus value is what the capitalist or landlord receives above any wages of management—that is, what they receive simply as owners of scarce factors of production which are in demand on the market. In Marx's view, it is the social system of capitalism that grants to certain classes the strategic position of ownership of the means of production, which allows them to demand returns in the form of profit, interest, and rent.

Note that when Marx talks about the land becoming "personified in the landlord," this somewhat mystifying mode of speech refers to the fact that it is the landlord, as an economic agent who owns the land, who steps forward on the market to receive payment for the use of the land. The system of markets with its various categories of agents existing over time makes the various kinds of payments—profit, interest, and rent along with wages—seem perfectly natural and to have existed "from time immemorial."

3. Let's look at the long paragraph (third from the end) of Chapter 48 (The Trinity Formula) in *Capital,* Vol. III, International Publishers, p. 830:

> In capital-profit, or still better capital-interest, land-rent, labor-wages, in this economic trinity represented as the component parts of value and wealth in general and its sources, we have the complete mystification of the capitalist mode of production, the conversion of social relations into things, the direct coalescence of material productive relations with their historical and social determination. It is an enchanted, perverted and topsy-turvy world . . . [yet] it is . . . natural for the actual agents of production to feel completely at home in these estranged and irrational forms of . . . illusion in which they move about and find their daily occupation . . . This formula [the trinity formula] . . . corresponds to the interests of the ruling classes by proclaiming the physical necessity and eternal justification of their sources of revenue and elevating them to a dogma.

Earlier Marx has referred to the trinity formula as presenting "a uniform and symmetrical incongruity" (Vol. III, International Publishers, p. 824). I believe that what he means by this is that the trinity formula presents capital, land, and labor as three co-equal partners in the process of production; and as co-equal partners each deserves to receive its share of the output according to its contribution. The formula presents the three factors of production as on a par—it presents them uniformly and symmetrically. The formula is an incongruity because, as we have said, on Marx's labor theory of value, labor is viewed as a special factor of production. From a social point of view, the total output of the production process is to be ascribed to past and present labor. The surface appearances of capitalist institutions conceal the extraction of surplus value and its conversion into profit, interest, and rent.[14]

It is important to keep in mind that Marx is not saying that, in the high period of capitalism when it is serving its historical role, the general belief in the justice of profit, interest, and rent is the result of deception, that is, a belief which arises as a result of clever manipulation of public beliefs by certain persons backstage who stand to gain from the misconceptions of others. Rather, Marx's view is that the widespread belief in the justice of profit, interest, and rent is perfectly natural—an illusion (as opposed to a delusion)—given the situation of economic agents in the system of capitalist institutions as a system of personal independence. This belief is part of a capitalist conception of justice adapted to the requirements of the capitalist mode of production. It characterizes the ideological (false) consciousness of capitalist society and is shared by workers and capitalists alike. It is an illusion which Marx's *Capital* hopes to dispel, now that capitalism has served its historical role.

---

14. Marx says in *Capital*, Vol. III, Ch. 48, part III, p. 825 (New York: International Publishers, 1967), also in *Selected Writings*, ed. David McLellan (Oxford: Oxford University Press, 1977): ". . . the respective part played by the earth as the original field of activity of labor . . . and the other respective part played by the produced means of production (instruments, raw materials, etc.) in the general process of production, must seem to be expressed in the respective shares claimed by them as capital and landed property, that is, which fall to the share of their social representatives in the form of profit (interest) and rent, like to [just as in the case of] the laborer—the part his labor plays in the process of production is expressed in wages. Rent, profit, and wages thus seem to grow out of the role played by the land, produced means of production, and labor in the simple labor-process, even when we consider this labor-process as one carried on merely between man and nature, leaving aside any historical determination" (McLellan, *Selected Writings*, p. 501).

§5. The Allocative and Distributive Role of Prices

1. In order to clarify Marx's view further and to bring out what his implicit conception of justice may be, let's distinguish between the allocative and the distributive role of prices.[15] The allocative role is connected with the use of prices to achieve economic efficiency, that is, to direct the use of scarce resources and factors of production to those employments in which they yield the greatest social benefit. The distributive role of prices is their determining the income to be received by individuals in return for what they contribute to production.

Now, it is perfectly consistent for a socialist regime to establish an interest rate, say by setting up a money-market on which worker-managed firms can borrow funds for capital expansion. This interest rate will allocate revenues among investment projects and will provide a basis for computing rental charges for the use of capital and scarce natural resources such as land and minerals. Indeed, this must be done if these means of production are to be employed in the best way from a social point of view. For even if these resources fall from the sky without human effort, they are nevertheless productive, as Marx recognizes and takes care to assert. When combined with other factors of production a greater output results.

It does not follow, however, that there must be private persons who as owners of these resources receive as their personal income the monetary equivalents of these evaluations. Rather, accounting prices in a socialist regime are economic indicators to be used in drawing up an efficient schedule of economic activities. Except in the case of work of all kinds—mental and physical—prices under socialism do not correspond to income paid to private persons. Instead, the prices imputed to natural resources and collective assets have no distributive role. In capitalism these prices do have a distributive role, and it is this role that characterizes what I have called pure ownership. This distinction between the two roles shows the importance of distinguishing between the use of the market to organize economic activities efficiently and a system of private property in which the worth of resources becomes the personal income of the owners. This latter use illustrates private property as a basis of exploitation.

15. See Rawls, *A Theory of Justice*, §42.

2. The point of Marx's labor theory of value can perhaps be brought out as follows. Consider the objection to Marx's view that says that just as Marx attributes the total output to labor, we can, if we like, attribute the total output to capital, or to land, and conclude that capital, or land, is exploited.[16] In this case, land or capital, whichever we pick, produces more than is necessary to reproduce itself and so it yields a surplus. If, as factors of production, capital, land, and labor are to be viewed as perfectly symmetrical, we can indeed do this. Marx would consider it a formal trick: his point, as I have said, is that capital, land, on the one hand, and labor, on the other, are not to be viewed symmetrically.

Rather, he thinks that human labor is the sole factor of production that is relevant from a social point of view in considering the justice of economic institutions. This being so, pure profit, interest, and rent, as returns of pure ownership, are to be attributed to labor. These returns are viewed as paid out of the product of surplus labor, and they are equal to the total value produced by labor minus the amount that is consumed by labor itself.

Thus, I take Marx to say that when we step back from the various modes of production that have existed historically, and which will exist, we must of course recognize that capital and land are productive. But from the point of view of the members of society, as they might consider together these modes of production, the only relevant social resource is their combined labor. What concerns them is how social and economic institutions are to be organized so that they can cooperate on fair terms and use their combined labor effectively with the forces of nature in ways to be decided by society as a whole. I think this idea underlies Marx's vision of a society of freely associated workers. See *Capital*, Vol. I, Chapter 1, §4 (Tucker, p. 327), where Marx says: "The life-process of society, which is based on the process of material production, does not strip off its mystical veil until it is treated as production by freely associated men, and is consciously regulated by them in accordance with a settled plan. This, however, demands for society a certain material ground-work or set of conditions of existence which in their turn are the spontaneous product of a long and painful process of development."

3. I believe that Marx takes for granted the idea that people's combined

16. See the Generalized Commodity Exploitation Theorem, as proved in John Roemer's *Value, Exploitation, and Class* (New York: Horwood, 1986), in §3.2.

labor is the only relevant social resource. For him, this basic point of view is obvious; and so, for him the basic idea of the labor theory of value is likewise obvious. A capital or a land theory of value that says that capital or land is exploited is simply frivolous. A society does hold and has control over certain productive natural resources; but from the point of view of the members of society in their social relations, the relevant resource they have as human beings is simply their labor and how they can best use it in accordance with a plan settled upon openly and democratically. This we will discuss in the next lecture.

Marx supposes, then, that all members of society equally have a claim, resting on justice, to full access to and the use of society's means of production and natural resources. The basic question is how those means are to be effectively used, the work shared and commodities goods produced, and the rest. Therefore, for him pure economic rent of property ownership is unjust because it in effect denies just claims to access and use, and any system instituting such rent is a system of domination and exploitation. And this is why he describes capitalists' appropriation of the product of surplus labor by such terms as robbery and embezzlement, forced labor and theft.

4. We have seen that Marx in *Capital* does not deny that capitalism as an economic and social mode of production has a fundamental historical role. It is the enormous achievement of capitalism to build up the means of production and to make possible the communist society of the future. That is the historical role of capitalism as a system of domination and exploitation. One aim of *Capital* is to explain this historical role and to describe the historical process by which it has been accomplished.

But in Marx's day, capitalism has already fulfilled its historical role, and another aim of Marx's *Capital* is to hasten its passing. Marx thinks that once we understand how capitalism works, we will recognize it as a system of exploitation—a system in which labor is made to work for a certain period of time in exchange for nothing (unpaid labor). We will see it as a system based on concealed theft. He assumes that we all implicitly accept the fundamental idea that labor is the only socially relevant resource as we all together, as a society, face nature. He assumes also that all of us should fairly share in doing the work of society and have an equal access to and use of its means of production and natural resources. This is why he rejects the legitimacy of private property in the means of production in its distributive role as inconsistent with basic justice.

I conclude by reminding you that I have not commented on whether Marx's various ideas about the justice and the injustice of capitalism are really consistent. Can we say that the basis on which he seems to say that capitalism is not unjust is consistent with his describing it as a system of forced labor and concealed theft? Is it consistent with his idea that human labor is the only relevant factor of production from a social point of view, and that all members of society equally have claim to have access to and to be able to use society's means of production and natural resources? I think Marx's various ideas about justice can be understood so as to be consistent with one another, and I begin with this in the next lecture.

MARX III

His Ideal: A Society of Freely Associated Producers

§1. Are Marx's Ideas about Justice Consistent?

1. In the last lecture I discussed three things:

(a) Passages in which Marx may appear to say that capitalism is just, or at least not unjust.

(b) Passages in which Marx says things that imply that capitalism is unjust, e.g. by characterizing the appropriation of surplus value with such expressions as "forced labor," "embezzlement, "concealed theft."

(c) What Marx would have said (if he had known about it) about the marginal productivity theory of distribution as justifying the resulting distribution under capitalism; after which I suggested that Marx thought that:

> (i) the total of human labor of society is the only relevant factor of production from a social point of view—from our point of view: the point of view of all the members of society as freely associated producers. And:

> (ii) all members of society—all freely associated producers—equally have a claim to have access to and use society's means of production and natural resources.

2. While the various things Marx says about justice may appear contradictory, I think they can be made consistent as follows:

(a) In regard to the passages in which Marx may appear to say that capitalism is just (by the conception of justice adequate to it in its historical period), we say that he is describing the ideological consciousness of capitalist societies and the juridical conception of justice expressed by the legal system of a capitalist social order. When Marx says that a certain juridical conception of justice is adequate to capitalism and is appropriately adapted to its operating requirements, he does not mean to endorse this conception of justice. He is commenting on the juridical conception of justice adequate to capitalism: on how this conception of justice works and its social role; and on the way it shapes ideas about justice held by capitalists and workers alike.

(b) If this interpretation of Marx's view of the juridical conception of justice is correct, then his ideas of justice are consistent. We simply say that in describing capitalist appropriation of surplus labor by such terms as "forced labor," "embezzlement," and "concealed theft," he is expressing his own convictions. He implies that capitalist appropriation is unjust, but he doesn't expressly say so in so many words, and may not be aware of the full implications of what he says.

(c) In regard to Marx's view that human labor is the only relevant factor of production from a social point of view, and the further claim that all equally have a claim to access and use of society's means of production and natural resources, let's say the following:

(i) This is the conception of justice that underlies Marx's describing capitalist appropriation as robbery, embezzlement, and the rest, since private property in the means of production violates that equal claim. Moreover,

(ii) This conception of justice is not relative to historical conditions in the way that the different juridical conceptions of justice were adequate to slavery in the ancient world, or to the feudalism of the medieval world, or are adequate to capitalism in the modern world. These conceptions are each relative to historical conditions and are adequate only in their particular historical period. In the same terms Marx condemns all these modes of production and their associated juridical conceptions of justice. The idea that human labor is the only relevant factor of production always holds, and so he rejects all the social forms of prehistory[1] as at bottom unjust in the light of this standard.

(iii) The fact that a society of freely associated producers cannot be realized under all historical conditions, and must wait for capitalism to build up the means of production and the accompanying technological know-how, does not make the ideal of such a

---

1. Marx speaks of the historical process leading up to capitalism (that of divorcing the producer from the means of production) as the "pre-historic stage of capitalism" (*Capital*, Vol. I, Tucker, pp. 714f); and of all the processes leading to his desired end stage of a society of freely associated producers as, simply, "prehistory."

society a relativist one. It simply means that Marx's own political conception of justice with its related ideals can only be fully realized under certain conditions; but this is true of all conceptions and ideals.

(iv) By contrast, the juridical conceptions of justice adequate to slavery, feudalism, and capitalism are never valid. Rather, they serve an essential historical and instrumental purpose during a certain period of time. At best the societies to whose modes of production they are adequate can be excused or mitigated, but only insofar as they are necessary stages on the way to a society of freely associated producers at the end of prehistory.

§2. Why Marx Does Not Discuss Ideas of Justice Explicitly

1. It is nevertheless puzzling that, if Marx's ideas about justice are consistent, he did not discuss them at least enough to remove the ambiguities as to what he believed. Of course, as I have said, he seems never to have thought systematically about justice and regarded many other topics as far more urgent. But there seem to have been other reasons that moved him. I mention several.

(a) One reason is that he opposed the utopian socialists. This connects with Marx's saying: "The philosophers have only *interpreted* the world in various ways; the point, however, is to *change* it" (*Thesis XI on Feuerbach,* Tucker, 145; Marx's italics). This connects also with Marx's effort in *Capital* to discern the "laws of motion" of capitalism and to figure out how it really worked, so that when historical conditions were ripe we would know how to act in a realistically informed way.

(b) A second reason for his not discussing his ideas of justice is that Marx opposes reformism and the tendency to focus on issues of distributive justice, that is, on the distribution of income and wealth and on raising wages, as narrowly conceived. Of course, he was not opposed to raising wages as such, and he urges workers to continue their struggle with capitalists to raise them. But he felt they should do so as part of their efforts to further the economic reconstruction of society. In a lecture given in London in 1865 to the General Council of the First International, he says: "Instead of the *conservative* motto, '*A fair day's wages for a fair day's work*,' they [the workers] ought to inscribe on their banner the *revolutionary* watch-word: *'Abolition of the wages system.'*"[2]

(c) Marx thinks the utopian socialists represent the initial attempts of the working class to realize its aims. The underdeveloped condition of that class, and the economic circumstances necessary for its emancipation, made it impossible for the utopian socialists to develop a realistic theoretical conception of the conditions required for the successful achievement of these aims. Instead, these writers suppose that there is some new social science based on a conception of the future that will enable them to create the necessary conditions for emancipation by personal intervention from above, or by moral persuasion. The utopian socialists do not regard the working class as the agent of its own emancipation, as Marx thinks it must be. Rather, they regard the working class simply as the most suffering class. It is not regarded, as Marx regards it, as politically active and as moved by the imperative needs of its social and class situation.

(d) A further point is this: the early phase which the utopian socialists represent is marked by an anarchy of thought and by many diverse conceptions of an ideal future society. This state of anarchy is entirely natural in view of the highly personal and non-historical nature of these doctrines. They are, after all, blueprints for an imagined future, and not the outcome of a realistic theoretical analysis of existing political and economic conditions. These blueprints, Marx thought, were drawn up in ignorance of what he calls the "laws of motion of capitalism," which laws will bring about in due course the conditions necessary for the complete abolition of classes. In Marx's view, the anarchism of conceptions of the future to be found in the utopian socialists can only be overcome by an accurate theoretical understanding of present circumstances and of what is possible: such an understanding will make clear what is to be done.[3]

(e) Another objection Marx had to the utopian socialists is that, in his view, they were attached to their own personal conceptions of the future, and since they thought they could impose these conceptions on society from above, or by moral persuasion, they believed that class struggle and revolutionary action are unnecessary. They sought to appeal to "humanity"

2. Marx, *Value, Price and Profit* (New York: International Publishers, 1935), Ch. XIV, p. 61. [Fifth paragraph from the end.]

3. Cf. Marx, *Selected Writings*, ed. David McLellan, 2nd ed., p. 149 (Oxford: Oxford University Press, 2000), from *Holy Family*.

as deeper and more basic than class. For this reason Marx thought they failed to grasp the class basis of capitalism and the depth of the transformation required to overcome it. From Marx's standpoint, the utopian socialists are reactionaries in the sense that their doctrines lead them to oppose the only realistic path to emancipation, namely, revolutionary struggle and the organization of the working class as a political force.

Marx believed, then, that the utopian socialists proceeded contrary to the correct procedure, namely, as he said in an early article, that of developing: "new principles to the world out of its own principles. We do not say to the world: 'Stop fighting; your struggle is of no account. We want to shout the true slogan of the struggle at you.' (Rather) We only show the world what it is fighting for, and consciousness is something that the world *must* acquire, like it or not."[4] Marx's (explicit) aim, then, is to show the world—that is, the working class as the developing and increasingly active political force—what it is, and not what it ought to be, fighting for. Marx aims to do this by explaining to the working class the meaning of its own experiences and actions in the present historical situation. He wants to elucidate the role that the working class must assume in its own emancipation. Thus, one aim of *Capital* is to spell out the laws of motion of capitalism as a social system so that the working class's understanding of its situation and of its historical role can have a realistic scientific basis, as opposed to personal and moral conceptions of the future espoused by doctrinaire visionaries.

(f) A final consideration is this: Marx is suspicious of mere talk about moral ideals, especially those of justice and liberty, equality and fraternity. He is suspicious of people with ostensibly idealistic reasons for supporting socialism. He thinks that the criticisms of capitalism made on the basis of these ideals are likely to be non-historical and to misunderstand the social and economic conditions necessary to improve matters even from the point of view of these ideals. For example, we are likely to think that justice in distribution can be improved more or less independent from the relations of production. This tempts us to look for the best account of distributive justice to guide us in doing this. But distribution is not independent from the relations of production, which are, Marx thinks, fundamental.[5]

4. Tucker, *Marx-Engels Reader*, 2nd ed., pp. 14f, "Letter to Arnold Ruge," Deutsch-Französicher Jahrbucher, 1844; see also Marx, *Selected Writings*, ed. McLellan, 2nd ed., pp. 44–45.

5. On this see Section I of the *Critique of the Gotha Program*.

Marx also thinks that in general, and leaving aside many individual exceptions, the ties of class interests (in a society divided into classes) are too strong. Unless we actually cast our lot with the working class, and join in its struggle and suffer its fate, we are not reliable allies of that class. Considerations of right and justice cannot usually be relied upon to move us that much. In Marx's view, we are normally moved by our more imperative needs, and in a class society these needs are shaped mainly by our class position. Not to recognize this is self-delusion.

To conclude: Marx might have been moved by many reasons for not saying in so many words that capitalism is unjust. But none of the reasons are such as to prevent him from having ideas of justice and sincerely thinking within himself that capitalism is unjust.

§3. Disappearance of Ideological Consciousness

1. I am now going to discuss what, in *Critique of the Gotha Program*, Marx thinks of as the first stage of communism, and later will take up a few questions about the second stage of full communism next time. I use the designation "a society of freely associated producers" to refer to Marx's ideal society, a designation he uses often in *Capital*. How can we briefly describe it?

Perhaps in the following way: a society of freely associated producers has two stages: a socialist stage and a stage of full communism. Each stage answers to the following two-part description, each part of which I shall discuss in some detail.

First, a society of freely associated producers is a society in which ideological consciousness has disappeared. Its members understand their social world and have no illusions about how it works. Moreover, because ideological consciousness has disappeared, they have no delusions about their role in society, nor do they need such delusions.

Second, a society of freely associated producers is a society in which there is neither alienation nor exploitation.

One might question whether the first stage, socialism, satisfies these requirements to a sufficient degree. For our limited aims here, I assume that it does.

2. I begin with the first of these requirements. For Marx ideological consciousness is false consciousness of a certain kind. To have an ideology

in Marx's sense is not merely to have a philosophy or a scheme of political principles and values, as the term "ideology" is often used today. Unhappily, the term has been abused and has lost the original, definite sense Marx gave it. For him an ideology was not merely false, but its falsehood serves a definite sociological or psychological role in maintaining society as a social system.

In Marx's sense, there are two kinds of ideological consciousness: illusions and delusions. As for illusions, they are real in that with fully normal powers of perception and inference we are taken in by the surface appearances of things. Similarly, we are taken in by the surface appearances of institutions and fail to see what is really happening beneath that surface. One's beliefs are false because one is fooled by the semblances that are indeed deceptive. These cases are analogous to optical illusions.

In *Capital*, Vol. I, Chapter 1: §4, Marx discusses at length how, by focusing on the relative prices of commodities and fixing on the relation between prices and objects, we fail to see the significance of the fact that commodities are produced by human labor and that prices express a social relation among producers. A clearer and simpler example is what Marx says about how the wage system conceals the ratio of necessary labor to surplus labor, as opposed to the clarity of the feudal system with the serf's surplus labor open to view (*Capital*, Vol. 1, Tucker, p. 365). There is nothing in how wages are paid that alerts workers to the amount paid for necessary and for surplus labor. Workers are probably not aware of the difference in any case.[6]

It is in part because of these illusions that Marx thinks we need an economic theory—in particular the labor theory of value—to penetrate beneath the misleading and deceptive surface appearances of capitalist institutions. He says: "All science would be superfluous if the outward appearance and the essence of things directly coincided." *Capital*, III, Chapter XLVIII: §3 (New York: International Publishers, 1967), p. 817.

In the society of freely associated producers the form of appearances and the essence of things in politics and economy do directly coincide. This is because society's economic activities are carried out in accordance with an economic plan publicly decided upon in accordance with democratic procedures. I will come back to this.

6. See the calculations in Duncan Foley, *Understanding Capital: Marx's Economic Theory* (Cambridge, Mass.: Harvard University Press, 1986), p. 46.

3. The other kind of ideological consciousness is delusions. These again are or involve false beliefs; but they may also involve false or irrational values. These are values we would not espouse were we fully aware of why we hold them, or were it not for certain psychological needs that press upon us and subject us to special strains characteristic of those in our social position and role.

As is well known, Marx thought religion was a form of ideological consciousness in this sense. But Marx thought it is quite pointless to criticize religion as Feuerbach and the young Hegelians did, by maintaining that religious alienation is a fixation on an imaginary fulfillment in an imaginary world. Much of Feuerbach's psychology of religion may be correct, but explaining it to people does not help them to overcome their religion.

The reason Marx thought such criticism pointless is that the psychological needs to which Feuerbach's account refers depend on existing social conditions. Religion is part of people's psychological adjustment to their class position and social role. Until social conditions are changed so that people's true human needs can be effectively satisfied in a society of freely associated producers, religion will persist. In *Capital*, I (Tucker, 327), Marx says: "The religious reflex of the real world can, in any case, only then finally vanish, when the practical relations of everyday life offer to man none but perfectly intelligible and reasonable [*durchsichtig vernunftig*] relations with regard to his fellowmen and to Nature."

This reminds us of the point of Marx's Thesis XI—the last thesis—on Feuerbach, which says, in its entirety, "The philosophers have only *interpreted* the world, in various ways; the point, however, is to *change* it." It reminds us also of Hegel's remark: "Once we look at the world rationally, it will look rationally back." To this Marx adds, in effect, that we can't look at the world rationally until we are rational; and we can't be rational until our social world is rational. Therefore, when conditions allow, we must change our social world so that it is made rational.

4. In Marx's view, another kind of delusion rests on the needs of the social system and on the needs of the individuals in it if the social system is to work properly. Now the capitalist system involves robbery and theft in that it involves the appropriation of the workers' surplus product in violation of their equal claim of access to society's means of production. Yet the capitalist mode of production has the historical role of building up the means of production so that a society of freely associated producers is possible. It is essential to the smooth working of capitalism (when it is serving its his-

torical role) that this robbery and theft be hidden from view. This is because, seeing both capitalists and workers as decent people, capitalists don't want to be, or to be seen as robbers, and workers don't want to be, or to be seen as robbed. This is, as it were, part of Hegel's *List der Vernunft*, "the cunning of reason."

So in its high period, the juridical conception of justice, which Marx sometimes mocks as "the very Eden of the innate rights of man" (*Capital,* Vol. I, Chapter VI, Tucker, p. 343), enables all economic agents, capitalists and workers alike, to think of their position as just and their income and wealth as deserved. This, along with the deceptive appearances of capitalist institutions, smoothes the operations of the social order.

In a society of freely associated producers, these delusions are no longer needed: the workings of the economy are guided by a publicly known democratic plan and so are open to view, and this without disturbing consequences.

§4. A Society without Alienation

1. The second of the requirements for a society of freely associated producers is that there be no alienation and no exploitation. In the Paris Manuscripts of 1844, in a section entitled "Estranged Labor" (Tucker, pp. 70–81), Marx discusses four aspects of the idea of alienation:

Under the capitalist mode of production the workers are alienated, first, from the product of their labor, from what they produce. It becomes an alien thing: that is, for one thing, it is owned and controlled by others—the capitalists—who may dispose of the product of workers' labor as they—the capitalists—decide.

But more than this, the surplus labor of the workers builds up the great mass of (real) capital, and hence it becomes the wealth of and in the control of the class whose interests are antagonistic to theirs. The products of labor also appear on the market, and the movement of prices—which are competitively determined—is not understood by the workers (or by anyone else), since there is no public democratically determined plan of production.

Thus the adjustment to market forces of the prices of what the workers produce appears to the workers as controlled by an alien power. This power is independent of them as producers, and it holds them in servitude to the products of their labor.

Second, the worker is alienated from the productive activity of labor it-self. That is, work is external to the workers, as it does not realize their na-ture. Their work does not exercise or develop their natural powers; nor is it voluntary, but forced, undertaken only as a means for satisfying other needs. In short, work is not meaningful.

2. Third, workers are alienated from their species and from their spe-cies-life *(Gattungswesen)*. So likewise are the capitalists. Now the idea of spe-cies-life is offhand rather obscure. But it is characteristic of German Ideal-ism, and it is important not to trivialize it. We trivialize it when, for example, we say that calling human beings "species beings" means that they are by nature social beings. Or that they have reason and self-con-sciousness, and that they are aware of themselves and other human beings as belonging to one species, each member of which likewise has reason and self-consciousness.

Rather, I think Marx's idea is much fuller than this. He means some-thing like the following: Human beings are a distinctive natural kind—or species—in the sense that they collectively produce and reproduce the con-ditions of their social life over time. Yet, along with this their social forms evolve historically and in a certain sequence until eventually a social form develops that is more or less adequate to their nature as rational and active beings who, as it were, create, working with the forces of nature, the condi-tions of their complete social self-realization. The activity by which this col-lective self-expression is accomplished is species-activity: that is, it is the co-operative work of many generations and is completed only after a long period of time. In short: it is the work of the species over its history. The species will enter the promised land—full communist society—but not all of its members will. (Recall Rousseau's idea of the perfectibility of man in the *Second Discourse.*)

An essential part of this social self-creation of human beings over time is economic activity. To be alienated from species activity is first of all not to comprehend or to understand this process; and second, it is not to partic-ipate in this activity in a self-realizing way.

If we ask what it means for all to participate in this way, the answer is provided by the kind of economic scheme that exists in a society of freely associated producers. We get some idea of what this is from what Marx says in *Gotha* about the first stage of socialism. I shall come back to this.

The fourth aspect of alienation is that we are alienated from other peo-ple. Under capitalism, this alienation takes the special form given by the free market. In this case the workers are subject to the power of the capitalists indirectly. Their power to extract surplus labor is via the market and not open to view. And the relation between capitalists and workers is one of antagonism; the members of these classes are alienated from one another, and are in an economic system which tends to make individuals mutually indifferent to one another's concerns.

3. Thus Marx's claim about the absence of alienation and exploitation in a society of freely associated producers I take to be this: If we survey these four kinds, or aspects, of alienation, then in a society of freely associated producers, alienation disappears, just as ideological consciousness disappears. This is because all may participate in the democratic and public planning process and everyone does their share in carrying out the plan that results.

§5. Absence of Exploitation

1. The second feature of the second requirement of a society of freely associated producers is the absence of exploitation. Recall that for there to be exploitation, it is not sufficient that $s/v > 0$, where s is surplus or unpaid labor, and v is labor necessary to produce goods for the worker's own consumption. This is satisfactory in capitalism since capitalists control and benefit from surplus value. But in a society of freely associated producers— a socialist society—there is no surplus or unpaid labor. This is because in a socialist society, as in any just society, there must be a surplus to be used for the benefit of the worker—for social expenses such as public health, education, and welfare. Also, as Marx says: "A definite quantity of surplus labor is required as insurance against accidents, and by the necessary and progressive expansion of the process of reproduction in keeping with the development of the needs and the growth of population" (*Capital*, Vol. I, Tucker, p. 440). Thus, as we saw, what makes $s/v > 0$ exploitation is the nature of the basic structure of society within which it arises. The reason there is no exploitation under socialism lies in the fact that economic activity follows a public democratic plan in which all participate equally. This respects the equal claim rooted on Marx's idea of justice that all have equal access to society's resources.

2. Recall the main features of the background institutions of capitalism

that lead to exploitation (make the ratio $s/v > 0$ an indicator of exploitation). They are simply the prerogatives of private ownership in the means of production, namely:

(a) The aggregate social surplus (total of things produced by surplus labor) falls into the hands of other people (than the workers) who own the means of production (via procedures of the legal order, just contracts, etc.). Thus the owners as a class own the output of production.

(b) The owners of the means of production also exercise autocratic control over the labor process within the firm and industry. They and not the workers decide on the introduction and use of new machinery, the extent and the details of the division of labor, and the rest.

(c) The owners of the means of production also determine the extent and the direction of the flow of new investment; they decide—each firm individually (assuming competition)—where their surplus funds are best invested to maximize long-run profit, etc. Thus, this class determines (as a whole but not jointly) the use to be made of the social surplus, and the rate of growth of the economy.

3. Thus, the upshot is that Marx thinks that when these prerogatives are in the hands of freely associated producers, and exercised through a public and democratic economic plan that all understand, and in the framing of which all may participate, there is no exploitation. Nor is there ideological consciousness or alienation. A society of freely associated producers achieves the "unity of theory and practice."

Put another way, their shared understanding of their social world, as expressed in the public economic plan, is a true description of their social world. It is also a description of a social world that is just and good. It is a world in which individuals fulfill their true human needs for freedom and self-development, while at the same time recognizing the claim of all to have equal access to society's resources.

§6. Full Communism: First Defect of Socialism Overcome

1. So far, in surveying the idea of a society of freely associated producers, my aim has been to stress the importance for Marx of the idea of a public and democratically arrived at economic plan, which all understand and in which all participate.

He believed that if a society of freely associated producers follows such a plan, ideological consciousness disappears and there is no alienation or exploitation. A unity of theory and practice obtains: we understand why we do what we do, and what we do realizes our natural powers under conditions of freedom. In the first stage of communism—following tradition, call this stage "socialism"—however, there is still much inequality, due to the inequality of native endowments and to the fact that labor is rewarded for its duration and intensity in consumption goods. This reward to unequal endowments has been called socialist exploitation.[7]

There is also still division of labor, since, as Marx suggests (*Gotha*, Tucker, p. 531), it is only in the higher phase of communist society—again, following tradition, call this "communism"—that division of labor is surpassed. Marx seems to think of these two defects of inequality and division of labor as inevitable in a society that has just emerged after a prolonged struggle from capitalist society, as in the case of the first stage, socialism.

I am going to accept, for our purposes here, Marx's idea of a public and democratic economic plan. I accept also his thought that such a plan eliminates ideological consciousness as well as alienation and exploitation (except possibly for the socialist exploitation, as defined by Roemer, above). There are many difficulties with the idea of a public and democratic economic plan, and Marx leaves the details extremely vague. He left it as a problem for the future. I shall not discuss those difficulties. Instead, I shall discuss several other questions closer to our concerns with Marx's ideas about justice and his criticism of the liberal tradition.

2. I start by discussing the first defect of socialism, the inequality of shares of consumption goods that results from unequal individual endowments, which results as a "natural privilege." Recall the passage from *Gotha* (Tucker, pp. 530–531):

> "Equal right . . . is still in principle bourgeois right."
> "Equal right is still . . . stigmatized by a bourgeois limitation."
> "The right of the producers is proportional to the labor they supply."
> "Equality consists [in applying] an equal standard, labor."
> "But one man is superior to another physically or mentally and so supplies more labor in the same time."
> "Equal right is an unequal right for unequal labor."

7. See John Roemer, *Value, Exploitation, and Class* (New York: Horwood, 1986), pp. 77f.

"Unequal individual endowment and thus productive capacity [are recognized] as natural privileges."

"It is therefore, a right of inequality in its content, like every right."

"Further, [some have larger families and other differing sound claims]."

"To avoid all these defects, right instead of being equal would have to be unequal."

3. Marx seems to accept this inequality as something inevitable in the first phase of communist society. He says: "Right can never be higher than the economic structure of society and its cultural development conditioned thereby" (*Gotha*, Tucker, p. 531). So, we have to wait for economic conditions to change.

But why do we simply have to wait for conditions to change? Why, e.g., can't society, adopting a principle like the Difference Principle,[8] impose various taxes etc. and adjust incentives so that the greater endowments of some work to the advantage of those with fewer endowments? Is it simply an oversight on Marx's part that he doesn't think of this?

Following G. A. Cohen, let's say that Marx holds what we may call a libertarian view that may be defined as follows:

(a) "Each person has full self-ownership in his own person and powers; and so each person has the moral right to do what he likes with himself, provided that he does not violate the self-ownership rights of anyone else." Therefore,

(b) "He may not be required on pain of coercive penalty to help anyone else, unless he has contracted to do so."

Proposition (b) is viewed as a consequence of (a).[9]

4. Still following Cohen, libertarianism, so defined, "may be combined with other . . . principles with respect to those productive resources which are not persons"—land and minerals and powers of nature. What we may call right-wing libertarianism (Robert Nozick in *Anarchy, State and Utopia*) "adds that self-owning persons can acquire similarly strong rights in un-

8. The Difference Principle is the second part of the second of the two principles of justice in justice as fairness, which states that social and economic inequalities are to satisfy two conditions: first, they are to be attached to offices and positions open to all under conditions of fair equality of opportunity; and second, they are to be to the greatest benefit of the least-advantaged members of society. Rawls, *Restatement*, pp. 42f.

9. G. A. Cohen: "Self Ownership, Communism, and Equality," *Proceedings of the Aristotelian Society* 64 (Supplement), 1990, pp. 1f.

equal amounts of external natural resources. Left-wing libertarianism is, by contrast, egalitarian with respect to the distribution of raw external resources: Henry George, Leon Walras, Herbert Spencer, and Hillel Steiner have occupied this position."[10]

I would not say that Marx is a left-libertarian, as he certainly would not put it this way. But it is a view that fits what he says in several respects:

(a) First, it fits his critique of capitalism as we have surveyed it. That critique bases exploitation on the fact that capitalists own all the means of production. Now, I have suggested that on Marx's view everyone has an equal claim of access to and use of these resources. It is the class monopoly of the means of production that is the root of exploitation.

(b) Marx does not suggest that the better endowed should be required to earn their greater consumption shares in ways that contribute to the well-being of those less well endowed. Beyond respecting everyone's equal right of access to external natural resources, no one owes anything to anyone else, other than what they want to do voluntarily. Those less well off don't lack access to external resources; they are simply less well endowed.

(c) This attitude is in line with Marx's view in *The German Ideology*. It is not one in which people are told to help one another; or have impressed on them by its culture various duties and obligations. Rather, it is a society without such moral teaching, a society in which people have no serious conflicts of interests with one another, and may do as they have a mind to do, with division of labor overcome (*The German Ideology*, Tucker, p. 160).

I conclude that Marx would reject the difference principle and similar principles. As Cohen puts it, he thinks of communism as radical egalitarianism—equal access to society's resources—without coercion. This last means that no one can be required to benefit himself only in ways that contribute to others' well-being. That would be coercive. It would amount to giving rights to some people (those being aided) as to how other people shall use their powers—granting that all respect the left-libertarian principle of right to equal access. I, on the other hand, think we must introduce principles like the Difference Principle or other such measures to maintain background justice over time.

10. Ibid., p. 118.

§7. Full Communism: Division of Labor Overcome

1. What makes it possible for division of labor to be overcome? But first, what is bad about division of labor? Well, many things, some listed in the well-known passage from *The German Ideology:* ". . . as soon as the distribution of labor comes into being, each man has a particular, exclusive sphere of activity, which is forced upon him and from which he cannot escape. He . . . must remain so [in that sphere of activity] if he does not want to lose his means of livelihood; while in communist society, where nobody has one exclusive sphere of activity but each can become accomplished in any branch he wishes, society regulates the general production and thus makes it possible for me to do one thing today and another thing tomorrow . . . just as I have a mind" (Tucker, p. 160).

2. What, for Marx, are the attractive features of this description of communism? First, we can do "just as we have a mind." Our activities proceed harmoniously with those of everyone else. We do as we please, they do as they please, and we may do things together. But there is no sense of moral constraint or moral obligation; no sense of being bound by principles of right and justice.

Communist society is one in which the daily awareness of a sense of right and justice and of moral obligation has disappeared. In Marx's view, it is no longer needed and it no longer has a social role.

3. Another attractive feature for Marx is that each of us may, if we wish, realize all our various powers and engage in the full range of human activities. We may all become—if we want to—all-around individuals exhibiting the full range of human possibilities. This is part of what it means to get around the division of labor.

Consider that if we were musicians we might want to take turns playing all the instruments in the orchestra. (If this seems far-fetched, let the orchestra represent the range of human activities.) On the other hand, there is a contrasting idea, stated by Wilhelm von Humboldt and further illustrated by the analogy of the orchestra in *A Theory of Justice*, §79, note 4. This idea [of social union] is that by a division of labor we can cooperate in realizing one another's full range of human powers and moreover enjoy together, in one joint activity, its realization.

This is a different idea: it sees the division of labor as making possible what would otherwise be unattainable, and as acceptable provided certain conditions are met—that it is not forced and exclusive—the same things Marx objects to. But this is not Marx's idea. His idea is that of our becoming all-around individuals and joining with others only as we have a mind to do so. This idea is consistent with the idea of self-ownership as defined earlier, and it is not restricted by an awareness of a sense of right and justice.

4. What makes the overcoming of the division of labor possible? It seems essentially three things:

(a) Limitless abundance, which results from the building up of the means of production.

(b) Labor becomes life's prime need: people need to work and it is no longer necessary to entice them to do so via incentives.

(c) Labor is also attractive—meaningful work—which is an aspect of (b).

Two passages in Marx are especially relevant for this. In a passage from *Gotha* (Tucker, p. 531; McLellan, p. 615), Marx says: Only in the higher phase of communism is "the narrow horizon of bourgeois right" surpassed (the inequality we discussed earlier). "The antithesis between mental and physical labor, has vanished." Labor has become "not only a means of life but life's prime want"; and Society puts on its banner: "From each according to his ability, to each according to his needs!"[11]

The other passage, from *Capital*, Vol. III (Tucker, p. 441), concerns the realm of freedom beginning "only where labor which is determined by necessity and mundane considerations ceases."

5. How should we interpret the precept "From each according to his ability, to each according to his needs"? It is not, I think, a precept of justice, or a principle of right. It is simply a descriptive precept or principle that is accurate to what is done and to how things happen in the higher phase of communism.

§8. Is the Higher Phase of Communism a Society Beyond Justice?

1. Many people have wanted to say that communism is a society beyond justice. But in what sense is it true? It depends on what aspect of com-

11. This precept is from Louis Blanc, added to his *Organization of Work*, 9th edition (Paris, 1850).

munist society we are considering. Recall that communism equals radical egalitarianism without coercion. This idea still holds and it involves:

(a) The equal claim of all to have equal access to and use of society's means of production.

(b) Everyone's equal claim to take part along with others in the public and democratic procedures by which the economic plan is formed.

(c) Equal sharing—I assume—in doing the necessary work that no one wants to perform, if there is such work (presumably there is some).

Hence the distribution of goods is just if we accept equality as just. Moreover, the equal right of all to the use of resources and to participation in democratic public planning is respected, so far as such planning is necessary. So in this sense—with this idea of justice—communist society is certainly just.

2. But in another sense, communist society is, it seems, beyond justice. That is, while it achieves justice in the sense just defined, it does so without any reliance on people's sense of right and justice. The members of communist society are not people moved by the principles and virtues of justice—that is, by the disposition to act from principles and precepts of justice. People may know what justice is, and they may recall that their ancestors were once moved by it; but a troubled concern about justice, and debates about what justice requires, are not part of their common life. These people are strange to us; it is hard to describe them.

However, this absence of concern with justice was a feature that attracted Marx. We should ask ourselves whether this is indeed an attractive feature. Can we really understand what it would be like? Consider what Mill says in *On Liberty*, III: 9.[12] It is easy to reject Marx's limitless abundance as utopian. But the question of the desirability of the evanescence of justice raises a much deeper question.

To me it is both undesirable as such, and also as a matter of practice. Just institutions will not, I think, come about of themselves, but depend to some degree—although not of course solely—on citizens having a sense of

---

12. Mill says that it is "by cultivating [what is individual in themselves] and calling it forth, within the limits imposed by the rights and interests of others, that human beings become a noble and beautiful object of contemplation. . . . As much compression as is necessary to prevent the stronger specimens of human nature from encroaching on the rights of others cannot be dispensed with. . . . To be held to rigid rules of justice for the sake of others, develops the feelings and capabilities which have the good of others for their object."

justice learned in the contexts of those very institutions themselves. The absence of concern with justice is undesirable as such, because having a sense of justice, and all that it involves, is part of human life and part of understanding other people and of recognizing their claims. To act always as we have a mind to act without worrying about or being aware of others' claims, would be a life lived without an awareness of the essential conditions of a decent human society.

Concluding Remarks

I have tried to explain the central place in Marx's view of the idea of a society of freely associated producers conducting their species-life—as he called it—in accordance with a public and democratically arrived at economic plan which all understand and in which all participate.

When society conducts itself in this way, ideological consciousness disappears and there is no alienation or exploitation. There is a unity of theory and practice: we all understand why we do what we do, and what we do realizes our natural powers under conditions of freedom. The idea of a society-wide public and democratic economic plan has very deep roots and fundamental consequences in Marx's thought. It is important to see this, especially now when the collapse of communism may easily tempt us to overlook these connections and to suppose that the very idea of a democratic economic plan is discredited. Although we may reject it, we must try to understand why this idea had such a central place in the socialist tradition and what significance it has for us now.

APPENDIXES

Four Lectures on Henry Sidgwick
Five Lectures on Joseph Butler
Course Outline

INDEX

FOUR LECTURES ON HENRY SIDGWICK

(Fall 1976, 1979)

LECTURE I

Sidgwick's *Methods of Ethics*

§1. Preliminary Remarks

(1) You will recall that in the first lecture on Hume, I remarked that the historical tradition of utilitarianism extends roughly from 1700 until 1900. And what I call the "classical line" within that tradition is represented by Bentham, Edgeworth, and Sidgwick (the "BES line," let's say). Sidgwick's *Methods of Ethics* (1st edition, 1874; 7th and last edition, 1907) is the most refined and complete philosophical statement of the doctrine (combining Bk. I, Ch. 9; Bk. II, Ch. 2; Bk. III, Chs. 13 & 14; Bk. IV, entire) and may be said to conclude that phase of the historical development. Bentham and Edgeworth are both more original in contributing basic ideas to the classical principle of utility as a sharp and definite notion subject to mathematical interpretation, in contrast to Hume's much looser notion of utility as the happiness and necessities of society; although if we press Hume's account of the point of view of the judicious spectator in a certain way, a natural transition to the classical principle is latent in it. (See Hume Lecture II and the discussion below.) Sidgwick's originality lies in his conception of moral philosophy itself: what it is, how to do it, and so on.

(2) In considering the three utilitarian writers—Hume, Sidgwick, and J. S. Mill—we are fixing in the first instance upon the notion of utility and paying attention to how it is defined and understood. And we shall find three quite different notions of utility in Hume, Sidgwick (or BES), and in J. S. Mill.

In Hume Lecture II we looked at Hume's account of the point of view of the judicious spectator[1] to see:

> (i) How Hume understood the role of this point of view in his psychological and naturalistic account of morality; and
>
> (ii) Whether it contained an intuitive way of arriving at a sharper (more exact) notion of utility than Hume uses in the *Treatise*, the *Enquiry*, and in "Of the Original Contract," which notion we saw did not present a clear contrast with Locke's Social Contract criterion, when both are used as normative principles.

I made the suggestion that such a natural or intuitive way can be found as follows:

(a) We pick up on Hume's idea that moral approvals and disapprovals are continuous with natural human emotions—original passions of our nature (and innate to it)—namely, love and hatred. Or in the *Enquiry*, continuous with the principle of humanity (benevolence).

(b) These approvals and disapprovals are founded on the principle of humanity as aroused from the point of view of the judicious spectator. In this connection note the important paragraph 5 of Sec. VI of the *Enquiry*, where Hume says: "The same endowments [qualities of character] of the mind, in every circumstance, are agreeable to the sentiment of morals and to that of humanity; the same temper is susceptible of high degrees of the one sentiment and of the other; and the same alteration in the objects, by their nearer approach or by connexions, enlivens the one and the other."

Hume goes on: "By all rules of philosophy, therefore, we must conclude that these sentiments are originally the same [he means, in origin they are the same in the self *now*]; since, in each particular, even the most minute, they are governed by the same laws [and to the same degree], and are moved by the same objects."[2]

(c) Then combine these presumptions to give an account of *comparative* moral judgments, and it is not unnatural to say that from the point of view of the judicious spectator we approve more strongly, to a higher degree, of one institution or set of qualities than another, if it produces (or seems designed to produce) more happiness. Greater happiness enlivens our senti-

---

1. For the term "judicious spectator" see *Treatise on Human Nature*, Bk. III, Pt. III, Sec. 1, ¶14.

2. *An Enquiry Concerning the Principles of Morals*, pp. 235–236.

ments more. And thus we are on the way to the Bentham-Edgeworth-Sidgwick definition of utility.

There are some signs of this sharper notion in Hume, but not many. At one point in the *Enquiry* he refers to the "balance of good" (App. III); and at another he shows an awareness of the principle of diminishing marginal utility: in the discussion of the impracticality of perfect equality (in Sec. III, par. 25, p. 194). But essentially, the sharper notion must wait for the BES line. By calling it "sharper" I do not mean to imply that all things considered the sharper notion is better, philosophically speaking. It does, however, pose a clearer contrast with other views, and that is a gain: we can now see more clearly, at least, where some of the differences lie between utilitarianism and the social contract tradition. It is partly to gain this sharpness and clarity that we take up Sidgwick.

(3) *The Methods of Ethics* as a philosophical work: I regard this book, no doubt somewhat eccentrically, as important both as a philosophical work and as having a distinctive historical significance.

(a) For one thing, the book is symbolic of the re-entry of Oxford and Cambridge into the English philosophical tradition in an unconstrained and serious way. Remember how recent all of this is; it can be dated from 1870 roughly. Sidgwick played some part in this by refusing to subscribe to the Thirty-nine Articles in 1869,[3] and resigning his fellowship at Trinity College. This is not to say that there were no important University figures before Sidgwick: for there were, for example, F. D. Maurice, Whewell, and John Grote; but they were all Anglicans and rejected utilitarianism and empiricism (as represented by Hume, Bentham, the Mills, etc.). One might say they were committed to opposing utilitarianism because they regarded it as inconsistent with their religious convictions. There is no harm in that, as such; but when it's a condition of being at the University, the picture changes.

(b) *The Methods of Ethics* is the clearest and most accessible formulation

---

3. [The Thirty-nine Articles were the principal confession of the Church of England, set forth in 1563, and approved by the Anglican Convocation and by Parliament in 1571. They were based in large part on the Lutheran Augsburg Confession (1530) and the Confession of Württemberg (1562). They affirm the orthodox Christian doctrines of the Trinity, the Person of Christ, and human sinfulness, and they are Protestant, or "Reformed Catholic," in character in their emphasis on justification by faith, the Scriptures, and only two holy sacraments. See Stephen Sykes and John Booty, eds., *The Study of Anglicanism* (New York: Fortress Press, 1988), pp. 134–137. —Ed.]

of the classical utilitarian doctrine. This classical doctrine holds that the ultimate moral end of social and individual action is the greatest net sum of the happiness of all sentient beings. Happiness is specified (as positive or negative) by the net balance of pleasure over pain, or, as Sidgwick preferred to say, as the net balance of agreeable over disagreeable consciousness. In Sidgwick's day the classical doctrine as just adumbrated had been long familiar from Bentham's works and their wide influence on subsequent writers. What makes *The Methods of Ethics* so important is that Sidgwick is more aware than other classical authors of the many difficulties this doctrine faces, and he attempts to deal with these difficulties in a consistent and thorough way while never departing from the strict doctrine, as for example J. S. Mill did. Sidgwick's book, therefore, is the most philosophically profound of the strictly classical works, and it may be said to bring to a close that period of the tradition.

(c) *The Methods of Ethics* is important for another reason. It is the first truly academic work in moral philosophy (in English), modern both in its method and in the spirit of its approach. It treats moral philosophy as any other branch of knowledge. It undertakes to provide a systematic comparative study of moral conceptions, starting with those which historically and by present assessment are the most significant. Sidgwick undertook this study because he thought that a reasoned and satisfactory justification of the classical doctrine (and indeed of any other moral conception) could be given in no other way. And such a justification he hoped to give. To this end Sidgwick tries to reduce all the main moral conceptions to three: egoistic hedonism, intuitionism, and universal hedonism (the classical utilitarian doctrine). After describing the subject of ethics and its boundaries in Book I, the three subsequent books take up these three conceptions in the above-mentioned order, although it should be observed that universal hedonism has been explained and argued for as superior to intuitionism by the end of Book III. The systematic justification of universalistic hedonism over intuitionism is given in Book IV. We expect Sidgwick to go on and to argue that universalistic hedonism is also superior to egoistic hedonism, since it is clear that his philosophical and moral sympathies are with the former. But he finds that he cannot do so. He believes that both forms of hedonism equally satisfy the standards of reasoned justification he has so carefully formulated. Sidgwick concludes with dismay that our practical reason seems to be divided against itself; and whether and how this division can be resolved he leaves as a problem, not for a work in ethics, but to be taken up only after we have made a general examination of the criteria of true and false beliefs.

(d) *The Methods of Ethics* has two serious defects that need not concern us now: (i) it undertakes a somewhat narrow range of comparisons and omits, I think, several fundamental aspects of a moral conception; (ii) Sidgwick fails to see Kant's doctrine as a distinct moral conception worth of study in its own right. Still, Sidgwick does present a full and well-done across-the-board comparison with intuitionism.

(e) Sidgwick's originality lies in his conception of the subject of moral philosophy, and in his view that a reasoned and satisfactory justification of any particular moral conception must proceed from a full knowledge and systematic comparison of the more significant moral conceptions in the philosophical tradition. *The Methods of Ethics* is a fundamental work because it develops and displays this conception of moral philosophy with a secure mastery and a full command of the necessary details. An accurate understanding and informed assessment of the classical utilitarian doctrine—which is still highly relevant for the moral philosophy of our time—may best start from a careful study of Sidgwick's treatise.

The academic nature of the work, and no doubt certain features of Sidgwick's style, make the work hard going; it can easily seem dull and tiring, but academic works are not seldom dull, even when of the first rank, unless one gets into the ideas and comes to the work sufficiently prepared. How could it be otherwise? So my job is to try to tell you enough about *The Methods of Ethics* and its background so that you are in a position to appreciate the argument at least. You won't find it entertaining. Take it a little bit at a time.

(4) Sidgwick's Life: Sidgwick's entire life fell within the reign of Queen Victoria (1837–1901): he was born on May 31, 1838, and died on August 28, 1900. Grandson of a well-to-do coffin manufacturer, his father went to Trinity College Cambridge and became an Anglican clergyman, and then was appointed master of the grammar school in Skipton, Yorkshire. He died in 1841.

Henry Sidgwick attended Rugby, then went to Trinity in 1855 and after a brilliant career as an undergraduate became a Fellow of Trinity in 1859 (at the age of 21). Sidgwick resigned his fellowship in 1869 (at age 31) because of his religious doubts; subscription to the Thirty-nine Articles of the

Church of England was required by law for the tenure of fellowship.[4] He was promptly given a special position that did not require subscription to the Articles; and he was re-appointed Fellow when the law requiring subscription was repealed. Sidgwick became Knightbridge Professor (following Birks, successor to F. D. Maurice) in 1883, at the age of 45. He never taught elsewhere. William James wanted him to come to Harvard for the year 1900, but Sidgwick seemed not interested in pursuing the opportunity.

In 1876 at age 39 Sidgwick married Eleanor Balfour, who was the sister of Arthur Balfour, subsequently the Prime Minister. She founded Newnham College, the first place of higher education for women in Cambridge.

Of G. E. Moore, his student, Sidgwick said: "His acumen—which is remarkable in degree—is in excess of his insight."[5]

§2. The Structure and Argument of *The Methods of Ethics*

(1) Perhaps the first thing to notice about *The Methods of Ethics* is that is does not set out to advocate or to justify some particular moral and philosophical, or theological, doctrine. In this way, it is different from most of the works that precede it: e.g. by Hobbes and Locke, Bentham and J. S. Mill. Of course, this is part of what I meant by saying that *The Methods of Ethics* treats moral philosophy as any other branch of knowledge.

But more than this, note Sidgwick's remark in the Preface to the first

4. [The following remarks were among Rawls's notes on Sidgwick, on the thoughts that led him to resign his fellowship. The remarks appear to follow J. B. Schneewind's discussion in *Sidgwick's Ethics and Victorian Moral Philosophy* (Oxford: Oxford University Press, 1977), pp. 48–52. —Ed.] "Sidgwick on 'The Ethics of Conformity and Subscription' (1870): What is the *duty* of progressive members of a religious community to that community, with regards to expressing dissenting views? Sidgwick thinks one must choose between two evils: loss of veracity and absolute unchangeability. One must accept *some insincerity,* the evil of which can be lessened only if: (1) there is some maximum thereof [of insincerity]; (2) we encourage open avowal of dissent. Three main features [of Sidgwick's essay]: (1) It is a realistic appraisal [of actual practice], not ideal [society]; (2) There are no clear common-sense rules to guide us in deciding how to act when two duties conflict [e.g. the duty of veracity and duty of fidelity to one's chosen church]; (3) Difficulties and conflicts are to be resolved by some form of appeal to the utilitarian principle."

5. See J. B. Schneewind, *Sidgwick's Ethics and Victorian Moral Philosophy,* pp. 15–17. For those who wish to consult a secondary work on Sidgwick's ethics, Schneewind's book is highly recommended. It provides a comprehensive discussion of Sidgwick's doctrine and locates it within the history of English moral philosophy.

edition (*Methods of Ethics*, p. vii; hereafter *ME*) that he aims to examine (and I would add compare and contrast) all "the different methods of obtaining reasoned [moral] convictions as to what ought to be done which are to be found—either explicit or implicit—in the moral consciousness of mankind generally." These methods "have been developed, either singly or in combination, by individual thinkers, and worked up into the systems now historical" (p. vii). Sidgwick wishes to describe and criticize (assess) these methods "from a neutral position, and as impartially as possible" (p. viii). Part of our task here is to see what this neutral and impartial position is.

What is a "Method of Ethics"? Sidgwick defines it as any rational procedure by which we determine what individual human beings ought to do; or determine what is right for them to do; or to seek to realize by (free) voluntary action (*ME*, p. 1). The phrase "individual human beings" distinguishes ethics from politics, which Sidgwick says studies what is right or good legislation,[6] but this distinction is not important for us, since the principle of utility applies to both and Sidgwick's discussion of justice really belongs to politics.

Note that Sidgwick assumes that, under any given circumstances, there is something (some definite alternate institution or custom, etc.) that it is right or reasonable to do, or to bring about (if this is possible); and that this may be known in principle. (See *ME*, Preface, 1st edition, p. vii.) In addition, Sidgwick assumes that a rational method is one that can be applied to all rational (and reasonable) human beings to get the same result, when the method is correctly followed (cf. *ME*, 27, 33). In sum: There is always *one right* or *best answer*, and this answer is the *same* for all rational minds. For Sidgwick this assumption is characteristic of science and the search for truth; he believes it holds for moral philosophy and ethical beliefs. Sidgwick says: it is implied in ". . . the very notion of Truth that it is essentially the same for all minds, [and so] the denial by another of a proposition that I have affirmed has a tendency to impair my confidence in its validity" (*ME*, p. 341).

This is said in explaining why a mark of self-evidence is *general agreement in judgment*. Thus Sidgwick holds the thesis of moral objectivity.

(2) Now the methods of ethics Sidgwick has in mind are those proce-

---

6. "Politics . . . seeks to determine the proper constitution and the right public conduct of governed societies." *ME*, p. 1.

dures embedded in the historical doctrines: the various forms of rational intuitionism and moral sense views; perfectionism and utilitarianism; and social contract doctrines insofar as they incorporate parts of such doctrines. Sidgwick also includes rational egoism as a method of ethics.

Note that Sidgwick wishes to concentrate on the methods themselves and their differences as methods, and not on their practical results. He wants to put aside the desire to edify which he thinks is a barrier to advance in ethics, and to study the methods from disinterested curiosity. He wants to forget about even "finding and adopting the true method of determining what we ought to do; and to consider simply what conclusions will be rationally reached if we start with certain ethical premises, and with what degree of certainty and precision" (ME, Preface, 1st edition, p. viii).

This statement does not quite describe Sidgwick's view accurately, since he is prepared to say that a *rational* method of ethics must answer to certain criteria; and these criteria serve, as we shall see, as the *neutral* standpoint from which the different methods can be assessed. Nevertheless, the desire to set out and to compare the various methods of ethics, from an impartial point of view, is an important feature of *Methods of Ethics*.

The implication of this feature is that we should not view *Methods of Ethics* as aiming to justify classical utilitarianism. It is plainly the doctrine Sidgwick prefers and the one to which he is most strongly drawn. But at the end of *ME* he thinks he is forced to recognize that while utilitarianism, from a neutral point of view, passes the criteria of a rational method of ethics far better than any form of intuitionism, and so is superior to intuitionism, nevertheless classical utilitarianism and rational egoism both seem to pass these standards equally well. Sidgwick comes to the unwelcome conclusion that there seems to be a conflict of reason within itself in the practical sphere.

(3) The structure of *ME* is roughly as follows (I go over this so that you can put Ch. 5 on Justice and Sidgwick's argument as a whole in its proper context):

(a) *ME* falls into 4 Books.

Book I: discusses preliminary matters: definitions of ethics and of moral judgment, ethical principles and methods; definition of free will and its relation to ethics; definitions of desire and of pleasure; of intuitionism vs. egoism and self-love, etc.

Book II—Egoism: since Sidgwick decides that there are essentially only three fundamentally distinct methods of ethics, rational egoism, intuitionism, and utilitarianism, he sets out to give a systematic comparison and description of these. Book II is devoted to rational egoism.

Book III—Intuitionism: covers the various kinds of intuitionism (together with Chapter 8 of Book I), and at the same time points out the weakness of intuitionism as a method and hints at the argument to come, that classical utilitarianism is superior. See especially Book III, Chapter 11, on the review of common-sense morality, then Chapter 13 on Philosophical Intuitionism, and Chapter 14 on Ultimate Good.

Book IV—Utilitarianism: begins with the definition of the principle of utility in its classical form. Chapter 1 presents part of the neutral and impartial point of view, or argument whereby methods of ethics can be assessed. Chapter 2 discusses the proof of the principle of utility; Chapter 3 surveys the relation between common sense and utilitarianism and argues that common sense is, as it were, unconsciously utilitarian. Chapters 4–5 lay out the method of utilitarianism; and Chapter 6 discusses the relations between the three methods of ethics and closes with the dilemma of the "dualism of practical reason."

(b) Strictly speaking, the argument of *Methods of Ethics* does not justify the classical utilitarian doctrine, although it is clearly the view to which Sidgwick is strongly inclined. The reason is that while utilitarianism wins out over intuitionism in Bks. III–IV, a tie exists between utilitarianism and rational egoism: that is, both satisfy equally well the objective criteria of a rational method of ethics. This offhand surprising conclusion is reached in the last chapter of Bk. IV; so we have, Sidgwick says, the dualism of practical reason and no objective resolution is in sight.

Thus, from this structure and outline it is clear that Sidgwick fails in his objective: While he is satisfied, for the moment, that he has described and compared the main methods of ethics correctly, it turns out that at least two of them—rational egoism and utilitarianism—pass equally, so far as he can tell, the rational and neutral tests of any such method. Therefore his initial assumption of *objectivity*—the thesis that there is always one right answer—is put in question. He suggests a way out via a theological assumption, but this we have not time to examine (I believe it well worth looking at, however convinced one may be that it cannot be correct).

(4) I should mention here (it will be relevant later), first, that Sidgwick reduces the main methods of ethics to three only—not, to be sure, without

examining the others of historical importance: rational egoism (Bk. II); intuitionism (Bk. III); and utilitarianism (Bk. IV). Thus perfectionism reduces to intuitionism; and Kant's doctrine reduces to a formal principle of equity or fairness in Sidgwick's terminology (cf. *ME*, p. 379). This is, in my opinion, too small a range of comparisons: it is defective, I think, in not seeing that Kant's doctrine, or a view similar to it, is a distinctive method of ethics; and *Theory of Justice* is such a view. Also, I think he wrongly assimilates perfectionism to intuitionism. This gap in Sidgwick's range of comparisons is one weakness of his overall view.

Secondly, I believe Sidgwick fails to include in his description of methods of ethics certain important aspects of a moral conception, but I shan't go into this at this point.

(5) The General Criteria of any Rational Method of Ethics:[7]

I call your attention to the footnote, p. 293 (of Ch. 5) where Sidgwick says that by "arbitrary" (as applied to definitions) he means definitions that include limitations (exceptions and qualifications) "as destroy the self-evidence of the principle; and, when closely examined, lead us to regard it as subordinate." Now in the background here is Sidgwick's view of the criteria for the 1st principles of a Rational Method of Ethics, which are:[8]

(a) First, Sidgwick holds that the 1st principles of a method of ethics must satisfy these conditions: (i) they must be at least as *certain* as any other moral principles, and (ii) of *superior validity* to other principles; (iii) they must be *really self-evident* and derive their validity, or evidence, from no other principles, moreover:

(b) Any such principles (iv) must be fully *rational* in the sense that they contain no limitations, or exceptions, or restrictions, unless these are self-imposed; that is, follow from the principle itself, and are not simply appended as unexplained provisos (cf. *Methods of Ethics*: 293n., the definition of "arbitrary"). In addition:

(c) (v) 1st principles must control, regulate, and *systematize* subordinate principles and standards (and lower-level moral precepts and beliefs) so as to organize them into a *complete and harmonious* scheme free of arbitrary elements. This requirement is connected to another: namely that (vi) 1st principles must define a method of ethics that determines (ascertains) ac-

---

7. Here I interpret Sidgwick's procedure and arguments, but see especially Book IV: 2.
8. Here you should see *Methods*, III, Ch. 11 and IV, Ch. 2; and Schneewind, Chs. 9–10.

tual rightness, and not merely prima facie rightness—1st principles must yield a correct judgment, all things considered; and so (vii) must serve for rational agents as an actual *guide to practice,* and so enable us to act rationally—hence first principles cannot be vague, imprecise, and ambiguous; and finally (viii) a first principle must be one that suitably *corrects* our pre-reflective judgments.

Sidgwick's account of justice (Bk. III, Ch. 5) is designed to show that none of the principles of justice found in common sense meet these criteria and hence are subordinate principles. It is particularly the last three conditions, (d)–(f), that he argues throughout Bk. III, Ch. 5, on Justice, although the first three are there also. We turn to Sidgwick's account of justice in the next lecture.

LECTURE II

Sidgwick on Justice and on the Classical Principle of Utility

§1. Sidgwick's Account of Justice

(1) You should read Sidgwick's account of justice in Book III, Chapter 5, as part of his long and careful account of the intuitive principles found in common sense, and refined by various writers in the effort to formulate them as bona fide and rational first principles. He believes that his survey of these principles shows that in every case, these principles prove to be vague and imprecise once we try to apply them in practice; and that they are subject to various exceptions and qualifications that are arbitrary in the sense that the principles themselves do not include any explanation of the rational basis of these exceptions and qualifications. Therefore, Sidgwick concludes, these principles cannot be bona fide rational and objective first principles. There must be *some other* and higher controlling principle or principles that accounts for these qualifications and provisos. And he hints throughout (and often more than hints) that this *higher* principle *must* be the principle of utility. All this, of course, on the assumption that there is always a right or true answer, and that we can know it and agree upon it (if we follow reason).

(2) Sidgwick discusses the notion of justice on three occasions: the fullest is that in *Methods,* Ch. 5 of Book III; the next is the brief summary of Ch. 5 that Sidgwick gives in his "Review of Common Sense," Ch. 11 of Book III, at 349–352; and finally there is the assessment in Ch. 3 of Bk. IV, at 440–448.

Sidgwick explains the different aims of these discussions as follows. In Ch. 5 of Book III the aim is "to ascertain impartially what the deliverances of Common Sense actually are" (*ME*, p. 343); while the aim in the "Review" of Ch. 11 is "to ask how far these enunciations [i.e. the deliverances of common sense] can be claimed to be classed as Intuitive Truths" (*ME*, p. 343). In Ch. 3 of Book III the aim is to show that in coping with the difficulties and ambiguities, etc., that arise in practice in defining and specifying its notions of justice, common sense is, as it were, unconsciously utilitarian, since the principle of utility is naturally invoked, even if only implicitly. (One of Sidgwick's definitions of common sense of mankind is this: what is "expressed generally by the body of persons on whose moral judgments [one] is prepared to rely"; *ME*, p. 343). So while these various accounts of justice are somewhat repetitive, their stated aim is different; and in fact Sidgwick's observations are not the same and they supplement each other to some extent.

(3) A rough outline of Ch. 5 is as follows:

(a) In §1 (*ME*, pp. 264–268) Sidgwick holds that while justice is connected in our minds with laws (cf. administration of justice), it cannot be identified with what is legal, since laws may be unjust. Again, while justice includes and implies the absence of arbitrary inequalities in framing and administering laws, it is not merely this either.

(b) In §2 (pp. 268–271) Sidgwick discusses what he calls *"conservative justice,"* that is: the fulfillment of (1) contracts and definite understandings, and (2) expectations that arise naturally out of the established practices and institutions of society. However, the duty of fulfilling the latter is not clearly defined; nor is it clear how much weight these expectations should have.

(c) In §3 (pp. 271–274): The social order itself may be held to be unjust as judged by the standard of *ideal justice.* But there are different conceptions of this standard.

(d) In (§4) (pp. 274–278): One view is that freedom is the absolute end; but the attempt to elaborate an ideal notion on this basis runs into insuperable difficulties.

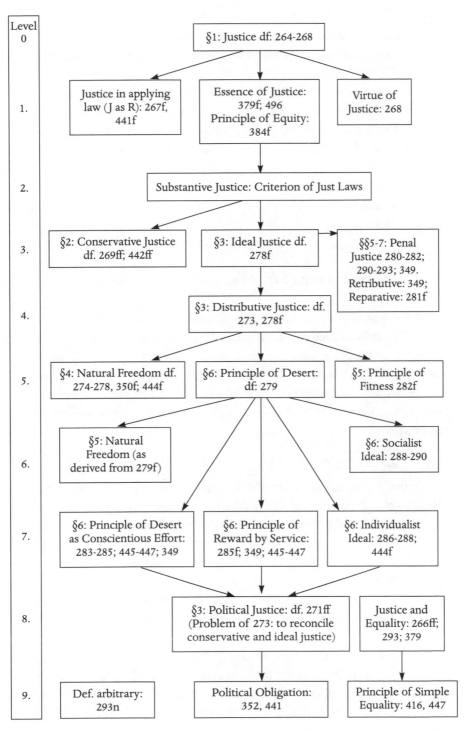

§1: Justice df: 264-268

Justice in applying law (J as R): 267f, 441f

Essence of Justice: 379f; 496
Principle of Equity: 384f

Virtue of Justice: 268

Substantive Justice: Criterion of Just Laws

§2: Conservative Justice df. 269ff; 442ff

§3: Ideal Justice df. 278f

§§5-7: Penal Justice 280-282; 290-293; 349. Retributive: 349; Reparative: 281f

§3: Distributive Justice: df. 273, 278f

§4: Natural Freedom df. 274-278, 350f; 444f

§6: Principle of Desert: df: 279

§5: Principle of Fitness 282f

§5: Natural Freedom (as derived from 279f)

§6: Socialist Ideal: 288-290

§6: Principle of Desert as Conscientious Effort: 283-285; 445-447; 349

§6: Principle of Reward by Service: 285f; 349; 445-447

§6: Individualist Ideal: 286-288; 444f

§3: Political Justice: df. 271ff (Problem of 273: to reconcile conservative and ideal justice)

Justice and Equality: 266ff; 293; 379

Def. arbitrary: 293n

Political Obligation: 352, 441

Principle of Simple Equality: 416, 447

Figure 8. Schema of Sidgwick's account of justice, *Methods*, Bk. III, Ch. 5

(e) In §5 (pp. 278–283): Nor does the realization of freedom answer to our common conception of ideal justice, which is rather that desert should be requited.

(f) In §6 (pp. 283–290): But the application of this principle likewise is very perplexing for it admits of different interpretations of desert: for example, desert may be estimated by conscientious effort, or by worth of what is done (of services); moreover, the principle of fitness is a complicating factor.

(g) §7 (pp. 290–294): Similarly, there are difficulties with *ill desert* in defining criminal justice. Sidgwick ends with a summary of his conclusions (pp. 293–294).

§2. Statement of the Classical Principle of Utility

Intuitively, the idea is to maximize the net balance of pleasure over pain.

(1) The principle applies quite generally to all subjects: in situations and practices, individual actions and traits of character, etc., and in all circumstances, both ideal and non-ideal. Thus: in any given situation, that institution or action, etc., is right, or that which ought to be done, if among all the feasible alternatives realizable in the circumstances, it is the one that maximizes:

$$\sum a_i u_i = a_1 u_1 + a_2 u_2 + \ldots + a_n u_n \text{ (a linear sum of the } u_i\text{'s)}$$

where the a_i's are real numbers (the weights of the u_i's) and the u_i's are real numbers that represent the utility (the net balance of pleasure over pain) for each individual *I*, these numbers taking into account all the consequences of the institution or action in question on every one of the individuals affected whatever their position in space or time, and so, e.g., however far into the future.

(2) To fix ideas assume that the individuals in question belong to the same society and leave aside all other individuals; however, include all persons for *m* generations into the future, when by hypothesis, the world comes to an end. The idea is the maximize utility over this stretch of time, leaving out the past, since bygones are bygones and not affected by human action.

(3) In the classical doctrine the weights a_i all $= 1$, for as J. S. Mill says this is implied by the notion of measuring pleasures and pains as objective

quantities given by their intensity and duration. Nothing so philosophical as an "equal right to happiness" is required contra Herbert Spencer (cf. J. S. Mill, *Utilitarianism*, Ch. 5: par. 36, footnote).

(4) The u_i's are, as stated, numbers that measure the net balance of happiness for each individual I over the relevant stretch of time (during which the institution or action in question has effects). We can imagine this stretch of time divided into unit intervals so each $u_i = u_{ij}, j = 1, \ldots, q$. But this is just frills, so no more of this kind of thing. You can see how it goes.

(5) The fundamental point is that the u_i's represent only one kind of information: namely the net balance of utility computed, or estimated, solely from the intensity and duration of the agreeable or disagreeable consciousness of pleasure and pain, regardless of any of the objective relations of individuals to one another that are conditions of these experiences, or the aims of the desires the satisfaction or dissatisfaction of which brings about pleasure or pain. In themselves, the pleasures of vindictive cruelty count equally with those of generosity and affection. As Bentham said: at the margin, push-pin is as good as poetry (a unit of one = a unit of the other).

§3. Some Comments about Interpersonal Comparisons of Utility (IP-Comparisons)

(1) In order to speak of maximizing a linear sum of utilities, we must assume that it makes sense to add the pleasures and pains of each individual and that the units in which these are estimated are the same for different individuals. The classical doctrine assumes full comparability of interpersonal comparisons: (a) that levels of happiness are comparable, and (b) in the same units. The Bentham-Edgeworth-Sidgwick line also assumes a natural zero, a point of indifference between pleasures and pains. On these matters, see Sidgwick's *Methods of Ethics*, Bk. II, Ch. 2.[9]

(2) The classical doctrine assumes that each individual can estimate and compare their own levels of happiness on the basis of introspection and memory: pleasures and pains are aspects directly known in experiences judged to be agreeable or disagreeable.

---

9. [See Sidgwick Lecture III of this volume for an extensive discussion of interpersonal comparisons of utility. —Ed.]

(3) Assuming the same natural zero for all individuals, and (following Edgeworth) the same just-noticeable difference in levels of happiness as the common unit for all individuals, as well as supposing that all individuals can rank consistently the differences between levels of happiness, it follows that the interpersonal comparisons required are forthcoming, and without relying on choices involving chance and risk. (These assumptions are extremely strong and seem implausible; but more on this later.)

§4. Some Features of the Principle of Utility as the First Principle of a Rational Method of Ethics

(1) We are especially concerned with those features of classical utilitarianism that lead Sidgwick to think it overcomes the defects of intuitionism, as shown in his discussion of justice (discussed in the previous lecture). With this in mind, notice first that utilitarianism is a single-principle conception: a conflict of first principles is impossible since there is only one such principle. This is a gain over intuitionism.

(2) Moreover, Sidgwick believes the principle of utility is the consequence of three self-evident (or seemingly self-evident) principles: (a) the principle of equity (or fairness) (*ME*, pp. 379f), which Sidgwick finds already formulated in essentials by Clarke (pp. 384f) and Kant (pp. 385f); (b) the Principle of Rational Self-Love (zero time preference) (p. 381); and (c) the Principle of Rational Benevolence (pp. 382f). These three principles, however, do not conflict but together yield the single principle of utility; and so the criterion of self-evidence is satisfied without giving up the criterion of having a guide in practice. (On this see Lecture I on Sidgwick at B: 5.)

(3) Sidgwick contends that the principle of utility is fully rational in that it is not limited or restricted by arbitrary exceptions or qualifications; it applies with full generality to all cases of practical reasoning; and the use of secondary rules or "middle axioms" (*ME*, p. 350) is explained by the principle itself, thus meeting the criterion discussed in Lecture I, B: 5.

(4) Finally, the utilitarian principle harmonizes and systematizes common-sense judgments and adjusts them in a coherent and consistent way. (See, for example, the discussion of ideal values in Bk. III, Ch. 14, and the conclusion (pp. 406f) that no principle but that of utility can organize these

judgments.) At the same time, this principle corrects our pre-reflective judgments and so criterion B: (5): (c): viii is also satisfied. Sidgwick assumes that our pre-reflective judgments (or some of them) have *some* prima facie validity, and so bringing order into them is further confirmation of the principle of utility. (See Bk. IV, Ch. 2, pp. 419–422.)

§5. Sidgwick's Critique of Natural Freedom as an Illustration

(1) In §4 of Bk. III, Ch. 5, Sidgwick argues that the Principle of Freedom—the principle that the whole of what people owe to one another, apart from contracts (including the enforcement of these), is freedom from interference—cannot be the first principle of a rational method of ethics. For one thing, (a) it contains arbitrary restrictions: for it does not itself account for why it doesn't apply to children and the mentally deficient and the like, but must tacitly invoke another principle, e.g. the utilitarian principle (*ME*, p. 275).

(2) Again, (b) it is ambiguous as between freedom of action allowing for all kinds of annoyances but barring constraint, or as including as well freedom from certain annoyances at least, although not presumably from all. But to find the mean between these two unacceptable extremes, some further principle is required, again, e.g. the utilitarian principle (pp. 275f).

(3) If a social order is to be possible using this principle, the Principle of Freedom must allow the right to limit one's freedom by contract. But this right itself must be limited since it hardly allows the right to sell oneself into slavery; yet to derive an appropriate limited right to limit one's freedom by contract from the Principle of Freedom alone seems impossible. We need some additional principle, which may then be superior in validity, etc. (p. 276).

(4) Turning to the question of the appropriation of material things and especially land (and here Sidgwick seems to have Locke in mind; in 1–3 above he has perhaps Spencer in mind), he argues that the principle of freedom would be best realized without any appropriation. If, in a society where all land is appropriated and some inherit no landed property, the argument is that everyone in society is nevertheless better off with appropriation than without, then the view is that interference with freedom can be compensated for. But this is, in effect, to appeal to another principle, and so

the realization of freedom cannot be "the one ultimate end of distributive justice" (pp. 276ff).

§6. Further Points Concerning Definition of the Principle of Utility

(1) The phrase "the greatest happiness of the greatest number" seems to occur first in Hutcheson's *Inquiry Concerning Moral Good and Evil* (1725): see III, §8. This phrase has led some to regard the principle as nonsense, since it presents two aims (happiness and numbers) to maximize. But this is a misunderstanding: the principle is to maximize total happiness, and this means that the *distribution* of happiness among existing people, or over generations, as well as the number of people (so far as social policy affects this), are all to be decided by what maximizes total (not average) utility. Sidgwick is clear on these points: see *ME*, pp. 415f (see also *A Theory of Justice*, pp. 161ff).

(2) Note that the principle of utility puts no weight at all on *equality* (in the sense of an equal distribution of utility): the *only* thing that counts is *total* utility. This is implied by the additive nature of the principle (to maximize a linear sum of the u_i's). Observe that if the principle were said to multiply utilities, there would be a push in favor of equality. Thus the mathematical form already incorporates an *ethical* notion: namely, distribution is not significant.

(3) In practice, regarding, e.g., legislation, utilitarians often assume people have similar capacities for pleasure and pain, and that the principle of diminished marginal utility holds: all this implies equality, *ceteris paribus*, in distributing the means of happiness.

LECTURE III

Sidgwick's Utilitarianism (Fall 1975)

§1. Introduction to Utilitarianism

(1) As I have said before, utilitarianism is the longest (oldest) continuous tradition in English moral philosophy. By English I mean: written in the

English language; many of the important utilitarian writers are Scottish—Francis Hutcheson, David Hume, and Adam Smith—and in this century it has had strong representatives in the United States. It is no exaggeration to say, I think, that beginning with the second quarter of the 18th century utilitarianism has more or less succeeded in dominating English moral philosophy. By dominating, I mean:

(a) It counts among its representatives an extraordinary sequence of writers—Hutcheson, Hume, Smith, Bentham, the two Mills, Sidgwick, and Edgeworth—who in numbers and intellectual power surpass that of any other line of moral philosophy, including social contract theory, idealism, intuitionism, and perfectionism. (Keep in mind that I am talking about English moral philosophy, and not that of the continent: Germany, France, etc.)

(b) Again, utilitarianism has tended to control the course of philosophical debate insofar as other traditions have labored to construct an alternative to it, often unsuccessfully. While intuitionism or idealism may succeed in establishing various weaknesses in utilitarianism, they fare less well in formulating an equally systematic doctrine that can match that of the best utilitarian writers. Primary among the intuitionists I have in mind are Butler, Price, Reid, and Whewell, while the main 19th-century British Idealists are Hamilton, Bradley, and Green.

(c) Further, utilitarianism has had very close ties with social theory, and its leading representatives have also been major political theorists and economists. Consider this striking fact: of all the great classical political economists, every single one—with the exception of Ricardo—has an equally important place in utilitarianism as a tradition of moral philosophy! One has only to list the names: thus,

18th century: Hume, Adam Smith, and Jeremy Bentham.

19th century: James and J. S. Mill, Edgeworth, and Sidgwick (the latter two more in economics and philosophy, respectively, but they had both interests). Sidgwick's third book, *The Principles of Political Economy* (1884; 3rd ed. 1901), is a short treatise in utilitarian welfare economics, in a sense the first.

In the 20th century, utilitarianism has had far more influence in economics than any other moral philosophy, where it was represented by Marshall and Pigou; only with the 1930s did the hold of the classical doctrine fail. But still today many economists hold what they call a very general form of utilitarianism. More on this later.

It is, therefore, absolutely necessary to give utilitarianism careful attention. A tradition of this force cannot be without great merit.

(2) Now, a few brief comments about the beginnings of utilitarianism in modern times. Like so much else of modern English moral philosophy and social theory, it is convenient to say: it starts with Hobbes and the reaction to Hobbes. We must keep in mind that Hobbes is an overwhelming figure—a marvelous writer with a vigorous style, and seemingly a perfect form of expression of his peculiarly deep, and somewhat terrifying, vision of political life. Hobbes aroused a violent intellectual reaction: to be regarded as a Hobbist was somewhat dangerous, and the reasons are easy to see: Hobbes was the chief representative of modern infidelity.

Consider and compare with Hobbes an orthodox Christian moralist like Cudworth, who espoused roughly the philosophical views shown in the left column of Figure 9.

Compare this with how he [Cudworth] interpreted Hobbes (as did much of the age (right column).[10] To see what Hobbes meant to his age, what violence he did to the Christian moral and philosophical tradition, there is no better source than Cudworth's *True Intellectual System* (1671) (imprimatur), (1678) (date of publication).

(3) However, the reaction of the leading utilitarians to Hobbes was, of course, very different from Cudworth's. (Here I leave aside the theological utilitarians—Gay, Paley, and Austin—as special cases; and some were theologians or theists, such as Hutcheson and Smith.) For the most part, what bothered them about Hobbes was not his atheism, if atheist he was, or his materialism, determinism, and individualism. In some reasonable sense, Hume, Bentham, the two Mills, and Sidgwick also held these views. What they rejected in Hobbes rather (or in what Hobbes was taken to mean or represent) was:

(i) The doctrine of psychological egoism and ethical egoism.

(ii) The idea that political authority is legitimated by superior power (though this is doubtfully Hobbes's view), or by agreements made in the face of superior power, or indeed that it rests on a social contract at all, or on any kind of contract (in the usual sense).

(iii) The thesis of ethical relativism.

10. John Passmore, *Ralph Cudworth* (1951), pp. 11f.

Thus, it is useful to think of classical utilitarianism (the line of writers from Hutcheson-Hume to Sidgwick-Edgeworth) roughly in this way, namely, as the attempt to formulate in reaction to Hobbes:

(a) a moral and political conception that gave an account of the grounds of political authority, not as based on power but on moral principles; and one that was not relativistic, nor based on psychological egoism, nor ethical egoism.

At the same time, classical utilitarianism accepted as conditions of the state of modern culture that a moral and political conception must be secular, that is:

(b) classical utilitarianism does not base moral first principles in the divine will, and it is fully compatible with the denial of theism (in the traditional sense). It is compatible also with: materialism, determinism, and individualism, and so with what are thought to be the conclusions of social theory and natural sciences.

In sum: classical utilitarianism was the first tradition to develop a systematic moral conception under the assumption of a secular society under modern conditions. Much of the effort of utilitarian writers is devoted to opposing the orthodox moral tradition and to establishing a moral basis for political institutions entirely free from any theological background; and designed to be compatible with secular assumptions and the trends of the modern world.

You will observe that the notion of a truly based well-ordered society as a reasonable political criterion rests on the same idea. So we may accept this objective: we can do this without implying that the orthodox [theological] assumptions are false. It suffices to develop a moral doctrine that does

Cudworth	Hobbes
Theism	Atheism
Dualism (mind and body)	Materialism
Free will (libertarianism)	Determinism
Organic theory of the state	Individualism
Eternal and immutable morality	Ethical relativism

Figure 9.

not presuppose this [theological] basis (if this is possible). I shall assume that all the views we discuss accept this background objective.

§2. The Statement of the Classical Principle of Utility (Sidgwick)

(1) Sidgwick gives a careful statement of the principle in *Methods of Ethics*, Bk. IV, Ch. I. I shall go over the main points, making a few comments for purposes of clarification: I define utilitarianism ("Universalistic Hedonism," as he sometimes says) as the ethical conception that holds that the (objectively) right institution or set of institutions, or the objectively right conduct (of individuals), in any given circumstances is that which will produce the greatest amount of happiness on the whole. Or which will lead to the greatest net balance of happiness (agreeable feeling).

In this sum of happiness that is to be maximized, we are to include all individuals (persons), whoever they are, that are affected by the institution or conduct (that is, whose happiness is affected positively, or negatively). Actually, the classical utilitarians thought that in principle it was necessary to include all sentient beings and therefore all animals or living things that can experience pleasure and pain. Capacity and liability for these feelings requires them to be included. This is an important aspect of utilitarianism that we shall note later; for the moment let's suppose that the consequences of institutions and actions are limited to human individuals and subsequent generations of individuals.

Formally, we can write the utilitarian principle the following way: Let $u_1, \ldots, u_n$ be the utilities (numbers representing the degree of happiness) of the n individuals affected by the institution (or system of institutions) or the actions in question: say the n individuals in society, or whatever [group]. Let $a_1, \ldots, a_n$ be the weight of these utilities. Then, the principle is:

$$\text{To maximize: } \sum a_i u_i = a_1 u_1 + \ldots + a_n u_n$$

That is: the right alternative (institution or act (or whatever)) is that alternative (institution or act) which belongs to the set of feasible (possible) alternatives that maximizes this function. (Assume for the moment that there are no ties.)

It is immediately obvious that this principle is not that of ethical egoism: everyone's happiness is taken into account and given some weight (assuming all the $a_i > 0$).

(2) Let us at this point notice a very important feature of this principle: the u_i's are numerical measures of happiness, and for Sidgwick the ultimate good is agreeable feelings or agreeable experiences (or consciousness) (more on this later). These are states of mind or aspects thereof, and they are known, as it were directly, by introspection: they are, so to speak, *complete in themselves* (over a certain interval of time) and *good* in themselves (or in the case of pain, bad in themselves). The recognition of these feelings does not presuppose, or use, any principle that involves the concept of right, or justice, etc., or any concepts that fall under these. Thus, classical utilitarianism uses a notion of happiness and of ultimate good that is defined *independently* and, as it were, *prior to all other moral notions,* or at any rate, prior to those of right and justice and of moral virtue and moral worth. This is characteristic of *teleological* conceptions, and so utilitarianism is a teleological doctrine.[11]

Where it differs from other teleological conceptions is in its definition of good—of what it is that is to be maximized. Thus perfectionism says that we are to maximize certain forms of excellence (human and other perfections) or certain other values: beautiful things, or knowledge of the world (or the main structural parts, etc. thereof), or some mix of these.[12] (Sometimes the term "ideal utilitarianism" is used for this view, but this is a misnomer.) Examples of perfectionism are found in G. E. Moore and Hastings Rashdall and many other writers who give some weight to perfectionist values.

But classical utilitarianism defines the good to be maximized subjectively, that is, in terms of agreeable feelings or experiences (consciousness) of (human) individuals.

(3) This may seem like an overly narrow definition of good. I have used it first because it has a certain clarity and simplicity about it; and second, because it is Sidgwick's (and Bentham's and Edgeworth's) view; and Sidgwick has several interesting arguments for it (which I shall mention later). His view is the sharpest statement of the strict classical doctrine and he resists all efforts to depart from it, especially those of Mill (whom we take up next); and Moore, etc.

If we wish, however, the utilitarian notion of goodness can be inter-

---

11. [See John Rawls, *A Theory of Justice* (Cambridge, Mass.: Harvard University Press, rev. ed., 1999), pp. 21–23, 35–36, 490–491, 495–496, for a discussion of teleological doctrines and their contrast with contract doctrines. —Ed.]

12. [See *A Theory of Justice*, section 50, on the Principle of Perfection. —Ed.]

preted much more widely; thus as the satisfaction or fulfillment of non-hedonistic human interests; or as the satisfaction or fulfillment of rational (human) interests, imposing certain tests of rationality, provided that these do not involve the other moral concepts (rights and moral worth, etc.): that is, we allow for a certain appropriately limited class of corrections to human interests or desires (by rational deliberation, etc.). Or more generally, we may think of the good as happiness defined as the successful execution of a rational plan of life (again with "rational" appropriately defined).[13] Utilitarianism can be enlarged to include these variations, and many common objections to the doctrine are not as plausible against these forms of utilitarianism. Certainly Mill, for example, wants to categorize the good to be maximized in this sort of way (at least).[14]

The crucial feature of the definition of the good in utilitarianism is this: (a) that it defines the good independently (from concepts of right and moral worth); and (b) subjectively: what is good is (i) agreeable feeling (or consciousness) (pleasure), or (ii) the satisfaction of rational individual interests—defined relative to people's actual interests—(with "rational" suitably limited), or (iii) execution of rational plans of life (happiness); and (c) it is in a certain sense individualistic: ultimate good is attributed solely to the conscious experience of individual persons and presupposes no objective relations. In any case, (d) it is the sum of this good (these goods of individuals) that is to be maximized. Perhaps the best way to be clear about what this sense of individualism amounts to is to contrast it with other views.

(4) Permissible Variations or Refinements: Let's explain in more detail the notion of a permissible variation (or refinement) of classical utilitarianism: namely, what is the point of this notion and what do we mean by it? First its point: there is a tendency to use the term "utilitarianism" extremely loosely, so that there are many distinctly different kinds of moral conceptions said to be utilitarian. This looseness has an unfortunate effect: it obscures the structure of different moral doctrines, and we fail to keep in mind what is special about each. So we need a notion of permissible variation of utilitarianism to specify those variations all of which share the characteristic or special structure of the classical utilitarian view.

Now what is this characteristic structure? (a) First, it is the characteristic

13. [See here Rawls's account of a person's good in terms of the rational plan of life that a person would choose under conditions of deliberative rationality, taking into account the Aristotelian Principle. *A Theory of Justice*, sections 63–66. —Ed.]

14. See the Appendix to this lecture on permissible variations of utilitarianism.

structure that utilitarianism shares with teleological doctrines generally: namely, that the notion of the good is defined prior to and independent from the right (and all the concepts that fall under it); and then right is defined as maximizing the good. This way of introducing the right is one aspect of the natural intuitive idea that underlies utilitarianism. It is the idea that rational conduct and decision is maximizing the good: striving for the greatest good. (Contrast Social Contract Theory.)

(b) Second, the characteristic feature of utilitarianism as distinct from other teleological conceptions is that it defines the good subjectively, roughly speaking from the point of view of the subject: the individual human agent. What this means in this case is this:

(i) The good is defined as agreeable or desirable consciousness; or pleasure rather than pain; or as the satisfaction of desire, according to its intensity and duration.

(ii) The capacities for pleasure and pain, or the relevant desires and aversions, are those which, at any given time, people actually have. We start at each moment in our deliberations from those aspects of people as they are, or can be foreseen to be. Practical reason is based upon *given* propensities and desires.

Thus what is characteristic of classical utilitarianism is that it treats the person according to its capacities for pleasure and pain, satisfaction, etc. Its claims upon social resources depend upon these. And this is in contrast with some other views which regard the claims of the person differently, e.g. Social Contract Theory, Kant's theory.

Now to define a permissible variation of utilitarianism: namely, one that preserves these features and does not introduce elements inconsistent with them. The idea is that in examining utilitarianism, we want to see if any view that has these features can be correct. It would be progress to show that all views with these features must be unsatisfactory.

For this reason, we might be willing (as I suggested earlier) to permit the view—when it strengthened its case and made it a better conception—to suppose that the good is defined as satisfaction of *rational* desires, where these are the desires individuals would have if they subjected their present actual desires to certain forms of rational assessment (by the principles of rational choice). This gives a different view (a variation), but we might want to count it as a permissible variation within the same structure.

The point is: we would not have found the basic fault of utilitarianism if we did not allow it this variation when it made the view better. (As discussed below, limits on actual desires via constraints of the concept of right are not allowed.)

§3. Points about Interpersonal Comparisons

(1) It is clear that the notion of summing up the pleasures (for simplicity) or degrees of happiness of different individuals presupposes that we have some way of comparing and estimating the pleasures experienced by distinct persons. We can say, for example, that individual A has twice the pleasures as individual B, etc.

Let us make a few observations about these points:

First, we assume that the a_i's are all equal and so let them be 1. This presumably is what Bentham meant (as quoted by Mill in *Utilitarianism*, Ch. V, par. 36) by: "everybody to count for one, nobody for more than one." Mill interprets this weighting rule correctly: it does not imply, as Spencer argues in *Social Statistics,* an equal right to happiness; instead it follows from the independent definition of good as pleasure, or satisfaction, etc. As Mill says: it supposes only that equal amounts of happiness (pleasure) are equally desirable (good) whether felt by the same or different persons. All of this is implicit in the idea of measurement applied to pleasures. It is part of the principle of utility itself, not a premise needed to support it.[15] So Mill says. This is fair enough given the understanding of good as pleasure (satisfaction) and nothing but pleasure. (Contrast Maine's Brahmin, who would weight the pleasure of one who is a Brahmin 20 times that of those who are not; he needs to modify the strict classical principle in some way to reach his conclusion.)[16]

15. Mill says: "Mr. Herbert Spencer . . . says the principle of utility presupposes the anterior principle that everybody has an equal right to happiness. It may be more correctly described as supposing that equal amounts of happiness are equally desirable, whether felt by the same or different persons. This, however, is not a *pre*supposition, not a premise needful to support the principle of utility, but the very principle itself; for what is the principle of utility if it be not that 'happiness' and 'desirable' are synonymous terms? If there is any anterior principle implied, it can be no other than this, that the truths of arithmetic are applicable to the valuation of happiness, as of all other measurable quantities." *Utilitarianism*, ch. V, footnote to paragraph 36.

16. Henry Maine, *Lectures on the Early History of Institutions* (London: Murray, 1897), pp. 397ff.

(2) Thus, henceforth, we assume that the weights are all = 1. We may add here that this is true of all individuals, however far distant in space or time; and since our actions are limited in their effects to the present or future, we can say (letting bygones be bygones) that the pleasures of all future persons have the same weights as those of present persons. There is then no pure time preference: this means that if we discount future pleasures, either our own or those of other people, this must be for some other reason than mere location in time or space alone; otherwise we apply the principle of utility incorrectly. For example, we must say: that some prospective pleasures are for various reasons more or less probable, their realization more or less uncertain. If so, they may be discounted, or weighted according to their estimated probability or likelihood; this gives the so-called mathematical expectation. But this form of discounting does not imply pure time preference: this discounting is based on reasonable estimates of uncertainty (probability) and not simply on the fact that a pleasure is distant (future) in time.

(3) Now for a few words about *interpersonal comparisons*. Evidently to arrive at interpersonal comparisons of utility we need two things at least:

(a) A cardinal measure of utility for each individual (all *n* of them) and

(b) A way of matching up the measures of utility of distinct individuals so that we can meaningfully relate and add: in short, we need correspondence rules that tell us how to compare and weight the pleasures of different persons.

To do (a) alone is not sufficient; only if we can do both (a) and (b), and do so in some satisfactory way, have we established a way to make interpersonal comparisons.

Some points about these cardinal measures: first, in the classical doctrine the individual cardinal measures of utility were based on individuals' estimates of their own happiness arrived at by introspection and reflection and by their comparisons among their various states of well-being: the intensity and duration of their states of agreeable or disagreeable consciousness. In a word: individuals were thought (a) to be able to rank their various levels of well-being in a consistent way; they could also say (b) the difference between the levels of states A and B is equal to (or greater or less than) the difference between C and D. On these two assumptions, a cardinal measure for each individual does exist; and such a measure is independent from choices (preferences) involving risk or uncertainty. (Another possible measure is based on a theory that goes back to Edgeworth; this measure too is independent from risks and uncertainty.)[17] Thus the classical measure is *not* to be confused with the von Neumann–Morgenstern measure of utility, which is based on consistent choices over lotteries (various combinations of probability weighted alternatives). (Perhaps we can say more on this later.)[18]

Second, in setting up the correspondence rules so that we can add the utility measures of distinct individuals, it is *not necessary* that we be able to compare the levels (absolute levels) of the well-being of these individuals. Unit comparability suffices; level comparability is unnecessary. (Full comparability = level plus unit comparability.) Since we are maximizing the sum of well-being, all that matters is how much (by how many units) each individual goes up or down, from where they are, as a result of realizing the various feasible alternatives. Whether individual A, say, goes up or down n units from a level higher or lower than the level of B does not matter, assuming unit comparability. The institution or policy or action that leads to the largest net increase (balance of $+$'s and $-$'s) from the present situation will maximize utility over those alternatives.[19]

17. [In *A Theory of Justice*, rev. ed., section 49, p. 282, Rawls says the following: —Ed.
"There are several ways of establishing an interpersonal measure of utility. One of these (going back at least to Edgeworth) is to suppose that an individual is able to distinguish only a finite number of utility levels. A person is said to be indifferent between alternatives that belong to the same discrimination level, and the cardinal measure of the utility difference between any two alternatives is defined by the number of distinguishable levels that separate them. The cardinal scale that results is unique, as it must be, up to a positive linear transformation. To set up a measure between persons one might assume that the difference between adjacent levels is the same for all individuals and the same between all levels. With this interpersonal correspondence rule the calculations are extremely simple. In comparing alternatives we ascertain the number of levels between them for each individual and then sum, taking account of the pluses and minuses. See A. K. Sen, *Collective Choice and Social Welfare* (San Francisco: Holden-Day, 1970), pp. 93f; for Edgeworth, see *Mathematical Psychics* (London: Kegan Paul, 1888), pp. 7–9, 60f."]

18. [See Rawls, *A Theory of Justice*, rev. ed., section 49, pp. 283–284, for a discussion of the von Neumann–Morgenstern definition of utility and problems with interpersonal comparisons of utility. —Ed.]

19. When economists speak of "adding utilities at the margin" they mean something like this, and precisely this if we suppose that the gains and losses (measured in goods and services) are sufficiently small so that the marginal utility of each individual stays approximately constant over the whole interval of possible gains and losses measured in goods and services, etc. [This sentence was crossed out in Rawls's handwritten lecture notes. —Ed.]

§4. Philosophical Constraints on a
Satisfactory Measure of Interpersonal Comparisons

(1) There are at least two very important philosophical constraints on any satisfactory set of correspondence rules for interpersonal comparisons. Unless these are fulfilled, we have not yet defined a plausible utilitarian view. The first constraint is that the correspondence rules must be both meaningful and acceptable from the moral point of view as interpreted by the particular form of utilitarianism in question—in the present case, the strict classical doctrine. Not any kind of correspondence will be admissible. Moreover, all correspondence rules seem to involve some rather strong ethical assumptions, or at least assumptions with ethical implications, and these presuppositions must accord with the view in question.

(2) To illustrate: there is the well-known *zero-one rule*. This says: assuming that we have individual cardinal measures, and assuming that these measures are bounded above and below, pair these corresponding lower and upper bounds each with zero and one respectively. This sets up an interpersonal cardinal measure, but is it a measure we want? Does it define an aim that we want to maximize (given the utilitarian view)? Think about this in the light of the following extreme (and no doubt non-serious) example: this example has the merit of clearly exhibiting the difficulty. Consider a society that at time t_0 consists of n people and m cats about equal in numbers (each person has their cat, as it were). Including all sentient beings, write: To maximize:

$$\sum u_i = u_1 + \ldots + u_n + u_{n+1} + \ldots + u_{n+m}$$

An amount of manna X falls each Hicksian week[20] (time period): how to distribute it? Now, cats are more easy to get near the bliss point ($u = 1$) than people (adopting the 0–1 rule), let's assume. So, perhaps over time, we maximize the sum of utilities by reducing the ratio of n/m so that at time t. (the optimum) there are relatively few people collecting and distributing the manna to lots of nearly blissfully happy cats. (I assume the amount of

---

20. [John R. Hicks (1904–1989), a British economist who won the Nobel Prize jointly with Kenneth Arrow in 1972. —Ed.]

manna is fixed at X for all t.) The explanation of this conclusion is that cats are more efficient producers of utility per unit of X, if we use the 0–1 rule.

This example is not offered as a serious objection, but rather to bring home vividly the difficulty. Namely, just because we can establish *some* interpersonal measure so far proves nothing: this measure must define an aim that from a philosophical standpoint the theory says we should maximize, or one that we can live with. If the interpersonal measure has unacceptable implications, the utilitarian presumably has something else in mind. The point then is this: any scheme of correspondence rules has, it seems, ethical implications, (a) via the implications of the resulting principle, and (b) via the embedding of ethical notions in the correspondence rules; and it has ethical implications even if the scheme *seems* to involve no moral notions or principles. It has these implications because it sets up an aim that we are to maximize; and to maximize as the sole end of institutions and actions. Moreover, sometimes it may be clear that some ethical conceptions are embedded in the correspondence rules, e.g., is the 0–1 rule a way of saying that sentient beings have equal rights, or (perhaps better) equal claims to maximize satisfaction? For contrast this case with Mill's reply to Spencer: that pleasures *qua* their intrinsic properties of intensity and duration (say) are equal regardless of whose pleasure they are. In the example above, we say simply: the total range of human pleasures (over all individuals) equals (by stipulation) the total range of feline pleasure (over all cats) regardless of variations between human individuals or between individual cats, or between cats and people. What justifies this stipulation? If we reject the 0–1 rule for cats and people, what is the correct ratio? Does the 0–1 rule hold for all people? Should we aim for simple pleasures, as the 0–1 rule implies?[21]

(3) Second, the correspondence scheme (for interpersonal comparisons) must not involve any ethical notions or principles that depend upon the notions of *right* or of *moral worth*. The reason for this is that the classical doctrine introduces the concept of right as that of maximizing some independently defined notion of good. (One clarifies this by giving examples: e.g., hedonism, human excellence, etc.)

We may have seen that the 0–1 rule may involve some ethical notion, for example of equal rights or equal claims to (maximized) satisfaction. Of

---

21. [See *A Theory of Justice*, rev. ed., pp. 284–285, for a related discussion of the value assumptions underlying interpersonal comparisons.]

course, this is no objection to the view that uses the resulting principle; but what we need to be clear about is that this principle is no longer the classical principle of utility: it is something else. We introduced a principle of equal claims for all sentient (or human) beings; and where did we get that? Not from its being the best way to maximize utility; for we have used it in defining utility. So it is a basic first principle perhaps; if so, then this needs to be made explicit. Finally, why *add* utilities? Why not take the greater product of utilities, which normally results in less inequality in the distribution of utility?

(4) Again, the standard assumptions that utilitarian writers often use may be covert ways of introducing or adding first principles.[22] This depends on how these assumptions are used and justified. If they are followed irrespective of the actual facts of individual psychology, then to this extent they are first principles; and mean in effect: always treat people as if these assumptions hold. If so, these first principles must be explicitly noted; and once again, we no longer have the strict classical doctrine.[23]

(5) Finally, a more subtle instance of the same problem is this: we must be careful to count among pleasures or satisfactions only states of consciousness or feelings that are suitably characterized: that is, solely by the good and by non-moral notions. Thus it is no argument against certain inequalities, say, from a utilitarian standpoint that people resent them; or that these inequalities make them indignant. For resentment and indignation are moral feelings: they imply that the individual affirms some conception of right and justice, etc., and presuppose a belief that the principles defining these conceptions are violated by these inequalities. Such an argument is

22. See Maine, *Lectures on the Early History of Institutions*, pp. 399f. [See *A Theory of Justice*, rev. ed., p. 285, where Rawls says the following of this same reference: —Ed.] "Maine's assumptions on the standard utilitarian assumptions are apropos here. He suggests that the grounds for these assumptions are clear once we see that they are simply a working rule of legislation, and that this is how Bentham regarded them. Given a populous and reasonably homogeneous society and an energetic modern legislature, the only principle that can guide legislation on a large scale is the principle of utility. The necessity to neglect differences between persons, even very real ones, leads to the maxim to count all equally, and to the similarity and marginal postulates. Surely the conventions for interpersonal comparisons are to be judged in the same light. The contract doctrine holds that once we see this, we shall also see that the idea of measuring and summing well-being is best abandoned entirely."

23. Cf. Lionel Robbins, *The Nature and Significance of Economic Science* (London: Macmillan, 1932), p. 141.

not permitted by the constraints on the classical view. What a classical utilitarian must argue instead is that certain inequalities cause so much envy and anguish, or so much apathy and depression (all, say, unpleasant states of mind), that the greater balance of happiness is generally achieved by eliminating these inequalities. Even if we take these moral feelings into account, we are to weight them solely by their intensity and duration as feelings. Is that appropriate?

(6) A further example to illustrate the way in which moral notions may be included in individual utility functions is the following. Suppose we include a variable that represents individuals' appraisal of, or attitude toward, the existing distribution of goods, or even of satisfaction (we assume that all individuals know what this distribution is). And assume that, for this purpose, the relevant feature of the existing distribution is based on the Gini-coefficient: each individual is pleased or displeased according to the degree of inequality as measured by this coefficient.[24] They are more pleased as equality increases, *ceteris parabis*, although individuals may differ in the desire for equality. Then each u_i looks something like this:

$$U_i = U_i \, (X, I, G) \text{ and so maximize } \sum U_i \text{ as defined}$$

where X is a vector of goods; I is income; and G is the Gini-coefficient.

Here we can assume that (to simplify) we have, for each individual, indifference curves something like those in Figure 10.

This scheme can fit into either an ordinal or coordinal theory. For our purposes here, let's assume that the indifference curves have meaningful cardinal measures that mesh appropriately, via correspondence rules, with the measures of other individuals (interpersonal comparisons are valid).

Now the point is this: we can formally proceed to maximize the net balance of utility. But the theory is no longer teleological in the required sense:

(a) By including an entry for the Gini-coefficient, individuals take distri-

24. [The Gini-coefficient, attributed to Gini (1912), is a measure of inequality.
"There are various ways of defining the Gini coefficient, and a bit of manipulation . . . reveals that it is exactly one-half of the relative mean difference, which is defined as the arithmetic average of the absolute values of differences between all pairs of incomes. . . . Undoubtedly one appeal of the Gini coefficient, or of the relative mean difference, lies in the fact that it is a very direct measure of income difference, taking note of differences between *every* pair of incomes." Amartya Sen, *On Economic Inequality* (Oxford: Oxford University Press, 1997), pp. 30–31.]

bution into account. Offhand it looks as if they have a pattern principle of the first kind (a principle based on the pattern of distribution as represented by some property computed from the distribution of goods and income (the X's and I's)).

(b) We need to know on what basis individuals are really taking distribution into account. Is it really that their response to G is based on:

(i) benevolence and sympathetic temperament
(ii) moral convictions springing from a view of the duties of beneficence
(iii) convictions of justice in distribution; and of what conception more specifically

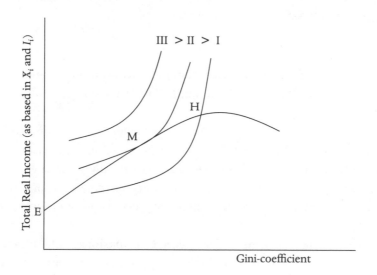

Figure 10.

EH curve = maximum output (given Gini-coefficient)[a]
So H = maximum output (over all Gini-coefficients)
So M = most preferred point (for individual i)[b]

   a. [notes on the graph: E labels the point of intersection between the vertical axis and the EH curve; M labels the point of intersection between the EH curve and II; H labels the point of intersection between the EH curve and I. —Ed.]

   b. Cf. William Breit, "Income Redistribution and Efficiency Norms," in Hochman and Peterson, *Redistribution Through Public Choice* (1974).

(iv) views about the advisability of greater equality for social stability

(v) views about general advisability of reducing envy and depression

(vi) views about insuring against possible losses in the future to oneself: risk aversion to greater inequalities and so a wish to establish public policy of less inequality

(c) The last three are compatible with teleological constraints; while the first three, with the possible exception of the first, (i), are not.

From the standpoint of moral theory, what we want to know is not on what basis people actually do take distribution into account (presumably all six above reasons and more influence this or that individual), but on what basis they think they should take them into account. And what their moral conceptions are in this respect. Thus, in particular, what allowance does classical utilitarianism make for distribution?

§5. Some Points Regarding Greatest Numbers and Happiness and Maximizing Total vs. Average Utility

(1) The phrase "the greatest happiness for the greatest numbers" occurs first, it seems, in Francis Hutcheson, *An Inquiry Concerning Moral Good and Evil* (1725), Sec. III, §8. This phrase has occasionally given rise to the confusion as to whether the principle of utility directs us to maximize total pleasure, or to maximize the number of persons, or some weighted mix of both.

The classical doctrine is clear: we are to maximize total pleasure (net balance of pleasure over pain). In the long run numbers (or the size of society) is to be adjusted accordingly. This is what the classical view says. To maximize a weighted mix of net pleasure (total) and numbers represents an intuitionist view and is no part of the classical doctrine. Perhaps it should also be said that the absurdity attributed to Bentham's utilitarianism by von Neumann and Morgenstern (in the 2nd edition of *Theory of Games,* 1947), namely, that Bentham wanted to maximize two things at once, aggregate happiness and numbers, is incorrect. Neither Bentham, Edgeworth, nor Sidgwick would fall into this foolishness.

(2) Second, there is the question whether we are to maximize *total* utility or *average* utility (well-being per capita over the members of society).

Here again the classical view is perfectly clear: we are to maximize *total*, not average, utility. Of course, the two are the same in the short run with n fixed (n = population of society). But in the long run n is not fixed, and under certain conditions the total and average views give different results for population policy or indeed for any social policies insofar as they influence the size of population (e.g., via effects on birth rate, death rate, etc.). Crucial among the conditions in determining population size is the relative rate at which average utility decreases if population increases. If average utility falls slowly enough, the loss in the average may *always* be less than the gain in the total from greater numbers, so one can theoretically be led to a very large population of very low (for each individual, positive > 0) utility; rather than a far smaller population that would maximize average utility. Perhaps, however, utilitarianism is not a feasible principle for population policy in any case. If so, then the question is, how is the classical utilitarian to get a complete view?

It is to be observed that Sidgwick is clear on both these points. (See *ME*, pp. 415f.) This is, among other reasons, why I say Sidgwick is the best representative of the classical view: he is aware of all these sorts of points and resolves them each time in ways consistent with that view. Note again that if we say average rather than total utility is what should be maximized, we seem to be introducing a new or distinct first principle. For if pleasure *alone* is the sole good, it seems clear that we are to maximize the sum of it. Why in this case does the average matter at all?

§6. Concluding Remarks

(1) It is important to emphasize the point of the preceding remarks. The introductory historical remarks are to highlight the long continuity of the utilitarian tradition; its striking dominance (in at least three respects) over the course of English (speaking) moral philosophy since the first quarter (at least) of the 18th century; and its close tie with social theory, especially political theory and economics: there is nothing else anywhere that approaches this pattern of features.

Also, we must realize that, with some but not much qualification, the leading utilitarians attempted to work out, in reaction to Hobbes, an acceptable moral theory for a secular society with the features of the modern world. Their reaction to Hobbes (in contrast with the orthodox Christian response, e.g. Cudworth) brings out this aspect of their work: they represent the first modern moral and political theory.

(2) Also, second, I have discussed Sidgwick as the last of the leading strict classical utilitarians: the Bentham-Edgeworth-Sidgwick trio. Sidgwick's presentation is the most detailed; he is fully aware of most (at least) of the problems (as not even all contemporary utilitarians are). One needs to recognize the many complications in formulating what seems at first sight a rather simple principle (conception). Actually, the initial simplicity makes the complexity easier to see.

(3) Finally, we went over quickly some of the matters that arise in establishing interpersonal comparisons of well-being. This was merely to highlight the problems, to illustrate the difficulties. For example, the 0–1 rule is not, I think, even approximately satisfactory over all sentient beings, though it's better over human beings. But it shows where many deep troubles lie. We shan't pursue these questions further now. Yet one must be aware of the problems.

Appendix to Lecture III:
Regarding Cardinal Interpersonal Comparisons

Points: The main points are these:

(1) We need two things to apply utilitarian principle:

   (a) A cardinal measure for each individual.

   (b) Meaningful correspondence rules to correlate these measures: at least unit comparability.

(2) Cardinal vs. Ordinal Measures:

   (a) Ordinal simply defines a complete ordering of better and worse, but not how much worse or better.

   (b) Cardinal measure defines a zero and a unit and says how many units between levels.

   (c) There is no unique scale but all scales in cardinal measures related by positive linear transformation (e.g. temperature scales). In ordinal, positive monotonic transformation.

(3) In classical cardinal individual measures, e.g. Sidgwick: *ME,* Bk. III, Ch. II:

(a) Individuals can rank levels of well-being by introspection (complete ordering).

(b) Individuals can rank differences between levels by introspection (complete ordering of differences between levels). These ((a) and (b)) give a cardinal individual measure.

(c) In making these rankings, no choices or decision involving risk or uncertainty are involved.

(4) Re Correspondence Rules: These are needed to match up the measures of distinct individuals:[25]

(a) Level comparability is a matching of levels.

(b) Unit comparability is a matching of units (how many units of individual A = 1 unit of individual B).

(c) Full comparability = Level plus unit. For application of utilitarianism we need only unit comparability (utilitarianism interested in totals, not levels).

(5) Zero-One Rule as Illustration:

(a) If we work out the consequences of this rule for a society of people and cats, we get what may be odd results. But if we reject the rule for people-cat correspondence, why do we do so? Is it just that we don't want to be slaves to cats? And what is the correct ratio, not exactly, but even roughly? Very roughly?

(b) If the 0–1 rule fails to hold for people and cats, does it hold between all people? Why can't the reasons that lead us to reject it for the people-cat correspondence lead us to reject it between different kinds of people? And can we, or should we, accept this implication? Again, how consistent are the reasons for rejection with the classical utilitarian view? Do they involve a doctrine of the different qualities of pleasure in a way utilitarianism can't allow? (e.g., J. S. Mill, although his view is unclear).

(c) Does the 0–1 rule imply that we should cultivate simple and easily satisfiable pleasures as a matter of social policy? Or even further: simple kinds of people who are easily made happy in ways that require few social resources?

(d) What moral principle is implicit in the 0–1 rule: is it a claim to

---

25. Here cf. Amartya Sen, *Collective Choice and Social Welfare* (San Francisco: Holden-Day, 1970), Chs. 7 and 7*.

equal or to maximal satisfaction on the part of all beings with a capacity for satisfaction?

The 0–1 rule is a useful way simply to illustrate the problem of cardinal interpersonal comparisons. And the conjecture is that any scheme of correspondence rules seems to embody deep ethical assumptions that are hard to get out of utilitarianism. It is here that the complexity of utilitarianism starts to appear.

LECTURE IV

Summary of Utilitarianism (1976)

(1) In the past three classes we have been discussing the classical utilitarian doctrine as formulated by Sidgwick in *Methods of Ethics*.[26] (Think of this as B-E-S utilitarianism, although there are variations between them. Sidgwick's statement is the most complete and consistent. He pushes the classical view to its philosophical limits.)

Recall that the classical utilitarian view says to maximize:

$$\sum \sum u_{ij} = u_{11} + u_{21} + \ldots + u_{nm};$$
where i = individuals and j = periods of time.

Where for each u_{ij}:

(a) The real number represents an interpersonal cardinal measure of net well-being for individual i in period j; and where this net well-being is interpreted *hedonistically* as the desirable feeling aspect of consciousness (cf. *ME*, I: ix; II: ii; III: x).

(b) This cardinal measure is based on introspection: assessment by the individual (who it is assumed can order levels of well-being and also order differences between these levels: and all this by judgments that do not involve risk and uncertainty (contra von Neumann–Morgenstern cardinal measure of utility)).

---

26. [The following remarks, entitled "Transition from Utilitarianism," constitute the first section of a 1976 lecture on "Locke and Social Contract Doctrine." —Ed.]

(c) The characterization of the u_{ij}'s is *teleological:* no notions of the right are required for the definition of utilities.

(2) Now the intuitive idea of classical utilitarianism has a number of attractive features. Indeed, it can seem *self-evident* that what we should do is maximize the good; or that we should *always* do that action which, in the circumstances, will most likely have the best consequences, all things considered. Classical utilitarianism seems a clear way of formulating this view.

So formulated, it has many admirable features:

(a) It is a *single* principle maximizing conception.

(b) Thus, it needs *no priority rules,* in theory; all working rules are approximations, rules of thumb, etc.

(c) It is a *completely general* conception, applying uniformly to *all* subjects.

(d) It has but one *basic* notion—the good; and then introduces others (right and moral worth) via the maximizing idea.

(e) It has often seemed to be readily expressible in mathematical form suitable for reasoning using calculus, and it has been so used in economics.

One should keep these features in mind. Throughout these lectures I have tried to stress the simple, underlying intuitive ideas that seem to guide the development and formulation of ethical and political conceptions. So understood:

> Classical utilitarianism evolves from the notion of *maximizing the good;* it readily fits with the idea of using all means for the *promotion* of good in the *best* way (the *most rational husbanding* of social instruments and resources).

Such is the structure of the classical view.

(3) In discussing this doctrine I have suggested that its simplicity may be deceptive:

(a) That in defining the good itself, what the u_{ij}'s are a measure of, we must be careful to abide by the constraints of a *teleological* theory: the u_{ij}'s cannot include an adjustment for feelings of *resentment,* or *disinterested* aversions to unreason (Sidgwick); for attitudes regarding distribution (Gini-coefficient), and so on.

(b) The procedures of interpersonal comparisons may themselves embed principles of right, which need to be then made explicit and require an explanation: e.g. zero-one rule; other standard assumptions.

(c) That the u_{ij}'s are to be *summed* rather than, e.g., multiplied is itself an *ethical assumption;* e.g. only summing is indifferent to distribution.

(d) Moreover, all the various constraints (a), (b), (c) above may naturally suggest, or even force, a certain conception of the person: e.g. that of a *container-person* (as found in Sidgwick).

Thus the thought is this: if we pay attention to what is going on in the classical doctrine we see that it is not so simple as it at first appears. Of course, this is no objection. But it alerts us to the fact that *any reasonable* political conception is bound to have a complex structure, even if it does develop from some simple intuitive idea. Presumably, social contract theory will show the same features.

(4) A final comment on the use of the notion of a *utility function.* This term is often used (in economics and elsewhere) as a mathematical representation of someone's preferences, choices, decisions, etc. For example, one could use a utility function to represent the decisions, or judgments, of an intuitionist (*TJ*, §7). Or these functions could be used to represent the collective social decisions made by a society; or by its members as they make choices via their constitution.

In my view, it is very unfortunate that the notion of utility function is used in this broad way: it would be much better to do the following:

(a) Adopt some other term as appropriate in each case: such as, (multiple) objective function; social decision function; or constitutional choice function. Avoid terms like "utility"- or "welfare-functions" that have special and restrictive connotations.

(b) Realize that such objective- or decision- or judgment-functions merely *represent* or *describe* for purposes of some theory what some agent's choices or decisions are (the agent may be a person, firm, association, society, etc.). The function may not take any account *at all* of *how* this agent decides, of what complex of principles they actually employ. E.g., take the case of an intuitionist judgment-function.

(c) Understand that the problem from the standpoint of moral theory is not *representation* in the thin sense, but grasping the complex of principles that enter into and regulate the *judgments* actually made, or that would be made in reflective equilibrium.

(d) Also, mathematically speaking, the representation-function may be such that there is no natural sense in which it describes the agent as *maximizing anything.* E.g., there may be multiple objectives; or lexical orderings (no continuous representative function).

(e) Finally, we will not have a classical utilitarian theory unless the representation-function observes all the restrictions of the appropriate teleological theory.

To sum up the main point overall:

Anyone's moral or political judgments can, let's assume, be represented by some mathematical function. In terms of this function, one can say: they judge as if they think that in each case society should maximize this function, promote the *best consequences* (as defined by this function).

But this way of speaking implies *no specific* political conception. The question then is: what is the *shape*, or what are the *special features* of this function; and what conceptions and principles stand behind it in the thought and judgments of agents (individuals and society)?

FIVE LECTURES ON JOSEPH BUTLER

LECTURE I

The Moral Constitution of Human Nature

§1. Introduction: Life (1692–1752), Works, and Aims

(1) Joseph Butler was born at Wantage, Berkshire, in 1692. His father was Presbyterian and wanted his son to enter the Presbyterian ministry. Butler attended a well-known Dissenting Academy at Gloucester (later moved to Tewksbury) where, in due course, he decided to convert to the Church of England. In 1714, at the rather mature age of 22, he entered Oriel College, Oxford, as a commoner, and took his arts degree in 1718. That same year he was ordained deacon and then raised to the priesthood by Bishop Talbot at St. James, Westminster. Also that year, 1718, he was made preacher at Rolls Chapel, London—a post he held until 1726. During these years he wrote the *Sermons* on which his reputation in moral philosophy largely rests. These were first published in 1726. Butler held various other positions, eventually becoming Bishop of the wealthy See of Durham in 1750. He died two years later.

Besides the *Sermons*, Butler is well known for his later work, *The Analogy of Religion*, published ten years after the Sermons, in 1736. I shall not say much about this work, but it is important to keep it in mind, as it tells us a great deal about Butler's background conceptions and the framework of ideas within which his moral philosophy is to be understood. To forget this background is precisely the kind of mistake in interpretation I want to avoid. I should add that the *Analogy* contains two short Appendices, one on personal identity, the other a brief dissertation (as he calls it) of virtue. The latter we shall also read.

(2) Although it is clear from his style that Butler did not enjoy the rough-and-tumble of controversy, his works are nevertheless designed to re-

fute certain definite views and writers in his day. Butler's aims were in the following sense practical:

(a) He did not trouble to prove truths that no one denied. He took no interest in finding new or more elegant ways of establishing received truths.

(b) He only attacks what he regards as dangerous, that is, morally corrupting or tending to undermine beliefs and virtues necessary for human society, or the integrity of Christian faith. Essentially, Butler is an apologist in the old sense: a defender of morals and reasonable belief. For him, philosophy is defense, as it is also, in an interestingly different way, for Kant.

(c) Butler always assumes as premises those he holds in common with his opponents. He is happy to recognize shared assumptions and to defend morals and reasonable religious belief from this common ground. His style is respectful and moderate, although there are occasionally strong statements concerning the pernicious consequences of the views he is attacking.

(3) Butler's philosophical temperament is practical also in another sense: he takes little interest in metaphysical or epistemological or other philosophical questions for their own sake. He avoids philosophical subtleties; speculative questions are beyond our reach. There are two chapters in the *Analogy*, the titles of which express this attitude: Part I, Chapter 7, "Of the Government of God, Considered as a Scheme or Constitution Imperfectly Comprehended," and Part II, Chapter 4, "Of Christianity, Considered as a Scheme or Constitution Imperfectly Comprehended."

Thus, Butler's practical aim is simply to confirm us in our moral and religious practice in everyday life. He is not concerned to elaborate new moral values or to work out a new basis for the moral virtues, and similarly for religious practice. He is a conservative, a defender of morals and reasonable Christian belief. We do not need philosophy for practical life in society; we do need it, however, when the basis of our practical life is attacked by philosophical means. We must, as it were, fight philosophy with philosophy, and only with philosophy so far as necessary.

§2. Butler's Opponents

We can divide Butler's opponents into two groups as follows:

(1) Certain moral philosophers, especially Hobbes, but also Shaftesbury and Hutcheson, among others. Where Butler differs from them is clear

from the *Sermons,* where the references are explicit. His main antagonist is Hobbes and the various writers Hobbes influenced, or who expressed related views, such as Mandeville. Concerning Hobbes, it is useful as a schema for looking at the history of modern philosophy to see it as beginning with him. Hobbes was seen in his day as the most dramatic expression of modern infidelity, and no wonder, in view of the enormous power of his work, *The Leviathan,* perhaps the greatest work on moral and political philosophy in the English language, even though its main thesis must be considered false. Hobbist doctrines we understand to imply materialism, determinism, and egoism. He was thought to deny a reasonable basis for morals—hence, Hobbism involved amoralism and recognized rational calculation of interests as the only kind of practical or rational deliberation. Hobbes was said to base political obligation on relations of power, and to deny any objective or shared basis for morals. It was left to the Sovereign to decide upon the content of society's laws, which represent, therefore, public conventions enforced by the Sovereign's monopoly of power when the Sovereign is effective.

Plainly, Butler is much concerned to refute this view (as were Cudworth and Clarke, and the utilitarians, Shaftesbury, Hutcheson, and Hume). Butler is concerned with this task not only in those places where Hobbes is explicitly referred to (e.g. Sermon I: 4, footnote), but Butler's conception of the constitution of human nature is itself the centerpiece of this reply. Clearly it differs from Hobbes (as interpreted) in ascribing to human nature a principle of benevolence and the supreme principle of conscience which directs us to the moral virtues and prompts us to act from them for their own sake.

Beyond these evident differences there is a more basic difference, namely: Hobbes had drawn a picture of human nature that often describes us as unfit for society—as driven by vanity and the desire for glory and self-display. Even our reason is a hazard to us; it leads us to speculate and to imagine that we can understand more things and to run society better than anyone else. Our reason can make us fanatics (Hobbes has in mind preachers of sects) and render society ungovernable, unless we somberly recognize our situation and coolly calculate on the basis of our fundamental interest in our self-preservation. What Hobbes took to be the madness of the English Civil War lies behind this picture of our unfitness for society. It is this picture of ourselves, as unfit for society, that Butler opposes with his conception of the moral constitution of human nature. This should become clear in a moment when I sketch the outlines of this constitution.

(2) The other group of Butler's opponents, although they are not of direct concern to us, are the English Deists of his day. These writers attacked the necessity of Revelation and of the Scheme of Christian Faith (to use Butler's term) as based on Revelation. The Deists believed that natural theology was sufficient: reason can establish the existence of God as creator of the world and a being of supreme intelligence and power, and an exemplar of justice and benevolence. Two of these writers were John Toland (1670–1722) who wrote *Christianity not Mysterious;* and Matthew Tindal, who wrote *Christianity as Old as the Creation,* which appeared after Butler's *Sermons* in 1730. It is works such as these that Butler attacks in the *Analogy* (1736).

Thus notice that Butler accepts as premises the Deist view, as just stated. Butler takes for granted that God exists as creator of the world, etc., both in the *Sermons* and in the *Analogy.* We must not forget these background premises in reading and interpreting the *Sermons.* For example, there appears to be in Butler an inconsistency in what he says about the supremacy of conscience and the claims of cool and reasonable self-love. Whether he is consistent here may depend on these background assumptions. We shall come back to this later.

§3. The Moral Constitution of Human Nature

This brings us to the main topic for today. But first let me make a remark about the content of the Preface and the first three sermons.

(1) The Preface was added in the second edition and gives a survey of the main theses of the *Sermons.* The prominence given to the constitution of human nature shows that Butler regarded it as the centerpiece of his moral doctrine. The first Sermon describes this constitution in greater detail; the second Sermon focuses on the notion of the authority of conscience vs. the influence of the promptings of conscience. This is an important distinction which Butler tries to explain and support by an appeal to our moral experience. Next time, I shall try to examine what he says here in more detail. The third Sermon takes up the question of the possible con-

flict between the authority of conscience and cool and reasonable self-love. Butler also discusses this question in the Preface: pars. 29 and 41, and in Sermon XI: 20–21.

(2) Let us turn to the notion of a constitution of human nature. Butler thinks this notion involves various features:

(a) Human nature has various parts, or psychologies, or intellectual powers and dispositions.

Butler distinguishes:

(i) Appetites, affections, and passions of various kinds, and here we should include attachments to particular persons, places, and things, including institutions and traditions.

(ii) The two general and rational or deliberative principles of benevolence and reasonable self-love. There is some ambiguity in Butler's account of benevolence; he sometimes describes it as an affection or passion, and at others as a general and deliberative principle. This is not a major difficulty, and we can clear it up when we come to Sermons XI–XII. For the time being, let's think of benevolence as a general and deliberative principle (and so, as a higher-order principle).

(iii) The supreme principle of reflection (as Butler sometimes says), of the principle of conscience. This is the principle or the power of moral judgment, and the judgments of conscience prompt us to act from the moral virtues—veracity, honesty, justice, gratitude, and so on, for their own sake.

(b) Such are the parts of human nature. The notion of a constitution requires that these parts stand in certain relations. They are organized in a hierarchy and governed or directed by a supreme regulative principle. With this requirement in mind, it appears that Butler describes the relation of organization as having three levels: the lowest, the affections and passions; next, the general and rational deliberative principles of benevolence and reasonable self-love; and the highest, the principle of reflection or conscience. Thus the idea of a constitution, for Butler, implies that normally an authoritative decision of judgment is given when such a decision is required. To ascribe to conscience this authoritative and supremely regulative role is to say that the deliverances or judgments of conscience, when they are called for, specify conclusive or decisive reasons for what we are to do. The appeal to conscience is final; it settles the matter.

(c) Butler thinks we must add a further point if the notion of a constitution is to apply. We must specify the end to which the constitution of human nature is directed and by reference to which its organization can be understood. In the Preface: par. 11, he compares human nature to a watch. We can talk about the constitution of a watch because a watch is organized to tell time. This purpose enables us to understand why its parts are organized as they are. Similarly, Butler describes the constitution of human nature as adapted to virtue: the parts are organized as they are—with the principle of reflection or conscience authoritative and supreme—in order that we may be prompted to act virtuously, to do what is right and good for their own sake.

(3) At first sight, this comparison between the constitution of human nature and the organization of a watch seems unsatisfactory. We are not artifacts designed to fulfill certain purposes of superior beings who have made us for their ends. But, as soon as we say this, we know that Butler does believe this; only for him there is but one such superior being, namely, God. Thus, speaking generally, we are made for God's purposes, although God's purposes and scheme of government, both in nature and in revelation, are imperfectly comprehended by us.

This religious doctrine might seem less foreign to us if we look at the details of our own moral constitution. Butler's view might be put more instructively if we said this: our constitution is adapted to virtue, and virtue is in turn those forms of conduct which adapt us to our daily life as members of society. The content of the virtues and of the deliverances of our conscience give due allowance both to the claims of society and to other persons, as well as to the claims of reasonable self-love (which, of course, is not the same as selfishness). We are beings who must be in part concerned with ourselves, since we have appetites and affections and attachments of various kinds; but also, we must live in society in view of our social nature, a point that Butler repeatedly emphasizes. Thus, when Butler says that our constitution is adapted to virtue, he can be taken to mean that our constitution is adapted to forms of conduct which enable us to be reasonable members of society.

We are able to engage in forms of social life which give due allowance and scope for our own and others' good. Regarded in this way, we can see how the notion of the constitution of human nature is directed against Hobbes. We shall see later how the notion of the authority of conscience is directed against Shaftesbury; and how Butler's conception of the content of conscience (of its judgments) is directed against Hutcheson (on the latter, see the *Dissertation of Virtue*).

LECTURE II

The Nature and Authority of Conscience

§1. Introduction

Last time I discussed the moral constitution of human nature, its parts or elements, the relations between these parts—how they are organized into a moral constitution by the supremacy and authoritative role of conscience—and finally, the end of this constitution which Butler describes as the adaptation of our nature to virtue. I glossed the adaptation of our nature to virtue as: Our nature is adapted to virtue, and virtue in turn is those principles and forms of action and conduct which adapt us to our life in society; that is, which make us fit to conduct ourselves as members of society concerned as we must be with our own interests and those of people we care for, but able to give due whether to the interests and concerns of others. Our moral constitution makes us fit for society by enabling us to act in accord with the due claims of the good of the community and of our private good. This emphasis on the moral constitution of human nature as making us fit for society, and Butler's emphasis on this moral constitution, is the centerpiece of Butler's reply to Hobbes.

(1) Today I shall make some observations on Butler's view concerning the nature and the authority of the *principle of reflection,* or *conscience*. It also proves useful here to note what he regards as the content of conscience. By this I mean the kinds of actions and forms of conduct, and the kind of temper and character in our nature, which conscience approves of. For example, in the *Dissertation on Virtue II* (an appendix in the *Analogy*), Butler argues against Hutcheson that the content of our conscience is not utilitarian. This means that the deliverances of our conscience are not in accordance with principles of utility; or as Butler puts it, "benevolence, and the want of it, singly considered" is not the "whole of virtue and vice" (par. 12). It is not the case that (slightly adapted) "we . . . approve of benevolence

to some persons rather than to others, or disapprove injustice and false-hood upon any other account, than merely as an overbalance of happiness was foreseen likely to be produced by the first, and misery by the second" (par. 12).

What is of interest here is not simply that Butler rejects utilitarianism as an account of the content of conscience (as a correct conception of right and virtue) but the kind of argument he uses to support his rejection, and the interpretation he gives of the conclusion he draws.

(2) Thus two preliminary comments: first, Butler's argument rests sim-ply on an appeal to our common-sense moral judgments, which he as-sumes everyone, or most everyone, agrees upon. The judgments he has in mind are those of any fair-minded person who is impartial and considers the matter in a cool hour. Here I have used Butler's phrases: "fair-minded," "impartial," "cool hour." Of course, he takes for granted various other con-ditions which I need not spell out here. Let's call such judgments "consid-ered judgments." Butler takes these as more or less given, that is, as com-monly recognized facts of our moral experience. His moral doctrine rests on this appeal to moral experience, as opposed to revelation or to rational-ist philosophical views. While he appears to agree with a rationalist such as Clarke, his argument takes another form. This feature of Butler's method is a distinctive shift. Moreover, he regards this moral experience as *sui generis;* he does not suppose that moral notions can be resolved into non-moral no-tions (assuming some such line between notions can be drawn indepen-dently in some useful way). Here he contrasts with Hobbes and possibly with Hume (this remains to be seen); and in this respect he does agree with Clarke and the rational intuitionists.

The second preliminary comment on Butler's rejection of utilitarianism (pars. 12–16) is that for him a moral doctrine is an account of the moral constitution of our human nature. Butler is prepared to entertain the view, as a speculative possibility, that God acts solely from the Principle of Benev-olence. But for him this is, I think, simply a speculative possibility; it is not our business to speculate about such matters so far beyond our comprehen-sion. Our conscience is to be our guide, given the station and place in the world God has called us to; and our conscience is not utilitarian. That we know, and that's all we need to know. Butler insists that the happiness of the world is God's happiness, not ours: ". . . nor do we know what we are about, when we endeavor to promote the good of mankind in any ways, but those which He [God] has directed; that is indeed in all ways, not contrary to veracity and justice . . . it is our business and our duty to endeavor, within the bounds of veracity and justice, to contribute ease, convenience, and even cheerfulness and diversion of our fellow creature" (par. 16).

For us the principle of benevolence is approved within the bounds and limits specified by justice and veracity and the other relevant virtues. Observe, further, here that a great shift will later come with Bentham, who will emphatically say that happiness of the world is our business (Hume does not say this, as we shall see). Ask yourself why this shift occurs and what lies behind it.

§2. Features of Our Moral Faculty

(1) It is this faculty of conscience and our moral nature that makes us capable of moral government. Here by our "moral nature" (as opposed to our moral faculty or conscience), Butler means our moral emotions: compassion, resentment, indignation, and so on; or our natural sense of gratitude, etc. We distinguish between harm and injury, as it were, spontaneously ("unavoidably," Butler says) (*Dissertation II*: par. 1).

(2) Nor are the deliverances of conscience on general matters, with respect to the particulars, doubtful. There is an acknowledged universal standard; it is that which in all ages and countries has been professed in public in the fundamental laws of all civil constitutions; namely, justice, veracity, and regard to the common good. There is no problem of lack of universality (par. 1).

(3) It is manifest that we have such a faculty of conscience. Some features of it are:

(a) Its object—what it judges and approves of—is those actions and active practical principles which, when fixed and habitual in us, specify our character (par. 2).

(b) Thus its object is actions—as distinct from events—where the notion of an action involves the notion of a person doing something from will and design, including under design the intention of bringing about such-and-such consequences (par. 2).

(c) Presuming also that such actions as are objects of this faculty are within our power, either in what we do or what we fail to do (par. 2).

(d) Such action and conduct is the natural object of the moral faculty, as speculative truth and falsity is the natural object of speculative reason (par. 2).

(4) The remainder of the *Dissertation* is an appeal to moral experience to show aspects of the content of conscience. (Here see the statement at the end of par. 1, p. 53: "And as to these inward feelings themselves; that they are real, that man has in his nature passions and affections, can be no more questioned, than that he has external senses." See also Sermon II, end par. 1.) For example:

(a) Our moral faculty associates with moral good or evil actions of good or ill desert; this association is natural (part of our constitution) and is not artificial or accidental (par. 3).

(b) Our moral faculty approves of prudence as a virtue and disapproves of folly as a vice (cf. pars. 6–7).

(c) Our moral faculty does not approve benevolence as the whole of virtue. Here Butler sets forth a critique of Hutcheson (pars. 8–10).

(5) Recall that in the Preface and Sermon I the role of the Principle of Reflection or conscience is supreme and regulative. Its office is to administer and to govern. In Sermon I, Butler's account is brief and found in pars. 8–9. In par. 8 he defines conscience and is concerned to prove its existence by describing two actions such that it would be absurd to deny that we approve of one and disapprove of the other when we coolly reflect.

§3. Outline of Butler's Arguments for Conscience's Authority: Sermon II

(References: Preface: pars. 24–30, esp. 26–28; Sermon I: pars. 8–9).

(1) Our constitution as a creature and its adaptation to certain ends is a reason to believe that the Author of our nature intended it for these ends. Note Butler's deistic-shared premises: see also par 3: lines 9–11 (par. 1).

(2) The objection to be resisted: granted there is such a faculty as the moral faculty, why is it authoritative? Why not say: let each follow their nature, so conscience directs only when it is strongest? What sign is there that the Author of our nature intends otherwise? (par. 5).

(3) The objection assumes there is no distinction between violating justice for the sake of present pleasure and acting justly when there is no

temptation to the contrary. Both are equally following our nature. But if this were true:

(a) The idea of deviating from our nature would be absurd;

(b) Then what Paul says re our being a law unto ourselves would be erroneous;

(c) Since following nature as an injunction would have no point.

Thus the objection rejects what Paul says, though seeming to allow it. Language shows that following nature is not acting as we please (par. 6).

(4) We need to explain what is meant by saying: every man is naturally a law unto himself, and may find within himself the value of right and obligation to follow it (par. 6).

(5) Two senses of nature are not relevant (pars. 7–9).

(6) The third sense is that of St. Paul and explains the sense in which a man is a law to himself. The argument is this (all from pars. 10–11):

(i) Our passions and affections to public and to private good conflict.

(ii) These passions and affections are in themselves natural and good, but there is no way of seeing how deeply each kind belongs to us by nature.

(iii) None of these passions and affections can be a law to us.

(iv) But there is a superior principle of conscience which asserts itself and approves or disapproves.

(v) This faculty makes us a law to ourselves.

(vi) It is not a principle of the heart to regulate us by its degree of influence but is a faculty different in kind and supreme over all the other elements of our nature and bears its own authority.

(vii) Still, it is a principle that does influence us and prompts us to comply with its dictates.

(7) The illustrative example Butler uses (an animal caught by bait) would be in the case of man an action disproportionate to our nature, and hence unnatural (par. 13). This action is unnatural not because it involves going against self-love merely as natural, since the same is true of repressing passion for the sake of self-love (merely, as natural) (par. 15).

(8) There must be another distinction: namely, the principle of self-love is superior to passions. To act from our nature, self-love must govern. This gives an example of a superior principle without invoking conscience (par. 16).

(9) Similarly, conscience is superior to the passions which directly seek objects without distinction of means necessary to obtain them. When these means injure others, conscience disapproves and is to be obeyed. Here self-

love is left out of consideration. Conscience is supreme without consider-ations of influence (par. 17).

(10) Thus we get the distinction between power and authority, here ap-plied not to civil law and the constitution of society, but to principles of hu-man nature. From its nature and role, conscience is manifestly superior; it involves judgment, direction, and superintending. And conscience has this authority and role, regardless of how often we rebel against it (pars. 18–19).

(11) Butler gives a second argument (pars. 20–22). Suppose the contrary. The bounds or limits of our conduct are then defined by our natural power on one side, or our not seeking harm for its own sake for ourselves or for others. This results from supposing that *only* their relative strength is the difference between principles of human nature. But the limits above make us morally indifferent between, e.g., patricide and filial duty. But this is absurd.

The Principles of this argument are:

(1) The way our nature works and is regulated indicates God's intention for how we should govern ourselves.

(2) For this knowledge of our nature, the appeal is to moral experience; e.g. how our feelings of shame affect us, etc.; and re faculty of conscience.

(3) Butler assumes rough agreement of judgments of conscience.

What is Butler's Argument for Conscience's Authority and Supremacy?

(A) One Form:

(1) God fashioned us as reasonable and rational beings capable of being a law unto ourselves.

(2) Such beings need a governing principle or faculty if, as we do, they have numerous passions, affections, and appetites, and competing more general affections such as benevolence and self-love.

(3) None of these other principles and passions, etc. can provide such a governing principle.

(4) Conscience claims superiority and authority as such a principle or faculty:

> (a) First, via its approvals and disapprovals, and the agreement in common content thereof between persons.
>
> (b) Second, by the fact that we experience ourselves as self-con-demned if we violate conscience.
>
> (c) No other principle or passion has these features: no other con-demns us if we violate it.

(5) The use of language supports the claims of conscience.

(6) It is shown very powerfully in the passion of resentment that conscience is supreme and authoritative.

(B) Another Form:

(1) Revise the first premise above by just supposing that we are capable of being a law unto ourselves. (Leave out the theological background.)

(2) Then proceed largely as before.

§4. Summary of Butler's Argument for the Authority of Conscience

(1) We have surveyed Butler's argument for the authority of conscience as he presents it in Sermon II, which is entirely devoted to this question, and have mentioned points which he makes elsewhere (particularly in the Preface, pars. 24–30, and Sermon I: 8–9). Let's now ask what the argument is, or indeed whether strictly speaking it is an argument at all. What I shall say is at best an interpretation of Butler's argument or presentation. Clearly he does not try to make a rigorous case for his view.

Butler takes for granted, I think, what I have called the Deistic Assumption, which implies that God is the Author of our nature, and that the design of our nature gives reasons for believing what God intended our nature to be and how its various elements are to work together. Butler also assumes that as reasonable and rational beings, we are capable of being a law unto ourselves and of taking part in the life of society. By "reasonable" I include what Butler means by "fair-minded." Reasonable and fair-minded are different notions from rationality. This latter has the sense roughly of adoption of the most effective means to given ends, or of adjusting given ends to one another when these ends compete and cannot be jointly satisfied.[1]

(2) Now if we are to be capable of being a law unto ourselves, our nature must have what Butler calls a moral constitution adapted to some aim and capable of governing itself. The question of the authority of conscience, or the lack of any such authority, is to be settled by looking at our moral experience to see if we find any appropriate authoritative element which can govern our nature and direct our conduct and adapt it to our life in society.

1. See the Lectures on Hobbes for the distinction between reasonable and rational.

Certainly given the many elements in our nature, we need some such governing or regulative principle. We have appetites, affections, and passions of various kinds, some more directly concerned with other persons, some more directly with ourselves. These appetites, affections, and passions focus on means to certain ends—states of affairs or whatever—and do not, as such, take into account the wider effects on other persons generally. These springs of conduct are, let's say, narrowly focused, whether the focus is on other persons or on ourselves. None of these springs of conduct can provide a governing or regulative principle. This follows from the nature of appetites, affections, and passions. They do not embody a reasonable or rational principle by which self-government or self-regulation is possible. Butler illustrates this by the example of the animal enticed into the baited trap by the prospect of gratifying its hunger. Were we to behave in similar fashion, contrary to the affection for ourselves expressed by the principle of reasonable self-love, we would be acting wrongly as well. Butler uses this example to exemplify the general idea of supremacy: the idea of how one principle in our nature can be governing—have authority rather than merely influence—over other elements in our nature.

(3) Next, I believe Butler holds that reasonable self-love is not the authoritative principle of our nature, although he is anxious to maintain that, in the long run at least, and given the moral government of God, there is no essential conflict between the authority of conscience and reasonable self-love. His view of ostensible conflict I shall postpone until later. But it is easy to see that reasonable self-love, although a general affection in the sense that it regulates particular appetites, affections, and passions, is an affection for ourselves. The object of reasonable self-love is always partial: it concerns the good of but one person among many. And so it cannot provide a principle suitable for our being a law unto ourselves as a member of society.

The same is true of benevolence: benevolence is likewise often a general affection (as self-love is) in that it regulates particular affections for other persons' good. This is the case when benevolence takes the form of public spirit, or love of country (patriotism), and the like. But whereas the persons who are the concern of reasonable self-love are always well-defined—namely the very person who is moved by self-love—the persons who are the concern of benevolence shift and vary, and criss-cross, in all sort of ways from person to person. C. D. Broad suggests that Butler means by benevolence the principle of utility: to maximize the happiness of society. But this is not to be found in the texts and is indeed contrary to it. The upshot then is that neither self-love nor benevolence, either general or particular, can provide the requisite authoritative principle so that we can be a law unto ourselves.

(4) Of course, there may be no such principle; although Butler does not entertain this possibility. To say that we are made in the image of God is to say that there is such a principle in our nature. Butler believes that our moral experience is sufficient testimony that this principle is to be found in conscience.

First, it is formal in the fact that every (normal) fair-minded person, when impartial and able to consider the matter in a cool hour, approves of some kinds of actions and not others. People recognize and judge that they ought to do some things and not others; and that these judgments are decisive and binding upon them. From these judgments there is no further appeal: they specify conclusive reasons for how we are to act. Moreover, the decisive and binding nature of these judgments does not depend upon their hold and effective influence on our character and springs of conduct. Thus, these judgments are authoritative: these features all together specify what authority is, as opposed to influence.

Second, it is important that persons generally agree in their approvals and disapprovals. Or to use the term introduced earlier, the content of the deliverances of conscience is more or less the same in all ages and in all countries. This enables the deliverances of conscience (imposing as always the conditions on them required for considered judgments) to provide an authoritative principle so that we can be a law unto ourselves as members of society. Plainly, if each person's conscience clashed with everyone else's, the requisite conditions would be lacking.

Third, Butler makes the further observation that when we act against our conscience, we condemn ourselves before ourselves and incur our self-dislike. I think he means to say that no other element in our nature has this feature. Self-sacrifices of various kinds we may reject having to make; but so long as they are reasonably necessary we don't in the least stand self-condemned. And even if in some cases we must sacrifice the interests of others in certain hard cases (for example, when someone must lose out and we are to decide, as it were, judiciously), we should be troubled by such diversions and actions, and often troubled deeply to do the best we can. We need not condemn and hate ourselves for this, assuming that the decision and action taken was the reasonable one in the circumstances and that these circumstances were not our doing or responsibility. This special feature of conscience, if indeed it is special, is one of the features of our moral experience Butler appeals to in contending for the authority of conscience.

Fourth, and last, Butler connects the authority of conscience and the self-condemnation we feel in acting contrary to it with the moral passions, for example, with our feelings of resentment and indignation, and the like. He says in Sermon VIII: 18 (pp. 148–149): "Why should men dispute concerning the reality of virtue, and whether it be founded on the nature of things, which yet surely is not matter of question; but why should this, I say, be disputed, when every man carries about him this passion, which affords him demonstration, that the rules of justice and equity are to be the guide of his actions? For every man naturally feels an indignation upon seeing instances of villainy and baseness, and therefore cannot commit the same without being self-condemned." Thus if we generalize (or universalize, to use a contemporary term) the principles implicit in the moral passions of resentment and indignation, these principles turn out to be what Butler calls the "rules of justice and equity." These rules are not simply rules of reason but he thinks of them as powerfully felt, as is shown by the moral passions. The reason we condemn ourselves when we go against our conscience is that we are doing things which we hate in others, and which arouse our resentment and indignation.

(5) For all these reasons, then, Butler takes the deliverances of conscience to be authoritative for us apart from their influence. This distinction between authority and influence is of great importance, and so I have tried to give one possible account of it. As a final point, I believe that Butler assumes that our moral experience is *sui generis* (and in this he agrees with Clarke and the intuitionists). This means roughly that the notions of moral approval and disapproval, the sense of "ought" involved in being a law unto ourselves, the notions of resentment and indignation as feelings directed to injury vs. harm (to wrongs), are based on one or more primitive moral notions, not further definable in terms of non-moral notions. How far Butler's account of the authority of conscience depends upon his Deistic assump-

tion I have not considered and shan't do so here. I suspect, however, that most of his account can be preserved intact, at least if we grant his taking moral experience as *sui generis*.

LECTURE III

The Economy of the Passions

§1. Introduction

Today I wish to discuss what I shall call the economy of the passions as illustrated by what Butler says about compassion in Sermons V–VII, and about resentment and the forgiveness of injuries in Sermons VIII–IX. But first, two brief comments.

(1) I want to emphasize once more the stress that Butler gives to the social character of human nature. Indeed, this is the main theme of Sermon I. Recall that the text of this sermon is Romans 12:4–5: "For as we have many members in one body, and all members have not the same office: so we, being many, are one body in Christ, and every one members one of another." Butler wishes to fill in the analogy which St. Paul suggests here between the parts of our body and how they constitute one body on the one hand, and how we, as many separate persons, constitute a society as opposed to a mere aggregate of individuals. The account of the moral (vs. physical) constitution of human nature is designed to display how it is that "we were made for society and to do good to our fellow-creatures" as well as that "we were intended to take care of our own life and health and private good" (Sermon I: 3, p. 35). (Recall here that in the eighteenth century the term "moral" had a wider use than today, and often meant "psychological," which is Butler's intended sense in inquiring into the "moral constitution of human nature.") Once this constitution is described, Butler sums up the theme of the social nature of human beings with the repetition of the statement just cited (I: 9, p. 44) and in the long and quite wonderful paragraph I: 10 (pp. 44f). The second sentence of this paragraph is: "Mankind are by nature so closely united, there is such a correspondence between the inward sensations of one man and

those of another, that disgrace is as much to be avoided as bodily pain, and to be the object of esteem and love as much desired as any external goods." You need to read the whole paragraph here.[2] Here, of course, Butler is stressing a long-standing Christian theme, not only against Hobbes's doctrine of man as unfit for society, but against various forms of individualism more generally. I mention these obvious points only so we shan't lose sight of them.

(2) In the quote above from I: 10, we see that Butler finds signs of our social nature in the passions, for example, in the fear of disgrace and the desire for esteem. Today we will discuss compassion and resentment as passions that are especially important, so Butler thinks, for our moral constitution as a whole. Compassion strengthens and supports our capacity to follow and act from the dictates of conscience and the claims of benevolence. Although, as it turns out, there is a sense in which compassion is a non-moral passion, whereas resentment on some occasions is needed to

---

2. [Sermon I, paragraph 10, says in its entirety the following. —Ed.]

"And from this whole review must be given a different draught of human nature from what we are often presented with. Mankind are by nature so closely united, there is such a correspondence between the inward sensations of one man and those of another, that disgrace is as much to be avoided as bodily pain, and to be the object of esteem and love as much desired as any external goods: and, in many particular cases, persons are carried on to do good to others, as the end their affections tend to, and rest in; and manifest that they find real satisfaction and enjoyment in this course of behaviour. There is such a natural principle of attraction in man towards man, that having trod the same track of land, having breathed in the same climate, barely having been born in the same artificial district, or division, becomes the occasion of contracting acquaintances and familiarities many years after: for any thing may serve the purpose. Thus, relations, merely nominal, are sought and invented, not by governors, but by the lowest of the people; which are found sufficient to hold mankind together in little fraternities and copartnerships: weak ties indeed, and what may afford fund enough for ridicule, if they are absurdly considered as the real principles of that union; but they are, in truth, merely the occasions, as any thing may be of any thing, upon which our nature carries us on according to its own previous bent and bias; which occasions, therefore, would be nothing at all, were there not this prior disposition and bias of nature. Men are so much one body, that in a peculiar manner they feel for each other, shame, sudden danger, resentment, honor, prosperity, distress: one or another, or all of these, from the social nature in general, from benevolence, upon the occasion of natural relation, acquaintance, protection, dependence; each of these being distinct cements of society. And, therefore, to have no restraint from, no regard to others in our behaviour, is the speculative absurdity of considering ourselves as single and independent, as having nothing in our nature which has respect to our fellow-creatures, reduced to action and practice. And this is the same absurdity, as to suppose a hand, or any part, to have no natural respect to any other, or to the whole body."

still compassion and to strengthen our capacity to carry out the dictates of justice, more accurately penal justice. But resentment is not to be confused with revenge, the gratification of which is always wrong; and resentment itself must be hedged and balanced by the precept to forgive those who injure us. It is this *balancing and working together* of the various passions and how they assist our capacity to act from the dictates of conscience, and a public spirit of good-will to others generally, that I mean to refer to by the phrase "the economy of the passions." The passions are, as it were, a subsystem within the moral constitution of human nature; they have an essential role, in Butler's view, in adapting that moral constitution to virtue, that is, to those forms of thought and conduct which enable us to take part in and to contribute to the life of society.

When we come to Hume and Kant we shall compare their accounts of the passions, and their role, with Butler's account.[3] Thus these intuitive common-sense psychological inquiries are an essential part of the material we want to cover.

§2. Butler's Method

Now for a few remarks about Butler's method of approaching the passions:

(1) First, keep in mind the theological background, or what I have called Butler's "Deistic Assumptions": namely, that God exists with the familiar theistic properties; that God created the world; that in addition to being omniscient and omnipotent, etc., God is also benevolent and just, and therefore intends the good of living things and of human beings in particular. This assumption Butler never argues for; he simply takes it for granted. While the *Sermons* are not limited to this assumption in the same way as the *Analogy* (the *Sermons* after all are sermons and take Scripture as their texts, etc.), it is useful for our purposes to note (what I believe is the case) that the Deistic Assumption by itself accounts for most, if not all, of what Butler thinks he needs.

Thus, it explains how Butler can say that our moral constitution (and

3. [See John Rawls, *Lectures on the History of Moral Philosophy,* ed. Barbara Herman (Cambridge, Mass.: Harvard University Press, 2000) for the lectures on Hume and Kant referred to here. —Ed.]

how it prompts us to think and act) is "the voice of God within us" (Sermon VI: 8, p. 114); and how he can say on another occasion that our human nature (that is, I take it, our moral constitution) is to be held sacred, for "in the image of God, made He man" (Sermon VIII: 19, p. 149). Further, there are a number of places where Butler assumes that our moral constitution correctly described provides a reason for believing how God intends our constitution to be. Thus in Sermon II: 1 (in which Butler gives his main argument for the authority of conscience) he says: "If the real nature of any creature leads him and is adapted to such and such purposes only, or more than to any other; this is a reason to believe the Author of that nature intended it for those purposes" (p. 51). Note that Butler is not arguing to the existence of God with such and such properties and intentions, etc. He assumes that God exists and has certain intentions, consistent with God's benevolence and justice in creating the world. Therefore, the moral constitution of our nature may reasonably be taken to disclose something about God's intentions concerning us; which intentions, given our relation to God, are law for us. Since the examination of our constitutions shows that we are bound to regard the deliverances of our conscience as authoritative and decisive (and not merely as having some influence, more or less, on this or that occasion), Butler speaks of our moral constitution as sacred and as the voice of God.

In paragraph (II: 3), he goes on later to say:

> Since then our inward feelings, and the perceptions we receive from
> our external senses, are equally real; to argue from the former to life
> and conduct is as little liable to exception, as to argue from the latter
> to absolute speculative truth . . . And allowing the inward feeling,
> shame; a man can as little doubt whether it was given to him to pre-
> vent his doing shameful actions, as he can doubt whether his eyes were
> given him to guide his steps. (p. 53)

Butler continues:

> . . . as to these inward feelings themselves; that they are real, that man
> has in his nature passions and affections, can no more be questioned,
> than that he has external senses. Neither can the former (the passions)

be wholly mistaken; though to a certain degree liable to greater mistakes than the latter (the senses). (p. 53)

Among the important points in the paragraph is Butler's belief that what he calls the passions (vs. appetites and affections and attachments) are an important part of our moral constitution, and help to disclose to us how we are intended by God to conduct ourselves.

(2) Among the consequences of the Deistic Assumption are these. First, that none of the passions are in themselves evil; for such passions could not have been part of God's intention. There are, to be sure, abuses of passions and letting them go beyond their proper use (Sermon VIII: 3–4, pp. 137–138). Revenge is an abuse of resentment and is our responsibility and fault (Sermon VIII: 14–15, pp. 145–146). What is a wicked and bad character is the disorder of our moral constitution; and the abuse and lack of control of its several elements, once this disorder occurs.

A second consequence of the Deistic Assumption is that a passion, at least an important and fundamental one, must have some proper role and task in our moral constitution as a whole. Of course, it may appear to us to have no such role and task. But on the Deistic Assumption this can't be so; and hence we are prompted to reflect on our makeup to see if we can work out what its role and task is. This is important for Butler in the case of resentment. The role and task of compassion he thinks are relatively straightforward; it assists the dictates of conscience and the concerns of good-will to others, particularly when others are in distress and need our help. But why should we have the passion of resentment, which Butler says is unique among the passions (as opposed to their abuse) in having as its aim the inflicting of pain and misery on another, even if only because of an injury (vs. harm) which this person has done? Thus Butler looks for the role and task that resentment must have; if we describe our moral constitution correctly, we may be able to work out what it is. Of course, we may not be able to, since the scheme of nature and our place in it is a moral scheme of God's government, but one imperfectly comprehended. (See *Analogy*: Pt. I, Ch. 7, "Of the Government of God, considered as a Scheme or Constitution, imperfectly comprehended.")

(3) A further observation is this, stated in the first paragraph of Sermon VIII, "Upon Resentment." When Butler examines our moral constitution

and its various parts, he always does so as the constitution of natural beings and within their natural circumstances. He assumes that our moral constitution is adjusted to these circumstances and natural conditions; our proper constitution is what it is because of our situation in nature. Thus he says that in this inquiry we are "to take human nature as it is, and the circumstances in which it is placed as they are; and then consider the correspondence between that nature and those circumstances, or what course of action and behavior, respecting those circumstances, any particular affection or passion leads us to" (p. 136). See also Sermon VI: 1, p. 108. He says he mentions this matter to distinguish his inquiry from those of another kind: namely, why aren't we more perfect creatures than we are (e.g., why doesn't conscience in us have power (influence) as it has authority); or why aren't we placed in better circumstances? But such questions as these we have nothing to do with. To pursue them is to run the danger of doing something "worse than impertinent curiosity" (Sermon VIII: 1, p. 137). Thus Butler sees his task as not that of asking "Why were we not made of such a nature, and placed in such circumstances, as to have no need of so harsh and turbulent passion as resentment?" but, taking our nature and condition as being what they are, "Why or for what end such a passion was given us?": and this chiefly in order to show what are the abuses of it (VIII: 2, p. 137). Thus, as his practical temper inclines him, Butler refuses to engage in philosophical speculation or subtle metaphysical inquiries. He really does, for the most part, stick to what he takes to be the plain facts concerning our moral constitution as manifest in our common moral experience; he thinks that these facts are open to view in the sense that we require no philosophical or other doctrine to uncover them, no special procedures or methods to make them available to us. Butler thinks, to be sure, that only someone who already has a systematic theory would describe our nature as Hobbes does (cf. Sermon I: 4, ftnt. b (pp. 35ff); V: 1, ftnt. a, pp. 93ff). But he thinks that it is clear to us that Hobbes is mistaken, once we carefully examine our common moral experience. What I have in mind is that we do not find in Butler the idea that the agreed facts of moral experience are peculiarly difficult to ascertain, even granting that partiality and pride, etc., can draw us into self-deception and self-deceit (Sermon X: "Upon Self-Deceit"). All of this gives Butler's discussion of the passions a rather straightforward empirical cast, not unlike that of natural history. It is this feature of Butler's *Sermons* which, despite their theological background, made them so important for Hume. Much if not most that Butler says doesn't depend on this background at all.

§3. Role of Compassion: As Part of Our Social Nature

(1) Its definition—from Sermon V: 1 we can say: Compassion is an affection for the good of our fellow creatures and delight from the affections being gratified, and an uneasiness from things going contrary to it.

Thus by definition compassion is related to others' good (as distinct from resentment which concerns a wrong, an injury). It is a general affection somewhat indeterminate in the range of persons it includes; but to some degree it often includes all human persons—and so is fellow-feeling, as Butler often says. In this respect it is distinct from attachments—affections for particular persons—and from self-love, a kind of general affection for oneself.

Butler's initial characterization of compassion is not quite right, and it's important to correct it for the purpose of understanding his view. He says (Sermon V): When we rejoice in the prosperity of others, and compassionate their distresses, we, as it were, substitute them for ourselves, their interest for our own; and have the same kind of pleasure in their prosperity, and sorrow in their distress, as we have from reflection upon our own (92–93). But it seems obvious that when others are in distress and we feel compassion for them we do not have the same kind of distress as they; nor do we feel as we would feel if we were to imagine (as far as we can) that we were in their situation. Very roughly, when you are ill and I feel compassion for you, I don't feel ill; but my compassion prompts me to help or to comfort you in some way. Moreover, my compassion doesn't make me dwell on how I would feel if I were ill in the way you are. I might start dwelling on that, but the point is: that's not what makes my feeling of compassion. What does this is my thinking what I can do to help and to comfort, accompanied by feelings of distress on my part, and so on. Of course, Butler knows this perfectly well, and says it correctly later in Sermon V: 5: "Whereas men in distress want [need] assistance; and compassion leads us directly to assist them . . . The object [of compassion] is the present misery of another [which needs] a particular affection for its relief. . . . [Compassion] does not rest in itself, but carries us on to assist the distressed" (97). Here Butler is contrasting compassion with rejoicing in the felicitation of another.

LECTURE IV

Butler's Argument against Egoism

§1. Introduction

Today I shall discuss Butler's argument against egoism as found in Sermon II, the first of two sermons on the love of our neighbor. By egoism in this connection we should understand Hobbes's psychological egoism and the various forms in which this was a fashionable view in Butler's day (in Mandeville, for example); or so Butler plainly believes. Keep in mind that Butler is engaged in apologetics, in the defense of the common-sense moral doctrines and virtues and in these as a part of Christian faith and belief. He is concerned to argue that a way of life informed by these common-sense virtues is not a way of folly unmindful of the proper good of our own person, but to the contrary, it is completely consistent with this good when correctly understood. Next time I shall discuss the supposed conflict between conscience and self-love and suggest how I think Butler resolves this conflict. In this connection Sermons XII–XIII are important.

In Sermon XI ("Upon the Love of our Neighbor") Butler examines four questions which appear in this order in the text:

(1) Whether private interest is likely to be promoted to the degree in which self-love engrosses us and prevails over other principles. It is in connection with this question that Butler introduces the so-called Paradox of Egoism (or paradox of hedonism): the idea that preoccupation with one's own concerns can be in various ways destructive of one's own happiness. This question is discussed in the long par. 7: 190ff.

(2) The second question is whether there is any peculiar incompatibility between the pursuit of public vs. private interest. By a peculiar incompatibility between public and private interest Butler means an incompatibility

which is other and greater than the incompatibility between any two affections, whether particular or general. Thus he observes (in par. 18) that the more time and thought we give to the good of others, the less time and thought we can give to the good of ourselves, and so on. His question is whether there is a peculiar or distinctive kind of incompatibility between private and public interest. He wishes to hold that there is not. The question is first discussed in pars. 10–11, pp. 194ff.

(3) The third question examines the nature, the object, and the end of self-love, as distinguished from other principles and affections of the mind. Butler believes that the answer to this third question must be taken up first; the answer to the other questions depends upon it, although as the discussion proceeds he says things that are relevant to it. The first discussion of this question is given in pars. 5–8, pp. 189–192ff.

(4) Once the first three questions are answered in the order (3) → (1) → (2), Butler takes up a 4th question which can be seen as a generalization of the 1st question. It asks whether a way of life, a devotion to benevolence and virtue and to public good, is likely to prove incompatible with a proper concern for our private good. He holds that it does not any more than any other particular affection or passion may prove incompatible. Indeed, he goes further, and enumerates several distinctive features of a way of life characterized by a devotion to benevolence and virtue that tend to reduce this incompatibility. This question is discussed in pars. 12–15, pp. 197–200. He considers an objection to his answer in pars. 17–19; and in pars. 20–21, pp. 204–206, there is a well-known passage on the alleged conflict between conscience and self-love which appears to concede the supremacy of self-love, in ostensible contradiction to Butler's earlier thesis of the supremacy of conscience: He says: "Let it be allowed, though virtue or moral rectitude does indeed consist in affection to and pursuit of what is right and good, as such; yet that when we sit down in a cool hour, we can neither justify to ourselves this or any other pursuit, 'till we are convinced that it will be for our happiness, or at least not contrary to it" (206). This passage and others related to it I take up next time. The question we have to ask is whether Butler is simply inconsistent; or whether, taking the troublesome passages in context and keeping in mind his overall view, we can work out a coherent doctrine. Of course we may have to supply some of the details and correct a few slips, but we should assume—as usual with any text we are prepared to read—that a coherent interpretation can be found.

§2. Butler's Argument contra Hedonistic Egoism

While Butler's argument contra hedonistic egoism (in pars. 4–7, with supplementary observations elsewhere)[4] is not altogether successful, he does make several essential points which pave the way for a useful refutation. These points are picked up by later writers (e.g., Hume, *Enquiry,* App. II of *An Enquiry into the Principles of Morals,* and Bradley in *Ethical Studies,* Essay VII, esp. pp. 251–276).[5] Bradley's argument is quite decisive, I think. Thus, rather than set out and comment upon Butler's argument as he presents it, I shall sketch in brief form what I take to be a version of Bradley's argument and then point out what Butler contributed to it. This will help us to see at the same time where Butler's formulations may need correction.

(1) Let's begin by noting certain features of the actions of reasonable and rational agents. We assume that agents can select between various alternative actions, depending on their circumstances and the various constraints to which they are subject. The class of alternatives is within their powers: they are able to do and not to do any of these actions. Which available action an agent will do depends upon the agent's beliefs, desires, and assessment of the consequences of the possible action, as understood by the agent. Here "desires" is a stand-in for Butler's appetites, affections, and passions both general and particular, and in these we have to include what in the passage just quoted Butler called the "affection to and pursuit of what is right and good, as such." Note that Butler calls this an affection.

(2) Next, think of the *object of desire* as that state of affairs the bringing about of which is the aim of the desire. When this object is brought about, we say the desire is *fulfilled;* it has achieved its aim by realizing its object. Let's say that a desire is *gratified* when the agent knows, or reasonably believes or experiences, that the desire is fulfilled.

The language here has to be rephrased a bit to accommodate desires to participate in or to engage in various activities, or to do various things, for their own sake. Sometimes it is awkward to think of activities as states of affairs, even if by certain locutions we can do this. We should also introduce the notion of a *final desire* as, for example, the desire to engage in an

---

4. Cf. especially the statement of one basic psychological principle in par. 13.

5. F. H. Bradley, *Ethical Studies* (Oxford: Oxford University Press, 1927).

activity, or to bring about a certain state of affairs, *for its own sake.* A *chain* of reasons—I want to do X to bring about Y, and Y to bring about Z, etc.—must stop, say, at Z, which I want to bring about for its own sake. A chain of reasons must not only be finite, but is usually reasonably short. As Butler notes, if this isn't the case, we are not moved by desire but by uneasiness—an aimless inclination to activity without apparent reason. This uneasiness is the emptiness of desire with[out] the possibility of any gratification except motion.

(3) Now very roughly we can characterize the *intention* of an action as those consequences of an action which are foreseen by the agent and recognized as part of the causal chain of events and processes essential or necessary for bringing about the state of affairs which specifies the object of desire. Other consequences may also be foreseen, e.g. those which are subsequent in time to the realization of the object of desire, and for the sake of which the action is done. Of course, even if we don't count these consequences as part of the agent's intention, we may still hold the agent accountable or responsible for them, provided they were, or should have been, foreseen. Different ways of drawing these lines may equally serve the same philosophical purposes.

Next we say that the *motive* of an action is the desired and presumptively foreseen consequences for the sake of which the action is done. So described, we should distinguish motive from the psychological element that moves the agent to act. This element can be described in various ways depending on the circumstances, ranging from an impulse to a deliberate plan the formulation in thought of which directs and moves the agent. Part of the context of this deliberate thought will be the thought of the desired and foreseen consequences, or what I have just referred to as the motive.

(4) The preceding is admittedly rather tedious. But going over these distinctions puts us into a position to make a simple and indeed obvious point which can break the hold of egoism over our thought. This point is the following: the gratification of desire is always pleasant, or enjoyable, or satisfying, (etc.)—whichever description is appropriate. But it does not follow that the *object* of desire is always to obtain (or to realize) the experience of pleasantness, or enjoyment, or satisfaction. That the gratification of desire is always pleasant, enjoyable, or satisfying does not imply that the *motive* is always pleasure, enjoyment, or satisfaction, nor that the thought of plea-

sure, enjoyment, or satisfaction is the psychological element that prompts our actions.

This enables us to see the fallacy in the following argument:

(1) Every deliberative and intentional action of ours is undertaken in order to bring about, or to try to bring about, some object of one or more of our desires, which desires belong to our person and prompt us to act.

(2) When a desire is fulfilled—when the object of desire is achieved and we know, or reasonably believe, or experience this fact—our desire is gratified.

(3) The gratification of desire is always pleasant, or enjoyable or satisfying; the frustration of desires is always unpleasant, etc. Therefore:

(4) The object of all our desires is really the pleasures (pleasant experiences) or the enjoyments which ensue upon the recognized fulfillment of our desires.

This conclusion does not follow, since the argument depends on a confusion between the *object of desire* and the *gratification of desire*. Desires have indefinitely many different kinds of objects, and their objects specify their *content*. The fallacy lies in supposing that the content of all desire is the pleasant and/or the enjoyable experience because the gratification of desire is pleasant and enjoyable.

It is this fallacy which Butler is after in his discussion of the third question in pars. 4–7. He is also after a second fallacy latent in the above argument; namely, the fallacy of supposing that because all of our actions are moved by one or more of our desires—Butler, Hume, and Kant all agree on this—and gratification of our desires is pleasant or enjoyable to us and not to someone else, then we must have been moved to act by these pleasant or enjoyable experiences as *objects* of our desire. Here the idea that the desires that move us to act are *our* desires, and the pleasantness and enjoyment of gratified desires are *our* experiences, somehow tempts us to suppose that our desires must take these experiences of ours as their objects. Against these errors Butler says: "Every particular affection, even the love of our neighbour, is as really our own affection [an affection of ours], as self-love; and the pleasure arising from its gratification is as much my own pleasure [a pleasure I experience and not someone else], as the pleasure self-love would have." There is an odd clause deleted here, the meaning of which I am uncertain. Butler goes on: "And if, because every particular affection is a man's own, and the pleasure arising from its gratification his own pleasure, . . . such particular affection must be called self-love; according to this way of speaking, no creature whatever can possibly act but merely from self-love; and every action and every affection whatever is to be resolved up into this one principle."

He adds: "But then this is not the language of mankind: or if it were, we should want words to express the difference, between the principle of an action, proceeding from cool consideration that it will be to my own ad-vantage; and an action, suppose of revenge, or of friendship, by which a man runs upon certain ruin, to do evil or good to another. It is manifest the principles of these actions are totally different, and so want different words to be distinguished by: all that they agree in is, that they both proceed from, and are done to gratify an inclination in a man's self" (188).

In these important paragraphs 4–7 we can see how Butler is making the distinctions we earlier rehearsed. One way to put his point is that psy-chological egoism overlooks essential distinctions. Either it is a truism that we always act from our own desires, which desires, when these action are successful, are gratified; and these gratifications of our desires are *our* grati-fications. (How could it be otherwise?) Or: psychological egoism is false. Looking at the plain facts of experience, our desires—appetites, affections, and passions—have many different objects, an extremely varied content which comprises much more than pleasure.

(5) Butler also wishes to make another psychological point which is important; namely, that it is impossible, given our psychological constitu-tion, for pleasure or enjoyment to be the object of desire. Put another way: something else other than pleasure must be desired; and indeed, fo-cusing on pleasures and enjoyments as a certain kind of self-love does pre-suppose desires—appetites, affections, and passions—which have by our constitution certain objects; and these desires could not be gratified unless there was a "prior suitableness" between these desires and their objects (par. 3).

Some further points:

(1) Regarding this last point: Butler calls these objects *external* things. He would have done better to say desires are desires to do things involving

or using external things. Take the example of eating; or helping another. This doesn't affect Butler's main point.

(2) It would have also clarified Butler's argument had he distinguished more explicitly various kinds of desires; for example:

(a) Desires *in* a self vs. desires *of* a self's, and among the former:

    (i) Self-centered desires: those for my *own* honor, power, glory; health and nourishment.

    (ii) Self-related desires: for the honor and power of persons and groups related to *me*—my family, my friends, my nation, etc.

Selfishness is specified by relation to such desires.

(b) Affections for others are neither self-centered nor self-related desires: they include desires for the other's good. Proper self-love is an affection for our good and is altogether different from selfishness, as I hope to discuss next time.

(3) Also I think Butler conflates two rather different notions of self-love and two different notions of happiness, which go with these.

(a) The first has hedonistic overtones, as when Butler says the object of self-love is "somewhat internal, our own happiness, enjoyment, satisfaction ... [it] never seeks anything external for the sake of the thing, but only as a means of happiness or good" (par. 3, p. 187).

(b) A planning or rational plan notion of self-love: ordering, scheduling, and arrangement of the fulfillment of desires aimed at securing our own good. See for example the second sentence of par. 16: "Happiness consists in the gratification of certain affections, appetites, passions, with objects which are by their nature adapted to them. Self-love may indeed set us to work to gratify these; but happiness or enjoyment has no immediate connection with self-love, but arises from such gratification alone. Love of our neighbour is one of those affections."

The trouble with the hedonistic notion is that it tends to absorb everything. The planning notion does not do this, but applies to ordering those affections and desires that more directly concern us so that they work for our proper good.

(4) Also Butler might have invoked a distinction mentioned by Bradley between the thought of pleasure and a pleasant thought. The latter has no hedonistic implications: it does not show pleasure to be the object of desire.

(5) Finally, Butler is concerned to show that a life devoted to benevolence and virtue has a natural compatibility with our *happiness*. See the whole Sermon XI and the 4th question, answered last. The affection to benevolence and virtue cannot be lacking from us without our being *disfigured*.

LECTURE V

Supposed Conflict between Conscience and Self-Love

§1. Introduction

I shall work into today's main questions via the supposed conflict or inconsistency in Butler's view between what he says about the Authority of Conscience on the one hand and the claims of self-love on the other. I emphasize that this matter is simply a way into the main question I hope to discuss; because I believe that for Butler there is no inconsistency or conflict. The important thing is to see why this is so: roughly, his idea is that the more our nature approaches its perfection, the more the love of virtue—of justice and veracity—and what Butler calls "real benevolence" (in XII: 4) become one and the same thing. Such benevolence is then the sum of the virtues; it is "a principle in reasonable creatures, and so to be directed by their reason" (XII: par. 19, p. 223). And so, we might better say: natural benevolence has been made more extensive and integrated with the direction of reason, that is, conscience or the principle of reflection.

On the other hand, Butler distinguishes various forms of self-love. There is self-love in the sense of our so-called interest, that is, our self-interest as fashionable worldly opinion thinks of it. There is what we may call *narrow* self-love, that of persons whose interests are mostly interests *in* themselves: in their own honor, power, position, wealth, and so on, persons whose natural benevolent affections and attachments are weak. Again, self-love differs according to its scope, that is, upon whether it is limited in its concerns to our temporal and imperfect state, or whether it also considers our state of possible perfection in the hereafter. If we introduce the notion of *reasonable self-love* as a settled affection to the proper good of our person as a reasonable creature (with the moral constitution as described in Sermons I–III), and if we take in the full scope of self-love, which includes the state of our possible perfection, then Butler believes that a life guided by the love of virtue—by an affection to right and justice and moved by real benevolence—is that way of life which best advances our good. It provides for the greatest happiness of which we are capable; a happiness we can reasonably have faith in and hope for. Thus, given our nature and our place in the world, there can be no conflict or inconsistency between conscience, the deliverances of which we are always to follow, and self-love. Here we must say that conscience is real benevolence informed by reason, and self-love is to be taken as reasonable self-love construed as a settled affection for the proper good of our person taken in full scope.

Offhand, this solution may seem to lack philosophical depth. You may say: "Of course, if we bring God into the picture and suppose that we are rewarded by the blessings of heaven for virtue and punished by hell-fire for vice, then there cannot be a conflict between conscience and self-love. The familiar question, 'Why be moral?' in this case has an obvious answer." But to interpret Butler's solution this way misses altogether what is in the text of Sermons XI–XIV: namely a moral psychology which sets out a number of different notions of benevolence and self-love; and which indicates a way in which we can think of these different notions as higher or more perfected forms of benevolence and self-love. This supposes that benevolence can be extended or generalized and thereby informed and guided by reason as the principle of reflection or conscience. This moral psychology then enables Butler to explain the love of our neighbor and the love of God in such a way that these loves are most congruent with our real happiness and hence with the highest form of self-love. What is to be learned from Butler is the principles of his moral psychology and how they are supposed to lead to this conclusion.

In studying Butler's moral psychology, I urge you to put aside altogether the idea of rewards of heaven and punishments. The notions of reward and punishment play no essential part. To a considerable extent—although not completely—we can interpret Butler's psychology in terms of secular analogies; and when we can't do this, we must think of God as the perfection of reason and goodness, and not as dispensing rewards and punishments. The *Visio Dei*—the vision of God—plays an important part in Butler's account in Sermons XIII–XIV; it is the consummation of our real happiness, or proper good. My suggestion is that whether or not we take this idea seriously, the principles of Butler's moral psychology and how they work are not affected.

§2. Why Suppose Butler Is Inconsistent: re: Conscience and Self-Love

Let's consider here several relevant passages:

(1) In the Preface, par. 21, of Butler's *Sermons,* Butler supposes that our own happiness is a manifest obligation; yet it may conflict with that of what conscience requires in certain cases: he resolves the conflict in favor of conscience. He says: "But the obligation on the side of interest really does not remain. For the natural authority of the principle of reflection is an obligation to the most near and intimate, the most certain and known: whereas the contrary obligation can at the utmost appear no more than probable; since no man can be *certain,* in any circumstances, that vice is his interest in the present world, much less can he be certain against another: and thus the certain obligation would entirely supersede and destroy the uncertain one; which yet would have been of real force without the former" (end of 21st paragraph, pp. 15–16). This passage settles the question by saying that conscience is more near and intimate, more certain and known. Butler says here that we can't be certain in *any* circumstances that vice is our interest in the *present* world. But one says sometimes we can. And in any case this is hardly a persuasive or sufficiently deep ground for the always overriding authority of conscience.

(2) The summarizing par. 13 of Sermon III gives a similar impression. It says that reasonable self-love and conscience are, it seems, co-equal and superior principles in human nature.

> Reasonable self-love and conscience are the chief or superior principles in the nature of man: because an action may be suitable to this nature, though all other principles be violated; but becomes unsuitable, if either of those are. Conscience and self-love, if we understand our true happiness, always lead us the same way. Duty and interest are perfectly coincident; for the most part in this world, but entirely and in every instance if we take in the future, and the whole; this being implied in the

notion of a good and perfect administration of things. Thus they who have been so wise in their generation as to regard only their own supposed interest, at the expense and to the injury of others, shall at last find, that he who has given up all the advantages of the present world, rather than violate his conscience and the relations of life, has infinitely better provided for himself, and secured his own interest and happiness. (p. 76)

Thus again it seems we are to follow conscience, since duty and interest are perfectly coincident; and presumably conscience is the safer guide; indeed for us, authoritative.

(3) The most striking passage is perhaps Sermon XI: 21: "Let it be allowed, though virtue or moral rectitude does indeed consist in affection to and pursuit of what is right and good, as such; yet, that when we sit down in a cool hour, we can neither justify to ourselves this or any other pursuit, till we are convinced that it will be for our happiness, or at least not contrary to it" (p. 206).

Butler here may be attempting to protect religion and common-sense morality from the scorn of fashionable self-interested doctrines. Since he doesn't say here what notion of self-love he is appealing to when we, as it were, sit down in a cool hour, this passage is not inconsistent with my general suggestion made at the outset. I don't think Butler ever goes back on the idea that for us conscience is supremely authoritative. We have to keep in mind what he says in par. 6 of III (p. 71): "Conscience does not only offer itself to show us the way we should walk in, but it likewise carries its own authority with it, that it is our natural guide; the guide assigned us by the Author of our nature: it therefore belongs to our condition of being, it is our duty to walk in that path, and follow this guide, without looking about to see whether we may not possibly forsake them with impunity." Thus it is the guide assigned to us by God, and our duty is to follow it. Recall also the *Dissertation of Virtue,* where our conscience has a content that is not the same as maximum happiness or benevolence interpreted in that way. *Real* benevolence is benevolence as an affection for right and justice, etc., for the good of others, within the limits these notions allow.

In sum, then, these passages—while to a certain degree troublesome—don't go counter to the general solution suggested. Part of the difficulty may be that Butler himself in the Preface to the *Sermons* says very little

about Sermons XIII–XIV. This may encourage us to overlook their importance for his view. Indeed, they are the culmination of his account of the
various notions of benevolence, self-love, and happiness, and so the principles of his moral psychology.

§3. Some Principles of Butler's Moral Psychology

(1) Let's start with the principle we discussed last time: "All particular affections whatever, resentment, benevolence, love of arts, equally lead to a
course of action for their own gratification, i.e. the gratification of ourselves; and the gratification of each gives delight: so far, then, it is manifest
they have all the same respect to private interest" (XI: par. 14, p. 197).

But: "This gratification is not the *object* of the affections; the deliberate
pursuit of *pleasure* as such presupposes the affections, which do *not* have
pleasures as their object." Note that in XIII: par. 13 (pp. 239–240) Butler says
that the question: Whether we ought to love God for God's own sake or for
our own is a mere mistake in language. He makes the same point here as
earlier contra Hobbes and others regarding egoism. We are to love God as
the highest and proper object of our perfected real benevolence (as informed and directed by our reason), but of course the delight we find in
this love constitutes the full gratification of our nature and therefore answers to our reasonable self-love which looks after our real happiness. Butler is using the distinctions we discussed earlier to say that there is no conflict between the perfected love of God and our proper good.

(2) There are several important psychological principles which apply to
benevolence as an affection for virtue and public good which distinguish it
from the affections generally:

(a) One is hinted at in par. 16 of XI (p. 201): "Love of our neighbor . . .
as a virtuous principle, is gratified by a consciousness of endeavoring to
promote the good of others; but considered as a natural affection, its gratification consists in the actual accomplishment of this endeavor."

But what is the explanation of this fact? Here Butler simply asserts it. Is
it a basic principle or a corollary of such a principle? We get an answer perhaps in XII: par. 23 (see also XIII: pars. 7–10). For Butler says here: "Human
nature is so constituted, that every good affection implies the love of itself;
i.e. becomes the object of a new affection in the same person. Thus, to be

righteous, implies in it the love of righteousness; to be benevolent, the love of benevolence; to be good, the love of goodness; whether this righteousness, benevolence, or goodness, be viewed as in our own mind, or in another's: and the love of God as a being perfectly good, is the love of perfect goodness contemplated in a being or person" (p. 228).

This is restated in XIII: 3 (p. 230); XIII: and par. 6 (pp. 234f), where Butler says: "To be a just, a good, a righteous man, plainly carries with it a peculiar affection to or love of justice, goodness, righteousness, when these principles are the objects of contemplation. Now if a man approves of, or hath an affection to, any principle in and for itself; incidental things allowed for, it will be the same whether he views it in his own mind, or in another; in himself, or in his neighbour. This is the account of our approbation of, our moral love and affection to good characters; which cannot but be in those who have any degrees of real goodness in themselves, and who discern and take notice of the same principle in others." Call this a basic principle of reflective affection: a good affection—an affection to virtue—generates an affection to itself.[6] It also explains why we can't violate conscience without self-condemnation: we must dislike vice in ourselves.

(b) Next there are two principles which generate love: First, the Principle of Superior Excellence, XIII: pars. 7–8 (pp. 234–235). Second, the Principle of Reciprocity: good intentions and actions for our benefit and good generate a natural gratitude and returning love (XIII: 9–11, pp. 236–238).

(c) Next there is a basic presumption: namely, these principles won't work—particularly Principle (a) of reflective love—unless we have some degree of moral goodness: i.e., an affection to goodness in our mind and character: XIII: 9, p. 236.

(d) Principle of Proper Aspiration: XIV: 3, p. 244, which Butler connects with Resignation = fear-hope-love:

"Resignation to the will of God is the whole of piety: it includes in it all that is good, and is a source of the most settled quiet and composure of mind. There is the general principle of submission in our nature."

(e) Principle of Continuity: XIII: 12, pp. 178f.[7]

---

6. See the statement in par. 16 of XI (p. 168) quoted above. See the selection immediately under section 2a above.

7. [It is not clear what this principle is. The lectures end here abruptly, without further elaboration or a summary. —Ed.]

APPENDIX: ADDITIONAL NOTES ON BUTLER

Important Points in Butler

(Hobbes and Butler, the two great sources of modern moral philosophy: Hobbes as posing the problem—the writer to refute. Butler supplied a deep answer to Hobbes.)

(1) Authority vs. Strength

(2) Dissertation notion of RE = starts here[8]

(3) On Method—Last par. Dissertation on personal identity

(4) Egoism contra Hobbes: Butler holds moral projects as much a part of the self as other parts of the self: our natural desires, etc. Kant deepens this by connecting ML (Moral Law) with the self as R+R (Rational and Reasonable).

(5) In Dissertation Butler attacks Hutcheson's explanation of the moral sense.

(6) Butler's general method is to appeal to experience; but there are different kinds of experience, moral vs. non-moral, memory vs. non-memory (as in Ref. in 3).

(7) Hume responds to Butler in two ways:

(a) Hume tries to allow for Butler's distinction of Authority vs. Strength by the distinction between the calm vs. violent passions.

(b) Hume tries to reply to Butler's critique of utilitarianism (Hutcheson) re justice by the distinction between the natural and the artificial virtues. (Hume concedes Butler is right in saying that justice is not always beneficial.)

(8) Butler does not want to explain everything; or to go beneath or to systematize the data of our moral experience. Systematic theory isn't his aim. We know enough for our salvation, and that knowledge we should be clear about and hold firm.

Sturgeon: on Butler *Phil. Review* (Schneewind thinks wrong)

Whewell's chapter on Butler in his *History of Ethics*: "Butler got the data right; our task is to work out the theory" (or something like that).

(9) Connect this up with Kant; including his notion of reasonable faith.

---

8. ["RE" seems to refer to reflective equilibrium, and "Dissertation notion of RE" refers either to Butler's "Dissertation: Of Personal Identity" or to Rawls's own dissertation and his initial account of reflective equilibrium worked out there, which was published in "Outline of a Decision Procedure for Ethics" (1951), in Rawls, *Collected Papers*, ed. Samuel Freeman (Cambridge, Mass.: Harvard University Press, 1999), Ch. 1. —Ed.]

(10) Butler proposes a new basis for the authority of morals—not revelation or divine will; but moral experience (as available to common sense
and conscience).

Conscience and the Authority of Conscience:
Preface: 24–30, esp. 26–28; Sermon I: 8–9; II: entire
Social Nature of Man:
Sermon I: 9–13; cf. esp. 10, 12
    There is no self-hatred in man, or the desire to hurt others for
their own sake, or of injustice, oppression, treachery, ingratitude, etc. (also
Kant).
    Preface: 26–28: to violate conscience is to be self-condemned, we can-
not so act without "real self-dislike."
Conflict [of] Conscience vs. Self-Love:
Preface: 16–30; esp. 24; III: 9; XI: 20
Analogy: 87 and 87n
    religious and temporal interest of self-love cf. 70f
Conscience in *Analogy:*
    (1) Cannot depart from with[out] self-condemnation: 111
    (2) Its dictates are the laws of God, laws as including sanctions: 111
Conflict [of] Conscience and Self-Love: (Passages)
Preface:
    Conflict with one's own interest, happiness left without a remedy by
        Shaftesbury: 26; 27–30 also relevant
    Conflict resolved by epistemic certainty [of] conscience: 26
Sermon I:
    Paragraph 15: appears to put conscience and self-love on a par
Sermon II: (avoids comparing conscience and self-love)
    Conscience principle in the heart, and supreme: 8, 15
Sermon III: discussion 6–9:
    Narrow self-interest impossible for us: 6–7
    Self-Interest (present and temporal) as maximizing satisfactions
        generally
        Coincides with virtue and its course of life: 8
        And will do so in the final distribution of things: 8
    Conscience and self-love properly understood co-equal, but we are to
        follow conscience always: 9
Sermon XI: 20–21

[453]

Butler's Aim: To Show Us to Ourselves: II: 1
    On Conscience:
    Its role in Constitution of Human Nature:
        The parts of Human Nature set out (Const = Econ): P:14
        Supremacy of conscience defs constitution of human nature: P:14
        All parts governed by conscience, gives idea of constitution or system of human nature: P:14; This system adapted to virtue: P:14
        That our constitution is at times disordered doesn't make it not a constitution: P:14
        In virtue of conscience and our constitution we are moral agents and accountable: P:14
        Nothing more contrary to our nature than vice and injustice: P:15
        Constitution of our nature requires us to govern ourselves by conscience: P:25
        Our constitution makes us a law to ourselves and liable to punishment, even when we doubt the sanction: P:29
    Its Authority: P:16–30
        Conscience as approbation of some principles or actions, etc.: P:19
        Conscience and its authority is what distinguishes man from animals: P:18–24
         Conscience claims absolute direction of our constitution: P:24
         This claim made independent of strength of influence: P:24
         Shaftesbury's error: to have a scheme where strength decides: P:26
        Why conscience overrides: epistemic argument from certainty and authority: P:26
        We cannot violate our conscience without self-condemnation and self-dislike: P:28
        Conflict of conscience and self-love: 16–30
        Does not depend on Religion but issues from our own mind: *Analogy* I: 7:11
        Conscience necessary for governing and regulating other elements of human nature: II: 8
        Argument from disproportion II: 40
    Method and Intuitionism
        Relation to Clarke, etc. P:12
        Appeal to moral facts as Butler's own method: P:12, 27; II: 1
        Appeal to moral experience as *sui generis*: P:16

Appeal to moral sense of each person's heart and natural conscience: II: 1

(Compares to appeal to the sense re knowledge of things)

Appeal to moral emotions and their role: e.g. shame: II: 1

They cannot be wholly mistaken: II: 1

Why is our nature social?

(1) Shown by appetites and affections, etc. (On resentment, on compassion, Sermons XI–XII)

(2) By general principle of benevolence

(3) By context of conscience

(4) By fact that reasonable self-love would lead us to be social

Is the Constitution of Human Nature Actual or Merely Ideal?

(1) The parts are actual, including conscience.

(2) It is ideal in that it can be disordered; and conscience is not generally followed.

(3) It is manifest in the actual deliverances of conscience of impartial and fair-minded persons, given a cool hour.

(4) The const. is then what we would be like in our actions if we generally followed conscience.

(5) This const. and supremacy of conscience makes us a law unto ourselves; it makes us responsible and accountable moral and reasonable agents.

(6) Butler would say: All this is based on facts of our moral experience.

Is Butler an intuitionist? e.g. like Clarke?

Preface

Butler's acceptance of intuitionism à la Clarke: Pref: 12

Butler's own method: Pref: 12f

appeal to moral experiences as matters of fact: 12, 27

Const. (or econ) of human nature: Pref: 12f; 14

the various parts: 14

relations of parts and supremacy of conscience: 14

purpose: adopted to virtue: 14

as watch to tell time: 14

Irrelevance of disorders: 14

Constitution of agents accountable for disorders in the const.: 14

COURSE OUTLINE

Philosophy 171:
Political and Social Philosophy—Spring 1983

This class will consider several social contract and utilitarian views which have been important in the development of liberalism as a philosophical doctrine. Attention will be given to Marx as a critic of liberalism; and time permitting, the class will end with some discussion of *TJ* [*A Theory of Justice*] and other contemporary views. The focus of the class is narrow in the hope of achieving some depth of understanding.

A. Introduction
B. Two Social Contract Doctrines: (3 weeks)
    1. Hobbes:
        a. Human Nature and the Instability of the State of Nature
        b. Hobbes's Thesis and the Articles of Peace
        c. Role and Powers of the Sovereign
    2. Locke:
        a. Doctrine of the FLN
        b. Social Contract and the Limits of Political Authority
        c. The Legitimate Constitution and Problem of Inequality
C. Two Utilitarian Doctrines: (3 weeks)
    1. Hume:
        a. Critique of the Social Contract Doctrine
        b. Justice, Property, and the Principle of Utility
    2. J. S. Mill:
        a. The Principle of Utility Revised
        b. The Principle of Liberty and Natural Rights
        c. Subjection of Women and Principles of the Modern World
        d. Private Property, Competitive Markets, and Socialism

D. Marx: (2½ weeks)
  a. The Role of Conceptions of Justice
  b. Theory of Ideological Consciousness
  c. Theory of Alienation and Exploitation
  d. Conception of a Rational Human Society
E. Conclusion: Some Contemporary Views
  a. Sketch of the Main Ideas of *TJ*
  b. Their Relation to Some Other Views

Texts

Hobbes, *Leviathan*, ed. Macpherson (Pelican Classics)
Locke, *Treatise of Government*, ed. Laslett (New American Library)
Hume, *Enquiry Concerning the Principles of Morals* (Liberal Arts)
J. S. Mill, *Utilitarianism* and *On Liberty* (Hackett); *Subjection of Women* (MIT)
Marx, *Selected Writings*, ed. McLellan (Oxford)

Readings

Leviathan, Pt. I, esp. Chs. 5–16, Pt. II entire; *Second Treatise*, entire; *Enquiry*, entire, and *Of the Original Contract* (Xerox); *Utilitarianism*, entire, *On Liberty*, esp. Chs. 1–3; *Subjection of Women*, entire; in McLellan, ed., *On the Jewish Question*, #6; *Economic and Philosophical Manuscripts*, #8; *On James Mill*, #10; *Theses on Feuerbach*, #13; *German Ideology*, #14; *Wage-Labor and Capital*, #19; Selections from *Grundrisse*, #29; and *Capital*; and *Critique of the Gotha Program*, #40.

Lectures are on Monday and Friday. There will be a final examination and a term paper of approximately 3,000 words.

Index

absolute regime, in Hobbes, 82–83
absolutism, 84; Locke on illegitimacy of,
  15; royal, and Robert Filmer, 106; royal,
  108; could not be contracted into
  (Locke), 130; and principle of utility, 175
Ackerman, Bruce, 4, 136n; discourse ethics
  of, 19
actions, as object of conscience, and the
  moral faculty in Butler, 424–425
activities, higher and lower (Mill), 307–308
Adam, and original sin, 208
Alembert, Jean le Rond d', 194
alienation: from others (Rousseau), 204; in
  Marx, 359; four aspects of (Marx), 362–
  363; from product of labor, 362–363;
  from productive activity of labor, 363;
  from species-life, 363; from other people,
  363–364
amour de soi (Rousseau), 230, 236; natural
  self love, 197, 201; vs. *amour propre*, 197–
  198, 206; proper form of, 217–218
amour propre (Rousseau), 230, 233, 236; natural vs. unnatural form of, 198–199; distinct form of self-concern in society, 198–
  200; as unnatural or perverted, 199, 201,
  205; Kant on, 199–200; wide view of,
  199–200; as natural desire for equality,
  200, 205; proper form of, 218
anarchy, and Hobbesian state of nature, 84
Aristotelian principle, in Mill, 269, 300
artificial duties: vs. natural duties (Hume),
  169; justice, fidelity, and allegiance to
  government (Hume), 169
artificial virtue(s): of justice, 177–184; in

Hume, 178, 180; justice as, 180–181; vs.
  natural virtue, 180–181
assurance, sovereign's role of providing,
  78–79
Augustine, dark mind of western thought,
  302
authority: of sovereign, achieved by its authorization, 79–80; vs. power (Butler),
  427; vs. influence, 429, 431. *See also* political authority
authority of conscience: in Butler, 420,
  426, 427–428, 453, 454; Butler's arguments for, 425–432. *See also* conscience
authorization: of sovereign, 79–80; nature
  of, 80

background culture, 6, 7
balance of powers: rejected by Hobbes,
  86; check on power, 87
Barber, Benjamin, 2n, 4
basic liberties: equal, list of, 12; in Mill's
  principle of liberty, 288
basic structure of society, 17; and social
  contract, 216; primary subject of justice, 234, 234n; and Mill, 267; and exploitation, 335, 346
benevolence: Hobbes recognizes, 40; and
  human nature, 46–47; as natural virtue,
  180–181; Butler's view of, 418; a higher-
  order principle (Butler), 420; and Butler's response to Hutcheson, 425; not
  authoritative principle of our nature,
  429; not the same as principle of utility,
  430; distinguished from affections